# RETHINKING PUNISHMENT

The age-old debate about what constitutes just punishment has become deadlocked. Retributivists continue to privilege desert over all else, and consequentialists continue to privilege punishment's expected positive consequences, such as deterrence or rehabilitation, over all else. In this important intervention into the debate, Leo Zaibert argues that, despite some obvious differences, these traditional positions are structurally very similar and that the deadlock between them stems from the fact they both oversimplify the problem of punishment. Proponents of these positions pay insufficient attention to the conflicts of values that punishment, even when justified, generates. Mobilizing recent developments in moral philosophy, Zaibert offers a properly pluralistic justification of punishment that is necessarily more complex than its traditional counterparts. An understanding of this complexity should promote a more cautious approach to inflicting punishment on individual wrongdoers and to developing punitive policies and institutions.

Leo Zaibert is Professor of Philosophy at Union College, Schenectady, New York.

# Rethinking Punishment

## Leo Zaibert

CAMBRIDGE
UNIVERSITY PRESS

# CAMBRIDGE
## UNIVERSITY PRESS

University Printing House, Cambridge CB2 8BS, United Kingdom

One Liberty Plaza, 20th Floor, New York, NY 10006, USA

477 Williamstown Road, Port Melbourne, VIC 3207, Australia

314–321, 3rd Floor, Plot 3, Splendor Forum, Jasola District Centre,
New Delhi – 110025, India

79 Anson Road, #06–04/06, Singapore 079906

Cambridge University Press is part of the University of Cambridge.

It furthers the University's mission by disseminating knowledge in the pursuit of
education, learning, and research at the highest international levels of excellence.

www.cambridge.org
Information on this title: www.cambridge.org/9781107194120
DOI: 10.1017/9781108151740

First published 2018

Printed in the United Kingdom by Clays, St Ives plc

*A catalogue record for this publication is available from the British Library.*

ISBN 978-1-107-19412-0 Hardback
ISBN 978-1-316-64539-0 Paperback

*For Anna*

# Contents

# Preface

The main questions I investigate in this book revolve around a truly important issue – the justification of punishment – and thus have attracted the attention of many thinkers throughout history. It may perhaps seem otiose to revisit them again. But the approach to the justification of punishment I undertake here is different from all others and indeed responsive to what appear to me as generally overlooked shortcomings of the previous efforts.

Necessarily, then, I spend considerable energy examining – often critically – the views of others, and to a considerable extent it is within the context of that critical examination that my own views gradually emerge. I here focus on contemporary authors, for two main reasons: first, because with the benefit of hindsight, and cognizant of the long history of punishment theory, contemporary authors have tended to avoid at least some earlier mistakes; second, because my own approach is in important ways informed by recent developments in moral philosophy. It would have been anachronistic, and pointless in other ways too, to mobilize these recent developments against past views that have been substantially refined or altogether abandoned. In other words, I here focus on what I take to be the real cutting edge in punishment theory, and I suggest that even cutting edge punishment theorists stand to benefit from embracing the sort of fundamental rethinking I recommend.

I have incurred many intellectual debts in the process of writing this book, and I would like to express my gratitude to the following people and institutions. In the summer of 2013, I was a visiting professor at the University of Toronto. I am grateful to Markus Dubber for arranging this visit and for many stimulating conversations. In the fall of 2013, I was the H. L. A. Hart Fellow at Oxford University's Centre for Ethics and Philosophy of Law. I am grateful to the Centre, to University College, to the Jurisprudence Discussion Group, and to John Gardner. In the fall of 2016, I was a Scholar-in-Residence at New York University under the auspices of the Faculty Resource Network. I am grateful to Anne Lydia Ward, to Samuel Scheffler, and to the conveners of the Colloquium in Legal, Political, and Social Philosophy that fall – Liam Murphy and Jeremy Waldron. I am grateful, too, to Union College for its continued support over the years. Finally, I am very grateful to Cambridge University Press, its referees, and especially to John Berger and his team. John shepherded this project from its beginning with warm enthusiasm and with utmost professionalism. Working with John and with Kristina Deusch, Becky Jackaman, Karin Kipp, and Karthik Orukaimani has been a genuine pleasure.

This book is much improved thanks to friends and colleagues who either have invited me to present parts of the manuscript at their institutions or have read parts (or, in a few cases, the entirety) of the manuscript and offered illuminating suggestions and criticisms. Without their input this book would not have been what it is. They are Vera Bergelson, Luis Chiesa, Felmon Davis, Julien Deonna, Steve de Wijze, Tony Dilloff, Markus Dubber, Kim Ferzan, George Fletcher, Stephen Garvey, Stuart Green, Adil Haque, Paul Hughes, Kyron Huigens, Doug Husak, Ingvar Johansson, John Kekes, Adam Kolber, Elena Larrauri, Ambrose Lee, Jae Lee, Harry Marten, Calum Miller, Kevin Mulligan, Alice Ristroph, José María Sauca Cano, Jonathan Simon, Barry Smith, Hillel Steiner, Mariam Thalos, Emma Tieffenbach, Jerry Vildostegui, Mark Wunderlich, and Ekow Yankah. Needless to say, they do not all agree with me, and they have not always succeeded in saving me from errors and infelicities.

While I have been writing about the themes discussed herein for most of my professional life, the material in this book is essentially all new. There are a handful of exceptions. Section 2.2 of Chapter 2 covers ground similar to that covered in my "Just Organic Wholes," in Leo Zaibert (ed.) *The Theory and Practice of Ontology*, London: Palgrave/Macmillan (2016): 135–156; Section 4.5 of Chapter 4 expands on some of the points I made in "Beyond Bad: Punishment Theory Meets the Problem of Evil," *Midwest Studies in Philosophy* 36 (2012): 93–111; and the appendix is a slightly edited version of my "On the Matter of Suffering: Derek Parfit and the Possibility of Deserved Suffering," *Criminal Law and Philosophy* 11 (2017): 1–18.

By far I owe my greatest debt to Anna Schur. She has helped me in more ways than I can count and probably in more ways than I will ever know. Without Anna's profound insights and without her unwavering support, this would have been a *really* very different book. I am very happy to dedicate the book to her.

# 1

# Punishment as a Problem

The expression "the problem of punishment" is extraordinarily common; in fact, it has become a cliché in the specialized literature.[1] Insofar as whatever else punishment seeks to do, it seeks to make wrongdoers suffer (by somehow diminishing their well-being or by visiting upon them something they do not want), it is immediately obvious that there is indeed something problematic about it, something in need of a justification. Understandably, much has been written about punishment and its justification. In spite of the ensuing voluminous and unwieldy literature, however, surprisingly little attention has been paid to the discussion of the *type* of problem – or indeed of the *types of problems* – that punishment generates.

These problems can usefully be broken down into two general types: practical and theoretical. When authors use the expression "the problem of punishment" (or its cognates), they above all have in mind the suffering brought about by the state (or other authorities). Throughout history states have often over-criminalized – that is, they have defined as punishable – far too many activities, and they have over-punished both those activities that should have been criminalized and those that should have not.[2] But the extremes to which modern, conspicuously democratic states have taken over-criminalization and over-punishment are particularly worrying. Commenting on the United States, Douglas Husak notes: "1 in every 138

---

[1] Compiling a comprehensive list of all uses of this expression is unnecessary. A few recent examples should suffice: "The Problem of Punishment" is the title of David Boonin's 2008 book (Cambridge: Cambridge University Press), and it is the title of chapters or sections in books by J. Angelo Corlett (ch. 3 of his *Responsibility and Punishment*, Dordrecht: Springer [2013]), by Whitley R. P. Kaufman (ch. 1 of his *Honor and Revenge: A Theory of Punishment*, Dordrecht: Springer [2012]), and by Victor Tadros (first section of the first chapter in his *The Ends of Harm: The Moral Foundation of the Criminal Law*, Oxford: Oxford University Press [2011]).

[2] For example, almost two millennia ago, commenting on the *Lex Papia Poppaea*, which criminalized (among other things) not marrying and not procreating, Tacitus complained: "[W]here the country once suffered from its vices, it was now in peril from its laws." Further, reacting to the "countless and complex statutes" of his day, Tacitus added: "[W]hen the state was most corrupt, laws were most abundant." See Tacitus, *Annals* (3.25) (John Jackson, trans.), Cambridge, MA: Harvard University Press (1931), 563.

residents is incarcerated. An estimated 1 in 20 children born in the United States is destined to serve time in a state or federal prison at some point in his life." The "grand total" of people under some form of supervision or another by the American criminal justice system is a staggering "over 7 million."[3]

By and large, it has been these sorts of practical problems that have attracted the attention of contemporary punishment theorists. This focus may partly explain the fact that "the problem of punishment" is often taken to be either exclusively or predominantly "the problem of *state* punishment."[4] There is no denying that these practical problems are both pressing and depressing. But this does not, I think, justify the comparatively little energy that has been expended in addressing the theoretical problem of punishment. In this book, thus, I attempt to shed much needed light on this theoretical problem.

I am moved by two convictions. First, I am convinced that the examination of theoretical problems, in general, is genuinely important in itself. For example, reflecting on his own views in "A Critique of Utilitarianism," Bernard Williams remarked: "[T]hese considerations do not themselves give solutions to practical dilemmas ... but I hope they help to provide other ways of thinking about them."[5] There can be little doubt that, say, Williams's view that utilitarianism is unable to cope with "the complexities of moral thought" has greatly advanced that general debate – even if it has not solved any practical problems.[6] My approach in this book is very similar to, and in some ways inspired by, Williams's, for I will defend the view that contemporary punishment theory is unable to cope with the complexity of moral thought and moral life. Thus, as a first approximation to my goals here, it can be said that I seek to deploy, within the specific context of punishment, criticisms similar to those more general criticisms Williams deployed against both utilitarianism and what he called "the morality system." Second, I am convinced that the specialized literature on punishment has reached a kind of stalemate (which I will explain shortly). In light of this stalemate, the examination of the theoretical problems surrounding punishment may in fact help us better understand – and

---

[3]  Douglas Husak, *Overcriminalization: The Limits of the Criminal Law*, Oxford: Oxford University Press (2008), 4–5. See also Markus Dirk Dubber, *Victims in the War on Crime: The Use and Abuse of Victims' Rights*, New York, NY: New York University Press (2002), and David Cole, "The Truth about Our Prison Crisis," *The New York Review of Books* 44, 11 (June 22, 2017): 29–31. For the international (mostly European) dimension of these problems, see Elena Larrauri, "La Economía Política del Castigo," *Revista Electrónica de Ciencia Penal y Criminológica* 6 (2009): 2–22.

[4]  I have criticized this view in Leo Zaibert, *Punishment and Retribution*, Aldershot: Ashgate (2006).

[5]  Bernard Williams "A Critique of Utilitarianism," in J. J. C. Smart and B. A. O. Williams, *Utilitarianism: For and Against*, Cambridge: Cambridge University Press (1973), 117. Consider another eloquent example: "This book is unabashedly devoted to solving these problems, though to put it that way suggests an incredible *hubris* on the part of the author, and might also mislead the reader into thinking that the book is intended to put these problems, once and for all, to rest. It would be just as accurate to describe the book's aim as to provide a way of understanding – or, if you like, interpreting – these problems," in Susan Wolf, *Freedom within Reason*, Oxford: Oxford University Press (1990), 4.

[6]  Williams, "A Critique ...," 149.

eventually even help us solve – some of those practical problems that have hitherto monopolized attention. A full appreciation of the importance of the overlooked theoretical problem will, of course, develop slowly, as the book progresses. For now, an account of what the theoretical problem *is* shall suffice.

We have just seen the essential conceptual connection between punishment and suffering (understood very generally). The other essential conceptual connection worth our attention links punishment and (perceived) wrongdoing.[7] The idea is that by making wrongdoers suffer, *justice* is achieved. Punishment is thus immediately revealed as generating the theoretical problem of having to bring justice *through* suffering. There is, I will assume, obvious *value* in diminishing suffering in the world and obvious *value* in imparting justice.[8] By and large, I will focus on one specific type of suffering-diminution – variously called forgiveness, mercy, leniency (etc.) – and on one specific type of justice-imparting – punishment. It is obvious, too, that these values can conflict with each other, independently of any practical problems.

Theoretically speaking, then, punishment presents us with a moral dilemma: Which of these conflicting values is weightier? Importantly, and in contradistinction to the virtually universally accepted position, I will not assume that the dilemma simply evaporates, in the sense of being fully resolved, when punishment is taken to be (or not taken to be) *justified*. The expression "justification" (and cognates), particularly in the way contemporary punishment theorists use it, is far too impoverished to match the complexity of punishment and concomitant phenomena. Thus, I will here attempt to place the discussion of punishment in much closer proximity to discussions of moral dilemmas in general. I will in fact suggest that punishment theory has developed in remarkable isolation from other general advances in moral philosophy – in particular those associated with the budding specialized literature on moral dilemmas.

Punishment, I will argue, presents us with precisely the sorts of famous quandaries generated by other moral dilemmas – above all those associated with forgiveness and related phenomena. I will evidently have much more to say about forgiveness later on, but I would at once wish to suggest two important features of my understanding of this concept. First, the essence of forgiveness is the idea of a deliberate refusal to punish – it is a form of sparing (deserved) suffering that is motivated by a *special* moral reason. Second, while the idea of mercy is admittedly more general than the idea of forgiveness, I will treat both as synonyms here. Surely one could show mercy

---

[7] For ease of exposition, I will henceforth ignore the "perceived" rider and assume that perceived wrongdoing is always *correctly* perceived wrongdoing.

[8] I do not think that this assumption is problematic. Humans do tend to disvalue both gratuitous suffering and obvious injustice. I will not engage in this book with those thoroughgoing forms of skepticism, fatalism, incompatibilism, or determinism that call into question moral responsibility in general. Noting this assumption would scarcely be necessary were it not for the fact that there are influential authors who, notwithstanding their opposition to these thoroughgoing forms of skepticism, defend forms of limited skepticism aimed specifically at the moral defensibility (or metaphysical possibility) of deserved punishment.

absent any wrongdoing: the "mercy killing" of a patient afflicted with a painful terminal disease is evidently not a matter of forgiving her; helping someone in need may be an act of mercy, but, again, it is not a matter of forgiving her; etc. But when authors talk about mercy within the context of punishment theory, they are often talking about what I am here calling forgiveness: mercy in this context means the deliberate sparing of a suffering that is deserved as a result of wrongdoing (again: based on a special moral reason).[9] The general, age-old tension between justice and mercy is, within the specific context of our reactions to wrongdoing, the tension between punishment and forgiveness.

In this chapter, I will begin to delineate the contours of a more comprehensive – and more complicated – approach to punishment. In the first section, I will place the (theoretical) problem of punishment within the context of general theodicies. One important goal of doing so is to highlight, as I do in Section 1.2, some central differences between axiological and deontic considerations. Although these differences are very well known in moral philosophy in general, they are typically overlooked by contemporary punishment theorists – to the detriment of that particular, specialized literature. In Section 1.3, I suggest a new way of understanding the central debate regarding the justification of punishment: instead of focusing on the distinction between retributivism and consequentialism, we should focus on the distinction between monistic and pluralistic justifications. The discussion of the differences between the axiological and the deontic on the one hand and of monism and pluralism on the other sets the stage for a general discussion, in Section 1.4, of the nature and structure of those moral dilemmas that I suggest are very similar to punishment and from whose consideration the specialized literature on punishment stands to benefit. With these initial pieces more or less in place – or at least in sight – I conclude the chapter with an overview of the remainder of the book.

### 1.1 PUNISHMENT, THEODICIES, AND MEANING

As plain as it is that punishment seeks to cause suffering, it is also plain – if not plainer – that punishment is not the only, or even the main, source of suffering in the world. The existence of suffering *in general* has always stood in need of an explanation. Helping us to overcome, to reduce, or at least to cope with suffering in general is an essential aspect of every major comprehensive worldview – from the most

---

[9] In an authoritative entry on "Forgiveness" in the *Stanford Encyclopedia of Philosophy*, Paul Hughes documented the proximity of forgiveness and mercy – particularly of mercy within the context of wrongdoing. See Paul M. Hughes, "Forgiveness," *The Stanford Encyclopedia of Philosophy* (Winter 2016 edn., Edward N. Zalta, ed.), https://plato.stanford.edu/archives/win2016/entries/forgiveness/. A new version of the entry – coauthored with Brandon Warmke – preserves, in attenuated form, this idea: https://plato.stanford.edu/archives/sum2017/entries/forgiveness/. A certain looseness regarding these terms goes back for centuries. See John M. Cooper and J. F. Procopé's "Introduction" to Seneca's *On Mercy* in their *Seneca: Moral and Political Writings*, Cambridge: Cambridge University Press (1995): 119–127.

secular to the most religious. G. W. Leibniz coined a very useful term to refer precisely to the systematic effort to explain why there is evil in the world: theodicy.[10] In their theistic version, theodicies seek to explain why an allegedly benevolent and omnipotent God allows suffering to exist. But secular theodicies, as Max Weber's towering work underscores, are also perfectly possible and illuminating.[11] Human beings, independently of their religious commitments and independently of their differing degrees of intellectual sophistication, have naturally been attracted to theodicies since long before the term was coined. Trying to make sense of the fact of misery in the world is an essential part of the human condition – and this is what theodicies seek to do.

The central question of theodicy can be posed in a variety of ways, and in the previous paragraph I have in fact deliberately phrased it using three different terms – "suffering," "evil," and "misery" – precisely in order to highlight the irrelevance, for my purposes, of terminological minutiae. We well know the meaning of claims to the effect that punishment causes suffering, and we well know what it is to wonder why there is evil or misery in the world. Investigating the precise meaning of these terms may be an important and worthwhile project in some contexts, but not in ours. The fundamental question of theodicy can be expressed very generally: Why do bad things happen?

The expression "bad things" is, within the context of theodicies, necessarily – and unproblematically – loose, and it is indeed consistent with things that cause "suffering," with "misery," with things that can be considered "evil," and with a host of other possible descriptions. Those who have felt the existential pull of the fundamental question of theodicy have not had, and have not needed, any precise definition of these terms. In fact, this unproblematic looseness regarding the "bad things" of interest to theodicies is conspicuous, too, in connection to the "bad things" that punishment is supposed to involve. The most influential contemporary definition of punishment, the Flew–Benn–Hart definition, clearly exhibits this looseness: in Hart's own words, punishment "must involve pain or other consequences normally considered unpleasant."[12] These things "normally considered unpleasant" in the definition of punishment evidently are among the "bad things" of concern to theodicies.

[10] Gottfried Wilhelm von Leibniz, *Theodicy: Essays on the Goodness of God, the Freedom of Man, and the Origin of Evil* (Austin Farrer, ed.), New Haven, CT: Yale University Press (1952).

[11] Max Weber, *Economy and Society: An Outline of Interpretive Sociology* (Guenther Roth, ed.), Berkeley, CA: University of California Press (1978). See also Frederick Neuhouser's *Rousseau's Theodicy of Self-Love: Evil, Rationality, and the Drive for Recognition*, Oxford: Oxford University Press (2008), where he argues that Rousseau is best seen as presenting a secular theodicy (of *amour-propre*) that is "more palatable" than Hegel's secular theodicy (4).

[12] H. L. A. Hart, *Punishment and Responsibility: Essays in the Philosophy of Law*, 2nd edn., Oxford: Oxford University Press (2008), 4. While I have objected to aspects of the Flew–Benn–Hart definition of punishment, I find this looseness unobjectionable. My own definition of punishment recognizes that the punisher wishes something to happen to the punishee that would "somehow offset" the "bad thing" that she has done. See my *Punishment and Retribution*, 31 ff.

The fundamental question of theodicy can only be meaningfully asked on the basis of assuming the truth of another view whereby the world would be better if fewer bad things happened. Other things equal, a world with less suffering in it is better than one with more suffering in it. And then the connection between theodicies and punishment theory begins to emerge, for punishment involves the deliberate creation of a bad thing – suffering. This confronts us with the particularly poignant question about punishment: while the fundamental question of theodicy in general inquires about what reason could be adduced for there *being* any suffering in the world (assuming, to repeat, that less suffering is better than more suffering), punishment theorists need to explain why it is sometimes good to deliberately choose to *create* more suffering in the world.

As soon as the connection emerges, however, a potential objection arises too. The objection is that punishment is *essentially* a matter not of inflicting suffering but of something else: a matter of denouncing some acts, educating society, preventing or reallocating harms, or defending ourselves or our societies. If this objection succeeded, the particular question of punishment would lose at least part of its poignancy – for what we would be deliberately choosing to do when we punish would be to cause not suffering but something else. Suffering would be merely a side effect (although a perfectly foreseeable side effect) of what we *really* choose to bring about: denunciation, education, prevention, defense, etc.

But the objection fails. It fails, firstly, because of the abusively stipulative determination of what exactly it is that we are choosing to do. If I *know* that my choosing to $\phi$ will cause you suffering (even if that is not my main or direct intention) – how compelling is it to say that by choosing to $\phi$ I am not, *eo ipso*, thereby choosing to cause you suffering? This is reminiscent of what Pascal mocked as the "grand method of directing the intention."[13] But, secondly, the objection fails more fundamentally as well, as it evinces a misunderstanding of what punishment itself must – on pain of incoherence – mean. As Wittgenstein, among myriad others, has put it: it is perfectly "clear" that just as "reward must be something acceptable [or pleasant]," punishment must be "something unacceptable [or unpleasant]."[14]

In an important article that will occupy my attention later on (in Chapter 5), John Tasioulas usefully traces the genealogy of a powerful response to this objection. Tasioulas cites Williams's pithy version of the response:

---

[13]  Blaise Pascal, "The Provincial Letters," in *Works of Pascal* (O. W. Wight, ed.), New York, NY: Derby & Jackson (1859), Vol. 1., 231 and ff.

[14]  Ludwig Wittgenstein, *Tractatus Logico-Philosophicus* (C. K. Ogden, trans.), London: Kegan Paul (1922), 88 (6.422). See also Ludwig Wittgenstein, *Notebooks 1914–1916* (G. H. von Wright and G. E. M. Anscombe, eds.), New York, NY: Harper/Blackwell (1961), 78e. The German terms translated as "acceptable" and "unacceptable" by Ogden and as "pleasant" and "unpleasant" by von Wright and Anscombe are *Angenehmes* and *Unangenehmes*. While I prefer the latter translation, this variation is useful for my purposes: rewards involve good things, punishments bad things.

The idea that traditional, painful, punishments are simply denunciations is incoherent, because it does not explain, without begging the question, why denunciations have to take the form of what Nietzsche identified as the constant of punishment, "the ceremony of pain."[15]

Whatever specific punishments turn out to be,[16] to the extent that they remain forms *of punishment*, they will necessarily have to (seek to) make the wrongdoer suffer. The point here is in no way specially linked to denunciatory or communicative theories of punishment in particular. The point applies with equal force to any account of punishment in which the conceptual connection between punishment and suffering is rejected.

Denunciatory theories of punishment are but an example of what in his *Theodicy* Leibniz usefully called "medicinal" punishments – those that seek "to correct the criminal, or at least to provide an example for others."[17] Rehabilitative, educative, preventive, or defensive approaches to punishment are all equally susceptible to Williams's point, as long as these lose sight of the fact that, when we punish, any of these (or other) goals are achieved *by means of* making wrongdoers suffer. Conceptually, inflicting this suffering is not optional: to refuse to inflict this suffering (whether or not this refusal entails abandoning other ulterior goals as well) is to thereby refuse to punish. To punish, then, is to (try to) inflict suffering (or pain or misery or a bad thing, etc.) on someone as a response to her wrongdoing. Punishment without trying to inflict suffering is like gifting an object without intending to transfer any right over the thing gifted or like feeding someone without intending to give her some nourishment. This is not to *abuse* any definition (in the sense of Hart's famous protestation)[18] – it is merely to *use* one.

Leaving the objection behind, then, we can return to the peculiar poignancy of the question regarding the suffering that punishment causes. There is plenty of suffering in the world: suffering arising from the inevitable clashes between human vulnerabilities and the brute forces of nature or from human malice and cruelty or

---

[15] John Tasioulas, "Punishment and Repentance," *Philosophy* 81 (2006): 279–322, at 287 ff. Tasioulas traces this view to Hart and, via Williams, to Nietzsche. Williams, however, does not give citation for the passage in Nietzsche to which he refers. Michel Foucault strikes me as a more appropriate source for the idea of a "ceremony of pain." In his *Discipline and Punish* (New York, NY: Vintage [1995]), the ceremonial aspects of state punishment are a central motif, and Foucault repeatedly talks about "the ceremony of punishment," "the penal ceremony," "the ceremony of public torture," "the ceremony of public execution," "the ceremony of power." Foucault specifically uses the expression that Williams attributes to Nietzsche, "the ceremony of pain," on page 257.

[16] On the variability of acceptable forms of state punishment, see Michel Foucault, *Discipline and Punish*, and my "Justifying Incarceration," in *The Universality of Punishment* (Antonio Incampo and Wojciech Zelaniec, eds.), Bari: Cacucci (2015): 135–154.

[17] Leibniz, *Theodicy* . . ., 424–425. I shall make ample use of the term "medicinal," in preference of the admittedly much more widespread (and perhaps less jarring) term "instrumental." I have chosen to revive Leibniz's term because it seems helpful in stressing the remarkable parallel between certain views of punishment and medicine.

[18] Hart, *Punishment and Responsibility* . . ., 5 ff.

from sheer accidents and bad luck. But to punish is to *deliberately* bring bad things about, and this may suggest that punishment is, in itself, a matter of making the world worse, not better. This is, in fact, exactly Jeremy Bentham's extraordinarily influential position on punishment: "[P]unishment in itself is evil," to which he immediately adds that therefore it should only be admitted (if at all) when "it promises to exclude some greater evil."[19] I will argue at length later (especially in Chapter 3) that the Benthamite position is as widespread as it is deficient.[20]

Cases in which suffering is deliberately inflicted and that do not seem to make the world worse are evidently easy to imagine. To continue with the Leibnizian motif, just consider any medical intervention that causes some suffering but is likely to prevent much greater suffering. Or consider any case in which a person or a group of people is made to suffer in order to spare greater suffering to a larger group of people. These inflictions of suffering do not really make the world worse, since they are best described, once we broaden the lens through which we look at them, as overall *diminutions* of suffering. Many popular justifications of punishment – such as the already-mentioned Benthamite utilitarian justification and the rehabilitative, educational, preventive, or defensive justifications – can be seen as medicinal in Leibniz's sense. Proponents of these justifications see the badness of the suffering that punishment brings about as compensated by that badness which, *ex hypothesi*, punishment prevents. And so, in their view, punishment actually makes the world better, not worse.

But some have argued that there is, somehow, something good, in itself, about the suffering that punishment inflicts, independently of whether it prevents greater suffering. Leibniz is one example; his use of the term "medicinal" in this context is a put-down: "[T]rue retributive justice," he tells us, goes – because it *ought* to go – "beyond the medicinal."[21] The "harmony of things" that is essential to Leibniz's theodicy demands "evil in the form of suffering."[22] If the medicinal justifications were the whole story, then punishment would not really contribute much to the problem of suffering, for it would be plain that the suffering it generates is just necessary to avoid greater suffering. We would simply need to ensure that our calculations are correct. The medicinal approach – so influential nowadays, as I will argue – *reduces* the real and deep moral and political problems associated with punishment to mere "technological" ones, to echo Isaiah Berlin's insightful deployment of this term, itself reminiscent of Leibniz's deployment of the term

---

[19]  Jeremy Bentham, "An Introduction to the Principles of Morals and Legislation," in *The Works of Jeremy Bentham* (John Bowring, ed.), Vol. 1, New York, NY: Russell & Russell (1962), 83.

[20]  Importantly (although also in accordance with standard usage), unless otherwise noted, I will use "Benthamite utilitarianism," "classical utilitarianism," "hedonistic utilitarianism," *and* "utilitarianism" interchangeably. See John Rawls, *A Theory of Justice*, rev. ed., Cambridge, MA: Harvard University Press (1992), especially 19–24; and Julia Driver, "The History of Utilitarianism," *The Stanford Encyclopedia of Philosophy* (Winter 2014 Edition) (Edward N. Zalta, ed.): http://plato .stanford.edu/archives/win2014/entries/utilitarianism-history.

[21]  Leibniz, *Theodicy . . .*, 425.    [22]  *Ibid.*

"medicinal."[23] Leibniz – along with myriad other thinkers – believes this is too reductionist because the suffering constitutive of punishment is sometimes *intrinsically* good, even if it does not contribute to reducing further suffering. *That* problem – i.e., how punishment can be in this way intrinsically good – is the serious, non-medicinal, non-technological problem worth our attention.

Often, however, theodicies – particularly some theistic theodicies – attempt to solve this problem in suspect ways, by ascribing inscrutable wisdom to God. So, for example, a common move in these theodicies – including, in a way, Leibniz's own – is to suggest that God, being not only all-good but also all-knowing, knows that the suffering in the world that strikes us as excessive is in fact optimal. Things are taken to be interconnected in ways that mere finite beings cannot understand: attempts to "eliminate" this or that episode of suffering in the world would have produced even more suffering – and God, unlike us, knows this. Aside from their obscurantism, these approaches may perhaps be guilty of simply *transferring* the reductive approach: it is not humans that do the number crunching but God – it is just that God's calculations are too complicated for us. God would understand how the medicine is indeed medicine, how the technology operates, but the reductionism *could* still be there, only hidden from us. Opponents of the reductionist approach would object to mere transfers: they would want to ensure that reductionism is clearly rejected.

Secular theodicies fare better, as they tend to emphasize that the problem of theodicy is the problem of *meaningful* existence; it is the problem of *making sense* of a world that, as Weber noted, is filled with "undeserved suffering, unpunished injustice, and incorrigible stupidity."[24] For obvious reasons, I will here ignore the problem of incorrigible stupidity; but the twin problems of undeserved suffering and of unpunished injustice are, just as obviously, central to my aims in this book.

It is important to underscore that according to Weber suffering is really a problem for secular theodicies only when it is not deserved, and injustices are more of a problem when they are not punished. These two problems are not merely calculative, medicinal, or technological: a world in which vice was commonly rewarded and virtue commonly punished would be problematic *even if* it could be shown that it contained the minimum amount of suffering possible. And it would be problematic, first and foremost, because this state of affairs would strike us as existentially *meaningless*. As Weber put it, "the need for an ethical interpretation of the 'meaning' of the distributions of fortunes among men increased with the growing rationality of conceptions of the world."[25]

---

[23]   Isaiah Berlin, "Two Concepts of Liberty," in *Liberty* (Henry Hardy, ed.), Oxford: Oxford University Press (2002), 167.

[24]   Max Weber, "Politics as a Vocation," in Peter Lassman and Ronald Speirs (eds.), *Weber: Political Writings*, Cambridge: Cambridge University Press (1994), 362.

[25]   H. H. Gerth and C. Wright Mills, *From Max Weber: Essays in Sociology*, New York, NY: Oxford University Press (1946), 275.

This search for meaning in the world is particularly urgent in the face of what Weber called "the incongruity between destiny and merit."[26] Gershon Shafir's insightful interpretation of what "destiny" and "merit" mean for Weber is illuminating. With Shafir, we can see that Weber understands "destiny" as the worldview according to which the distribution of suffering in the world is disordered, arbitrary, and random – and *thereby* meaningless. "Merit," in contrast, is for Weber related to a worldview according to which the distribution of suffering in the world is somehow "ordered" – and *thereby* meaningful.[27] With Weber and Shafir, we see that humans can create meaning in an otherwise meaningless world by "infusing it with a rationalized ethic" so as to make "merit and destiny coincide."[28]

And we can then see, too, the reason for the pejorative sense in which Leibniz uses the term "medicinal" to refer to some justifications of punishment. As Shafir reminds us, Weber also had (in this context) a negative view of the medicinal, for although medicine "is capable of diminishing suffering," "the point of view of medicine" is "itself meaningless."[29] Needless to say, this is not supposed to be an attack on medicine as such or on any other technological mechanism that seeks to reduce suffering. Rather, it is both a criticism of the strategy of *reducing* the world of value to mere medicine, to mere technology, and a reminder of the relatively tenuous connection between medicinal strategies and the larger story concerning the relation between punishment and the meaning of life.

The fact that, on this view, distributions according to *merit* suffuse the world with meaning shall be very important in the remainder of the book. Admittedly, merit is not the only means of infusing meaning into the world – though it surely is one important such means.[30] To merit something means to deserve something; one's merit is one's desert. That these expressions are indeed synonymous is brought out by the fact that in some languages there simply is no word for "desert" other than "merit," in the sense that to translate the English proposition that "she deserves X" one would in those other languages have to say "she merits X."[31] The importance of merit – reflected not only in Leibniz and Weber but also in many other thinkers who

---

26  *Ibid.*
27  Gershon Shafir, "The Incongruity between Destiny and Merit: Max Weber on Meaningful Existence and Modernity," *The British Journal of Sociology* 36.4 (1985): 516–530.
28  *Ibid.*, 521.    29  *Ibid.*, 524.
30  In *The Book of Job in Medieval Jewish Thought* (Oxford: Oxford University Press [2004]), Robert Eisen suggests that prominent among the reasons why Job has remained so fascinating through the ages is that it deals with "one of humanity's deepest and most vexing problems." This problem is none other than "the suffering of the righteous" – i.e., the problem of *undeserved* suffering (*ibid.*, 3). Job's protestations are predicated on the fact that he (rightly) considers himself undeserving of suffering. In many interpretations (illuminatingly discussed by Eisen) Job comes to accept that God's decision to inflict undeserved suffering upon the righteous in order to *test their devotion* is another means to infuse meaning into the world. One need not agree with this other means in order to see that *Job* is centrally concerned with finding meaning in suffering.
31  This is explicitly the case at least in Spanish and other Romance languages. Comparisons between "ordinary" ways of saying things in different languages reveals obvious – though overlooked – problems for versions of the "ordinary language" approach to philosophy. Not that the intimate

have written about morality and the meaning of life – is undeniable. And yet many of the ablest contemporary philosophers doubt (or deny) the importance of desert (merit) in affecting the way we react to the possibility of inflicting suffering.

Leibniz and Weber, then, do not find suffering *as such* so philosophically problematic: it is specifically *undeserved* suffering that they consider meaningless and therefore deeply problematic.[32] Not only are these authors by no means alone in holding this position, but if Weber's towering and wide-ranging historical and sociological investigations are correct, this is – and has always been – the typical position of ordinary folk. That is why many have seen the quintessentially *human* urge to make sense of (meaningless) suffering as "a psychological, rather than a deontic [or normative] claim."[33]

In the next chapter, I will have much more to say about how desert confers (non-medicinal) meaning to suffering. But let us first take stock of what is clear already: punishment is incoherent without it being an attempt to inflict suffering, and (undeserved) suffering is the main problem that gives rise to theodicies. In light of these facts, the scarcity of systematic efforts to place the problem of punishment within the framework of theodicies is startling. Seeking to fill this gap is already a reason for writing this book. But there are also two specific reasons why such framing is likely to be particularly fecund.

First, this framing will allow me to connect the discussion of punishment to the discussion of authors not typically registering on contemporary punishment theorists' radars. This may already be visible, given my engagement with Leibniz and Weber, but there will be many more such instances in the book. I will, of course, engage with the work of leading contemporary punishment theorists and philosophers of law, but I will also discuss authors and sources not typically discussed by these contemporary punishment theorists. Engaging with these authors and sources can, as I hope to show, significantly contribute to refreshing and revitalizing contemporary debates over the justification of punishment.

Second, and more substantively, this framing reveals that the fundamental question of theodicy concerns *values*: it concerns itself with why *the world* is good (or bad). Theodicy is not necessarily (and certainly not primarily) action-guiding, it being rather connected to our understanding and evaluation of the world such as it is

---

connection between these two terms is lost in English. The connection is famously prominent in Adam Smith, for example, who understood "merit and demerit" as "the qualities of deserving reward, and of deserving punishment." See Adam Smith, *The Theory of Moral Sentiments*, London: Bohn (1853): 93 and ff.

[32] See also Bernard Williams, "Unbearable Suffering," in *The Sense of the Past*: Princeton, NJ: Princeton University Press (2007): 331–337.

[33] Tamsin Shaw, "The 'Last Man' Problem: Nietzsche and Weber on Political Attitudes to Suffering," in *Nietzsche as Political Philosopher* (Manuel Knoll and Barry Stocker, eds.), Berlin: de Gruyter (2014): 345–380. Or, as Nietzsche himself famously put it: "What actually arouses indignation over suffering is not the suffering itself, but the senselessness of suffering," in his *On the Genealogy of Morality* (Keith Ansell-Pearson, ed.), Cambridge: Cambridge University Press (2006), 44. See also Ansell-Pearson's useful "Introduction" to this edition of the *Genealogy* (xiii–xxx).

(or as it is assumed to be).[34] The same is true of punishment theory. And yet this concern with value as such has been largely absent from contemporary discussions of punishment – in my opinion, to their detriment. As I will argue in the next section, one of the consequences of this absence is that it has prevented contemporary punishment theorists from properly understanding what they themselves claim is the central debate regarding punishment.

## 1.2 THE AXIOLOGICAL AND THE DEONTIC

While many aspects of the philosophical discussion of punishment have for millennia been taken to be very difficult, and have been widely contested, there is at least one aspect regarding which there appears to be great clarity: the central debate regarding the justification of punishment is between retributivism and consequentialism.[35] The standard interpretation of the debate goes roughly as follows: retributivists justify punishment by its being *deserved*, whereas consequentialists, in contrast, justify punishment by the positive *consequences* that punishment is supposed (or known) to cause. To put this in the terms introduced previously: consequentialist approaches, seeking to prevent, deter, incapacitate, rehabilitate, communicate, denounce, and so on, are *medicinal*; only retributivism is non-medicinally concerned with justice as such.

So far, so good. But since *all* these rationales – medicinal and non-medicinal – seem desirable, a wide variety of efforts to combine them have been offered and in fact enjoy widespread popularity.[36] In spite of this popularity, however, these famous "mixed justifications" have generated more heat than light, and I have elsewhere argued against them.[37] But here I wish to put forth a new and more general explanation for their failure. I am afraid that, on first approximation, this explanation may perhaps sound too grand for its own good, but I will attempt to show that the explanation is indeed correct.

The mixed justifications have failed because their proponents have *misunderstood* what exactly is being opposed to what when retributivism is opposed to consequentialism and what exactly is involved in "justifying" punishment. That the debate

---

[34] I am here focusing on the world, such as it is, as the locus of meaning, conceivably independently of our intervention.

[35] As is well known, "consequentialism" can refer both to a general moral doctrine and specifically to a justification of punishment. Unless otherwise noted, I will throughout this book use "consequentialism" in the narrow sense of "consequentialism about the justification of punishment."

[36] See the seminal versions in A. M. Quinton, "On Punishment," *Analysis* 14 (1954): 133–142; in John Rawls, "Two Concepts of Rules," in Samuel Freeman (ed.), *John Rawls: Collected Papers*, Cambridge, MA: Harvard University Press (2001): 20–46; and in H. L. A. Hart, *Punishment and Responsibility*, 2 ff.

[37] Zaibert, *Punishment and Retribution*, 10 ff. For similar criticisms, see also Ted Honderich, *Punishment: The Supposed Justifications Revisited*, London: Pluto Press (2005), *passim*; and (regarding Rawls) Stanley Cavell, *The Claim of Reason: Wittgenstein, Skepticism, Morality, and Tragedy*, Oxford: Oxford University Press (1999), 292 ff., especially at 302–303.

between retributivists and consequentialists had been historically misunderstood was, however, the rallying cry of some of the early proponents of these famous mixed justifications themselves. So it may seem puzzling that I would claim that their views were such failures. The puzzle is not too difficult to resolve, however, for my view is that while those proponents of mixed justifications were formally correct in thinking that the central distinction had been misunderstood, they themselves were substantially wrong – *wildly* wrong, in fact – as to the nature of the misunderstanding.

More than half a century ago, A. M. Quinton famously proposed that the "antinomy" opposing retributivism and consequentialism "can be resolved" by making sure that we have "properly understood" retributivism.[38] Though I think that it is not only retributivism that needs to be properly understood – since "consequentialism" too is commonly misunderstood – *formally* I agree with Quinton. But that is where the agreement ends: regarding *substance* I disagree with Quinton deeply. Quinton (whose influence on other proponents of mixed justification is considerable)[39] held that "retributivism, properly understood, is not a moral but a logical doctrine."[40] Briefly, Quinton believes that retributivism reduces to the claim that the talk of punishing the undeserving evinces ignorance as to what the word "punishment" *means* and that this semantic point is all retributivists have ever cared about.

This is a serious mistake. Retributivism is not a logical or semantic thesis – and I know of no retributivist who has ever seen her own thesis in such a reductive fashion. Retributivists contend that retributivism *is* a moral doctrine: a doctrine that concerns itself with the moral defensibility of inflicting on wrongdoers the punishment that they deserve. Retributivism, moreover, is a special type of moral doctrine in a sense that has not been hitherto sufficiently recognized. If the apparently straightforward distinction between retributivism and consequentialism is to make any sense – and if it is to be of any help in advancing the debate concerning punishment's justification – it needs to be properly framed within the more general distinction pertaining to moral philosophy adumbrated by our discussion of theodicy: the distinction between the axiological and the deontic.

By "axiology" I – like others – refer to "the area of moral philosophy that is concerned with theoretical questions about value and goodness of all varieties," and I thus take it to be a synonym for "value theory."[41] By "deontic" I here refer to considerations that lead us to *act* in certain ways. It is evident that axiological and deontic concerns interact with each other in a great variety of ways: for example, that something is (or is not) good surely has some relevance regarding our deliberation as to what we ought (or ought not) to do. Perhaps we should act in such ways so as to

---

[38] Quinton, "On Punishment," 134.
[39] Rawls acknowledges the similarities between Quinton's views and his own in "Two Concept of Rules," fn. 4.
[40] Quinton, "On Punishment," 134.
[41] Mark Schroeder, "Value Theory," *The Stanford Encyclopedia of Philosophy* (Summer 2012 Edition) (Edward N. Zalta, ed.): http://plato.stanford.edu/archives/sum2012/entries/value-theory/.

bring about as much goodness as possible; at the very least our belief that something is good provides us with a reason or a motive for bringing it about. But it is no less evident that the two sorts of concerns are different: one thing is to say, for example, that showing affection is a good thing, and another is to say that we ought to show affection. To employ a bit of contemporary jargon: deontic concerns are essentially "action-guiding," whereas axiological concerns are not essentially, or directly, or decisively, "action-guiding." Some problems – such as the theoretical problem of punishment that is my focus in this book – can only, or at least more profoundly, manifest themselves within the axiological realm.

With the aid of the distinction between the axiological and the deontic, we can then begin to clarify the distinction between retributivism and consequentialism. Retributivism, first and foremost, *should* be seen as an *axiological* doctrine, not a deontic one (and much less a merely logical or semantic one, as Quinton and other "mixed theorists" would have it). Retributivists assert that there *is* value in deserved suffering *itself*, in the deserved suffering that is constitutive of punishment *itself*. (My emphasis on "itself" in the previous sentence is meant to underscore, once more, that this value is non-medicinal.) The fact that deserved suffering has value of course enters into the retributivist's deontic deliberations as to whether punishment should, in this or that case, be inflicted – but it does not commit her to any deontic position. The fact that deserved suffering is valuable does not necessarily justify *inflicting* it.

By no means do I wish to deny that there also exist "deontic retributivists," that is, thinkers who believe that because deserved suffering is valuable then it ought to be inflicted. As a matter of fact, many leading retributivists – with Kant at the forefront – often present their position as an amalgamation of both axiological and deontic elements.[42] Much confusion surrounds this issue. These retributivists simultaneously (or, as the case may be, intermittently) assert that retributivism is the *axiological* view that deserved punishment is intrinsically good and that retributivism is the *deontic* view that we ought to punish the deserving.[43] And yet, both for reasons I have discussed elsewhere[44] and for other reasons I will present later (particularly in Chapter 4), deontic versions of retributivism ought to be rejected.

This is not mere stipulation. There is one succinct and straightforward argument (albeit not hitherto sufficiently recognized) why retributivism ought to be seen as essentially axiological. Retributivists can disagree as to the complicated questions

---

[42]  Immanuel Kant, *The Philosophy of Law: An Exposition of the Fundamentals Principles of Jurisprudence as the Science of Right* (W. Hastie, trans.), Edinburgh: T. & T. Clark (1887), *passim* but particularly 194 ff.

[43]  The amalgamation is conspicuous not only in Kant's retributivism but in its most sophisticated contemporary defense, Michael Moore's (see his *Placing Blame*, Oxford: Oxford University Press [1997]) as well. I will discuss these matters in Chapter 4.

[44]  See Zaibert, *Punishment and Retribution*, 155 ff. See also David Dolinko, "Retributivism, Consequentialism, and the Intrinsic Goodness of Punishment," *Law and Philosophy* 16 (1997): 507–528.

concerning the deontic implications of their axiological commitments. But no retributivist can deny the axiological point that deserved punishment is intrinsically valuable. In this sense, then, this axiological commitment is revealed as absolutely essential to retributivism in ways that no other commitment is. Without adhering to this axiological commitment, you are not a retributivist.

Furthermore, it is precisely this essential retributivist commitment that the consequentialist denies. It is *this* disagreement, then, that allows us to properly understand the debate between retributivists and consequentialists. Situating the discussion of punishment within the framework of the more fundamental distinction between the axiological and the deontic gives us a particularly crisp and straightforward way of reframing the contemporary debate over the justification of punishment: the debate can be seen, in the first instance, as axiological. The retributivist asserts that deserved punishment is intrinsically valuable, and the consequentialist denies it. Not only is this way of drawing the distinction between these opposing camps sharper than traditional alternatives: it also packs much additional explanatory power. This is particularly true in the sense that so doing clarifies the true nature *both* of retributivism *and* of consequentialism. For to focus on the consequentialist's denial of the essential retributive commitment to the intrinsic value of deserved punishment allows us to see her for what she really is, independently of whatever assuaging, euphemistic words she may choose to characterize her own position.

Consequentialists are, in a very important sense, classical utilitarians: as such, they see punishment as evil, but as an evil that could nonetheless be "justified" (in the remarkably humble sense of "tolerated") if it can be reasonably expected to reduce greater evil. Consequentialists are classical utilitarians at least in the sense that they apply the classical utilitarian axiology to the case of punishment. Admittedly, it is possible to be a classical utilitarian about punishment and yet not endorse classical utilitarianism as a comprehensive moral doctrine; or, in other words, it is possible to be a classical utilitarian about punishment but not about other things. Independently of those possibilities, the point remains: extant consequentialist justifications of punishment are classical utilitarian in the sense just explained.

### 1.3 MONISM AND PLURALISM

Classical utilitarians, however, are not typically concerned with axiological matters *as such*. Typically, their interests are fundamentally deontic: we ought only *act* (punitively and otherwise) when so doing is likely to be useful, *à la* Bentham. This something useful is, a fortiori, the diminution of suffering (or the augmentation of pleasure).[45] Classical utilitarians are above all concerned with what is to be *done*: if they care much about axiological matters, it is only about those that are effectively

---

45   These are not two different goods. Unless otherwise noted, I will throughout mean "both" of these goods whenever I mention one of them. As Williams has pithily put it, "very roughly speaking" utilitarianism is the view "that the only thing that ultimately matters is how much suffering there

linked to the diminution of suffering, and this is why it is a hedonistic doctrine. But this is not because classical utilitarians *lack* an axiological position but because they move beyond their axiological position very quickly. Still, and since this fact has been so systematically neglected, it is worth emphasizing that the most fundamental point of contention between consequentialists and retributivists is, at its root, axiological.

In denying the essential axiological commitment of retributivism, consequentialists are *eo ipso* putting forth their own axiological position, just as Bentham did, namely that there necessarily is disvalue in suffering (deserved or otherwise): in accordance to their founding credo, "punishment [because it necessarily involves suffering] in itself is evil." Importantly, this particular axiological position is not a staple of all forms of utilitarianism; rather, it is characteristic only of its classical, Benthamite incarnation. But it is specifically this classical, Benthamite utilitarianism that is overwhelmingly at play in the contemporary discussion of punishment. The much richer – and much more promising – version of non-Benthamite utilitarianism that I will discuss in this book (above all in Chapter 2) is very rarely addressed by contemporary punishment theorists. The contemporary debate proceeds as if distinctions between different versions of utilitarianism either did not exist or did not matter.[46]

Independently of the higher-order problems with the debate itself, what is immediately clear is that the axiological worldview of classical utilitarianism is rather simple: there is but one good, in terms of which all other putative goods are to be expressed and understood – pleasure (which, as just explained, is in this context equivalent to the absence of pain). This axiological position is not just simple but problematically *simpleminded*. While evidently the word "simpleminded" is meant to express criticism, I do not mean it acrimoniously: I use it throughout in a somewhat technical sense.

In what I think is the most enlightening criticism of classical utilitarianism ever (perhaps with the exception of G. E. Moore's *Principia Ethica*), Williams defined simplemindedness as "having too few thoughts and feelings to match the world as it really is."[47] It is exactly in Williams's sense that I use the term "simpleminded" here.[48] As Williams also pointed out, so understood simplemindedness entails neither "lack of intellectual sophistication" nor "simple-heartedness."[49] Given its foundational axiology, classical utilitarianism is, for reasons that will become clearer

---

is" – see Bernard Williams, "The Human Prejudice," in *Philosophy as a Humanistic Discipline*, Princeton, NJ: Princeton University Press (2006): 135–154, at 144.

[46] There are many versions of utilitarianism. I will concentrate on the distinction between classical utilitarianism and *ideal* utilitarianism (to be defined in due course). So, I will ignore the distinction between act- and rule-utilitarianism, and I will ignore too all other versions of this most malleable of doctrines. Notwithstanding their differences, all versions of utilitarianism accept that, absent medicinal considerations, suffering is in itself evil.

[47] Williams, "A Critique of Utilitarianism," 149.

[48] I do not think that Williams's sense of "simplemindedness" should evoke quite the idea of "moral clumsiness." See Samuel Scheffler, *The Rejection of Consequentialism*, Oxford: Oxford University Press (1982), 3.

[49] Williams, "A Critique of Utilitarianism," 149.

as the book progresses, accurately described as simpleminded, for it unhelpfully reduces – and at times caricaturizes – both the phenomena it seeks to explain and the positions with which it disagrees. There are cases in which one may agree with the course of action classical utilitarianism recommends despite rejecting the explanations that utilitarians would adduce for it. Life just does not reduce to the perennial diminution of suffering, even if on many occasions reducing suffering may be the right thing to do.

As we shall see in due course, Bentham's dictum whereby "punishment is evil" is repeated either verbatim (or almost verbatim) or endorsed in spirit by a large number of contemporary philosophers – even by some who deny that they are utilitarians, let alone *hedonistic* utilitarians. A few of these contemporary philosophers admit that there is intrinsic value in things other than pleasure. For example, a currently popular suggestion among punishment theorists is that there is intrinsic value in the wrongdoer's recognizing that she has done wrong, in her coming to terms with the significance of what she has done, even if this recognition is not pleasant. But these authors are not to be seen as pluralists in my sense, for two reasons. First, because when we examine the details of these authors' theories, we find that their dominant suffering-reducing agendas tend to crowd out other considerations. Second, because the pluralism that I think is worth defending in our context is one that centrally opposes the value of punishment and the value of *forgiveness*. As will become clear later on (above all in Chapter 7), forgiveness is a very special form of diminishing suffering – and in fact a form of suffering diminution that is surprisingly difficult for utilitarians to even countenance. But a certain dismissal of the axiological significance of forgiveness goes beyond the utilitarians. Even those contemporary punishment theorists who properly see themselves as pluralists and who do not succumb to the indiscriminate suffering-reduction agenda of utilitarianism fail to take forgiveness seriously.

To be sure, not all forms of utilitarianism are wedded to hedonism. As we shall see in full detail in the next chapter, *ideal* utilitarians explicitly – and wisely – deny that pleasure is the only valuable thing. The axiology of *ideal* utilitarianism explains the otherwise probably confusing – and hitherto insufficiently investigated – fact that an ideal utilitarian can also embrace retributivism. Insofar as ideal utilitarians deny that pleasure is the only good, their adherents can endorse richer, *pluralistic* axiologies than the simpleminded axiology under whose monolithic heaviness classical utilitarianism groans. (This is so even if their pluralism may be not quite the one I defend here.) Ideal utilitarians can unproblematically embrace (axiological) retributivism, since their pluralistic axiology may allow them to recognize that giving people what they deserve – even if what they deserve is to suffer – is valuable. Moreover, ideal utilitarians can also understand that the value of forgiveness is not to be found in the fact that it reduces suffering simpliciter. These are things that, as I will explain in due course, the immensely more influential classical utilitarian simply cannot do.

The preceding remarks help us foreground four interesting and interrelated characteristics of the contemporary debate concerning the justification of punishment. First, as it turns out, the debate opposes thinkers (the retributivists) who believe that, whatever else may be relevant, the fact that punishment is deserved surely is part of the story of its justification and thinkers (the consequentialists) who believe that, since deserved punishment is at best valueless, the story of punishment's justification should simply be the story of our efforts to diminish suffering in the world. Second, although the core of the debate is axiological (to repeat: whether or not there is value in deserved punishment itself), insofar as the hedonistic utilitarian quickly abandons her own axiological concerns and moves to advance her deontic goals, the debate typically plays out – unhelpfully – as a confrontation between what should be recognized as an essentially axiological doctrine (retributivism) and a doctrine that recognizes itself as essentially deontic (consequentialism). At the very least, distinguishing between the axiological and the deontic dimensions of the debate is likely to help us explain – and sometimes explain away – some of the vexing problems surrounding the way in which the debate over punishment's justification plays out. Third, both consequentialism and *deontic* retributivism are simplemindedly monistic, and it is between these two alternatives that the contemporary debate over the justification of punishment plays out. In this book, I wish to explore the consequences of taking a richer and non-simpleminded pluralistic axiology (with which only *axiological* retributivism is consistent) seriously.

Fourth, and as a corollary to the first three characteristics noted previously, I am here suggesting a new way of mapping the relevant territory. Rather than seeing the difference between retributivism and consequentialism as central to the debate surrounding the justification of punishment, I propose that we recognize that the central distinction is in fact that which opposes monistic and pluralistic justifications of punishment. In this new map, many retributivist justifications, along with many "mixed" justifications of punishment, belong, together with consequentialist justifications, under the category of "monistic" justifications. For example, under this new light, Kant's retributivism and Michael S. Moore's retributivism, just as much as Quinton's and Rawls's and Hart's "mixed justifications," are revealed to be as monistic as Benthamite utilitarianism – and they are thus all grouped together under the general heading "monism."[50] There are, in fact, very few truly pluralistic justifications of punishment.[51]

---

[50]   Famously, Rawls distinguishes between justification from the perspective of a judge and from the perspective of the legislator, and Hart distinguishes between justification at the level of the "general justifying aims" of punishment and at the level of its "distribution." Each of these perspectives in itself is, however, monistic. See Rawls, "Two Concepts of Rules," and Hart, *Punishment and Responsibility, op. cit.* Quinton's "mixed justification" is even more obviously, and more unqualifiedly, monistic (since it is utilitarian through and through).

[51]   The contemporary author who explicitly comes closest to the type of pluralism I defend is John Tasioulas, above all in his "Punishment and Repentance," and in his "Mercy," *Proceedings of the Aristotelian Society* 103 (2003): 101–132. I will discuss him in Chapter 5.

To suggest this new map is not to thereby decree the absolute end of (something like) the distinction between retributivism and consequentialism. For it is possible that this distinction (or one like it) can resurface downstream, as it were. Consider two different pluralistic justifications, one that values desert much more decisively than it values medicinal considerations and one that values medicinal considerations much more decisively than it values desert. It may be thought useful to refer to the former as retributive and to the latter as consequentialist. I am not sure that it *would* indeed be useful to continue employing these labels (at least not without important qualifications), for this may confuse rather than clarify, given that they would refer to justifications that would still be importantly different from what we now call consequentialism and (deontic) retributivism. But even if these labels were used in this way, the distinction would still be operating only *within* the broader category of pluralistic justifications (or, as the case may be, *within* the broader category of monistic justifications, since the possibility discussed in this paragraph could evidently also be imagined under that other heading). And, thus, the fundamental importance of the distinction between monistic and pluralistic justifications that I am championing would remain intact.

These characteristics of the contemporary philosophical debate regarding the justification of punishment – above all the new map of the justifications of punishment I am proposing – are probably surprising to many. At the very least, it is plain that these characteristics and this new map are not generally acknowledged, and I suspect that they may be outright rejected by the orthodoxy among punishment theorists. But understanding what the debate really is about strikes me as crucial to advancing it, and I think that the way in which I frame the debate in this book gets us closer to such understanding.

While proposing a new map is indeed an important contribution to the debate, my goals in this book go beyond that. My more systematic goals are to defend a pluralistic approach to punishment and to show a series of hitherto under-investigated theoretical consequences that flow from taking pluralism seriously. Under this light, it should be clear that I am not interested in defending retributivism as such: what matters most is the pluralism with which axiological retributivism is consistent. Retributivism, understood as an axiological thesis, allows for a richer and pluralistic axiology, one that admits that there is value in both justice (in the form of deserved punishment) and forgiveness, understood as a very specific form of suffering diminution. This is why the pluralistic approach is preferable to consequentialism.

Of course, if retributivism is merely consistent with a pluralistic axiology, it follows that its defenders owe us an explanation as to the deontic import of the intrinsic value of deserved punishment. There are two possible extremes. One extreme is to insist that axiological considerations are completely independent from deontic considerations, so that they have no practical significance whatsoever. The other extreme is to link axiological considerations so tightly to deontic (action-guiding) considerations that the very distinction between the axiological and the deontic becomes moot (in a vein similar to that in which classical utilitarians link their simpleminded monistic axiology to the deontic agenda of diminishing suffering at all costs). Both of these extremes are problematic and, I think, evidently so: one extreme renders retributivism utterly inert regarding practical matters; the other extreme renders the distinction between the axiological and the deontic pointless, thus turning retributivism into as simpleminded and monistic a position as classical utilitarianism.[52] But somewhere along the space separating these extremes there exist sensible positions, from whose consideration the contemporary discussion of punishment stands to benefit.

### 1.4 CONFLICTS, REMAINDERS, AND FORGIVENESS

There are many reasons why sometimes refraining from punishing a deserving wrong-doer is more valuable than punishing him – even if one believes that there is value in inflicting deserved punishment. Perhaps the most conspicuous cases are those in which the refraining is related to resource-allocation and opportunity costs. It is easy to see how the effort to punish wrongdoers could easily come at a high price – financial and otherwise. Sometimes only by not punishing this deserving wrongdoer may we be able to punish a much more deserving wrongdoer. Other times, efforts to punish wrongdoers could be replaced by efforts to reward "rightdoers." And, of course, sometimes resources spent on keeping up the exorbitantly expensive penitentiary apparatuses of modern states could be put to use in much wiser and humane ways – including educational programs that are likely to prevent crime in the first place. Even at the purely interpersonal level, emotional energy expended in punishing those who have wronged us can often be better spent in more productive and meaningful ways.

To acknowledge the existence of these cases is not to thereby *deny* the value of deserved punishment: it is simply to recognize that this value, like any value, can be – and often is – lesser than other values. Again, this is something that pluralists can accept but that monists cannot. Paradoxically, then, it is precisely the *axiological* retributivist, insofar as she is a pluralist, who can accept that the value of desert may, on this or that occasion, be less important than other values (though, of course, she could also accept that the value of desert may, on this or that occasion, be more important than other values). The classical utilitarian cannot see a conflict between desert and other values here: since pleasure is the only value, then pleasure, as a value, simply cannot be greater or lesser than any other (putative) value because there are no other such values.[53] By her lights, deserved suffering is, like all suffering,

---

[52] For more on the connection between the axiological and the deontic, see Bas C. Van Fraasen, "Values and the Heart's Command," *Journal of Philosophy* 70.1 (1973): 5–19.

[53] See John Stuart Mill's unsuccessful attempt to distinguish between the *quality* of pleasures in "Utilitarianism," in *John Stuart Mill: On Liberty, Utilitarianism and Other Essays* (John Gray, ed.), Oxford: Oxford University Press (2008), 136 ff.

always a disvalue. The only way in which she could possibly see a "conflict" in these cases is if she contrasts the amount of pleasure that each of these possible courses of action would generate.

Accepting a pluralistic framework for the justification of punishment, however, is to *thereby* create the possibility of a different type of conflict – the type of conflict with which I will be chiefly concerned in this book. Imagine that we stipulated that resources were not scarce and that punishing the deserving would in no way affect the pursuit of any other worthy goals. It would seem that punishment in these cases would create some goodness "for free," as it were. The classical utilitarian, of course, would reject that this really is "for free," since as long as these inflictions of deserved punishment necessarily cause suffering, she would continue to flatly oppose them (again, assuming no medicinal benefits were obtained).

In trying to avoid the flatness of the utilitarian rejection, we may naturally turn toward retributivism, which would surely recommend punishing the deserving, particularly when (as we have just stipulated) we could do this "for free." But retributivism, in its widespread deontic version, quickly runs into problems too. For we can also imagine cases in which although punishing a deserving wrongdoer would not preclude punishing even more deserving wrongdoers, or rewarding others deserving of reward, or building schools, or channeling funds toward a variety of (more) important projects, *refraining* from punishing a wrongdoer (under certain circumstances) may strike us as producing a more valuable state of affairs than punishing her. In other words, there are cases in which we think that either the sheer sparing of suffering or, much more importantly for my purposes, that peculiar sparing of suffering that is constitutive of *forgiveness* is more valuable than punishment. The *deontic* retributivist cannot possibly countenance these cases: for if deserved punishment is valuable, and it is stipulated that there exist cases in which inflicting said deserved punishment costs us nothing, she should see no reason whatsoever why we should not simply go ahead and punish the deserving.

Monistic approaches – whether utilitarian or (deontic) retributivist – are unable to deal with the fact that the value of punishment and the value of forgiveness are in tension. Both classical utilitarianism and deontic retributivism would implausibly deny that there is a conflict at all: either there is only value in diminishing suffering or there is only value in deserved punishment. The former would, stubbornly, refuse to punish the deserving even when this has no costs, and the latter would, depressingly, never find forgiveness appropriate. Both classical utilitarianism and deontic retributivism exhibit a failure to engage with the axiological complexity this type of conflict reveals. The only way in which these monistic approaches – which dominate punishment theory – could be correct is if it turns out that there *never* is value in meting out deserved suffering or *never* value in its merciful remission. On its face, this possibility strikes me as very implausible. But as the book progresses specific reasons to reject it will be presented.

There is no denying that comparing the values of inflicting deserved suffering against, say, the value of building schools (or of rewarding the deserving, etc.) is often very difficult to do. But it is not *conceptually* difficult, in the sense that if we were able to reliably ascertain the value of each of the states of affairs to be compared, then what would be left to do would be simply a matter of computation. Again, I am not suggesting that these computations are easy – they often are not; what I am suggesting is that the difficulties in such situations are a matter of accountancy, exclusively related to determining the value that each compared constituent part is supposed to have and then adding and deducting those quantified values. The theoretical problem of punishment, in contrast, is not simply a matter of computational accountancy, and the moral mathematics that monism presupposes is incapable of dealing with those problems.

An example may help us to initially fix ideas. Imagine that a friend has done you some wrong, and imagine that you inflict on him what you take to be the punishment that he deserves: say, you end your friendship with him altogether.[54] Imagine further that as a result of your inflicting this punishment, your friend suffers a great deal and that you are aware of his suffering. Being *ex hypothesi* correct in thinking that your friend deserves this punishment does not preclude you from feeling bad about it and about how things turned out. Feeling bad about these things need not cause you to cease inflicting your friend's deserved punishment or to welcome him back into your life. Your distress about his suffering can coexist with your conviction that he deserves to suffer in the ways you are causing him to suffer and that your friendship should not be reestablished.[55] Evidently, these examples can be extended to include state punishment. And they are precisely the examples that monistic approaches cannot explain very well: they cannot explain how, if you create as much value as possible, you should feel bad about it.[56]

The monistic approach will seek to arrive at a final number, a *bottom line*, which will clearly and unequivocally indicate what the all-things-considered most valuable option is – and that single number would be whatever it is independently of how one arrived at it. Punishing your deserving friend, in the preceding example, is *ex hypothesi* the most valuable state of affairs – and with this determination difficulties allegedly end. Still, the suffering you cause your friend *is* suffering,[57] and it does not fully disappear by the fact that inflicting it may be on this or that occasion the correct

---

[54]  For a defense of the (surprisingly contentious) claim that punishment can occur outside the context of the state (or other thickly institutional contexts), see Leo Zaibert, *Punishment and Retribution*, 16 ff.

[55]  It may be thought that the famous image of a parent saying, as she is about to punish her child, "This will hurt me more than it hurts you," is another example of this phenomenon. Often, however, what parents are doing in these sorts of cases is *disciplining* their children, not punishing them: if they could teach the lesson without causing any suffering, they would rather do so. See my *Punishment and Retribution*, 33 ff.

[56]  What exactly this "feeling bad" entails will occupy my attention later on, above all in Chapters 4 and 8.

[57]  Importantly, it is not only the wrongdoer who suffers: her loved ones, who typically are innocent and underserving, suffer as well.

response to his wrongdoing. These moral conflicts do not resolve neatly: they necessarily leave *remainders* or *residues*.[58] But in the simpleminded approach of monism remainders do not really remain.

The eminently *axiological* conflict between the two particularly important values we have been considering – justice and empathy, punishment and forgiveness – is persistent and complex, and it leaves remainders that do not just vanish into thin air once we determine that we are "justified" in *acting* in this or that way. Being justified in doing this or that does not entail that those elements that called for a justification in the first place (which only a properly pluralistic axiology can countenance) altogether disappear. As noted, this axiology ought to recognize the central importance of *precisely* these two values – the value of deserved punishment and the value of its merciful remission – even if it is meant to be broad enough so as to recognize other values too. About this, the mixed theorists were also on the right track, for it was specifically justice and empathy that they were trying (however unsuccessfully) to combine. It is not an insignificant accident, then, that it would be the conflict between these two specific values that Berlin used as an example of the moral conflict that his pluralism can countenance:

> [V]alues may easily clash within the breast of one single individual; and it does not follow that, if they do, some must be true and others false. Justice, rigorous justice, is for some people an absolute value, but it is not compatible with what may be no less ultimate values for them – mercy, compassion – as arises in concrete cases.[59]

I will defend two closely interrelated theses in this book: first, that punishment is *necessarily* morally dilemmatic[60] and, second, that it is dilemmatic in a fundamentally theoretical, axiological (non-medicinal) sense captured by Berlin in this famous passage. Punishment is necessarily dilemmatic in the sense that realizing the value of that justice that is accomplished via the infliction of deserved suffering entails not realizing the value of mercifully remitting said suffering (and vice versa). In other words, both to do justice (in the form of giving wrongdoers the suffering that they deserve) and to try to diminish suffering in the world (particularly in the specific form of forgiveness) realize values. And punishment evidently involves a conflict between these values, in the sense that one cannot realize the value of just punishment without thereby failing to realize the value of forgiveness (and vice versa) – even if there are no indirect costs arising from pragmatic considerations at all. This conflict is much more

---

[58]   I will discuss remainders later, above all in Chapters 4 and 8.

[59]   Isaiah Berlin, "The Pursuit of the Ideal," in *The Crooked Timber of Humanity*, Princeton, NJ: Princeton University Press (1990): 12. This conflict is known by other names too, as the conflict between "justice and charity," "justice and equity," "justice and mercy," "justice and sympathy," "punishment and forgiveness," "punishment and mercy," etc. I take this variety of names to be further, indirect evidence of the centrality of this specific axiological conflict.

[60]   Unless otherwise indicated, I will throughout use "moral dilemma" and "moral conflict" as synonyms.

complicated than contemporary punishment theorists have acknowledged. In this book I will attempt to contribute to remedying this situation.

My task is made easier by the fact that the general discussion of axiological, theoretical moral conflicts constitutes, at present, a quite active area of research. Alasdair MacIntyre has described both the current interest in these moral dilemmas and their peculiar history eloquently:

> [I]f one were to publish two volumes, the first containing the entire preceding philosophical literature dealing with this topic, broadly construed, from Plato to W. D. Ross through Gregory, Aquinas, Kant, Hegel, Mill, Sidgwick, and Bradley while the second was devoted to the publications of the last thirty years, the second volume would be by far the larger.[61]

I will delay exploring the reasons for this peculiar history until Chapter 6, though one could at once point out that to many it has seemed that the very cogency of moral philosophy as such depends on denying that these moral dilemmas can arise. The idea of inescapable wrong seems to erode the very essence of morality. As Christopher Gowans has put it, "most philosophers in this [Western] tradition have assumed that circumstances always make it possible to avoid" moral dilemmas.[62]

What I wish to emphasize at the outset is that contemporary punishment theory has remained largely – and to its detriment – isolated from this rich, insightful, and particularly active contemporary specialized literature on moral dilemmas. This isolation is all the more remarkable in that the contemporary punishment theory with which I engage developed more or less coetaneously with the explosion of interest in ethical dilemmas identified by MacIntyre and others. One can imagine writers in future generations looking back in perplexity at that period – ours – that saw so much important work done in each of these two related areas in so much unhelpful isolation from each other.

Both when we forgive and when we punish we are pulled in different directions by the different values that are in conflict. In its most general form, the conflict revolves around the demands flowing from our sense of justice and the demands flowing from our capacity for empathy (although in both cases the demands need to be supported by *special* moral reasons, to be explained in due course). The conflict resolves in favor of justice in cases of punishment and in favor of empathy in cases of forgiveness. In other words, when we punish, we let the goodness of imparting justice "defeat" the badness of inflicting suffering, and when we forgive, we let the badness of suffering (which belongs to even justified punishment) be "defeated" by the goodness of a certain form of suffering reduction. But – and this is one of the most

---

[61] Alasdair MacIntyre, *Ethics and Politics: Selected Essays*, Vol. 2, Cambridge: Cambridge University Press (2006), 85.

[62] Christopher Gowans, *Innocence Lost: An Examination of Inescapable Moral Wrongdoing*, Oxford: Oxford University Press (1994), 4.

important insights found in the contemporary specialized literature on moral dilemmas – whether the conflict is resolved one way or the other, the value of the "defeated" considerations need not thereby disappear. These conflicts are not zero-sum games.

Insofar as I will seek to connect punishment theory to the specialized literature on moral dilemmas, and in particular insofar as I will take remainders seriously, my approach to the justification of punishment in this book will significantly differ from extant approaches. I have already tried to demonstrate how my approach differs from traditional consequentialist justifications of punishment, from traditional deontic retributivist justifications of punishment, and from traditional mixed justifications of punishments. But, in closing this section, consider also how my approach differs from other recent attempts to see punishment as a form of self-defense or modeled after defensive war or after cases in which someone is sacrificed for the benefit of others. While the "aggressor" in cases of self-defense and in cases of war *may* indeed deserve to be punished for her actions, she *need not* so deserve that (she may not be in the wrong at all). Repelling an attack need not at all be an instance of punishment. Typical sacrificeable characters – say, in trolley problems – are assumed to be innocent. And yet there are cases in which we may be justified in repelling threats or attacks, in causing undeserved suffering, and indeed in *sacrificing* completely innocent people, independently of whether these actions may realize any values of justice.

An obvious and crucial difference between any potential punishee on the one hand and any potential aggressor, threat, or innocent sacrificeable person on the other is that only the former necessarily *deserves* the suffering she is about to endure. Desert is inseparable from punishment in ways that render punishment very different from these other cases in which desert is inessential.[63] If in any of these other cases the goal could be achieved without causing suffering, that would clearly be preferable – and that is not true of punishment, where deserved suffering is in itself valuable. These other cases may perhaps generate conflicts, and we may indeed feel

---

[63] Jeff McMahan, for example, tends to underplay the differences between punishment and these other phenomena. McMahan thinks that punishment can be a just cause of war. But he further thinks that just war *must* be defensive and that punishment *must* be a medicinal matter or, in his own terms, a matter of "defense or deterrence" – further adding that "just war is never retributive." See his "Aggression and Punishment," in *War: Essays in Political Philosophy* (Larry May, ed.), Cambridge: Cambridge University Press (2008): 67–84, at 84. Similarly, in his recent and ambitious *The Ends of Harm* . . ., Victor Tadros defends a justification of punishment explicitly based on a medicinal view of punishment, one that models punishment on self-defense (whereby wrongdoers owe duties of protection to innocents) and that explicitly excludes desert. Daniel M. Farrell, in his "The Justification of General Deterrence," *The Philosophical Review* 94.3 (1985): 367–394, and Warren Quinn, in his "The Right to Threaten and the Right to Punish," *Philosophy and Public Affairs* 14.4 (1985): 327–373, also explicitly draw parallels between punishment and self-defense. For a different effort (in my opinion more interesting, since it shines needed light on the *reality* of suffering) to examine some connections between the justification of punishment and just war theory, see Alice Ristroph, "Just Violence," *Arizona Law Review* (2014): 1017–1063.

bad for having to kill people at war or for having to sacrifice innocents in some contexts. But these cases do not generate quite the type of moral conflict that punishment as such generates. These other cases do not generate the specific form of moral distress that punishment generates – because they do not generate the remainders that punishment generates. And so the strategy to model punishment after any of these other phenomena is doomed to fail as well, as it disengages from one of the essential values that punishment is supposed to realize: the value of justice achieved via the infliction of deserved suffering.

To repeat, this book is not about emphasizing the value of deserved suffering as such – it is about recognizing its inescapable relevance for the justification of punishment and the inescapable way in which it conflicts with the value of the merciful remission of said deserved suffering. To discuss punishment without paying attention to the moral conflict it generates (and its attendant remainders) is not only an impoverished exercise but truly an exercise in futility: a way of unwittingly ensuring that the central debate over punishment's justification will remain mired in an unproductive stalemate. If the debate over punishment's justification is to be advanced, we need to play much closer attention to the central conflict opposing the value of deserved suffering and the value of its merciful remission. Punishment is intrinsically dilemmatic, even if all *practical* problems are stipulated away and even if we are justified in inflicting it, because punishment involves inescapable wrongdoing and thus necessarily generates remainders. The devil is, so to speak, in those remainders.

## 1.5 OVERVIEW

Thus far I have, via an emphasis on the connections between punishment and theodicies, argued for the importance of paying attention to the distinction between the axiological and the deontic, which has been largely ignored by punishment theorists. I have suggested that this distinction allows us to draw a new map of the justifications of punishment centrally based on the distinction between pluralism and monism (rather than on the traditional distinction between retributivism and consequentialism) and that the pluralism on which I focus is particularly attuned to the values of deserved punishment and of forgiveness. I have also sketched some general reasons why pluralism is to be preferred over monism, and discussed some consequences of embracing a properly pluralistic justification of punishment.

In Chapter 2 ("Prolegomena to Any Future Axiology"), I seek to lay bare the essential contours of any reasonable axiology of punishment. Taking as point of departure the consideration of the intrinsic value of desert, I will expand on the appeal of a pluralistic axiology. A major goal of the chapter is to correct one of the most firmly entrenched misconceptions in punishment theory (no doubt anchored in the traditional map I think should be abandoned): that desert matters only to retributivists and that this is essentially a Kantian motif. I will show that, analytically speaking, there is nothing particularly Kantian about the importance of desert and that the intrinsic value of desert is recognized by some influential utilitarians. Desert is an essential aspect of any even minimally attractive axiology of punishment, quite independently of whether one *also* endorses retributivism. I highlight the value of desert, again, because insofar as I also take for granted the value of the diminution of suffering (and in particular the value of the *merciful* diminution of suffering), this begins to delineate the characteristics of the pluralism I defend.

The main authors I will discuss in the chapter are, then, all profoundly anti-Kantian and all fundamentally committed to pluralism: e.g., G. E. Moore and Franz Brentano. Of particular interest for my project are their views on organic wholes. I will try to show that the framework of organic wholes is very helpful for advancing our understanding of the justification of punishment.

In Chapters 3 and 4 – "The Persistence of Consequentialism" and "The Gerrymandering Gambit: Retributivism in the Budget Room" – I explore the different ways in which the vast majority of contemporary punishment theorists fail to embrace the pluralism that I suggest is indispensable for a correct axiology of punishment. Both punishment theorists and influential generalists espouse a variety of views about punishment that are, with respect to punishment, simpleminded and at odds with the pluralism that I recommend here. These uninspiring views, moreover, are evident across the board, indeed visible in both consequentialist and deontic retributivist approaches.

In Chapter 3, I will seek to expose the truly immense influence that classical utilitarianism continues to exert among punishment theorists. Rather than taking the well-trodden path of criticizing famous classical utilitarians (who can perhaps be seen as too-easy targets), I will focus instead on authors whose comprehensive moral doctrines officially eschew utilitarianism. And I will argue that when it comes to their views on punishment in particular, they remain (sometimes in spite of their protestations to the contrary) classical utilitarians. These thinkers see no value (absent medicinal benefits) in giving wrongdoers the punishment they deserve because they so deserve it. Like Bentham, they see punishment as bad in itself and thus as only *tolerable* when its infliction is deemed necessary for diminishing greater suffering. They are so focused on the (admittedly excessive) amount of suffering that contemporary criminal justice systems generate that their vision is clouded: *all* that they seek to do is to reduce suffering. As a result, I will suggest that these thinkers are not only classical utilitarians about punishment but also proto-abolitionists about it as well (although not all of them are aware of this): if they could reduce suffering in the world without inflicting any punishment, they would do so.[64] (Derek Parfit's

---

[64] Among the explicit defenders of full-blown abolitionism, see David Boonin (*The Problem of Punishment, op. cit.*). Among those who see their approach as at least a "stepping stone" on the road to full-blown abolitionism, see Victor Tadros (*The Ends of Harm . . ., op. cit.*). For criticisms of Boonin's position, see Leo Zaibert, "Punishment, Restitution, and the Formidable Method of Directing the Intention" *Criminal Justice Ethics* 29.1 (2010) 41–53; for criticism of Tadros's position,

belongs in this group too. But since his view is actually metaphysical – that while many things can be deserved, suffering *cannot* be deserved – I discuss, and reject, his arguments in an appendix.)

Although the failure to take pluralism seriously is most commonly the result of a monistic obsession with diminishing suffering, in Chapter 4 I show how influential deontic retributivists are also trapped in a monistic axiology. It is of course not the effort to diminish suffering that causes the retributivist's monism but her exaggerated concern with desert. I will in that chapter focus on the most famous historical defense of retributivism – Immanuel Kant's – and on today's most systematic and ambitious defense of retributivism – Michael Moore's. Rightly, Moore rejects the traditional mixed justifications of punishment, but he glibly explains this rejection by suggesting that retributivism cannot "share the stage with any other punishment goal."[65] Those other goals are, in Moore's mind, demoted to the level of a "happy surplus," and thus they play, for him, no role whatsoever in the justification of punishment.[66] I will argue that Moore has, perhaps unwittingly, constructed a justification of punishment that is as monistic and narrow as the classical utilitarian justifications that he so insightfully criticizes.

In so doing, Moore has missed the real enemy. The enemy is not utilitarianism as such but the monistic axiology upon which its (admittedly widespread) classical version rests. Discussing the ways in which Moore (and Kant) have replaced a monistic axiology with another monistic axiology is instructive in delineating the importance of taking pluralistic axiologies – and the moral conflicts that they generate – seriously. I will in this chapter discuss two specific consequences of these retributivists' failure to engage with moral conflicts. First, they miss the opportunity to offer a coherent account of the emotional dimensions of punishment, thus yielding an impoverished account of punishment whereby its difference from revenge is elusive. Second, they have very little to say regarding how to react to *evil* (understood as a form of wrongdoing qualitatively different from the merely bad).

In Chapter 5 – "Communication, Forgiveness, and Topography" – I turn my attention to what I take to be the most promising contemporary approach to the justification of punishment: the understandably popular communicative theory. In ways that I will discuss in the chapter, the communicative framework may be seen as the most amenable to the pluralism that I wish to defend. But I will explore two closely interrelated potential shortcomings of this framework. First, the framework could be deployed in such a way that it turns out to be but a new version of consequentialism, inheriting its problems. Second, even if not fully consequentialist, the framework could turn out to be axiologically monistic nonetheless. This could happen if the framework ends up being a matter of mainly substituting either

---

see Leo Zaibert, "The Instruments of Abolition, or Why Retributivism Is the Only Real Justification of Punishment," *Law and Philosophy* 32 (2012): 33–58.
[65] Moore, *Placing Blame*, 28.    [66] *Ibid.*, 153.

"deserved punishment" or "suffering diminution" with "communicating right messages," in a way that the monism is preserved.

In fact, R. A. Duff, one of today's leading champions of the communicative approach to punishment, has deliberately combined this approach with a self-consciously narrow view of punishment. Duff defends an "avowedly limited, and in an important sense shallow, institution [of criminal law, and of punishment in general]."[67] Duff believes that this is necessary in order to assure manageability. I will argue that Duff buys manageability at too high a price – and faux manageability anyhow: matters really *are* more complicated than Duff takes them to be.[68] Duff's efforts to keep things manageable lead him to underestimate the importance of those moral conflicts that a rich and properly pluralistic axiology engenders.

John Tasioulas, although squarely within the influence of Duff's communicative approach, nonetheless objects to Duff's endorsement of this odd shallowness regarding punishment.[69] I agree with a lot of what Tasioulas says, and I think that the spirit that motivates him is very similar to the spirit that motivates me. But I think that the differences between us are nonetheless important – and that their consideration may help advance the debate over punishment's justification. To a large extent, Tasioulas endorses the communicate framework because he thinks that it is in fact the best framework to accommodate the pluralism that we both think is important – a pluralism capable of registering both the value of deserved suffering and its merciful remission. In contrast, I will argue that axiological pluralism and communicative enterprises are rather independent matters. While Tasioulas comes as close as any contemporary author to what I believe is the right sort of pluralism, his emphasizing the communicative approach to punishment rather than the axiological approach I recommend causes him to ultimately offer a problematic account of forgiveness. And this problematic account of forgiveness renders his approach to the justification of punishment also problematic.

Up to this point in the book, I will have mostly been interested in advancing two interrelated goals: first, to present, incrementally, most of the essential tenets of my approach to the justification of punishment and, second, to show that extant justifications of punishment are indeed monistic and problematically simple-minded. The obvious corollary to these two goals is that my approach is to be preferred to its alternatives. In Chapter 6 – "The Allure of the Ledger: Better Than a Dog Anyhow" – I engage with possible reasons to resist my approach. I undertake to present a genealogy of these reasons, and I locate their origin in famous positions

---

[67] R. A. Duff, "The Intrusion of Mercy," *Ohio Journal of Criminal Law* 4 (2007): 360–387, at 376.

[68] Allegedly more manageable approaches, say, like classical utilitarianism, are not without problems and complexities of their own anyhow. For example, even the staunchest defenders of utilitarianism admit that it lacks "an adequate theory of *objective* probability" and that therefore it lacks "a secure theoretical basis" – though they add that such secure theoretical basis is also missing from deontological ethical systems or from ethical systems based on "ordinary prudence." See, e.g., J. J. C. Smart, "An Outline of a System of Utilitarian Ethics," in J. J. C. Smart and B. A. O. Williams, 41, and *passim*.

[69] Tasioulas, "Mercy," and Tasioulas, "Punishment and Repentance."

within moral philosophy more generally. While these positions are admittedly widespread, they have also been famously and powerfully criticized. Regrettably, the debate that has ensued (between the defenders of these positions and their critics) at the level of moral philosophy in general has had no counterpart within punishment theory in particular.

To a large extent, the debate relates to our very understanding of moral thinking and to whether it is to be modeled after mathematics and economics. One important aspect of this understanding (whether consciously acknowledged or not) is that moral "items" can easily – and at any rate profitably – be ledgered. Mobilizing Williams's notion of moral luck, and in particular its connection to Williams' criticism of "the morality system," I reject such an alluring approach – both at the general level of moral philosophy and in particular regarding the justification of punishment. This rejection, however, seems to leave us with an unmanageably messy situation in which we lack enough guidance as to what is to be done – including, as the case may be, whether punishment ought to be inflicted. I explore the extent to which this relative indeterminacy is or is not a serious problem. One prominent reason why my approach is not as messy as it may on first approximation appear to be is that, while my pluralism allows many (possibly innumerably many) factors to be relevant to the justification of punishment, I nonetheless focus on just two. These two factors – which are, as I have already noted, quintessential to a *properly* pluralistic approach to punishment – are the (antithetical) values of inflicting deserved suffering and of its merciful remission.[70]

While my decision to focus on two (the two most important) of the many values that are possibly relevant to the justification of punishment may *ceteris paribus* render matters more manageable than if I were discussing many values, it does not solve all problems. For my understanding of forgiveness does not see it as ever issuing in duties to forgive. This account of forgiveness may seem to render the tension of its value and the value of punishment particularly unstable. In Chapter 7 – "The Right Kind of Complexity" – I undertake to show why this instability is in fact to be welcomed because it is a relatively small price to pay for the ability to engage with a wide variety of values and reasons for action.

For example, in that chapter I defend the perhaps perplexing view that classical utilitarianism simply has no theoretical room for forgiveness, for it simply has no room for the kind of reason that would turn a garden-variety diminution of suffering into a bona fide instance of forgiveness. Axiological retributivism, in contrast, can accommodate forgiveness and its underlying constitutive reasons. Martha Nussbaum, however, suggests that axiological retributivism can only do this – just as it can only posit value in deserved suffering – as a result of engaging in "magical

---

[70]  At one given time, one given person can either punish or forgive. I will ignore cases involving many agents (some of whom punish and some of whom forgive), agents who first punish and then forgive (or vice versa), and cases of partial forgiveness.

thinking." I defend axiological retributivism from this charge and in fact show that Nussbaum's recent rapprochement with utilitarianism is regrettable and unhelpful.

Earlier in her career, Nussbaum insightfully sharpened our understanding of the complexity of moral life. Her recent overtures toward more simpleminded philosophical doctrines seem to me to undermine her own early contributions. Although her being distressed by the dysfunctional aspects of criminal justice systems noted at the outset is understandable, Nussbaum's wholesale ejection of punishment and punishment theory is not. Nussbaum flatly – with the same simplemindedness of the utilitarianism she now courts – rejects that there is any value in deserved suffering. And this position prevents her from even seeing precisely those difficult but crucially important conflicts generated by the tension between the value of deserved suffering and the value of its merciful remission. And it is only by engaging with these conflicts that the much needed and elusive progress regarding the justification of punishment is to be attained.

Thus, in Chapter 8 – "The Jugglery of Circumstances: Dirty Hands and Impossible Stories" – I follow Nussbaum's recommendation (from earlier in her career) and turn to a literary text in order to capture the type of moral dilemma that punishment is. It is not literature as such that interests me – though I have nothing against it; it is rather the fact that literature tends to present matters with much more complexity than schematic thought experiments. And it tends, too, to much more faithfully capture the axiological complexity of punishment and our responses to wrongdoing in general. I undertake to show how punishment can generate remainders: the wrongness of inflicting suffering does not just vanish in thin air because we are sometimes justified in inflicting it. I am not skeptical about justification: we really are sometimes justified in punishing wrongdoers – and sometimes even absent any medicinal considerations. But I will show how the structure of punishment's justification is more complicated than typically assumed.

The remainders that punishment generates can sometimes emotionally affect punishers; sometimes punishment – even if justified – *taints* us. These taints tend to have emotional repercussions. Of course, sometimes the value realized by punishing a certain wrongdoer is so much greater than the value that would have been realized by forgiving her that the taint arising from its infliction is minimal and its potential emotional repercussions negligible. But not all cases are like this. So, I discuss cases in which the sight of a punisher *not* emotionally affected by having had to punish rightly strikes us as disturbing. In other words, in some cases we respect and admire precisely those punishers who are emotionally affected for what they did. Their emotional distress reveals that they are able to judge with nuance and with depth. The consideration of taints should affect the way in which we think about – and ultimately inflict – punishment.

## 2

# Prolegomena to Any Future Axiology

The title of this chapter evidently evokes the title of Kant's famous book.[1] But the point I wish to make by this evocation is the opposite of what may probably be expected: there is very little Kantian in this chapter. And this may seem surprising, since part of what I will argue here is that desert ought to be admitted, alongside the merciful diminution of suffering, as a valuable element in any plausible axiology, particularly where punishment is concerned. As is well known, desert has traditionally been seen as the quintessential feature of retributivism, and Kant has traditionally been seen as – if not *the* – at least *a* quintessential retributivist. Part of what this chapter will reveal, however, is that there is no necessary connection between Kant (or Kantian views) and the ways in which I will argue desert ought to figure in any plausible axiology of punishment.

It is not merely that Kant plays no role in my views in this chapter – it is that some of the most important authors who do play central roles in the chapter happen to be profoundly anti-Kantian. Independently of whatever contributions this chapter may offer vis-à-vis the history of ideas as such or vis-à-vis our historical understanding of the thorny problem of the justification of punishment, I here seek to advance two main analytical goals. First, I wish to show *why* deserved punishment is valuable. Second, and no less importantly, I wish to argue that once we understand why desert is valuable, we should understand also why any plausible axiology of punishment must recognize this value.

The chapter breaks down into three sections and a conclusion. In Section 2.1, as I examine some typically overlooked connections between G. E. Moore's and Franz Brentano's axiological views, I will show that both these decidedly anti-Kantian and indeed utilitarian thinkers (utilitarians of a certain sort, to be explained in due course) admitted that desert – including, conspicuously, deserved suffering – is an indispensible part of any plausible axiology of punishment. I will further argue that even one of

[1] Immanuel Kant, *Prolegomena to Any Future Metaphysics* (Gary Hatfield, ed.), Cambridge: Cambridge University Press (2009).

the world's most important contemporary defenders of a straightforward hedonistic utilitarianism, Fred Feldman, incorporates desert into his axiology. In the second section, I discuss one way (the best way, in my opinion) in which desert can enter into one's axiology: the framework of organic wholes.[2] Although this framework is often and rightly associated with G. E. Moore, it has also been endorsed by many other thinkers. A consequence of the views discussed in this section is that since there are very few limits as to what can possibly be a part of any given organic whole, the framework of organic wholes is particularly conducive for richly pluralistic approaches to punishment. In the third section and in the conclusion, I will discuss a couple of possible objections to the appeal to organic wholes. Discussing these objections, I think, clarifies both the nature of the axiology of punishment defended in the chapter and some of the general goals defended in the book.

## 2.1 IDEAL UTILITARIANISM, DESERT, AND THE RICHNESS OF THE MORAL UNIVERSE

In the very first sentence of his review of Brentano's *The Origin of Our Knowledge of Right and Wrong*, Moore claimed that it contained "a far better discussion of the most fundamental principles of Ethics than any others with which [he was] acquainted."[3] Although he detects a certain arrogance in Brentano's "confidence both in the originality and in the value of his own work," Moore nonetheless admits that such self-confidence is "completely justified" for "it would be difficult to exaggerate the importance" of Brentano's work.[4] Alas, Moore's reasons for such an extraordinary assessment – particularly against the backdrop of the rich tradition of superb British moralists with which Moore was so well acquainted – remain under-investigated, even among those familiar with Moore's review of Brentano. The most notable exception, among generalists, has been Roderick M. Chisholm, whose *Brentano and Intrinsic Value* is not only the best presentation of Brentano's ethics in the English language but also the best study of its connection to Moore's views.[5] Among punishment theorists, these matters are almost completely ignored.

As Chisholm reminds us, "Brentano's theory is a theory of intrinsic value. It is concerned with that which is 'good and bad in itself' or 'good or bad as an end' and not with that which is merely good or bad as a means."[6] In other words, Brentano is interested in things that are non-medicinally good. Moreover, Chisholm also points out that Brentano's theory ought to be sharply distinguished from

> the theories of Bentham, Mill, and Sidgwick, who had held that pleasure alone [including the diminution of pain] is intrinsically good. Some pleasure is not intrinsically good, according to Brentano, and some displeasure is not intrinsically

---

[2] Following standard practice, I will use "organic wholes" and "organic unities" interchangeably.
[3] G. E. Moore, "Review" in *International Journal of Ethics* 14.1 (1903): 115–123, at 115.    [4] *Ibid.*, 115.
[5] Roderick M. Chisholm, *Brentano and Intrinsic Value*, Cambridge: Cambridge University Press (1986).
[6] *Ibid.*, 3.

bad. Moreover, some things other than pleasure are intrinsically good, and some things other than displeasure [or suffering] are intrinsically bad.[7]

Brentano's theory, then, is not just concerned above all with intrinsic value but also evidently "pluralistic," in the sense that it allows a variety of things other than pleasure to be intrinsically valuable.[8] These two characteristics are also conspicuously present in Moore's ethics. These shared characteristics explain why some have pointed out that "Brentano's ethical theory was an ideal utilitarianism that had yet to acquire the name" – an ideal utilitarianism *avant la lettre*.[9] After all, it is Moore himself who is generally regarded as the most influential exponent of ideal utilitarianism.[10]

For my purposes here, there is a crucial distinction between ideal utilitarianism and *the* version of utilitarianism that has received overwhelming attention within the context of punishment theory: classical utilitarianism. As we saw in the previous chapter, classical utilitarianism is both hedonistic and non-pluralistic, whereas, we now see, ideal utilitarianism is emphatically neither. Brentano denies that there exists "one sort of thing that would be under all circumstances the best thing attainable." Neither the maximal augmentation of pleasure nor the maximal diminution of suffering would be necessarily the best thing to do: "[F]or Brentano's ideal consequentialism, there is no concrete, non-formal end the pursuit of which would always be a positive value."[11] And the same can be said of Moore's ideal utilitarianism.

While evidently pluralistic and non-hedonistic, ideal utilitarianism is still utilitarianism in the sense that its adherents believe that the right thing to do is to maximize the amount of intrinsic goodness in the world, however variegated and indeed plural the contours and the constitutive elements of such goodness may turn out to be. Ideal utilitarianism represents an obvious improvement over classical utilitarianism: because of its pluralism, because of its allowing many – potentially infinite – things to be valuable in themselves, ideal utilitarianism is able to engage with a much richer moral universe than does classical utilitarianism. As we have seen, the classical utilitarian is simpleminded in the sense that, in the final analysis, she has only one goal in life – to seek pleasure (or to avoid suffering) – and only one simple

---

[7]   *Ibid.*, 4. As mentioned in the previous chapter, one should pause before including Mill in this group without qualification, given Mill's (admittedly problematic though not for that any less real) view whereby there exist higher and lower pleasures. Mill was neither fully Benthamite nor fully "ideal" (in a sense of "ideal" to become clear immediately).

[8]   Roderick Chisholm, *Brentano . . .*, 4.

[9]   Robert Welsh Jordan, "Review of Edmund Husserl's *Vorlesungen über Ethik und Wertlehre 1908–1914 Edited by Ullrich Melle* (Husserliana, Vol. XXVIII). Dordrecht/Boston/London: Kluwer Academic Publishers, 1988," *Husserl Studies* 8 (1992): 221–232, at 221.

[10]  Even if the term itself was coined by Hastings Rashdall in *The Theory of Good and Evil: A Treatise on Moral Philosophy*, Oxford: Oxford University Press (1907). And even if some central aspects of ideal utilitarianism can be seen as developments of Henry Sidgwick's views in *The Methods of Ethics*, Indianapolis, IN: Hackett 1981).

[11]  Welsh Jordan, "Review . . .," 222.

formula for establishing value – the more pleasure (or the less suffering), the more value.[12] And since this is the only goal, she hardly has space for moral conflicts in her worldview, and, in fact, she hardly has space for *really* difficult choices (i.e., choices where the difficulty goes beyond computational matters).

I think that even the most cursory reflection on our moral lives, on "what experience makes evident to us,"[13] lends all the support that is needed to the view that a richer axiology does a better job of capturing the moral universe as it really is than does an impoverished one. We value many different things: knowledge, love, friendship, art, sports, food, and so on; and, unlike classical utilitarians, we do not think that we could easily – if at all – express the value of some of these things in terms of anything else without thereby caricaturizing them. Recall Brentano's famous example:

> Consider how ridiculous it would be if someone said that the amount of pleasure he has in smoking a good cigar is such that, if it were multiplied by 127, or say by 1077, it would be precisely equal to the amount of pleasure he has in listening to a symphony of Beethoven or in viewing one of Raphael's madonnas.[14]

It is precisely this type of fungibility that classical utilitarians require – everything has to be expressible in the homogenizing terms of the amount of pleasure it generates – and that pluralists reject.

As a way to further bolster axiological pluralism, consider the way in which the most ingenious contemporary defenders of the axiological monism enshrined in classical utilitarianism, Fred Feldman, deals with Brentano's powerful objection, and with two other even more famous – and in my opinion even more powerful – objections to hedonism. Feldman links Brentano's point to a similar point made by John Rawls in A *Theory of Justice*:

> there are different sorts of agreeable feelings themselves incomparable, as well as the quantitative dimensions of pleasure, intensity and duration. How are we to balance these when they conflict? Are we to choose a brief but intense pleasant experience of one kind of feeling over a less intense pleasant experience of another?[15]

---

[12]   Again, I do not think these are two different goals. When philosophers speak of hedonism's concern with producing pleasure, they typically mean to include the avoidance of suffering as well. The *urgency* of a particular action tending to alleviate suffering, however, may be greater than that of a particular action tending toward increasing pleasure, as, for example, Karl Popper suggested in *The Open Society and Its Enemies*, London: Routledge (1945), 205.

[13]   Franz Brentano, *The Origins of Our Knowledge of Right and Wrong* (Oskar Kraus and Roderick M. Chisholm, eds.), London: Routledge (1969), 31. I will return to this phenomenological reflection in Chapter 8.

[14]   Brentano, *The Origins . . .*, 31.

[15]   John Rawls, *A Theory of Justice* (revised edn.), Cambridge, MA: Harvard University Press (1999), 488. See also Fred Feldman, *Pleasure and the Good Life: Concerning the Nature, Varieties, and Plausibility of Hedonism*, Oxford: Clarendon Press (2004), 45–46.

Immediately after citing this passage by Rawls, however, Feldman claims that although "the general drift of the passages [Brentano's and Rawls] is fairly clear," he thinks that "the details of the argument remain obscure." In light of this alleged obscurity, Feldman's response is rather humble: in his own words, "really just a suggestion."[16]

Feldman's suggestion is to offer three different detailed interpretations of what Brentano and Rawls may be after in these passages. Feldman's first interpretation sees the passages as "just an application of the principle that 'ought' implies 'can.'"[17] The passages may be read as offering the following objection: sometimes we are under an obligation to determine the relative pleasantness of two experiences, and we cannot do this in cases such as Brentano's cigar. Feldman's second interpretation is that Brentano and Rawls are in fact suggesting that hedonistic utilitarians cannot admit that different pleasant experiences can indeed be phenomenologically different. Finally, Feldman's third interpretation posits that the passages seek to question the possibility that pleasant episodes "come in precise amounts,"[18] so that the passages may merely seek to challenge the computational accountancy of classical utilitarianism.

I think that the passages, in any of Feldman's interpretations, pose obvious and serious problems for hedonism. But Feldman disagrees, for, in his view, the hedonistic utilitarian may, addressing each of these three possible objections in order, admit that (1) she may in fact be unable to "calculate accurately the number of hedons in any episode of pleasure";[19] that (2) she needs to endorse a more complicated ontology whereby in addition to any experiences we have (which could be phenomenologically very different from each other), we also have "the feeling of pleasure itself" that is always phenomenologically identical;[20] and that (3) pleasure and pains cannot be measured anyhow.

These are not inconsequential admissions. So, unlike Feldman, I do not think that hedonistic utilitarianism can survive unscathed after its proponents make any of these admissions. Rather than digressing on why these are problems for hedonistic utilitarians, I want to suggest that Feldman misses the essential point of the objection in these passages, what he calls their "drift." The gist of the objection is that hedonistic utilitarianism is *reductive*: more precisely, that it reduces the complexity of our moral life to an impoverished monism. In other words, the gist of the objection is that there is more to life than pleasure. The point is quite clear in Rawls, who is here above all arguing against the "dominant-end conception of deliberation," that is, against the view that there is one single end that renders all rational choice in principle possible.[21] These Rawlsian motifs are integral parts of his overall position that while it may perhaps be "a simple matter to show that hedonism gets us nowhere," it is nonetheless worthwhile to

[16] Feldman, *Pleasure* . . ., 46.    [17] *Ibid.*, 46.    [18] *Ibid.*, 48.    [19] *Ibid.*, 47.    [20] *Ibid.*, 48.
[21] Rawls, A *Theory* . . ., 486.

examine why so many have been "driven to resort to such a desperate expedient."[22]

These motifs are central, too, to Brentano's project, predicated as it is on the view that one thing being better than another sometimes has "nothing to do with [the] comparative intensity" of the bare pleasures each generates, but rather with the "peculiar type of phenomenon ... of preferring" – a phenomenon linked to the idea of it being *correct* to value one thing more than another, independently of any consideration regarding pleasure.[23] One reason why we may be correct in preferring one thing over another is that that thing *deserves* to be so preferred. Neither Brentano nor Rawls (though for different reasons) was at all concerned in these passages with the problem of quantifying pleasures or suffering as such; rather both were concerned with exposing the axiological monism of classical utilitarianism.

This essential point of the objections that Feldman finds obscure – i.e., the injunction against the monism involved in seeing one overarching type of good (i.e., pleasure) as exhausting the moral universe – is crucially important for my purposes. Of course, classical utilitarianism is a paradigmatic example of this simplemindedness, and since I will argue (in the next chapter) that, in spite of protestations to the contrary, the hedonistic approach continues to be extraordinarily influential within the context of punishment theory, the importance of engaging with these objections to hedonism should be evident. Pluralism – extremely rare among punishment theorists – is, other things being equal, less simpleminded than monism.[24]

Let us then turn to Feldman's reaction to two other famous objections that Feldman seems to think pose more serious problems to hedonistic utilitarianism and to the impoverished axiology it presupposes: Moore's "Heap of Filth" thought experiment and W. D. Ross's "Two Worlds" thought experiment. Feldman groups together these two thought experiments in what is effectively the last chapter of his book, titled "Problems about Beauty and Justice."[25] I think that this reveals the importance that Feldman, rightly, attaches to the objections embedded in the thought experiments. But, again, I do not think that Feldman is in the end convincing – I think that these objections do reveal insurmountable difficulties for the

---

[22]　*Ibid.*, 490. As I will argue, even those who agree with Rawls in general have nonetheless been "driven to resort to such a desperate expedient" when it comes to punishment.

[23]　Brentano, *The Origins* . . ., 26. While Brentano is famously credited with presenting a seminal "fitting attitude theory of value," I need not here decide the *grounds* on which this valuing is correct. As Daniel Jacobson has put it, "all sides grant that it is fitting to approve of the good and disapprove of the bad; what differentiates [the fitting attitude theory of value from others] is its ambition to explicate value by way of (fitting) evaluative attitudes" in his "Fitting Attitude Theories of Value," *The Stanford Encyclopedia of Philosophy* (Spring 2011 edn., Edward N. Zalta, ed.), https://plato.stanford.edu/archives/spr2011/entries/fitting-attitude-theories/.

[24]　In Chapter 4, I will argue that influential versions of retributivism are monistic too.

[25]　Strictly speaking, this is the penultimate chapter, but the actual last chapter, "Themes and Puzzles," is just a brief summation of sundry matters.

reductionist axiology of hedonistic utilitarianism. Consider first Moore's famous thought experiment:

> Let us imagine one world exceedingly beautiful. Imagine it as beautiful as you can; put into it whatever on this earth you most admire – mountains, rivers, the sea; trees, and sunsets, stars and moon. Imagine all these combined in the most exquisite proportions, so that no one thing jars against another, but each contributes to increase the beauty of the whole. And then imagine the ugliest world you can possibly conceive. Imagine it simply one heap of filth, containing everything that is most disgusting to us, for whatever reason, as far as may be, without one redeeming feature. Such a pair of worlds we are entitled to compare . . . The only thing we are not entitled to imagine is that any human being ever has or ever, by any possibility, *can*, live in either, can ever see and enjoy the beauty of the one or hate the foulness of the other.

And Moore's no less famous reaction to this comparison:

> Well, even so, supposing them quite apart from any possible contemplation by human beings; still, is it irrational to hold that it is better that the beautiful world should exist, than the one which is ugly? Would it not be well, in any case, to do what we could to produce it rather than the other? Certainly I cannot help thinking that it would; and I hope that some may agree with me in this extreme instance.[26]

This constitutes a problem for classical utilitarianism in the sense that, if one agrees with Moore, there exists, then, something more valuable than something else, and this is completely independent from considerations regarding pleasure or suffering, since after all neither of Moore's two worlds contains any of either. Feldman, however, disagrees: "[W]hen considered in itself, devoid of population as it is stipulated to be, the beautiful world is intrinsically no better than the ugly one."[27] I find it difficult to agree with Feldman on this. But it could be argued that this is one of those cases in which we have reached a point of disagreement about bedrock intuitions, and that is that. The hedonistic utilitarian's claim that the beautiful world is better *only* insofar as this world "has the capacity (if only it could be populated!) to produce pleasure in those who contemplate it"[28] is evidently not absurd. And this is a position that could, moreover, in the final analysis be correct. But we can, I think, avoid this stalemate of intuitions by considering the next objection to hedonistic utilitarianism, in which the stalemate does not seem to obtain.

Ross writes:

> If we compare two imaginary states of the universe, alike in the total amounts of virtue and vice and of pleasure and pain present in the two, but in one of which the virtuous were all happy and the vicious miserable, while in the other the virtuous

---

[26] Moore, *Principia*, 135.    [27] Feldman, *Pleasure . . .*, 192.    [28] *Ibid.*

were miserable and the vicious happy, very few people would hesitate to say that the first was a much better state of the universe than the second.[29]

Feldman begins his reply by admitting that "Ross's objection is a tougher nut to crack [than is Moore's]."[30] And he immediately adds: "[W]hereas we can reasonably say that in itself the beautiful world is no better than the ugly one, it may seem somewhat unreasonable to say that the just world is no better than the unjust one." In spite of a certain air of evasiveness in Feldman's "may seem somewhat unreasonable" rider, he does more or less straightforwardly admit that he is "prepared to acknowledge that the more fitting allocation of pleasures and pains in [the just world] makes it better in itself than [the unjust world]."[31] Moreover, Feldman recognizes that scenarios such as Ross's two worlds, unlike Moore's, do call "for further refinements in [his] formulation of hedonism"[32] – a project to which he turns, however, only on page 193 of an essentially 198-page-long book and which thus unfortunately remains woefully inchoate.

The reason why Feldman thinks that replying to Ross's objection is harder than to Moore's should by now be clear. Even if perhaps this could be seen as an unwillingness to engage with the objections at hand, it really is not absurd to react to Moore's thought experiment by protesting that the very talk of worlds that no one could ever experience is fancifully improbable or otherwise unrealistic. Maybe really the only way in which the beautiful and the ugly universes can be said to differ is by smuggling sentient beings into the picture – either as (potential) inhabitants of those worlds or simply as a result of having been asked Moore's questions about these worlds. Ross's thought experiment, in contrast, does not permit this move: his two worlds *are* supposed to be populated by ordinary sentient beings like ourselves. Moreover, while modifications to Moore's thought experiments so as to suggest instances that we could actually experience are necessarily impossible – since the thought experiment requires the absence of sentient beings – situations resembling Ross's thought experiments are perfectly familiar in our everyday life. We commonly experience wrongdoers getting away with it (i.e., vicious people enjoying pleasures) as well as deserving people not getting the rewards they deserve (i.e., virtuous people undeservedly suffering) – and when we witness these events we are, understandably, distressed. Other things being equal, we prefer (i.e., we think it is better, more valuable) – and we are *correct* in so preferring – justice to injustice. To deny this strikes me not only as utterly implausible but as downright perverse – as Feldman himself may be taken to have conceded.

The reason why Feldman thinks that despite this difficulty he can in fact reply to objections having to do with the intrinsic value of justice such as Ross's (a value that, as we have seen, is not a function of the *amount* of pleasure and suffering in the world) is the following. Feldman thinks that hedonistic utilitarianism can incorporate considerations related to desert and, via desert, to justice. So, Feldman believes

[29] Ross, *The Right* ..., 138.   [30] Feldman, *Pleasure* ..., 192.   [31] *Ibid.*   [32] *Ibid.*, 193.

that a hedonistic utilitarian can indeed recognize that there are "worthless pleasures (and worthwhile pains)." And just as the "objects of pleasure and pain" can in different degrees "deserve to be objects of pleasure and pain," the *subjects* of pleasure and pain can, too, be said to "deserve to be experiencing them" in different degrees.[33]

So, Feldman admits that, in order to avoid very serious problems, his "hedonistic" theory needs to be "adjusted" by considerations of desert – both regarding objects and subjects. Unfortunately, however, Feldman also admits that in order to "spell out these versions of the theory in their full glory, one would need to explain . . . what makes an object deserve to be an object of pleasure (pain)" and "what makes a person deserve to be a subject of pleasure [pain]" and that he has "not completed either of these jobs."[34]

It is not surprising, then, that Feldman would include a chapter in his book titled "But Is It Really 'Hedonism'?" or that the theme of determining whether his theory is really hedonistic is a veritable leitmotif in the book. To the extent that Feldman's view incorporates desert, it is, I think, less hedonistic and more pluralistic. But I wish to conclude this section by emphasizing that my main goal has not been to evaluate whether the credentials of Feldman's (or anyone else's) hedonism are at stake when these systems incorporate desert (or values other than pleasure). What matters to me here is that the utilitarian recognition of the intrinsic value of desert entails *eo ipso* the abandonment of monistic axiologies and of the simplemindedness they presuppose (since, after all, the utilitarian *also* values suffering reduction).

## 2.2 ORGANIC WHOLES AND THE SOUNDS OF JUSTICE

Despite his many agreements with Brentano, Moore criticized him for not giving enough importance to "the principle of organic unities."[35] Chisholm admits that "the principle of summation [Brentano] had offered [in *The Origin of Our Knowledge of Right and Wrong*] is inconsistent with the principle of organic unities," as Moore alleges.[36] But Chisholm also points out more than one way in which Brentano's view therein "presupposes Moore's principle [of organic wholes]" and that in fact many a remark by Brentano "enables us better to understand the concept of organic unity."[37] Chisholm also refers to passages in Brentano's unpublished manuscripts that clearly reveal that he was operating with something very much like the framework of organic wholes in mind. And I think that the usefulness of this framework for understanding the morality of punishment continues to be regrettably under-researched. The question in front of us now is: What is it exactly about the framework of organic wholes that is so helpful for understanding punishment? The answer is somewhat circuitous.

---

[33] *Ibid.*    [34] *Ibid.*, 206.    [35] Moore, *Principia*, 36.    [36] Chisholm, *Brentano* . . ., 69–70.
[37] *Ibid.*, 70.

The most salient – and most famous – characteristic of organic wholes is that their value is additively independent from the value of their parts. Imagine a whole formed by, say, three parts, a, b, and c, and assume that the values of these parts – in isolation – is, in order, 2, 3, and 5. The theory of organic wholes states that it is not necessary that the value of a whole containing only a, b, and c be 10 – it could be more or less than 10. Initially, perhaps, this may appear mysterious: What could possibly be the source of this differential value? The mystery can, however, be dispelled – and much more easily than usually assumed.

Consider the examples offered by another important philosopher who, like Moore, spoke in superlative terms of Brentano's seminal work on axiology (even though, also like Moore, he thought that Brentano's treatment of organic wholes was too "preliminary"). As he sought to develop Brentano's views, Edmund Husserl offered as perfectly non-mysterious examples of organic wholes "any melodic or color harmony whatsoever."[38] I can, for example, gather together in my own way the same piano *parts* that form Modest Mussorgsky's *Pictures at an Exhibition*, and what I will thereby produce will be unfathomably less valuable than Mussorgsky's original masterpiece. Independently of the *parts* of any whole themselves, the specific *ordering* of these parts generates – or fails to generate – value in different degrees.

The value of these orderings in examples such as the one contrasting my arrangement of notes to Mussorgsky's arrangement is so great that it actually tilts the scale in the opposite direction from the prima facie skepticism with which we began: What, *other than this ordering*, could possibly be the source of the differential value of wholes containing the same parts? Needless to say, to deny that these wholes have different values in these cases is to admit that all melodic (or color) harmonies are equally valuable – not really a serious proposition.

The skeptic may perhaps find Husserl's examples unpersuasive because she may believe that musical notes, by themselves, or colors, by themselves, are valueless – that the color green is as valueless as is the note G. But I think that this skeptical effort risks proving the opposite of what it wants: if the notes that make up a musical composition (or the colors that make up a certain painting, etc.) are indeed taken to be valueless, then it would seem that the value of any musical (or color, etc.) composition does after all flow *entirely form the ordering* of notes (or colors, etc.) itself – since *ex hypothesi* there would simply be nothing else from where it could flow. So, I find it hard to avoid the conclusion that Husserl's examples indeed dispel any mystery regarding Brentano's point that "the value of a whole is not a function merely of the value of the parts of the whole. 'Goodness also lies in the relations which are exhibited within the whole,'"[39] or Moore's point that an organic whole "has an intrinsic value different in amount from the sum of the values of its parts."[40]

---

[38] Edmund Husserl, *Gesammelte Werke, Band XXVIII: Vorlesungen über Ethik und Wertlehre 1908: 1914*, Dordrecht: Kluwer (1988), 96.

[39] Chisholm, *Brentano* . . ., 70, citing an unpublished manuscript Brentano wrote "probably in the 1890s."

[40] Moore, *Principia* . . ., 87.

Given my purposes, Husserl's examples of harmonies are helpful mainly in the explanatory sense: they help explain what organic wholes are and how they can indeed exist. But I wish to turn our attention back to examples of organic wholes in contexts that are closer to the axiological evaluation of punishment. Elsewhere I have explained how significant I find the fact that a utilitarian (albeit an ideal one), like Moore, could endorse – or at least feel the pull of – retributivism.[41] I still find this fact significant (and not sufficiently discussed by contemporary punishment theorists), though it is in this book that I advance for the first time what I take to be the most complete explanation as to how it is possible and what its significance is. And that explanation is also the answer as to what exactly is so helpful about the framework of organic wholes for the debate concerning the justification of punishment.

The beginning of wisdom is to recall the difference I introduced in the previous chapter between deontic and axiological retributivism: Moore's retributivism is purely axiological. There is value in deserved punishment, in the sense that deserved punishment can add value by belonging to this or that organic whole. This admission is not at odds with *his* utilitarianism, even though indeed it is anathema for *classical* utilitarianism. Furthermore, by deploying the framework of organic wholes, he avoids the evidently inappropriate moral mathematics of simpleminded accountancy. An organic whole in which a wrongdoer suffers to the extent that she deserves may be more intrinsically valuable than one in which all remains the same except that this deserving wrongdoer does not suffer.

As Moore turned his attention to organic wholes "exclusively composed of two great positive evils – wickedness and pain," he suggested that

> quite apart from *consequences* or any value which an evil may have as a mere means, it may, supposing one evil already exists, be worth while to create another, since, by the mere creation of this second, there may be constituted a whole less bad than if the original evil had been left to exist by itself . . . [W]here an evil already exists, as in this world evils do exist, the existence of the other part of these wholes will constitute a thing desirable *for its own sake* – that is to say, not merely a means to future goods, but one of the *ends* which must be taken into account in estimating what that best possible state of things is, to which every right action must be a means.[42]

In other words, Moore believes that an organic whole in which wrongdoers enjoy impunity could, other things being equal, be less valuable than an organic whole in which these very same wrongdoers suffer (to the extent that they deserve) – even if the former organic whole contains less suffering than the latter and even though suffering, considered in isolation, is a very bad thing indeed.

The other seminal *avant la lettre* ideal utilitarian thinker we have been discussing, Brentano, was interested in exactly this type of case – and his reaction was very similar to Moore's. Brentano identified three different general types of organic

---

[41]   The last section of my *Punishment and Retribution* is devoted to this topic. See *ibid.*, 208 ff.

[42]   Moore, *Principia* . . ., 264–265. Italics in the original.

wholes: "(1) the *bonum variationis*; (2) the *bonum progressionis*; and (3) the value of retribution or requital."[43] I will here ignore the first two types but would like to note that Chisholm helpfully reminds us that it was precisely because of the third type of organic whole, involving the case of retributivism in particular, that Brentano "had revised his original views."[44] Chisholm further calls our attention to Brentano's view whereby

> if at the Last Judgment a greater amount of bliss were given to a person who actually deserved it less, then he would have a greater amount of good than he otherwise would have, but the good in the universe, considered as a whole, would be less.[45]

And Chisholm reports that in an unpublished fragment titled "On the Good That There Is in Order or Arrangement," Brentano defended the view that "wickedness accompanied by sorrow is better than wickedness accompanied by pleasure" and that this fact "may justify the sorrow that is involved in repentance and the pain that is involved in vindictive punishment." Chisholm ascribes to Brentano the following view: "If A is a wicked deed and if B is the suffering involved in the sinner's remorse or in his retribution, then the two evils, A and B, may be preferable to A without B."[46]

Neither Moore nor Brentano mentions the term "desert" in these passages, but it is evident that their concern with "retribution" and "retributive punishment" is a concern with *deserved* punishment. If these remarkable similarities between the concerns and the views of our two (ideal) utilitarians were not impressive enough, even our self-proclaimed hedonistic utilitarian (Feldman) admits that desert needs to play a role in any credible axiology (as we saw in the previous section). As I pointed out earlier, the prominence of desert for the justification of punishment is important for more than one reason – not simply in itself but also for what it suggests regarding the convenience of adopting a pluralistic justification of punishment.

Linking the notion of desert to the discussion of organic wholes – and, indirectly, also to our discussion of theodicies in the previous chapter – reveals something important. The reason why all our authors agree that deserved punishment can, other things being equal, be better than impunity is because desert gives a certain *order* – a certain *meaning* – to the whole in which it appears, and this in turn generates intrinsic, non-medicinal, value. In Brentano's Last Judgment example, the whole he had in mind was, presumably, the world as such – precisely the world that is a central interest to those concerned with theodicies. What is at stake in Brentano's example is evidently the question as to what bestows meaning to the world. As we saw in the previous chapter (with Weber's help), this question is the cornerstone of every secular theodicy, of every effort to make sense of the world.

This order is not meant to be mere temporal sequence, though it could be just that. Consider two organic wholes, whose parts are stipulated to have the same exact values qua parts. The first organic whole contains a person who after raping and

---

[43] Chisholm, *Brentano* . . ., 70.   [44] *Ibid.*, 71.
[45] Brentano, *The Origins* . . ., 149; Chisholm, *Brentano* . . ., 72.   [46] Chisholm, *Brentano* . . ., 72.

burning someone has a car accident, in which he suffers injuries causing him a certain amount of pain. In the second organic whole, someone witnessed the crimes and then decided to beat up the rapist murderer, causing exactly the same amount of pain as the car accident in the previous case. In principle, the value of these two organic wholes could turn out to be different, even though the chronology of events is assumed to be the same.

One important way in which these orderings create meaning is by providing *plots* to the world and to our lives. The richer these plots are, the least amenable they are to be treated in simpleminded ways. Peter Goldie usefully draws a curve of ascending plot richness going from mere lists, to annals, to chronicles, to diaries, and finally to narratives (say, with complex novels at the very top). The "bare description of events" typical of the relative plot-less levels at the bottom of this curve gains in "coherence, meaningfulness, and evaluative and emotional import" as we ascend on the curve.[47] At the very bottom of this curve, we simply encounter "one damn thing after another."[48] Evidently, it is not chronology alone, or even mainly, that helps us distinguish between bare and rich plots.

The consequentialist who eschews the pluralism that the framework of organic wholes affords appears to assume that the moral phenomena associated with punishment exist at that very uninspiring bottom of the emplotment curve. In other words, she will have difficulty seeing why any difference should be admitted between the organic wholes just introduced – whether suffering is the result of an accident or of deserved punishment does not matter: suffering is suffering is suffering. Moreover, consider a third imagined organic whole: someone is hit by lightning when he is twenty-five years old, and this event causes the same amount of pain as in the two previous examples; later, when he is thirty years old, unrelatedly, he rapes and murders someone (causing the same amount of pain as in the previous examples, etc.). The consequentialist will again have difficulty explaining why any difference between these three cases – all assumed to generate the exact same amount of pain – should be admitted. The order, the plot, is in principle (excluding medicinal considerations, which we are in these examples excluding) irrelevant: what matters to the consequentialist is the bottom line – and in all these examples the bottom line is assumed to be numerically the same.

None of this should be taken to entail that the intrinsic value that desert generates cannot be defeated by other values. Rather, it is to say that this value is not as mysterious as many thinkers have claimed it is.[49] The value of desert is

---

[47] Peter Goldie, *The Mess Inside*, Oxford: Oxford University Press (2012), 9.

[48] As Goldie credits Elbert Hubbard for eloquently putting it, *ibid.*, 13.

[49] It is a well-worn trope that retributivism is somehow "mysterious." Famous exemplars include John Cottingham, "Varieties of Retribution," *The Philosophical Quarterly* 29 (1979): 238–246; Ted Honderich, *Punishment: The Supposed Justifications Revisited*, London: Pluto Press (2005); J. L. Mackie, "Retributivism: A Test Case for Ethical Objectivity," in Joel Feinberg and Jules Coleman (eds.), *Philosophy of Law* (sixth edn.), Belmont, CA: Wadsworth (2000). In Chapter 7, I will discuss Martha Nussbaum's version of the mysteriousness charge.

the result of it being a form of order, an arrangement, an emplotment. The very imposition of this order adds value to the organic whole whose parts have been so ordered. Just consider how different the following sequence of numbers – 0, 1, 1, 2, 3, 5, 8, 13, 21, 34, ... – must be for someone who knows of Fibonacci and for someone who does not. And even if one imagines two people, neither of whom are familiar with Fibonacci's sequence, the difference between the one who recognizes a pattern and the one who sees this as, in Hubbard's phrase, "one damn number after another" is significant: the former has recognized much more meaning than the latter.

Granting, *arguendo*, that the "problem of beauty" captured by Moore's heap of filth thought experiment is less devastating for monistic axiologies than the "problem of justice" captured by Ross's two worlds thought experiment is not to deny the structural similarities between them. We can now also see structural similarities between these thought experiments and deserved punishment. Beauty is the result of imposing a certain order (arrangement, structure, etc.) upon a group of entities. Justice, too, is the result of imposing a certain order (arrangement, structure, etc.) upon a group of entities. And to give someone what she deserves – even when what she deserves is suffering – is to impose a certain order (arrangement, structure, etc.) to certain entities or events. All these orderings, arrangements, and structuring convey *meaning* to a given situation and to our lives in general.

One need only recall the age-old views whereby justice is a matter of *harmony* in the soul and of rendering to each his due – views that are nothing short of cornerstones of our intellectual tradition going at least as far back as Plato, if not cornerstones of our very fabric as human beings. To take but one example among many, consider how Francis Ellingwood Abbot put it when he described justice as "the one absolute and all-inclusive word in ethics" and he suggested that justice is "grounded in reciprocity of ends and means as organic harmony" and that "its ethical formula is, perhaps, the ancient *cuique suum* – 'to each his own,' 'give every man his due.'"[50] There can be no harmony in these contexts without desert: the "due" just mentioned does not refer to what by this or that convention or positive law she is *entitled* to – it refers to what she *deserves*. The sense in which there is justice in my receiving the money I won in a raffle – to which I am no doubt *entitled* – is too humble to have so exercised every thinker ever to care about this topic. The sense of the *suum cuique* maxim has always included people getting what they *deserve* and not merely what they are otherwise entitled to receive. And this applies not only to "retributive justice" (understood here as connected not to retributivism as such but to the ways in which we respond to wrongdoing generally) but also to distributive justice. That is why it is so common to quote Aristotle: "[A]ll men agree that what is just in distribution

---

[50] Francis Ellingwood Abbot, "The Advancement of Ethics," *The Monist* 5 (1895): 192–222, at 216.

must be according to desert in some sense."[51] The connection between this idea and secular theodicy is obvious.

By invoking these venerable conceptions of justice here, I mean to illustrate the thread connecting desert, justice, organicity, and eventually value. The point is to indicate where the value of giving people what they deserve comes form – not to endorse any particular deontic policy or any particular view of distributive or retributive justice. Throughout history, the *suum cuique* maxim has been invoked in order to support different political agendas – and perversions of the principle are no doubt possible: say, the Nazis cynically invoking the maxim (*Jedem das Seine*) at the gates of the Buchenwald concentration camp. None of these aberrations, however, affects the purely axiological point being made here.

Consider the typical classical utilitarian, non-pluralist approach: if, say, a crime has already been committed, that crime has brought about some suffering – and suffering is always, undifferentiatedly, bad; to now punish the criminal is simply to add more suffering to the world. So, the non-pluralist hedonist concludes that, unless there would be some good medicinal consequences in inflicting this additional suffering, some likelihood that this additional suffering that is concomitant to punishment will actually tend to reduce suffering down the road (via prevention, rehabilitation, deterrence, etc.), there is nothing valuable in inflicting "deserved" punishment in itself. But this is simply to refuse to recognize the value that the very arrangement or order that desert imposes on some organic wholes. It is to assume that the axiological significance of the connection between the different episodes of pain in the world is identical to the axiological significance of entirely *random* collections of said episodes.

Rawls's criticism of those who assume "one single end for all moral deliberation" can be applied to the non-pluralist hedonist, given her exaggerated desire to see one single source of value. The non-pluralist hedonist would claim not to see the value in any ordering qua ordering. She would see the moral universe as perfectly, and uninspiringly, commutative. Consider R, who rapes V, and who thereby causes great suffering to V, and who, let us assume, does not himself suffer at all. If R were to be made to suffer, the non-pluralistic hedonist would think that this state of affairs is worse than the first one, since the only difference she will see is that now there is more suffering (unless, of course, if by making R suffer, we could reasonably – medicinally – expect overall suffering to diminish, but we continue to exclude these considerations in these thought experiments). *Who* gets to suffer and *why* are remarkably irrelevant considerations for the non-pluralistic hedonist. So, the state

51  Serena Olsaretti "Introduction: Debating Desert and Justice," in her edited volume *Desert and Justice*, Oxford: Oxford University Press (2003): 1–24, at 1. This is of course not to endorse any particular theory of distributive justice or even to suggest that the correct theory of distributive justice needs to incorporate considerations of desert in any significant way – there are many competing values at play in this context. It is merely to indicate how, even regarding distributive justice, desert has often been thought to be important. See also Geoffrey Cupit, *Justice as Fittingness*, Oxford: Oxford University Press (1996).

of affairs in which R rapes V and then B (a random bystander utterly unrelated to R and V) is made to suffer exactly the same amount as R may have been made to suffer via punishment would appear *equally* bad to our hedonistic non-pluralist. Moreover, if, after R rapes V, it turns out that by making V suffer far and beyond what she already suffered as result of having been raped, we could reasonably expect overall suffering to diminish, then the non-pluralist hedonist would find value in medicinally making V suffer.

Of course, the last scenario is a variation on the famous objection to utilitarianism whereby it can recommend "punishing" an innocent person. It is, admittedly, a particularly perverse variation (in that it scapegoats the very victim) but one that the classical utilitarian just cannot avoid: without access to the idea that there is an axiological significance to desert, she may have trouble even explaining what exactly is perverse about this variation. Classical utilitarians have typically defended them-selves by pointing out that in real life it is extraordinarily unlikely that scapegoating innocent people (or, in my version, scapegoating the very victims) would really reduce suffering in the world. This is likely true. But such a defense is an evasion of the theoretical point at hand: even if it is true that, say, in "real life" it would not be optimific to scapegoat, the classical utilitarian cannot deny that, in theory, there is nothing wrong with scapegoating. And my discussion of axiology here is theoretical: the classical utilitarian needs to deny that there is value in the distribution of suffering as such, and so is (other things being equal) committed to seeing the additional suffering of R to be neither less nor more deplorable than the suffering of any other random person (including V).

I find these considerations sufficient in showing that the order that desert adds to an organic whole *matters*. But it is still not clear that it is specifically the order that desert imposes that is valuable and not some other order. Imagine a whole whose parts are three random human beings, and imagine that someone arranges these three people according to the order in which she will murder them. I do not believe that this organic whole is, in the final analysis, made more intrinsically valuable by containing this particular order. Orderings can be themselves evaluated, and some are more intrinsically valuable than others.[52]

But then it could perhaps seem as if to introduce organic wholes and the values of orderings, arrangement, and structures is merely to relaunch the traditional debates regarding the justification of punishment, only now within a somewhat different framework. I think that this would be a misunderstanding of what the discussion of organic wholes in fact accomplishes. First, this discussion adds a concern with intrinsic value, and with axiology as such, that is often absent from the traditional discussion among punishment theorists: an organic whole with a certain order has more intrinsic value than the same whole without any ordering. Second, admitting

---

[52] This is not to say that orderings are to be seen as additional "parts" of organic wholes – for otherwise an infinite regress would obtain.

that a given ordering may be better or worse than other(s) is not to deny that the mere fact that an ordering is imposed on an organic whole adds *eo ipso* some value. Of course, perhaps the order is in itself so repugnant that the overall value of the organic whole actually diminishes – but the ordering as such, formally, adds some value. In other words, giving people the suffering that they deserve adds *eo ipso* some value, even if so doing, and given the additive independence of the value of the whole and the value of its parts or the value of its order, could also make the organic whole less valuable. It is important to emphasize, moreover, that the non-pluralistic classical utilitarian we have been considering does not have an alternative ordering to offer instead of the ordering created by considerations related to desert. The whole axiological discussion of orderings and their values has to necessarily strike her as *pointless*. She simply wants as little suffering in the world as possible, and that is that.

Third, and perhaps most importantly, recognizing the axiological significance of order does not only stave off flatfooted commutative axiologies, but it is also to further argue for the recognition of pluralism. Mobilizing organic wholes allows us to see how many types of factors can affect the overall value of any state of affairs and how this is as true of instances of punishment as of any other states of affairs. Only a superficial reading would see the discussion of the axiology of organic wholes as a mere euphemistic move. Turning to organic wholes allows us to see how pluralism is both possible and important, how an ideal utilitarian can be a retributivist, and how complicated the axiology of punishment is. And it does this without introducing, say, the more than a little bewildering Hegelian talk of punishment being "the negation of the negation [i.e., the negation of *crime*, which itself is the negation of *right*]."[53]

In fact, discussing these axiological dimensions of organic wholes highlights some of the perplexing oddities of the overly deontic approaches that dominate the specialized literature on punishment. For example, consider a common move in this literature: to suggest that if any of the essential components of justified punishment is missing, then the organic whole constituted by said punishment loses the *entirety* of whatever value it originally had. So, to inflict suffering on, say, a rapist, may be admitted to be of some value if done by someone with the authority to do so but (implausibly) suggested to be *completely* devoid of value (and barbaric, etc.) if done by someone without said authority.[54] There are excellent, typically overriding reasons to prevent vigilantism, but this is not because what a vigilante does is

---

[53] See G. W. F. Hegel, *Elements of the Philosophy of Right* (Allen Wood, ed.), Cambridge: Cambridge University Press (1991): 123 ff.

[54] This is one of the typical gambits in distinguishing (retributive) punishment from revenge: the former is done by an authority and of some value, the latter (insofar as not done by an authority) is completely valueless. A recent example of this move, found in Alon Harel's *Why Law Matters* (Oxford: Oxford University Press, 2014), says: "[I]t is not that it is impermissible for non-state agents to punish; it is rather that no other agent can punish, and any attempt to punish on the part of such agents is bound to fail, and constitute a mere (impermissible) act of violence," *ibid.*, 81. Harel sees punishment's value *entirely* disappear as it magically transforms into mere and valueless violence. For discussion of Harel's views, see Leo Zaibert, "Tragic Choices and the Law," *Critical Analysis of Law* 2.2 (2015): 257–267.

*completely* valueless – particularly if it is very similar to what an authority would have done. And the best way of avoiding these deeply counterintuitive implications is to recognize the axiological importance of both organic wholes and the orderings of their parts. Furthermore, to turn to the axiological flexibility and pluralism of organic wholes is, to echo Williams's pithy take on G. E. Moore, a way of rejecting "at once the stuffiness of duty and the vulgarity of utilitarianism."[55]

## 2.3 VARIANCE AND ITS DISCONTENTS

I would like to consider two possible objections to the views that I have presented thus far. These objections do not concern the claim, which I also endorse (and that I will further discuss in the next chapter), that deserved punishment is intrinsically valuable. The objections concern some structural aspects of the very axiology that organic wholes, as I understand them, presuppose.

The first objection stems from the views of Thomas Baldwin, the author of the very useful introduction to a recent and authoritative edition of Moore's *Principia Ethica*. Interestingly, Baldwin says very little about organic wholes in this introduction because he believes that the "principle of organic unities" is not among Moore's "most important contribution[s] to ethical theory."[56] In his equally useful *G. E. Moore: The Arguments of the Philosophers*, we get an idea as to why Baldwin thinks this way. Baldwin notes that except for a brief period in his youth, Moore was highly critical of absolute idealism and of its *metaphysical* organic wholes. And Baldwin seems to think that in spite of Moore's efforts to distinguish his view from absolute idealism, the organic wholes at the center of Moore's ethics should have suffered the same fate as the metaphysical organic wholes of said absolute idealism.

Baldwin thus wishes to explore whether "Moore can have his principle of organic unities without a commitment to the organic wholes of Absolute idealism."[57] And he is not sure that Moore can do this, for he thinks that "it seems irrational to hold that any 'whole' is no more than the sum of its parts (this is Moore's metaphysical doctrine) but that the intrinsic value of such a whole is not determined by the values of its parts." Baldwin's main worry, then, is that "the intrinsic value of a whole as a whole seems to be a *deus ex machina* which is liable to interfere with evaluation of situations in a random fashion."[58] Or, in other words, that the proponent of organic wholes can cherry-pick when and how to invoke them and their parts as they seek to determine the value of any given state of affairs.

---

55 Bernard Williams, *Ethics and the Limits of Philosophy*, London: Routledge (2006), 8.
56 Baldwin, "Introduction" in Moore, *Principia* ..., xxxvi. Contrast Baldwin's position to that of, for example, Derek Parfit, who, although highly critical of Moore, acknowledges the importance of his theory of organic wholes. See the references in the appendix.
57 Thomas Baldwin, *G. E. Moore: The Arguments of the Philosophers*, London: Routledge (1990) 127.
58 *Ibid.*, 127.

I am not sure that the irrationality Baldwin fears is really there. When Moore introduces organic wholes in *Principia Ethica*, he indeed goes to great lengths in order to distance himself from absolute idealism, particularly in the Hegelian version that had exerted considerable influence in Great Britain.[59] And that is why, when he defines organic wholes succinctly, namely as those whose intrinsic value is "different from the sum of the value of the parts," Moore emphasizes that this commits him to no metaphysical view as to countenancing "any causal relation whatever between the parts" or to accepting any view asserting that "the parts are inconceivable except as parts of that whole."[60] This is, I think, the gist of Moore's rejection of absolute idealism – and I do not think that this creates a problematic tension between his rejection of metaphysical organicity and his championing of axiological organicity, such as Baldwin suggests. From Moore's perspective, the metaphysical issues relating to causality and mereology need not affect the problem of value as such.

If Baldwin were right, however, Moore's problems would run much deeper, for there would appear to be irrationality, too, in Moore's simultaneous endorsement of metaphysical naturalism and of axiological non-naturalism. In other words, if Baldwin were right, Moore's simultaneous rejection of absolute idealism and his endorsement of organic wholes would affect his entire moral philosophy. For, allegedly, Moore could not have been a naturalist regarding metaphysics (which would follow from his particular rejection of idealism) and a non-naturalist regarding ethics in general. Thus, it would turn out that it would be not only organic wholes that could be criticized as unconvincing deployments of *deus ex machina* explanations but Moore's entire ethical apparatus. I find this to be too extreme an indictment.

In any case, since Baldwin sees an air of irrationality here, he does try to understand "why [Moore] thought that he required" the principle of axiological organic wholes.[61] Baldwin identifies two main possible kinds of cases regarding which Moore may have thought he needed the principle: first, the existence of organic wholes composed of beautiful things and someone's consciousness of such beautiful things, which possess, in Moore's view, much more value than the mere sum of the value of their parts. For reasons that are not important for my purposes here, Baldwin suspects that while there may be some "merit" to the use of organic wholes in these contexts, he nonetheless thinks that other alternatives would have been better than the appeal to organic wholes.

The second type of case why Moore may have been attracted to axiological organic wholes that Baldwin discusses is, in contrast, crucial for my purposes:

> [A]t one point [Moore] uses it to defend a retributive theory of punishment, according to which "the infliction of pain on a person whose state of mind is bad, may, if the pain be not too intense, create a state of things that is better on the whole

---

[59] Moore, *Principia* . . ., 78 ff.     [60] *Ibid.*, 87.     [61] Baldwin, *G. E. Moore* . . ., 128.

than if the evil state of mind had existed unpunished." Moore is here using the principle because it enables him to present an alternative to the familiar utilitarian justifications of punishment. The trouble here is that the principle's role is just that of a *deus ex machina*: somehow, the infliction of pain – a condition that is, for Moore, intrinsically evil – produces an outcome that is intrinsically better than without it. This is the irrational use of the principle which will permit a theodicy. Moore's ethics and the retributive theory of punishment are better off without it.[62]

It should come as no surprise that I find this unsatisfactory. First of all, Baldwin does not explore why Moore – remember: an ideal utilitarian himself – thought that he needed an alternative to those "familiar utilitarian justifications" of punishment. If Baldwin does not see problems with those utilitarian justifications, then he is just pushing the question one level up, and his question should really be: Why did Moore believe that there were problems with the "familiar utilitarian justifications" of punishment? If, on the other hand, Baldwin agrees with Moore in that there are problems with the "familiar utilitarian justifications" of punishment, it then strikes me as too cavalier to simply say that Moore's effort to correct those problems (by introducing axiological organic wholes and the pluralistic axiology that they presuppose) does not work and then leave it at that. "Theodicy," as I argued in the previous chapter, is not a bad word – and in fact I have argued that theodicies (particularly secular theodicies) are useful in advancing our understanding of the justification of punishment. To breezily link theodicies to irrationality, as Baldwin does, is, within the context of writing an introduction to Moore's overall philosophy, perhaps not a serious problem. But when discussing the justification of punishment as such, as I do here, such a facile linkage is unacceptable. Moore was indeed discussing theodicies (even if he did not use the very word) – and, for reasons I presented in the previous chapter, this was very much to his credit.

Second, and here the value of connecting Moore's views to those of others, such as above all Brentano's, becomes apparent. For Brentano also eschewed absolute idealism, and yet he too appealed to axiological organic wholes in remarkably similar ways to Moore. Why not ask the question about Brentano? As we have seen, Husserl too was sympathetic to the framework of organic wholes, and while there is considerable scholarly dispute as to whether Husserl was an idealist – a dispute that does not concern me here – at least early in his career Husserl was not an idealist.[63] Why not ask the question about Husserl? But there is more: as we have also seen, even Feldman, a self-confessed *hedonistic* utilitarian with no discernible

[62] *Ibid.*

[63] Discussing Roman Ingarden, Amie Thomasson says, "[L]ike many of Husserl's students from the Göttingen period, Ingarden is a realist phenomenologist who ardently resisted Husserl's apparent turn to transcendental idealism in the *Ideas* and thereafter," thus recognizing that at least early on Husserl was not an idealist. (Amie Thomasson, "Roman Ingarden," *The Stanford Encyclopedia of Philosophy* (Fall 2012 edn., Edward N. Zalta, ed.), http://plato.stanford.edu/archives/fall2012/entries/ingarden/). For the view that even the late Husserl should be seen as a realist (a possibility Thomasson leaves open), see Karl Ameriks, "Husserl's Realism," *The Philosophical Review* 86.4

commitment to any form of idealism, has admitted that hedonistic utilitarianism needs to be adjusted by considerations having to do with desert. And these considerations are best explained by the appeal to axiological organic wholes. So, why not ask the question about Feldman? And indeed why not ask it about any of the many philosophers who find axiological organic wholes attractive? It is not a minor accident that many disparate philosophers – including many non-idealist philosophers – are attracted to axiological organic wholes, and I find it doubtful that they are all thereby "irrational."

But my third and final worry about Baldwin's rejection of the importance of axiological organic wholes (and, summarily and *en passant*, of the "retributivist justification of punishment") is the most important: Baldwin does not really argue for his view. When he begins his discussion of Moore's appeal to organic wholes, Baldwin expresses his fear that they may be invoked capriciously, in a *deus ex machina* fashion. When he "pursues further" and discusses Moore's deployment of the principle within the context of punishment, Baldwin merely repeats his worry but now more assertively, as if he had somehow argued for it – although he did not.

A certain unmanageability of organic wholes is a legitimate and important worry, but simply repeating *deus ex machina* is neither to present an argument for its existence nor at any rate likely to help us cope with this worry. Needless to say, this entire book is an effort to show why the worry is worth having and to suggest ways of dealing with this worry within the context of punishment without succumbing to simplemindedness. The first steps involve the recognition that (a) the notion of desert is indispensable for understanding the axiology of punishment, that (b) the notion of desert is best understood via its presence in organic wholes, and that (c) desert does add an order (a plot, meaning, etc.) to the parts of organic wholes and that this order adds – in non-mysterious ways – value to those wholes. But I will conclude this section by discussing a related take on organic wholes, as presented by Jonathan Dancy in his "Are There Organic Unities?" and in his *Ethics without Principles*.[64]

The title of Dancy's article may sound ominous for my case, in the sense that if the question it poses is answered negatively, my main thesis in this chapter seems to lose its footing. But I will argue that, in the final analysis, rather than undermining my positions, Dancy's views strengthen them and in fact help clarify some of my main goals. There are thus two versions of my reaction to Dancy's position. The short version is to point out that, in spite of the title of his article, Dancy is not in fact

(1977): 498–519; Dallas Willard, "World Well Won (The): Husserl's Epistemic Realism One Hundred Years Later," in *One Hundred Years of Phenomenology* (D. Zahavi and F. Stjernfelt, eds.), Dordrecht: Kluwer (2002): 69–78; and Ingvar Johansson, "Fictions in the Spatiotemporal World – In the Light of Ingarden," *Polish Journal of Philosophy* 4.2 (2010): 81–103.

[64] Jonathan Dancy, "Are There Organic Unities?," *Ethics* 113 (2003): 629–650; Jonathan Dancy, *Ethics without Principles*, Oxford: Clarendon Press (2004).

opposed to organic wholes as such but only to what he takes to be some specific aspects of Moore's understanding of them. This is apparent in the article itself, but it is more explicit and in fact expressly stated in Dancy's *Ethics without Principles* – an excellent book published a mere year later and containing a chapter also titled "Are There Organic Unities?" that includes the bulk of the first half of the article. So, for example, as he accepts a principle asserting that "the value of one object can be affected by the nature (or value) of others," Dancy adds that "in accepting a doctrine of organic unities (not Moore's, of course) we have committed ourself [sic] to this principle."[65]

Dancy's rejection of Moore's organic wholes is particularly interesting to me because it seems, in a way, to come at things from the opposite direction as does Baldwin's. As we have just seen, Baldwin's worry concerns a certain instability about moral values that follows from the admission of Moorean organic wholes. But Dancy's main objection to Moore's theory is that he thinks that it is somehow *too* stable: Dancy believes that Moore is mistaken in combining two claims: that (1) "parts retain their intrinsic value regardless of variations in context" and (2) "parts may contribute either more or less value to a whole than they themselves have."[66] Contrariwise, Dancy believes that although "parts may have value which they do not contribute to the value of the whole," no part can ever "contribute value that it has not got."[67] Or, to summarize Dancy's general thesis, he thinks that entities could have some value when they are a part of one organic whole and a different value when they are part of another whole. And he objects to Moore's view that whatever value a part has *qua* part remains the same no matter of what organic whole it happens to be a part.

The sense in which Dancy appears to embrace precisely that instability that worries Baldwin is in full view now. And Dancy is aware of the worry, for he admits that "at this point some will see a difficulty," which he describes as follows:

> The picture we are now offering suggests that there is nothing constant in the realm of value, or at least that if there is something constant, that itself is some sort of anomaly. Everything appears to be, at least in principle, context-dependent. If one wants to know whether some feature is of value here, one cannot get one's answer by looking to see how it behaves elsewhere. No matter what it does elsewhere, it might be doing something different here. So there are few props for judgment, and one might reasonably wonder whether we are really able to cope if things are as variable as that.[68]

This picture is the direct result of Dancy's "particularist conception of morality, or of ethics more generally," which he forcefully defends in *Ethics without Principles*. Dancy admits that he sees "little if any role for moral principles" and that he thinks that "morality is in perfectly good shape and functioning quite happily, and that abandoning the mistaken link between morality and principles is if anything a

---

[65] Dancy, *Ethics without . . .*, 200.  [66] *Ibid.*, 176.  [67] *Ibid.*, 182.  [68] *Ibid.*, 184.

defence of morality rather than an attack on it."[69] How can Dancy defend this position, which he admits "can seem rather startling"?[70]

The gist of his defense is to distinguish two versions of context dependence. The first version, which he calls "extreme holism," asserts that "no feature has any value other than that which it acquires as a relation to a context." In contrast, however, there is a second version, which he calls "moderate holism" and which "allows the possibility of what we might call 'default value.'"[71] Dancy's example of the difference between these two versions is, again, very helpful:

> [W]e might distinguish between features such as, "that the train is about to leave," which in a certain context may increase the value of running, but in others does nothing of the sort, and features such as, "that this is causing needless pain," which seems to be already set up so as to diminish the value of a whole of which it is a part, even though, if holism is right, there may be contexts in which it does not do that.[72]

Extreme holism would see all features in the world as "neutral" as "the train is about to leave." But moderate holism can perfectly well countenance that some features are somehow "switched on already, as it were, though they can be switched off by other features."[73] Wisely, Dancy fastens his particularism to a *moderate* holism – and this allows him, I think, to deal with the apparent unmanageability that worries Baldwin. Moderate holism is consistent with particularism, and it is not very amenable to capricious cherry-picking. That something causes suffering is not completely neutral: hence my (not particularly bold) admission that there is *prima facie* value in diminishing suffering in the world. The fact that something causes suffering makes it the default position that its presence in a given organic whole should diminish the value of said whole. But this default position is defeasible, and this defeasibility comes via argument – not necessarily via *deus ex machina* stipulations. The fact that suffering is deserved is a way of defeating its default disvalue.

More wisely still (at least for my purposes), Dancy stresses that even the most moderate of holistic thinkers needs to recognize "that a default value is nothing like an unvarying value."[74] Of course, formally speaking, Dancy needs to appeal to something along the lines of this distinction between the default and the invariant, for if he did not, he would thereby lose his central objection to Moore's axiology. But the reason why the distinction between the default and the invariant is so important for my purposes connects substantively to the problem of punishment. It strikes me as sheer perversity – and in any case as extraordinarily implausible – to deny that suffering should be recognized as a *default* negative value. But, contrary to the prevalent position – a position that I will show in the next chapter is endorsed by many able and influential thinkers – this is not to say that suffering's value is *invariant*, i.e., that it is always bad, or that its presence in any organic whole necessarily decreases its value.

[69]  *Ibid.*, 1.    [70]  *Ibid.*    [71]  *Ibid.*, 185.    [72]  *Ibid.*    [73]  *Ibid.*    [74]  *Ibid.*

An example may help bring the point home. Consider the case of Leon Goldensohn, who was the prison psychiatrist during the famous Nuremberg trials, and, in particular of his notes on the interviews he conducted with the defendants on trial. There tends to be rather little editorializing or sentimentalism in his report. Goldensohn's remarks come across as rather detached and "scientific." But consider what Goldensohn says in the context of his interviews with Otto Ohlendorf, an SS member on trial for having been directly responsible for the murder of a reported ninety thousand (innocent) Jews. Ohlendorf seemed bizarrely invested in rejecting that specific number, repeatedly clarifying that he thought that there were "only sixty to seventy thousand" murdered. Calmly, Ohlendorf admitted that the victims included "men, women, and children"; that they were killed "in a military manner in a cordon"; that he commanded "fifteen-men firing squads"; and that they killed fifteen Jews at a time, efficiently using "one bullet per Jew."[75] In his report, Goldensohn writes that Ohlendorf "feels no remorse now except nominally. He looks like a burned-out ghoul, and his conscience, if it can be called such, is clean as a whistle and as empty. There is a dearth of affect, but nothing clinically remarkable."[76]

It appears that Ohlendorf was experiencing no suffering. But I would like to suggest that even though suffering is, by default, a negative value, it is not invariantly so: the organic whole that is formed by Ohlendorf suffering is better than that containing Ohlendorf not suffering. Of course, there are many possibilities: the organic whole in which Ohlendorf suffers as a result of being punished for what he did is arguably more valuable than that in which he suffers random headaches; the organic whole in which he suffers as a result of understanding the significance of what he did is arguably more valuable than one in which he does not understand this. Perhaps the organic whole in which he is repentant is more valuable than the one in which he is not repentant; perhaps the organic whole in which Ohlendorf makes himself suffer (as self-punishment) is more valuable than the one in which he is punished by others. Finally, even though we are assuming that the organic whole in which Ohlendorf suffers as much as he deserves is more valuable than the one in which he does not suffer *at all*, it is not clear that this organic whole is necessarily more valuable than one in which he does not enjoy impunity but nonetheless suffers less than he deserves.

Evaluating these sorts of variations is terribly important for our efforts to better understand punishment and its justification. What should be stressed now is that these variations are independent from Dancy's objections to Moore. What these variations show is that, in different degrees, organic wholes can be made more or less valuable by the presence of suffering and by both quantitative and qualitative

---

75  Robert Gellately (ed.), *The Nuremberg Interviews Conducted by Leon Goldensohn*, Knopf: New York, NY: (2004) 389.

76  *Ibid.*, 390. Goldensohn's reference to the (inappropriate) cleanliness of Ohlendorf's "conscience" portends my discussion of dirty hands in Chapter 8.

variations regarding said suffering. Given the default disvalue of suffering, this may still seem odd (along the lines that worry Baldwin). But I do not think that this oddity is paralyzing: things have default values that nonetheless vary in different contexts. And I think it is preferable to deal with this oddity than to explain it away by endorsing a reductive, monistic axiology. Brentano, Husserl, Feldman, and Dancy – among many others throughout history – were exercised by this oddity. This oddity is admittedly complicated, but it is not mysterious, magical thinking (as some have claimed, as we shall see later) or otherwise unmanageable: suffering changes its default value when it is deserved, and it is deserved when it produces a certain valuable arrangement between the parts of an organic whole.

Although I have just suggested comparisons in terms of more or less value regarding the distribution of suffering in hypothetical variations on Ohlendorf-like scenarios, I am by no means certain that I got them right. Like Dancy, however, I do not believe that trying to find immutable principles that would give us certainty regarding these comparisons will help: no "principles are anything like flexible enough to cover the ground and do the job we require of them."[77] And yet I do not think that this probably unavoidable dearth of absolute certainties stands in the way of understanding punishment better or that it should force us to capitulate into monism's facile (or spurious) certainties.

## 2.4 CONCLUSION

Immediately after explaining why – given the prominence of principles in ethics – particularists like him "face an uphill battle," Dancy suggests that there are two possible ways of trying to win such battle. The first one is to recognize that moral life "is just too messy, and the situations we encounter differ from each other in subtle ways that no panoply of principles could ever manage to capture. Principles deal in samenesses, and there just aren't enough samenesses to go round."[78] This, Dancy tells us, is not his strategy in his book:

> The book I have not written would really be an investigation of the subtleties of our moral thought and the actual complexities of life. The book I have written is about how to understand the way in which reasons work, and deals largely with theories about reasons rather than with life. As you can see, I would like to have been able to write the other book, the one about life, but this one is all I could manage.[79]

Against the background of the elegant way in which Dancy has put it, my claim that my own book in a sense aspires to be the type of book that Dancy could not manage to write comes across as brash. I of course do not mean it that way: what I wish to do by contrasting my approach to Dancy's is to underscore that I am not here interested in theories of reasons, the connections between reasons and values, the overall

---

[77] Dancy, *Ethics without . . .*, 2.    [78] *Ibid.*    [79] *Ibid.*

cogency of particularism, or most of the largely metaethical issues Dancy so aptly discusses.

A "book about life" such as the one that Dancy describes, moreover, is one that I cannot manage to write either. But my book is about *a slice of life*: about that aspect of life concerning the value of making people suffer as a result of their wrongdoing. I am further aided in my task by the narrower focus that guides me: I am interested in showing how the contemporary specialized literature on punishment has assumed that life is much simpler than it really is, how efforts to justify punishment have suffered as a result, and how axiological pluralism points to a way forward.

In the introduction to his book, Dancy suggests that many a moral theory "gives the wrong sense of the notion of moral conflict"[80] and has difficulty giving "any decent sense to the notion of regret."[81] The regret that Dancy has in mind is "the regret we feel when, though what we did was the right thing to do, still there were strong reasons to do something else."[82] Dancy never really returns in earnest to the consideration of these sorts of cases. In contrast, and as I sketched in the previous chapter, in this book I plan to address these important topics.

Punishment is the hitherto-unnoticed paradigmatic example of a moral conflict: sometimes the organic whole that contains deserved punishment is more intrinsically valuable because of its presence, even though (a) deserved punishment involves deliberately making someone suffer, (b) the *default* value of suffering is negative, and (c) there is value in forgiveness too. Even when punishment is "justified," the fact that we have to inflict it should, in different degrees, cause a form of remorse. Needless to say, I would not feel remorse in making Ohlendorf suffer, though I would very much feel it in having to inflict suffering on, say, someone found guilty of a one-off incident of reckless driving or of a one-off nonviolent criminal offense.[83] How to determine these degrees and what exactly gives rise to this peculiar sense of remorse in the first place are complicated issues that are not amenable to formulaic approaches. But these complications do not justify, in my opinion, the way in which contemporary punishment theorists have dismissed them.

Thus, in this chapter, I have tried to argue that part of the "mess" involved in adequately reacting to wrongdoing is to recognize that the notion of desert is, first, not nearly as mysterious as often suggested. Second, the power that desert has to alter the default negative value of suffering is not terribly different from what happens in morality in general: it is explained, *grosso modo*, by the existence of organic wholes and by an appeal to what Dancy calls moderate

---

[80] *Ibid.*, 3.    [81] *Ibid.*, 4.    [82] *Ibid.*

[83] I refrain here from using drug crimes as examples. Most "drug crimes" are to be regretted all right, not so much because they represent a moral conflict but rather because they should not have been criminalized in the first place.

holism. A moral phenomenon may perhaps have default value, but this is importantly different from invariant value.[84] Third, any effort to morally assess punishment that does not recognize these facts, and that is therefore not committed to a certain form of axiological pluralism, is simpleminded and doomed to fail.

---

[84] Adopting moderate holism within the context of punishment does not commit me to particularism as a full-blown metaethical doctrine (although, evidently, I am sympathetic to it). For the general debate over moral particularism, see Brad Hooker and Margaret Olivia Little, *Moral Particularism*, Oxford: Oxford University Press (2000).

# 3

## The Persistence of Consequentialism

Recognizing that deserved suffering is intrinsically valuable and a necessary and important part of the whole story regarding the justification of punishment points in the direction of a rich, pluralistic axiology. At the very least, such axiology will recognize intrinsic value *both* in the diminution of suffering (and, as I will explain in detail in Chapters 5 through 7, particularly in those diminutions of suffering that constitute forgiveness) *and* in the imparting of justice (even when such imparting may involve inflicting deserved suffering). But I have also claimed that this pluralistic axiology is widely rejected, both by consequentialists and by retributivists. In this chapter, I wish to discuss the ways in which by bluntly rejecting the value of deserved suffering, consequentialists perforce reject this pluralistic axiology too. (In the next chapter, I will show that insofar as retributivists reject *any* source of value other than deserved suffering, retributivists also reject axiological pluralism.)

To the uninitiated, however, my suggestion regarding the widespread contemporary rejection of the value of deserved punishment may seem unbelievable. She may assume that the idea of desert – which, as noted before, is the idea of *merit* and is inseparable from the idea of justice – is too foundational to be seriously doubted, let alone widely rejected. She may not be familiar with the forms of thoroughgoing skepticism that are only well known among academics, skepticisms that sometimes suggest that the very notions of moral responsibility and justice are mirages produced by our naïve clinging to unscientific notions of free will.[1] And she may be unfamiliar,

---

[1] Influential contemporary versions of this sort of skepticism include Galen Strawson, "The Impossibility of Moral Responsibility," *Philosophical Studies* 75 (1994): 5–24; Bruce Waller, *Against Moral Responsibility*, Cambridge, MA: MIT Press (2011); and Derk Pereboom, *Living without Free Will*, Cambridge: Cambridge University Press (2001), reworked and expanded a few years later as *Free Will, Agency, and Meaning in Life*, Oxford: Oxford University Press (2012). Engaging with thoroughgoing skepticism about moral responsibility and free will would entail a different book altogether. I must confess that I find it hard not to agree with Shelly Kagan's pithy way of explaining why he too avoided writing such a book: "I find myself far more confident of the claim that some people are more morally deserving than others than I am of any particular philosophical theses concerning the supposed metaphysical preconditions of desert." See Shelly Kagan, *The Geometry of Desert*, Oxford: Oxford

too, with that specific form of skepticism that is my target here: the skepticism espoused by thinkers who do not deny moral responsibility in general and who do not believe that the notion of justice is the offshoot of naïve sentimentalism but who nonetheless specifically single out deserved punishment as something that is invariantly disvaluable.

One version of this more narrowly focused skepticism I will leave aside and discuss at the end of the book, in an appendix. (Some readers may want to read the appendix at once, but that is not necessary: the arguments here do not depend on the arguments in the appendix.) That version is Derek Parfit's view that deserved suffering is not quite valueless, but *impossible*.[2] Parfit believes that we can deserve many things, but never suffering: so, for Parfit, Ohlendorf, to recall the example from the previous chapter, does not deserve to suffer because he – just like everyone else – *cannot* deserve to suffer. I know of no one else who has ever systematically defended this view.[3] I discuss it for two main reasons: first, because Parfit was an extraordinarily influential philosopher, and thus his views deserve special attention; and second, and more substantively, because the *spirit* of his metaphysical view that deserved suffering is impossible, is in fact but another manifestation of the hedonistic credo that animates the views that I criticize in this chapter: that suffering ought to be reduced at all costs.

Before advancing any further, it may be worthwhile to repeat a clarification I made already in Chapter 1. My target in this chapter is consequentialism, and by this I mean consequentialism-about-punishment. The consequentialists on whom I will focus in this chapter are, admittedly, not always consequentialists in general but only consequentialists-about-punishment. (Or so I shall argue – some of them in fact deny that they are consequentialists-about-punishment.) Choosing to engage with them rather than with authors who are consequentialist *tout court* highlights how pervasive consequentialism-about-punishment really is: even those who eschew consequentialism in general fall prey (perhaps unwittingly) to its allure when it comes to punishment. Whether consequentialism in general can survive the attacks

---

University Press (2012): 13. Thus, I will focus here on a narrower form of skepticism that attaches only to deserved suffering. The authors with whom I will engage do not deny that justice, moral responsibility, or free will exist, but they deny that any of these notions can possibly justify inflicting punishment simply because it is deserved.

2   In Derek Parfit, *On What Matters*, Oxford: Oxford University Press (2011).

3   Again, this is the view that while everything else *can* be deserved, only suffering *cannot*. It may be thought that Susan Wolf has *en passant* defended such a view in *Freedom within Reason* (Oxford: Oxford University Press, 1990). She seems (indirectly) committed to "the curious claim that being psychologically determined to perform good actions is compatible with deserving praise for them, but that being psychologically determined to perform bad actions is not compatible with deserving blame." This is so, however, only insofar as her position, unlike Parfit's, is not purely "metaphysical." "From a purely metaphysical perspective," Wolf tells us "it seems that either both determined agents [determined to do good or determined to do bad] must be responsible or neither can be," *ibid.*, 79. I cannot address here Wolf's overall insightful and ambitious thesis in that book. But this "curious" asymmetry is not central to her main aims. It is itself partly supported by appeals to intuitions and to ordinary language (*ibid.*, 80 ff.) that do not really constitute a *systematic* defense.

I mount against consequentialism-about-punishment and in particular whether it can be compatible with a flexible and pluralistic axiology (and whether even if it is indeed so compatible, it can survive other attacks) are interesting questions whose discussion is orthogonal to my goals in this book.

By way of introduction to this chapter, consider two very different thinkers: one, Martha Nussbaum, a wide-ranging author who has left an indelible mark in many different areas of philosophy; and the other, Victor Tadros, an important specialist in punishment theory in particular. Neither of them is a thoroughgoing skeptic about moral responsibility. And yet both of them display a similar skepticism for deserved suffering.

In a recent article, Nussbaum asserts that to think that the value of the suffering a person may experience can change in accordance with the nature or extent of her wrongdoing is to engage in "magical thinking."[4] Nussbaum's invariantist position implies not only that desert is morally inert (at least when it relates to suffering) but that the complexity of moral life – the complexity with which the theories of organic wholes and of modest holism seek to engage – is a chimera. Moral life, Nussbaum is in effect asserting, is relatively simple, and simple in a way that evidently resembles Benthamite utilitarianism: the less suffering the better; desert, merit, and justice are incapable of altering what she takes to be the invariant badness of suffering.

Nussbaum admits that by so asserting she is now "renouncing a range of things" she has said before and that her views about punishment now are "very Utilitarian."[5] To be sure, Nussbaum's article is not specifically about the justification of punishment as such. But, independently of context, she is perfectly explicit in her preceding views. She is also perfectly explicit when she claims that while she used to have "little sympathy with Utilitarian views of punishment," she now finds it "hard to avoid the conclusion that Bentham had a deep insight."[6] I do not think that to recognize that suffering is *prima facie* bad, as Bentham did, and as I have actually taken for granted, is a terribly *deep* insight. Given the previous two chapters, moreover, it should come as no surprise that I lament Nussbaum's rapprochement with

---

4 See Martha Nussbaum, "Transitional Anger," *Journal of the American Philosophical Association*, 1.1 (2015): 41–56. I will return to Nussbaum in much greater detail in Chapter 7.

5 Nussbaum, "Transitional Anger," 51. Benthamite utilitarianism does conflict – stridently – with some of Nussbaum's views as to the important connections between philosophy and literature, as developed in, say, her *Poetic Justice: The Literary Imagination and Public Life*, Boston, MA: Beacon Press (1995), and in some of her articles in *Love's Knowledge: Essays in Philosophy and Literature*, New York, NY: Oxford University Press (1990). It conflicts, too, with Nussbaum's inspiring rejection of the simple-minded avoidance of pluralism in her extraordinary *The Fragility of Goodness* (Cambridge: Cambridge University Press [1986]), where she claims that "the drive toward hedonism and utilitarianism" visible in "both Bentham and Sidgwick" was the result of a perceived "need for commensurability in order to deal with messy deliberative problems," 112.

6 Nussbaum, "Transitional Anger," 51. Given her prodigious pace, although this rapprochement with Bentham is a very recent development in Nussbaum's position, she appears to have changed her mind again. I will discuss Nussbaum at length in Chapter 7.

Benthamite utilitarianism – for Benthamite utilitarianism foists upon us an impoverished monistic axiology of invariant value.

Commenting on Shelly Kagan's recent treatise on desert – on desert in general, not just on deserved suffering in particular – Tadros asserts:

> *The Geometry of Desert* reveals that Shelly Kagan is the Charlie Parker of moral philosophy – a master of variations on a theme. As Parker's variations on *White Christmas* demonstrate, the impressiveness of musical variations doesn't depend on the brilliance of the theme. The same goes for philosophers, it seems. Desert, I think, is not much of a theme.[7]

Tadros is right that Kagan's work on desert is highly original – but not quite because "work on desert prior to Kagan's book" is "underdeveloped."[8] It is plain that many a philosophical treatise contains desert as a "theme" and very developed themes at that: from Plato's *Republic* to many of the writings of thinkers as dissimilar as the author of the *Book of Job*, Leibniz, Kant, Nietzsche, Moore, Brentano, Weber, Husserl, and Ross – to refer only to those few mentioned in the first two chapters of this book. Desert, given its intimate connection to merit and to justice, is, contra Tadros, rather than "not much of a theme," actually a *canonical* theme in the history of ideas: virtually every thinker who has ever engaged with moral philosophy or with the human condition has perforce dealt with desert.

In denying the axiological significance of desert, Tadros is reiterating his systematic invariantist defense of suffering's disvalue, which he develops in *The Ends of Harm*.[9] In so doing, Tadros is rejecting the pluralism for which I am here arguing and (in spite of his protestation to the contrary) endorsing (when it comes to punishment) the monism of classical, Benthamite utilitarianism.[10] In the final analysis, the only thing that matters for Tadros is reducing suffering in the world: the moral valence of suffering is unaffected by the fact that suffering may be sometimes a response (let alone a fitting response) to wrongdoing.

---

[7]   Victor Tadros, "Moving Mountains: Variations on a Theme by Shelly Kagan," *Criminal Law and Philosophy* 11.2 (2017): 393–405.

[8]   Tadros, "Moving Mountains . . .," *op. cit.*

[9]   Victor Tadros, *The Ends of Harm: The Moral Foundations of the Criminal Law*, Oxford: Oxford University Press (2011): 9, 25 ff., 45 ff., 66 ff., and *passim*. For criticisms, see Leo Zaibert, "The Instruments of Abolition, or Why Retributivism Is the Only Real Justification of Punishment," *Law and Philosophy* 32 (2013): 33–58. For Tadros's reaction (to me and to others), see his "Responses," *Law and Philosophy* 32 (2013): 241–325.

[10]  Tadros attempts to distinguish his position from Benthamite utilitarianism. In his "Responses" *Law and Philosophy* 32 (2013): 241–325, he claims that his view "shares with Benthamite utilitarianism only the idea that the suffering that punishment causes is not intrinsically good" and he adds that "[o]ther than that, [his view] and Benthamite utilitarianism have little in common" (244). It is true that Tadros's general position sees intrinsic value in things other than pleasure, but these things do not figure, at least not centrally, in his justification of punishment. I think Tadros underestimates the significance and implications of the quite major concession that he makes regarding the axiological similarity between his view and Benthamite utilitarianism.

Nussbaum and Tadros are by no means alone.[11] I cite them at the outset only insofar as they eloquently showcase the consequentialism (in the sense I defined in Chapter 1) that is so widespread nowadays and that, as noted before, amounts to classical utilitarianism – and is wedded to its impoverished monistic axiology. This is the view that the fact that someone deserves to suffer, insofar as it is a disvalue (or, at best, valueless), *by itself* does not justify inflicting that deserved suffering. Rather than simply adding names to the list of those who – consciously or otherwise – endorse consequentialism, I will in the rest of this chapter focus on a handful of themes as discussed by a relatively small number of influential authors in the hopes that this focus will help us further understand both the allure of consequentialism and its poverty.[12]

My point of departure in the first section that follows is Thomas Scanlon's recent crisp endorsement of consequentialism. While Scanlon's positions in this regard are, as are his positions in so many other topics, fair-minded, insightful, and penetrating, I suggest that some of them bear problematic resemblances to what in his rightly celebrated *Freedom and Resentment* P. F. Strawson referred to as a certain "panic." In the second section, I discuss some of the ways in which consequentialist positions can come perilously close to endorsing impunity ("perilously" in the sense of becoming problematically simpleminded). Finally, in the third section, I enlist arguments originally deployed by Isaiah Berlin, Bertrand Russell, and Jon Elster in other contexts in order to support my thesis that the monistic axiology on which contemporary consequentialism is built, when analyzed carefully, is indeed remarkably impoverished.

### 3.1 GIVING DESERT ITS DUE

In a recent article (to whose title this section's heading pays tribute), Scanlon admits that he has somehow reconciled himself with the idea of desert: in so doing, Scanlon claims to be "departing from positions [he had] taken in earlier work, in which [he] expressed skepticism about justifications of this kind [i.e., desert-based justifications in general]."[13] In other words, Scanlon has come around to seeing that sometimes a certain "treatment is made appropriate *simply* by certain facts" about what someone has done.[14] Scanlon's emphasis on "simply" is salutary: it "is intended to exclude

---

[11] Obviously, classical utilitarians have to reject retributivism. But many non-utilitarians reject it too – including many authors discussed in this book. Christine Tappolet has suggested that retributive emotions are "quite incompatible with a number of ideals of human flourishing, such as Epicurean ataraxia, Stoic apatheia, or Buddhist anatta," in her *Emotions, Values, and Agency*, Oxford: Oxford University Press (2016), 145. Doubtless this alleged incompatibility might explain the widespread antipathy.

[12] Since, as noted, by "consequentialism" (and cognates) I mean "consequentialism-about-punishment," when I affirm that "to be a consequentialist is to endorse classical utilitarianism," I mean that "to be a consequentialist-about-punishment is to endorse classical utilitarianism in the case of punishment."

[13] Thomas M. Scanlon, "Giving Desert Its Due," *Philosophical Explorations* 16 (2013), 102.

[14] *Ibid.*, 101.

justifications by appeal to the effects of treating the person in that way."[15] In other words, a desert-based justification of $\Phi$ justifies $\Phi$ wholly in terms of the fact that $\Phi$ is deserved – with no medicinal considerations. Scanlon further explains his change of heart:

> I was earlier led to reject desert altogether because I identified desert with the thesis that it is a good thing for people who have done wrong to suffer or at least that this is less bad than the comparable suffering of people who have done no wrong. It now seems to me a mistake to identify desert with these retributivist ideas.[16]

It is worth underscoring that Scanlon thinks that his mistake consisted in thinking that the idea of desert was necessarily linked to retributivism. This is a striking mistake. Students deserve certain grades, employees deserve certain salaries, and admirable people deserve admiration, just like criminals deserve punishment. Inasmuch as to "deserve something" is simply to "merit something" or to "being worthy of something" or to "being due something," it is not clear why – notwithstanding the protagonist role that desert has admittedly played for retributivists – anyone should think that there exists an exclusive relationship between desert and punishment theory. When, for example, Weber claims humans struggle with "the incongruity between destiny and merit" (as we saw in Chapter 1), he does not restrict merit to merited punishment. And what goes for Weber here goes also for Brentano, Husserl, Moore, Feldman, and virtually every other thinker who ever thought about a meaningful and just world.

But one thing is clear: while Scanlon now accepts many desert-based justifications of a variety of things, he continues to believe that desert-based justifications *of punishment* are to be rejected. Scanlon continues to endorse a position that has accompanied him throughout his career: that the view that "it is good that people who have done wrong should suffer" is "morally repugnant."[17] One has to assume that the "it" to which Scanlon refers in the previous citation can be substituted by "an organic whole": what Scanlon finds morally repugnant is the view that an organic whole in which people who have done wrong suffer is better than one in which they enjoy impunity. In other words, it is the very variance of suffering that Scanlon finds morally repugnant.

Furthermore, Scanlon appears to suggest that this moral repugnance attaches already to the *mere thought* whereby those deserving of suffering should suffer (or whereby their suffering is less bad than the suffering of the undeserving). Imagine someone who deserves to suffer in certain ways, and imagine that (for a variety of reasons) you do not wish anyone to inflict said suffering on her. But further suppose that this person comes to experience this suffering through a completely fortuitous act of nature and that you believe that this episode of "divine" or "poetic" justice is good – or at least not as bad as if this person had not deserved this suffering. For

---

[15] *Ibid.*   [16] *Ibid.*, 104.   [17] *Ibid.*, 102.

Scanlon *this belief* (in itself, unaccompanied by any action) may already be morally repugnant. So, it appears that it is the very possibility of reconciling ourselves – even if only in our minds – with deserved suffering that so vexes Scanlon. Still, in other places it appears that Scanlon's view is that what is really repugnant is to inflict suffering on those who deserve it (not to merely think that their suffering is good or not as bad as the same suffering experienced by someone who did not deserve it). I think that Scanlon's confused presentation, together with the relatively capricious isolation of punishment as the only case regarding which Scanlon continues to reject desert-based justifications, is the result of an understandable, but nonetheless exaggerated, "panic" regarding suffering.

Echoing some of Strawson's ideas, Scanlon admits that it is sometimes appropriate – i.e., not morally repugnant or even bad – to respond to a wrongdoer with "withdrawals of good will,"[18] such as, for example, when we display "a decreased tendency to hope that things go well for a person and to be sad or regretful if they do not."[19] But Scanlon disagrees with Strawson as to what exactly these withdrawals of good will entail. Scanlon reminds us that Strawson's view is that the

> withdrawal of good will can involve "modification of the general demand that another should, if possible, be spared suffering" and a "preparedness to acquiesce in that infliction of suffering on the offender which is an essential part of punishment."[20]

The difference between the two authors, then, is that Strawson's "withdrawals of good will" go further than Scanlon's. Strawson recognizes that withdrawals of good will can involve the infliction of suffering on those deserving to suffer, whereas Scanlon only allows for something considerably more pious.[21] For Scanlon, withdrawals of good will appear to at most warrant a certain tendency to stop *hoping* that a wrongdoer's life goes well or a certain state of affairs whereby we *feel less sad* when we learn that this wrongdoer's life does not go very well. In fact, many of Scanlon's "withdrawals of good will" take place wholly within the interior life of the "responder" to wrongdoing; they are consistent with the wrongdoer never even knowing that there was a "response" to his wrongdoing. In these cases, we are in the presence of a solipsistic position. But even if perhaps some of these responses can project beyond the interior life of the "responder," they should, in Scanlon's view, fall short of actually *inflicting suffering*.

It is of course hard to disagree with Scanlon that some of our reactions to wrongdoing can be private (even if one would may then perhaps want to insist on a difference between "reaction" and "response"). But it is also hard to agree that if

---

[18] *Ibid.*, 107.   [19]   *Ibid.*, 108.   [20]   *Ibid.*

[21] Some have suggested that it is possible to "strip" Strawson's position from these "retributive sentiments." See, e.g., Gary Watson "Responsibility and the Limits of Evil: Variations on a Strawsonian Theme," in his *Agency and Answerability: Selected Essays*, Oxford: Clarendon Press (2004), 258; see also Tappolet, *Emotions, Values, and Agency*, 146.

someone went beyond this private sphere and actually *punished* a wrongdoer (simply because he deserved it) this action would necessarily be morally repugnant. Imagine that you learn about Ohlendorf being punished for his crimes and that (independently of any medicinal consideration) you do not feel too sad about this punishment making his life not go well. From Scanlon's perspective, *perhaps* this could be morally acceptable. But if you *punished* Ohlendorf simply because you thought he deserved it (absent medicinal considerations), according to Scanlon you would have done something morally repugnant.

This is reminiscent of the views that eschew the analysis afforded by the theories of organic wholes and of moderate holism, which we have encountered before. Recall, for example, those authors who think that whatever value authorized punishment may happen to have, it *completely* disappears when the same "punishment" is administered by someone without proper authority. Similarly, Scanlon may be willing to recognize value in your privately reconciling yourself with someone's deserved suffering – but this value would *completely* disappear if you did anything seeking to inflict said deserved suffering. This immense normative difference reveals the lack of concern with the nuances of contexts and with the axiological perspective as such (let alone with the *pluralistic* axiology) for which I have been arguing.

Scanlon's emphasis on blame as a private phenomenon notwithstanding, he does believe that sometimes your blaming someone may, non-repugnantly, lead you to go beyond the solipsistic privacy of your own mind. Scanlon offers the following example, worth our sustained attention:

> Suppose I learn that at a party last week some acquaintances were talking about me, and making some cruel jokes at my expense. I further learn that my close friend Joe was at the party, and that rather than coming to my defense or adopting a stony silence, he was laughing heartily and even contributed a few barbs, revealing some embarrassing facts about me that I had told him in confidence.[22]

As he discusses his possible responses to Joe's behavior, Scanlon claims that these "fall into three categories":

> First, I might consider whether I should continue to regard Joe as a friend . . . Second, I may revise my attitude toward Joe . . . I might, for example, cease to value spending time with him in the way one does with a friend . . . Third, I might complain to Joe about his conduct, demand an explanation or justification, or indicate in some other way that I no longer see him as a friend.[23]

Of these three categories, the first two consist of mere revisions of private beliefs and attitudes unaccompanied by any overt action: my previous remarks thus apply to

---

[22]    Thomas M. Scanlon, *Moral Dimensions: Permissibility, Meaning, Blame*, Cambridge, MA: Harvard University Press (2008), 129.

[23]    *Ibid.*, 129–130.

them as well. The third category, however, does involve overt action, though only actions of a carefully qualified sort. Two such qualifications are particularly important. First, these actions fall within the context of Scanlon's friendship with Joe (although this is also true of the more passive "responses" in Scanlon's two other categories). Outside of a relationship – such as friendship – between Scanlon and Joe, blame appears inapposite. About this Scanlon is perfectly explicit: "To *blame* a person is to judge him or her to be blameworthy and to take your relationship with him or her to be modified in a way that this judgment of impaired relations holds to be appropriate."[24]

The second qualification is that when blame does issue in action, this action is mostly a matter of communication: Scanlon blaming Joe amounts to Scanlon wishing to have a conversation with Joe. Admittedly, the conversation may not be very pleasant for Joe (or, indeed, for Scanlon), and yet the point of blaming Joe to his face is to have him *understand* how badly he behaved and to elicit an explanation from him. But then we are immediately confronted with the following question: What if it is impossible to have this conversation with Joe (say, because he is really callous and would not care or because he died before Scanlon learned of his behavior at the party)? It seems that, by his own lights, Scanlon can no longer blame Joe: it is hard to see how we could possibly blame wrongdoers absent some *reparable* relation between us and them. In light of these two qualifications, it is hard to see how, from Scanlon's perspective, we could blame strangers, dead people, and ourselves. This is a strange sense of blame, to which I will return shortly.[25]

But my immediate emphasis is on the following: even that solitary case in which Scanlon's view of blame may survive the charge of solipsistic passivity strikes me as perhaps too misguidedly benevolent. Imagine that we attempted to enrich the unavoidably under-described Scanlonian account of his relationship with Joe. To completely avoid oversimplification, we would need many pages of felicitous psychological prose – and this is evidently not an option. But even a modest departure from schematism should help. Imagine, then, that at great cost to himself, Scanlon had helped Joe in significant ways for many years: without Scanlon's help, Joe would not have had a good job, indeed, would not have had a career at all, would not have even married his wife, etc. Suppose further that Scanlon came to realize that Joe had for many years been moved by a combination of malice (say, he was

---

[24] *Ibid.*, 128–129.

[25] Scanlon admits that sometimes we can blame outside the context of meaningful relationships such as friendships. I think that his admission is in tension with some of his other views. Outside relationships, Scanlon sees "blame" as mere "disapproval" (*ibid.*, 137). Moreover, while Scanlon admits that we can perhaps blame people who we never met or who are now dead, he also recognizes that such "relationships" obviously cannot be repaired. Discussing Scanlon's efforts to solve the tension between his view that blame involves repairing relationships and his view that sometimes we can blame absent such reparable relationships (think too about the problem of blaming *oneself*) would take me far afield. It suffices for my purposes here to say that, for Scanlon, more or less intimate relationships constitute, at the very least, the *paradigmatic* context for blame. See *ibid.*, 139–152.

always ungrateful and deeply envious of Scanlon) and brazen careerism (say, he thought that by celebrating these cruel jokes at Scanlon's expense, he was likely to gain favors from others). Does Joe's viciousness not make him deserving of something *other* than a conversation? Could Scanlon be justified if, without uttering a word, he were to show up at one of Joe's lectures, slap him publicly, and then leave, perfectly certain that he would never want to exchange another word with Joe and that he would never want to repair their relationship? Or if, without slapping Joe at all, Scanlon decided never to see or talk to Joe again (not wishing to repair their relationship)?[26]

As it turns out, then, the main point of disagreement between Strawson and Scanlon concerns, precisely, the role that suffering is supposed to play in our responding to wrongdoing: Strawson admits that sometimes we are morally justified in inflicting deserved suffering, whereas Scanlon, who finds that position morally repugnant, opts instead for remarkable passivity. This is how Scanlon reflects on the disagreement:

> It makes a big difference what kind of suffering is envisaged here. Decreased sympathetic concern ... as well as other reactions such as withdrawal of trust, withdrawal of affection and concern, and refusal of some kinds of aid and associa-tion all involve willingness to acquiesce in forms of *loss* for the person toward whom they are directed, since they all involve withholding things that person has reasons to want. In my view, as I have said, willingness to "acquiesce" in such losses is made appropriate simply by a person's deficient attitudes toward others. However, readi-ness to inflict the kind of suffering typically involved in the hard treatment aspect of punishment is an entirely different matter. It can be justified only on some basis other than pure desert, such as the beneficial consequences of a policy of threaten-ing and inflicting treatment of this kind. This divergence between my view and Strawson is a first-order moral disagreement about which kinds of concern are owed to others unconditionally and which are conditional upon their having the relevant moral attitudes toward others.[27]

While I think it is clear that the disagreement between Scanlon and Strawson is specifically about the normative implications – both axiological and deontic – of the suffering of the deserving, I wish to highlight a way in which this passage may be open to more than one interpretation. When Scanlon talks about "this divergence" between himself and Strawson, he cannot possibly be referring to his own rejection of "pure desert" as the justification of punishment. For about this Strawson was explicit too: although Strawson admits that he could "acquiesce in the infliction of suffering" when deserved, he denies that "we should be ready to acquiesce in the infliction of injury on offenders in a fashion which we saw to be quite indiscriminate or in accordance with procedures which we knew to be wholly useless."[28]

---

[26]   It is worthwhile to think of these questions in the context of Ohlendorf, Hitler, Iago, Claggart, etc.
[27]   Scanlon, "Giving Desert Its Due," 108.
[28]   P. F. Strawson, *Freedom and Resentment and Other Essays*, London: Routledge (2008), 24.

Strawson's preoccupation with *usefulness* here clearly shows that he, like Scanlon, rejects justifications of punishment based on "pure desert." Strawson, however, *also* rejected justifications of the "infliction of suffering on the offender which is an essential part of punishment"[29] that focus exclusively on the "social utility" of these inflictions of injury or suffering. *That*, in fact, is one of the – in not *the* – main messages of Strawson's *Freedom and Resentment*: "to speak in terms of social utility alone is to leave out something vital in our conceptions of these practices."[30] This way of speaking is the result of "a characteristically incomplete empiricism, a one-eyed utilitarianism."[31] (This "one-eyed utilitarianism" is, as we have seen, classical utilitarianism; *ideal* utilitarianism is *not* "one-eyed.") This is why Strawson insisted on the fact that it is a mistake

> to forget that these practices [which include inflicting deserved suffering, and believing that inflicting deserved suffering can add value to organic wholes], and their reception, the reactions to them, really *are* expressions of our moral attitudes and not merely devices we calculatingly employ for regulative purposes. Our practices do not merely exploit our natures, they express them.[32]

I would like to suggest that what Strawson rejects is simpleminded monism. And I would thus like to mobilize this passage as at least an indirect endorsement of the rich, pluralist axiology I defend here. Strawson's felicitous image of a one-eyed utilitarianism certainly points, I think, in that direction. Things other than the diminution of suffering are of value, and they are part of the story of punishment's justification. The pressing question is whether Scanlon agrees with Strawson on *this* point. We know that, like Strawson, Scanlon rejects "pure desert" justifications of punishment. But does Scanlon, again like Strawson, also reject the classical utilitarian justification of punishment?

It seems to me that Scanlon does not. In spite of Scanlon's nuanced rejection of purely teleological accounts of value and of his endorsing a pluralist account of value and valuing *at the general level*,[33] when it comes to punishment specifically, his view appears to be yet another exemplar of classical utilitarianism. Scanlon appears committed to the view that the *only* end of punishment is to medicinally alleviate suffering (mainly by repairing relationships, though perhaps otherwise too). In itself, punishment is of no value.

I cannot help noting a similarity between Strawson's point about our natures (with which Scanlon disagrees) and one of the central themes in Williams's criticism of (classical) utilitarianism we encountered earlier: "[W]e cannot regard our moral feelings merely as objects of utilitarian value ..., to regard those feelings from a purely utilitarian point of view, that is to say, as happenings outside one's moral self, is to lose a sense of one's moral identity; to lose, in the most literal way, one's

---

[29]  *Ibid.*, 23.    [30]  *Ibid.*, 24.    [31]  *Ibid.*, 25.    [32]  *Ibid.*, 27.
[33]  Thomas Scanlon, *What We Owe to Each Other*, Cambridge, MA: Harvard University Press (1998): 78–113 and *passim*.

integrity."[34] The view that, when it comes to punishment, Scanlon defends is the type of view that not only Strawson and Williams but Berlin, too, rejected. When ends are settled too confidently (as utilitarianism does), Berlin famously said, "the only questions left are those of means, and these are not political [or moral] but technical, that is to say, capable of being settled by experts or machines, like arguments between engineers or doctors."[35] As Berlin also points out:

> [T]hose who put their faith in some immense, world-transforming phenomenon, like the final triumph of reason or the proletarian revolution [or the avoidance of suffering, or the repairing of relationships, or the communication of right messages], must believe that all political and moral problems can thereby be turned into technological ones.[36]

Scanlon's "giving desert its due," at least within the context of punishment theory, turns out to be a very humble due indeed. Despite coming around to recognizing that there is something important about desert, and about desert-based justifications, Scanlon has not come around quite enough. He has not been able to rid himself of the excessive panic regarding suffering so ingrained in the contemporary thinking about punishment.

As is well known, Strawson's investigations into reactive attitudes sought to vindicate a "radical" modification of the view of those thinkers he called "optimists." The optimists are, roughly, compatibilists: they believe that our practices of blame and punishing can survive the truth of determinism – unlike both the "pessimists" (who think that determinism entails the demise of our practices of blame and punishment) and the "libertarians" (who perhaps too facilely reject the possibility of determinism). Strawson's modification simultaneously avoids the "conceptual deficiencies" of the optimists and wards off the "obscure and panicky metaphysics" of the libertarians.[37]

But I would like to suggest that the optimists share the panic Strawson attributes to the libertarians: while among libertarians the panic issues in odd metaphysical commitments and among optimists it issues in soothing (but ultimately unconvincing) simplifications, the panic is *about* the same: about the possibility that moral

---

[34] See Bernard Williams, "A Critique of Utilitarianism," in J. J. C. Smart and Bernard Williams, *Utilitarianism: For and Against*, Cambridge: Cambridge University Press (1973), 103–104.

[35] Isaiah Berlin, "Two Concepts of Liberty," in *Liberty* (Henry Hardy, ed.), Oxford: Oxford University Press (2002), 166.

[36] *Ibid.*, 167.

[37] Strawson, *Freedom and Resentment*, 27. I am here disagreeing with one aspect of Nomy Arpaly's otherwise admirable *Merit, Meaning, and Human Bondage: An Essay on Free Will* (Princeton, NJ: Princeton University Press [2006]). Arpaly thinks, for example, that "Strawson was wrong" in thinking that if someone (on gunpoint, say) were to command, "Praise me, or I'll kill you all!" she would thereby become praiseworthy (Arpaly, *ibid.*, 6). Arpaly argues that while in this case we would have *a reason* to praise the person who commanded us, the person would not thereby become praise*worthy* (for this is the wrong kind of reason). I agree with Arpaly. But I think that Strawson would have agreed too.

responsibility is a mirage. The optimist buys moral responsibility at too high a price: at the price of turning moral responsibility into a purely medicinal matter; the libertarian, in contrast, problematically gets moral responsibility for free. Scanlon's *ethics* is, I think, immune to many of the criticisms that Strawson leveled against optimists and libertarians, but when it comes to punishment, it remains, in these Strawsonian terms, "panicky" – as panicky as all contemporary treatments of punishment that take refuge behind a monistic axiology that exclusively (or almost exclusively) values the diminution of suffering. The targets of Strawson's criticism panic about a world without moral responsibility; as a good consequentialist (about punishment), Scanlon panics about failing to reduce as much suffering as possible, thus inheriting the "conceptual deficiencies" of Strawson's optimists.

### 3.2 THE PIETIES OF IMPUNITY

Scanlon thinks that by acquiescing in wrongdoers' "losses" we are in fact acquiescing in wrongdoers experiencing some suffering. Crucially, however, he thinks that this suffering is significantly different from the suffering typically involved in the "hard treatment aspect of punishment." Notwithstanding my rejection of what, mobilizing Strawson's use of the term, I have called Scanlon's "panicky" ethics, I agree that the suffering typically involved in the hard treatment aspect of punishment as meted by criminal justice systems *is* typically morally repugnant. *One* of my chief reasons for so agreeing, however, is that such suffering is too often *undeserved*.

To the extent that the axiology behind consequentialism is the monistic axiology of classical utilitarianism, consequentialists (like Scanlon but evidently also like the recent Nussbaum cited at the outset of this chapter, Tadros, and many other contemporary authors) cannot join me (or Leibniz or Moore or Brentano or Weber or so many others throughout history) in seeing the fact that suffering is *undeserved* as a point against it at all. As a matter of fact, and as we saw in Chapter 1, if it turned out that this undeserved suffering was the only medicinally efficacious way of reducing further suffering, the classical utilitarian would have *no* reason to object to it. In any case, if Scanlon's position is that the suffering that is to be diminished at all costs is only a *specific* type of suffering, what then is that type of suffering? How does it differ from other types of suffering? That punishment necessarily involves *some* type of suffering makes it all the more urgent for Scanlon to tell us more about *which* forms of suffering he finds acceptable and which he finds morally repugnant – and why. (Are all unacceptable forms of suffering infliction equally repugnant?)

At this point, the following strategy may be attempted: suffering, it may be assumed, is acceptable when not intentionally inflicted or when not taken to be intrinsically or "simply" (in Scanlon's sense) good. To see how this strategy fares, let us return to Scanlon's friend. The only non-solipsistic response to Joe's behavior that Scanlon envisages – and thus the only candidate for being an instance of punishment – is to have a conversation with him in order to "complain," to "demand an explanation," or to simply let him know that Scanlon "no longer see[s] him as a friend." Let us stipulate, in the first instance, that Scanlon's words have an effect on Joe: Joe is made aware of his despicable behavior, and he comes to understand what an ungrateful and indecent person he is. Surely this should cause Joe considerable suffering. But since it appears that this suffering is intentionally inflicted, and since Scanlon does not object to this conversation, the strategy will not do.

However, it could perhaps be suggested that what Scanlon *intended* was to have a conversation with Joe. What is intrinsically good would be the conversation itself – which is indeed intended – not its concomitant suffering – which is neither intrinsically good nor directly intended. (But consider: it is very likely, and at any rate *possible*, that the conversation between Scanlon and Joe would cause suffering to Scanlon himself, even if not to Joe. So, even if somehow it could be argued that by precipitating the conversation with Joe Scanlon is not intentionally inflicting suffering on Joe, Scanlon would surely be intentionally inflicting suffering at least on himself.) Of course, Scanlon must have *foreseen* that Joe's suffering was likely to ensue, but that was not his intention.

Distinguishing between intention and foresight is admittedly a time-honored strategy, though its shortcomings are also well known: as was briefly mentioned in Chapter 1, already in the seventeenth century Pascal had dubbed the doctrine of double effect the "method of directing the intention."[38] This strategy reeks of stipulative, self-serving casuistry – and in fact Scanlon has himself very convincingly criticized it:[39] one can often *claim* that one's intention is (almost) whatever one wants it to be.

Deploying strategies of this sort faces at least three additional problems. First, if all the potential goodness of inflicting suffering is taken to be in this way medicinal, then we would be embracing the uninspiringly "technological," "one-eyed" hedonistic utilitarianism (in Berlin's and Strawson's senses, respectively) that we have discussed previously. "Punishment," in a case like Joe's, would then be facilely *reduced* to a mechanism for repairing relationships. Second, in those cases in which relationships are irreparable (for whatever reason), we would be thrown back into solipsism. This passivity may in fact encourage people to become impenetrable (or to feign impenetrability), since this is likely to buy them impunity. Where relations – for whatever reason – cannot be repaired, punishment would, in principle, be morally repugnant.

The third problem goes even deeper, and its treatment will be lengthier. These strategies presuppose an implausible moral psychology, according to which we can neatly separate the normative and the emotional significance of our intending to do

---

[38]  See Blaise Pascal, *The Provincial Letters: Moral Teachings of the Jesuit Fathers Opposed to the Church of Rome and Latin Vulgate*, Toronto: William Briggs (1893). See also Leo Zaibert, "Punishment, Restitution, and the Marvelous Method of Directing the Intention," *Criminal Justice Ethics* 29.1 (2010): 41–53.

[39]  The first chapter of Scanlon's *Moral Dimensions* is titled "The Illusory Appeal of Double Effect."

$\Phi$, on the one hand, from the normative and emotional significance of our foreseeing that we are about to do $\Psi$, on the other – even when $\Phi$ and $\Psi$ are intimately linked. Only by assuming such implausible separation can the attempt to "direct the intention," suspicious as it is, even get off the ground.

Elsewhere Scanlon has endorsed something like this strategy:

> It is important that terrible wrongs be recognized by an appropriate response, and the victims of such wrongs are demeaned when the victimizers are treated as respected citizens with no mention of their crimes. But what makes it appropriate to recognize these wrongs is not that this involves suffering or loss on the part of the wrongdoers. It is rather that the absence of such recognition reflects indifference on the part of society toward the wrongs and those who suffered them. What is crucial is recognition, not suffering. Ideally, of course, one wants the perpetrators themselves to acknowledge these wrongs and express contrition for them. This will be painful, but it is not the pain that makes it desirable.[40]

At this point, I wish to bring Tadros's views back into focus. For Tadros has defended a position that, while strikingly similar to Scanlon's, nonetheless surpasses it in explicitness when it comes to the endorsement of precisely this problematic strategy. Like Scanlon, Tadros believes that getting wrongdoers to understand (or "recognize") that they did wrong is "a strong candidate for an intrinsic good." And, again like Scanlon, he believes that the concomitant suffering of such recognition is merely "an inevitable but negative side effect of the good of recognition" and clearly not an intrinsic good.[41] It could perhaps be argued that insofar as both Scanlon and Tadros admit intrinsic goods *other* than pleasure (and the diminution of suffering) – although never deserved suffering – they are not really monistic after all. I am not sure that this is correct, for three reasons. First, the non-hedonistic intrinsic goods they recognize do not really figure prominently in their justification of punishment. Second, it seems to me that sometimes the "intrinsic" good of recognition that they mention is not really intrinsic but medicinal in the sense of being conducive to preventing further harm. (I will return to the discussion of this issue in Chapter 5 when I discuss communicative justifications of punishment.) Third, as explained in Chapter 1, the pluralistic axiology worth championing ought to revolve around two values: the value of deserved suffering and the value of its merciful remission. A pluralistic axiology that did not include the value of deserved suffering would be a seriously *impoverished* view, even if formally speaking not fully monistic. An axiology that admits the intrinsic value of deserved suffering is, *other things being equal*, always richer than an axiology that does not admit it.

Facing an objection to the effect that he would be forced to recommend the use of an imagined moral anesthetic pill that would spare suffering to wrongdoers

---

[40]  Thomas Scanlon, *The Difficulty of Tolerance: Essays on Political Philosophy*, Cambridge: Cambridge University Press (2003), 223.

[41]  Tadros, *The Ends of Harm* ..., 45.

(provided they understood the wrongness of their actions), Tadros doubled down.[42] Tadros emphatically insisted that if such an anesthetic pill really existed, the more people took it, the better the world would be (again, provided that such people somehow understood those things that Tadros want them to understand). From Tadros's perspective – the perspective of classical utilitarianism – there is nothing objectionable about this moral lobotomy whereby a wrongdoer pops a moral anesthetic pill immediately after committing whatever atrocity one could imagine in order to avoid suffering – provided, that is, that she would "understand" the wrongness of her actions.

The moral psychology Tadros presupposes hardly resembles *human* psychology. Imagine that Joe, for example, is somehow made to understand the wrongness of his behavior, the baseness of his motives, and the extent of his invidious ingratitude, all against the backdrop of Scanlon's kindness and generosity. It is hard to resist the thought that Joe will *thereby* suffer, so much so that the very intelligibility of the alleged moral anesthetic pill is called into question. A pill that could numb the enlightened Joe's suffering would have to *eo ipso* numb his intellect as well. It is just too difficult to see how Joe could really understand what he has done without *thereby* suffering. One is tempted to suggest that understanding that one has done wrong is an *essentially painful state*, just as, for example, finding out that our romantic love is reciprocated is an *essentially pleasant state*. So, if this understanding (or recognition) truly is inseparable from this suffering, it is hard to deny that suffering is sometimes, if not itself intrinsically good, at least an *inseparable* part of organic wholes that are intrinsically better than other organic wholes from which they differ only because they do contain suffering.

Not distinguishing between acceptable and unacceptable forms of suffering is, I think, a problem for Tadros's position. But I think it is a greater problem for Scanlon's. After all, Scanlon is much more explicit in that some forms of suffering are acceptable whereas others are not (recall: not merely not acceptable but downright morally repugnant). Yet Scanlon does not distinguish, as he crucially needed to do, between the different types of suffering that he himself postulates. What appears to be the case is that, in spite of his explicit invocation of a distinction between different forms of suffering, Scanlon in fact believes that *all* inflictions of suffering are morally repugnant, unless they are instrumental – medicinal – in allowing us to attain some other good consequences.

In Tadros's case, however, there is no doubt about his rejection of all forms of suffering: suffering is for him invariantly disvaluable. Tadros asks us to imagine that Hitler has ended up in an otherwise deserted island: there is plenty of food there, but there is no way he would ever be found or that he would escape. We (somehow) can give Hitler nice weather (of the sort he loves) or rainy weather (of the sort he hates).

---

[42]   The objection is raised in very similar ways by Douglas Husak in his "Retributivism in Extremis," *Law and Philosophy* 31 (2012): 3–31; and by me in "The Instruments of Abolition . . .,".

Hitler will never know that someone controlled the weather. (Imagine that in either case Hitler will live the same number of additional years, etc.) Tadros wonders what would be better: for Hitler to enjoy nice weather or for him to be constantly bothered by the bad weather. Under these conditions, Tadros prefers it to be sunny – there is, in his view, nothing to be *gained* by Hitler's suffering. "Imagining Hitler suffering in the rain," Tadros points out, "is simply sad," and he adds: "Hitler's life was already going disastrously. In the imagined world [the rainy island] it is going even worse."[43]

Tadros's thought experiment can evidently be seen as a variation on J. J. C. Smart's famous example (deployed in order to defend utilitarianism) of an otherwise deserted universe in which there is "one sentient being only [a sadist], who falsely believes that there are other sentient beings and that they are undergoing exquisite torment [thus enjoying himself very much]."[44] As a consistent classical utilitarian, Smart used this example to bolster his claim that it is better for this solitary sadist to take delight rather than to feel sorrow for the (imagined) suffering of others. Although Tadros denies that he is a Benthamite utilitarian when it comes to punishment, his example is in a way even more utilitarian than Smart's, at least in the sense that the suffering Smart wishes the sadist to avoid would be after all the result of no longer being *deluded* and not suffering that he *deserved*, whereas the suffering that Tadros wishes to spare Hitler would have been suffering that Hitler deserved.

Others, of course, believe that since Hitler deserves much more suffering than the weather-induced suffering of Tadros's thought experiment, in the current scenario he should "suffer" the bad weather, independently of the fact that *ex hypothesi* no positive consequences may flow from this suffering. Making Hitler suffer via bad weather (the only way the thought experiment allows) is not to fail to appreciate the obvious fact that suffering's *default* value is negative and that in principle we wish to avoid it. It is rather to insist on the fact that the value of suffering, including deserved suffering inflicted via punishment, is not *invariant* and that it can enter into organic wholes that are made better because of its presence. (And it is not to deny that other forms of suffering – not allowed in this thought experiment – may be even more valuable.) To think otherwise is to display the panicky ethics I have been discussing and to cling to an uninspiring monistic axiology.

Let us return to Joe one last time. So far our assumption has been that Scanlon's words have an effect on Joe – that Joe suffers as a result of Scanlon's words. Imagine now that Joe dismisses Scanlon's complaint or that he offers no explanation or that he does not care about the fact that Scanlon no longer sees him as a friend. He is not made to suffer, and, effectively adding insult to injury, as Scanlon carries on with his reproach, Joe laughs to his face. Imagine, in other words, that Joe is *impenetrable*: he will not care about what Scanlon says and will, perversely, just keep laughing.

43  Tadros, "Responses," 259.
44  J. J. C. Smart, "An Outline of a System of Utilitarian Ethics," in Smart and Williams, *Utilitarianism: For and Against*, 25.

The point of a conversation in such a case eludes me.[45] Assuming that Joe is in this sense impenetrable renders this scenario very similar to that of Hitler in the island: the value – if any – of inflicting suffering on either of them would have to be intrinsic. But this infliction would be, for Scanlon, morally repugnant (and for Tadros barbaric). Scanlon's view that to do more than (pointlessly, as the case may be) converse with Joe or that for anyone to cause bad weather in Hitler's island would be to do something morally repugnant strikes me as a remarkably unattractive position.

But is there a way to *prove* that this position is indeed unattractive? Or have we reached a dead end, in the sense that the only thing left to do is to appeal to intuitions? Smart happens to have the intuition that a happy sadist is better than a sad-but-decent person (in his thought experiment), Tadros happens to have the intuition that to give bad weather to Hitler in the island is bad, Scanlon happens to have the intuition that the suffering that is due to Joe is at most the one that may perhaps result from a conversation, and I (and others) happen to have opposing intuitions. Is that all?

In a sense, a mere conflict of intuitions need not hurt my case, for at least five reasons, which I present in a roughly increasing order of importance. First, in general, the appeal to intuitions is not as problematic as often assumed; as John Rawls famously put it:

> [While] we should do what we can to reduce the direct appeal to our considered judgments ... there is nothing necessarily irrational in the appeal to intuition ... We must recognize the possibility that there is no way to get beyond a plurality of principles. No doubt any conception of justice will have to rely on intuition to some degree ... the dependence on intuition cannot be eliminated entirely.[46]

Thus, I would not be too worried if, regarding some ultimate questions, I, *just like my opponents*, relied, at some point or another, on some (ineliminable) appeal to intuition. I can echo John Elster (to whom I will return later): "I do not see how a theory of justice can dispense with intuitions altogether."[47] Second, outside the sometimes rarefied air of academic circles, the sorts of intuitions I am here opposing are not widely shared. For whatever it is worth, most human beings – now and throughout history – agree with my position that sometimes people should get the suffering they deserve – and sometimes simply because they deserve it. There is of course no denying that sometimes human beings are mistaken and that they go overboard – now and throughout history – in their vindictiveness, but that is beyond the point. The fact remains that the "intuitions" that I endorse are much more

---

[45] Imagine that the conversation was private, thus incapable of having any medicinal effects.

[46] John Rawls, *A Theory of Justice* (revised edn.), Cambridge, MA: Harvard University Press (1999): 36, 37.

[47] John Elster, *Sour Grapes: Studies in the Subversion of Rationality*, Cambridge: Cambridge University Press (1983), 137.

widely shared than the ones I oppose. Third, the appeal of classical utilitarianism *among contemporary punishment theorists* is so great and surreptitious that it is worthwhile to expose the ways in which it does conflict with ordinary people's deep-seated intuitions.

Fourth, in light of the considerations I have presented in the previous chapters, it has to be admitted that at the very least the burden of proof in this conflict of intuitions (if this is indeed what it is) has to fall on the defenders of invariance and on the defenders of the view that the ordering of the parts of organic wholes does not have any value. To deny that there is non-medicinal value in Hitler's suffering is to – simplemindedly – refuse to see any *meaning* in deserved suffering. As we saw in Chapter 1, many influential thinkers throughout history have found that the most serious problem of suffering is not with suffering as such but with *meaningless, underserved* suffering. But this denial is also a stubborn refusal to admit that a world in which Hitler does not suffer is less valuable than one in which he does suffer, along the lines we discussed in connection to Ross's thought experiment in Chapter 2. Even a hedonist utilitarian, like Feldman, avoided this stubbornness. This denial is, in fact, to treat any and all instances of suffering as utterly random: the suffering that Hitler would experience in the island has to be *computed* just as crudely and non-narratively as if he would have experienced it when he was a child, before he committed any atrocity, or as if it would have been inflicted by a sadist, who knew nothing about Hitler or his deeds, or as a result of a natural calamity. Whatever its context, suffering just needs to be entered into the utilitarian ledger and mechanically computed: the least of it, the better. The fact that this suffering is a *response* to Hitler's wrongdoing (even if Hitler himself does not know it) is, for my opponents, irrelevant. These four reasons show that even if I may not have quite *proven* their position wrong, I have showed that it is at least highly implausible.

Fifth, and finally, there is an important difference between our intuitive responses to token thought experiments and situations (or even to a series of token thought experiments and situations), on the one hand, and our "intuitive" responses to entire systems for evaluating phenomena, such as axiologies, on the other. Someone can say, for example, that she intuitively sees the wrongness (or rightness) of the death penalty. Admittedly, this move is often an off-putting conversation stopper, a refusal to engage with arguments. But at least it is an intelligible position: and sometimes invoking an intuition can also be shorthand for perfectly defensible positions such as those captured by the "one thought too many" line Williams has made famous.[48] In other words, the invocation can be taken to be a suggestion that some courses of action are just too *obvious* to need a justification or even a discussion. Imagine, in contrast, that someone would say that she "intuitively" sees the wrongness (or rightness) of Kantian ethics or of Sartre's existentialism. It is hard to see what, absent specific *arguments*, this could possibly entail.

---

[48]  See Bernard Williams, *Moral Luck*, Cambridge: Cambridge University Press (1981), 18.

Thought experiments such as Scanlon's Joe, Tadros's Hitler, Smart's deluded sadist, and so on, are of interest to me insofar as they allow me to expose problems *with their underlying monistic axiology*. The many problems these thought experiments face actually point in the direction of a coherentist justification for my position: the "intuition" I oppose clashes with a much larger number of our beliefs than does the "intuition" I endorse.[49] Endorsing (or rejecting) a given axiology is not only (or mainly) a matter of intuitions: arguments are needed. The disagreement in these cases is a matter of disagreeing about the underlying theories and the strength of the arguments that support them. Of course, perhaps our arguments and our very theories *ultimately* depend on, or are at least influenced by, some intuitions that, perhaps even unconsciously, we may espouse (along the lines Rawls and Elster suggest). But this does not deny the difference between the two kinds of appeal to intuition I am here suggesting. Independently of at least some intuitions, I have argued that there are problems and limitations with monistic axiologies. My rejection of some authors' responses to this or that thought experiment is based on what – for good or for bad – I have argued are problems with the theoretical underpinnings of their views. And in the remainder of this chapter, I will attempt to show how some of my misgivings about monistic axiologies actually play out in other contexts as well.

### 3.3 THE AVOIDANCE OF SUFFERING AND SOUR GRAPES

I will have much more to say about the use of thought experiments in moral philosophy later on. For now I merely want to steer clear of Tadros's thought experiment of Hitler in the desert island (or Smart's deluded sadist) and consider instead a more realistic (and thus less far-fetched) scenario. Consider Ricardo Klement, who allegedly lived an innocuous and drab life in Argentina until he was seized by Israeli agents and brought to trial in Jerusalem. Klement was, of course, Adolf Eichmann, who, like many other surviving Nazis, had changed his name after the war in order to escape justice. Metaphorically, Eichmann could be seen as inhabiting Tadros's island: he was, *ex hypothesi*, as deserving of suffering as was Hitler. Imagine that Eichmann had succeeded in faking his death, that he had carried on living a uneventful and law-abiding life in Argentina, and that he would have never been exposed as Eichmann (and assume further that he had even transformed himself into a great benefactor of humanity and that no good medicinal consequence would flow from inflicting on him the suffering that he deserved or from otherwise punishing him). Under these circumstances, why not let him enjoy

---

[49] For coherentism in general, see Laurence Bonjour, *The Structure of Empirical Knowledge*, Cambridge, MA: Harvard University Press (1985), *passim* but above all 87–156. Within the context of punishment theory in particular, Michael S. Moore has insightfully defended retributivism along coherentist lines. See, e.g., his *Placing Blame: A General Theory of the Criminal Law*, Oxford: Clarendon Press (1997), 165 ff.

life, like Hitler in his island (or like Smart's sadist in his lonely universe)? Independently of the historical facts as to whether the real Klement was really harmless, cases of this sort *can* indeed exist. And if we deny that there could be value in their suffering *as such* (in the sense that this suffering can add value to the organic whole in which it appears), then we are committed to saying, with Tadros, that like Hitler in his island, Klement should have carried on living a happy life in Argentina (again, stipulating medicinal considerations away).

By way of contrast, think of another utilitarian (albeit, as we have noted previously, neither Benthamite nor ideal): John Stuart Mill. Mill thought that there are cases in which someone has done something we find blameworthy, and yet our blame can only properly amount to something relatively passive, like mere moral dispraise of the sort Scanlon seems to recommend. Regarding some type of wrongdoer, Mill said that we are "not bound, for example, to seek his society"; about our association with this person, Mill thought that "we have a right to avoid it (though [interestingly] not to parade the avoidance)."[50] Mill's parenthetical remark seeks, precisely, to limit our response in these cases to something akin to moral dispraise, to prevent us from becoming too punitive: *parading* our avoidance of someone's company can evidently be a form of shaming punishment.

Importantly, however, the type of wrongdoer Mill had in mind in these cases was a person who harmed only himself. Dealing with people who commit "acts injurious to others," Mill, whose humanism and whose aversion to over-criminalization and over-punishment are second to none, was perfectly clear: this type of case "requires a totally different treatment." Mill saw these other wrongdoers as "fit objects of moral reprobation [understood as more than mere moral dispraise, as more than conversations, etc.], and, in grave cases, of moral retribution and punishment."[51] Mill's "totally different treatment" is predicated on the fact that some acts *harm* others.

One could of course harbor doubts about whether Mill's harm principle offers enough or correct guidance regarding criminalization policy. These doubts, however, do not affect its (much less frequently discussed) usefulness in allowing us to normatively distinguish between different kinds of *suffering* – along the lines that Scanlon needed to distinguish. Harm to others, in Mill's opinion, warrants the infliction of a type of suffering that is radically different from the much more placid and pious suffering contingently associated with expressions of moral dispraise. Since Mill was after all a utilitarian, the reason why he underwrites the infliction of this "totally different treatment" has more to do with the fact that he believes that this suffering has a tendency to reduce further suffering than with the possibility that this suffering is intrinsically valuable. In other words, Mill was (almost) as quick to move away from the axiological realm and toward the deontic realm as was Bentham. Be that as it may, Mill seems less committed to axiological monism

---

[50] John Stuart Mill, "On Liberty," in *On Liberty and Other Essays* (John Gray, ed.), Oxford: Oxford University Press (2008), 86.
[51] *Ibid.*, 87.

than Bentham and his contemporary heirs endorsing consequentialist justifications of punishment. Perhaps nowhere is this clearer than in his (unsuccessful) effort to distinguish higher from lower pleasures.[52]

A society that shows *no* commitment to give *some* wrongdoers the suffering that they deserve, sometimes simply because the deserve it, is not likely to be a *stable* society. The widespread view that justice *matters* is in fact an indispensable aspect of social peace; if history is to be trusted, where a large segment of the population thinks that a government neglects this aspect, sooner or later, social unrest is likely to ensue. This explains why the need to *do justice*, even if it involves inflicting deserved suffering for its own sake, is so crucial, for example, in cases of "transitional justice." There is no question that the first priority of nations who are recovering from long-standing totalitarian regimes or whose populations have been the victims of genocide or other forms of mass human rights violations is to establish solid institutional foundations for their new, incipient, and weak governments. And there is no question that *sometimes* pragmatic considerations defeat, or at the very least temper, considerations related to retributive justice. But there is no question, either, that considerations having to do with justice as such sometimes defeat – and almost always temper – those pragmatic considerations.

As it turns out, complete blindness to the demands of justice, such as that heralded by the overly pious position that flows from the axiological monism of classical utilitarianism, would be disastrous for the very forward-looking, pragmatic efforts to rebuild nations and for other practical matters with which classical utilitarians are so concerned.[53] And while sometimes those demands can be met by public denunciation, by formal declarations of the wrongness of certain acts, by truth and reconciliation commissions, etc., some other times these demands can only be met by ensuring that the perpetrators of these atrocities get to experience the suffering that they deserve *because* they deserve it.[54] Paradoxically, then, the overly pious consequentialist I am here criticizing can end up resembling the Talmudic figure of the *hasid shoteh* – i.e., the pious fool – who, for example, refuses to save a drowning woman out of fear that rescuing her from the water would necessarily involve touching her (or looking at her) inappropriately.[55]

The point of this brief Millian excursion into practical matters is simply to highlight that there is a danger inherent to the allegedly very pious effort to minimize suffering at all costs: danger, that is, that the effort may backfire.

---

[52]  *Ibid.*, 136–146. In his fine "Introduction" to the volume, Gray correctly points out that Mill's distinction between higher and lower pleasures "shows him moving away from the Benthamite utilitarianism" (xii).

[53]  See, for example, the contributions in *The Handbook of Reparations* (Pablo De Greiff, ed.), Oxford: Oxford University Press (2006).

[54]  See Scanlon, *The Difficulty of Tolerance: Essays on Political Philosophy*, 219–233.

[55]  *The Soncino Babylonian Talmud*, "Tractate *Sotah*," I. (Epstein, ed.) 21b, (pp. 72–73): www.halakhah .com/rst/nashim/28%20-%20Sotah%20-%2021a-49b.pdf.

The Benthamite obsession with reducing suffering may end up causing more suffering than it prevents. While I do not deny that medicinal considerations often matter, my discussion of the possible positive consequences of giving people the suffering that they deserve is not to thereby instrumentalize desert through the back door somehow. Rather, it is to suggest that Benthamite utilitarians better think twice before too quickly jettisoning the intrinsic value of deserved punishment. Of course, they could turn toward forms of self-effacing, esoteric, or "Government House" utilitarianism and *pretend* that they value deserved punishment even if they do not.[56] While I do not believe those options are promising, I do not need to discuss them here. For it suffices for current purposes that such options would evade answering the obvious question: Why would this pretending work? The answer is that deserved punishment is part of what justice entails, and humans unavoidably care about justice.

In an effort to further highlight the poverty of consequentialism (and its monistic axiology), I would like to suggest an unexplored – and instructive – parallel between it and a certain poverty other authors have discussed elsewhere. For example, Berlin famously claimed that to conceptualize liberty simply as the ability to do what one wishes is problematic. Sarcastically, Berlin pointed out: "[I]f I find that I am able to do little or nothing of what I wish, I need only contract or extinguish my wishes, and I am made free."[57] Despots of all stripes have sought to mold people's desires to whatever form of life they have invented for them, such that in a perverted sense, the new regimes would in effect be "liberating" them. To put it in terms of the slogan Berlin made famous, these regimes would be curtailing people's *negative* freedom but with the alleged goal of expanding their *positive* freedom. Perceptively, Berlin pointed out that

> the doctrine that maintains that what I cannot have I must teach myself not to desire, that a desire eliminated, or successfully resisted, is as good as a desire satisfied, is a sublime, but, it seems to me, unmistakable, form of the doctrine of sour grapes: what I cannot be sure of, I cannot truly want.[58]

Liberty, Berlin thus understandably insisted, has to be more complicated than this:

> [A]scetic self-denial may be a source of integrity or serenity and spiritual strength, but it is difficult to see how it can be called an enlargement of liberty. If I save myself from an adversary by retreating indoors and locking every entrance and exit, I may remain freer than if I had been captured by him, but am I freer than if I had defeated or captured him?

Berlin surely goes too far when he agrees with Schopenhauer in that "total liberation ... is conferred only by death"[59] or when he claims that "the logical culmination of the process of destroying everything through which I can possibly be

---

[56]  See Bernard Williams, *Ethics and the Limits of Philosophy*, London: Routledge (2006), 108 ff.
[57]  Berlin, "Two Concepts of Liberty," 186.     [58]  *Ibid.*     [59]  *Ibid.*, 186–187.

wounded is suicide."[60] Death can be seen as freer than life only in the sense in which a nonworking watch is more accurate than one that slows down a second per day. And that is not quite the sense of liberty that even the most simpleminded political philosophers have ever had in mind. The stipulation that we can only speak about liberty in connection to beings capable of making choices (or the stipulation that we can only apply the concept of accuracy in connection to *minimally working* watches) should obviously be admitted. Still, the force of Berlin's overall point remains strong: a life devoted to avoiding having unfulfilled desires can take the path of drastically reducing our desires, to the point of not resembling a human life. That is a path of uninspiring passivity.

The connection between the passivity with which Berlin was concerned and the passivity I have been discussing here thus emerges. Just as some *desires* are worth *having* even though they may cause suffering, some *actions* are worth *carrying out* even though they may cause suffering because, as we have seen, some organic wholes are made *more valuable* because they contain suffering. The passivity that is the target of Berlin's criticism is, famously, a matter of his deploying the stoic theme of a retreat to an "inner citadel," in which we will protect ourselves from the suffering that unfulfilled desires may cause. The passivity with which I am concerned is also a matter of strategic retreat to an inner citadel, one in which we will refuse to ever inflict suffering on anyone – no matter how deserving – unless it is a way of diminishing greater suffering. Both strategic retreats have a similar mono-maniacal, panicky (in the Strawsonian sense explained above) basis: the monistic axiology that enshrines the indiscriminate avoidance of suffering as the only locus of value.

It may appear, however, that the parallel I suggest faces a problem, since the retreaters I am criticizing – consequentialists-about-punishment – can after all endorse inflictions of suffering (based on medicinal considerations), presumably unlike Berlin's retreaters who are more unqualifiedly intent on exiling themselves to the inner citadel. But this alleged problem is mere appearance. The infliction of suffering that consequentialists accept, as we have seen, is *only* justified insofar as it tends to reduce further suffering. Their acquiescing in inflictions of suffering is not a concession to a more meaningful existence – it is merely a *strategy* seeking to maximize suffering reduction. And a similar maximizing, strategic retreater can be constructed in Berlin's case. Imagine that there existed some desires such that although they themselves were potential sources of suffering, having them would greatly reduce our overall suffering. Allowing ourselves to have these desires would be a perfectly sensible strategy for those seeking exile to the inner citadel in Berlin's case as well.

Just as strategically retreating to an inner citadel vis-à-vis desires that may cause us suffering is a passive position that may lead to an impoverished existence, refusing to

---

[60]  *Ibid.*, 186.

inflict suffering on those who deserve it is to retreat into an axiological citadel too, one that leads to an impoverished *world*. A world in which Eichmann and Ohlendorf, for example, suffer as a result of their active role in genocide is, *ceteris paribus*, better than a world in which they do not – and this is true independently of the potentially medicinal consequences inflicting such suffering may cause. In embracing invariantism, the misguidedly benevolent worldview presupposed by classical utilitarianism not only reduces any and all moral conflict to mere computational (medicinal, technological) problems, but it reduces human existence to a simpleminded monism whereby the only point of life is to reduce (undifferentiated) suffering.

Only a few years before Berlin's famous remarks on liberty, Bertrand Russell had made essentially the same point about this position. Commenting on stoicism, Russell had said:

> [There is, in fact, an element of sour grapes in Stoicism. We can't be happy, but we can be good; let us therefore pretend that, so long as we are good, it doesn't matter being unhappy. This doctrine is heroic, and, in a bad world, useful; but it is neither quite true nor, in a fundamental sense, quite sincere.[61]

The fact that both Berlin and Russell mobilize sour grapes here allows me to connect their views to Elster's insightful discussion of sour grapes and related phenomena.[62] Elster's work is extraordinarily far-reaching. And while his overall interest is in theories of rationality and rational choice (rather than in punishment), there is an aspect of his work that is helpful for my purposes. That crucial aspect consists in the fact that Elster thinks that sour grapes (and related phenomena) pose a problem not so much for stoicism but for *utilitarianism*: "[F]or the utilitarian, there would be no welfare loss if the fox were excluded from consumption of the grapes, since he thought them sour anyway."[63] The immediate, in a sense *formal*, problem is that "the cause of him holding them sour was his conviction that he would be excluded from consuming them, and then it is difficult to justify the allocation by invoking his preferences."[64] Only a bit less immediately, though considerably more substantively, the problem is that just as the fox can turn himself into someone who believes or perceives that the grapes are sour (it is irrelevant for my purposes to decide whether sour grapes is a perceptual or a cognitive phenomenon), we can turn ourselves into quite uninspiring beings. We can exile ourselves in various "inner citadels," and we can convince ourselves that we do not feel the pulls of justice or that to feel these pulls is to be a naïve victim of "magical thinking" or, worse, that one is "barbaric" or that one's views are "morally repugnant."

---

[61] Bertrand Russell, *A History of Western Philosophy*, New York, NY: Simon and Schuster (1945), 269.

[62] Above all in Jon Elster, *Sour Grapes . . .*, but also in Jon Elster, *Alchemies of the Mind: Rationality and the Emotions*, Cambridge: Cambridge University Press (1999).

[63] Elster, *Sour Grapes . . .*, 109. Elster does not say it explicitly, but it is scarcely necessary to do so: when he talks about "utilitarianism," he has in mind classical utilitarianism and clearly *not* ideal utilitarianism.

[64] *Ibid.*

In exploring utilitarianism's foibles, Elster addresses the famous discussion as to whether events we tend to assume are clearly positive, and indeed paradigms of human progress, can be embarrassing for utilitarianism. Thus, Elster discusses whether, for example, the Industrial Revolution may be a problem for utilitarians in that it may have "made wants rise faster than the capacity for satisfying them"[65] and that this may have caused people to suffer more than before. Insofar as Elster believes that since this was at least partially true, he did conclude (for reasons I need not explore here) that utilitarians could indeed be "led into a wholesale rejection of the Industrial Revolution."[66] My concern, of course, has nothing to do with the Industrial Revolution but deals with the fact that utilitarianism, quite generally, can recommend and foster lives remarkably devoid of meaning, taking place in ever more confining inner citadels, as Berlin and Russell point out. Thus, utilitarians may object to serious self-cultivation and to our efforts to refine our sensibilities, insofar as these endeavors could cause us to suffer much more intensely than otherwise.

The objection that Berlin and Russell raise against stoicism is in fact very similar to Elster's objection against (classical) utilitarianism. The aspect of stoicism that Berlin and Russell criticize is indeed the *same* aspect of utilitarianism that Elster criticizes. This common aspect is, precisely, the endorsement of a certain type of existence that conflicts not only with our most widespread and deep-seated intuitions but with our considered judgments as well. This existence would optimally protect us from suffering, albeit for all the wrong reasons. And the culprit, in the final analysis, is axiological monism.

To be sure, Elster does not explicitly identify monism as the culprit, but he comes close, and it is in any case quite natural to suggest that this interpretation is consistent with what he does explicitly say. Consider the following passage, which I will edit in order to highlight the overlap between his views and mine.

> It cannot be true that the smallest loss in welfare [or the smallest amount of suffering] always count for more than the largest increase in autonomy [or in any other value, such as justice]. There must be cases [organic wholes] in which the autonomy of wants overrides the satisfaction of wants, and in which frustration, unhappiness and revolt [or suffering] should be positively welcomed [in the sense of their making these organic wholes become more valuable] ... We do not want to solve social problems [or reduce suffering] by issuing vast doses of tranquilizers [or imagined moral anesthetics], nor do we want people to tranquilize themselves through adaptive preference change [such as sour grapes, etc.]. Engels may have overestimated the mindless bliss of pre-industrial society and underrates the mindless misery, but this does not detract from his observation that "this existence, cosily romantic as it was, nevertheless was not worthy of human beings."[67]

---

[65] *Ibid.*, 133.  [66] *Ibid.*, 134.

[67] *Ibid.*, 135–136. My parenthetical additions do no violence to Elster's views, but they allow me to overcome minor differences in terminology and emphasis that may render less explicit the intimate

What is not worthy of human beings is a life obsessively devoted to avoiding suffering, as if suffering were invariantly disvaluable. My cat, the fulfillment of whose needs is guaranteed, has really very little suffering in her life – yet this cannot really be the ideal for a human to follow. Some of us, after all, do prefer – and, for reasons we have discussed previously, are *correct* in so preferring – to be Socrates dissatisfied than a pig satisfied.

## 3.4 CONCLUSION

Imagine another island in which all is identical to Hitler's, except for the fact that this one is inhabited by Mother Teresa (or by your favorite benevolent hero). According to consequentialism and its monistic axiology, you have the *same* reason to press the button that gives good weather in Mother Teresa's case as you do in Hitler's case. In each case, you would be increasing the amount of pleasure in the world by the exact same amount (the cases are constructed as having no possible ulterior consequences), and that is *all* that matters. Furthermore, if someone would give Mother Teresa bad weather, this would be just as disvaluable as giving it to Hitler.

This conclusion may perhaps appear hyperbolic. It is not. Consider the unequivocal way in which Parfit has put it: "[T]hough we believe that innocent people do not deserve to be punished, we also believe that guilty people do not deserve to be punished. On our view, all punishment is in itself [equally] bad."[68] I find it hard not to see this wholesale rejection of all suffering – whether deserved or not, whether in this context or in that one – as too invariant and too monistic to be plausible. This position strikes me as too misguidedly pious and as too panicky a reaction to the default disvalue of suffering. It is an endorsement of the monism that underwrites that "one-eyed utilitarianism" that threatens our integrity and our very identity as moral beings and that in different – but surprisingly relevant – contexts Berlin, Russell, and Elster have convincingly criticized.

Utilitarianism can at best *tolerate* punishment, and only when it is supposed to have these or those medicinal effects. As Stanley Cavell has put it: "Utilitarianism can justify one sentence over another, or the practice of punishment by imprisonment rather than by death; but Punishment, the practice *überhaupt*, it cannot, and would not wish to, justify."[69] The reason for this has been my main concern in this

---

proximity between his desire-satisfaction formulation and my suffering-avoidance formulation of utilitarianism.

68  Derek Parfit, *On What Matters*, Vol. 2, 651. In this same vein, and evoking themes I addressed in my "The Instruments of Abolition ...," Patrick Tomlin has recently discussed Tadros's views and has rightly concluded that the approach "cannot morally distinguish between permissible punishment of the innocent [whatever this may mean] and permissible punishment of the guilty." See his "Innocence Lost: A Problem for Punishment as Duty," *Law and Philosophy* 36 (2017): 225–254, at 253.

69  Stanley Cavell, *The Claim of Reason: Wittgenstein, Skepticism, Morality, and Tragedy*, Oxford: Oxford University Press (1999), 300.

chapter: it is impossible to truly *justify* punishment, the practice *überhaupt*, without recognizing that there is value in deserved suffering.

I cannot think of a pithier way to end this chapter than by (slightly) editing Russell's version of the argument against stoicism in order to underscore how remarkably well it applies to consequentialism (again: about punishment). This should by now come as no surprise, since we have seen that the underlying problem in all the cases we have discussed in this chapter is consequentialism's invariant axiological monism:

> [T]here is, in fact, an element of sour grapes in consequentialism. We can't be just without making wrongdoers suffer because they so deserve it, but we can be benevolent; let us therefore pretend that, so long as we are benevolent, it doesn't matter being unjust. This doctrine is heroic, and, in a bad world, useful; but it is neither quite true nor, in a fundamental sense, quite sincere.

# 4

## The Gerrymandering Gambit: Retributivism in the Budget Room

More than forty years ago, George P. Fletcher began his influential *Rethinking Criminal Law* noting that both "Anglo-American criminal law and its underlying theory" had been "inhibited" in their "refinement" because "for over a century the prevailing philosophy of criminal law ha[d] been the [Benthamite, classical] utilitarian theory of sanction."[1] In light of what we have discussed in the previous chapter, it is easy to understand Fletcher's position. Fletcher was concerned with the fact that utilitarians endorse the view that the "good of the whole," i.e. the overall reduction of suffering, is "all that is thought necessary to justify the suffering of the individual confined."[2] And he was concerned with the concomitant ways in which "social interest" could then come at the expense of "the more basic inquiry whether the punishment of the accused is morally justified."[3]

Fletcher harbored some optimism that "the tide may change" and that perhaps our minds would eventually "come unstuck from the calculus of utility."[4] As I have been arguing, however, the tide has not changed, and our minds have not come fully unstuck. Classical utilitarianism, in part thanks to its formidable malleability but also to its seductive appearance of benevolent progressivism – of being the right antidote to a dysfunctional criminal justice system, for example – continues to hold sway. The common assumption continues to be – unwittingly or otherwise – that a necessary condition for justifying an infliction of suffering is its (reasonably supposed) tendency to reduce overall suffering.

Understandably, Fletcher saw a tension between a concern with justice as such and utilitarianism, and he thought, moreover, that the 1970s' "search for justice ha[d] revived retribution as the rationale of punishment."[5] In fact, it is now

---

[1] George P. Fletcher, *Rethinking Criminal Law*, Oxford: Oxford University Press (2000), xix.  [2] *Ibid.*
[3] *Ibid.*  [4] *Ibid.*, xx.  [5] *Ibid.*

commonplace to talk about a retributivist revival.[6] In light of what I deem the widespread influence of classical utilitarianism, I am unsure as to what to make about this alleged revival. But it cannot be denied that at least among punishment theorists, some such revival is real: several leading punishment theorists are, if not quite full-throttle retributivists, at least not unfriendly to retributivism.[7]

In other words, Fletcher and others have come to see retributivism as a viable alternative to the vagaries of utilitarianism. To the extent that retributivism does recognize the intrinsic value of deserved punishment, and to the extent that in so doing it is at least consistent with richer axiologies, seeing it as superior to Benthamite-inspired monisms is perfectly appropriate. The axiological retributivism I defend here, for example, is offered as more viable alternative to the monistic axiology of classical utilitarianism. But in this chapter I will argue that, *pace* Fletcher and others, retributivism, as it has typically been defended, has not really been as much of an improvement to utilitarian simplemindedness as one would have hoped. I will thus make good on my earlier promise to show that important versions of retributivism turn out to be as simpleminded as the consequentialism I have criticized previously. Unlike views based on classical utilitarianism, however, retributivism does not *need* to be simpleminded in these ways, and so its narrowness is in a way more startling. It is particularly unfortunate that many retributivists, aware of at least some of the seriously problematic aspects of classical utilitarianism, have failed to see how they in fact perpetuate arguably the most fundamental of those problems: an impoverished monistic axiology.

The chapter will proceed as follows. In the first section, I discuss the shortcomings of two very influential versions of retributivism – Immanuel Kant's and Michael Moore's. Eschewing the importance of the distinction between the axiological and the deontic, these authors advance a problematic, overly deontic version of retributivism. Moreover, they simultaneously under-define and over-define retributivism: they under-define it in the sense that they strip it of its axiological richness, and they over-define it in the sense that they link it (too closely) to other doctrines and theories from which it should be kept separate. In the end, these retributivists too easily relegate values other than desert to a position of relative unimportance.

In the second section, I consider the ways in which these forms of retributivism gesture toward recognizing the importance of moral emotions both to the evaluations of agents and ultimately to the justification of punishment. I do this by placing them against the background of the seminal articles by Bernard Williams and

---

[6] See the references to this "revival," "resurgence," and "renaissance," as it has been variedly called, in Russell Christopher's comprehensive "Deterring Retributivism: The Injustice of 'Just' Punishment," *Northwestern University Law Review* 96.3 (2002): 843–976.

[7] This is true of Fletcher himself but also of Herbert Morris, Michael Moore, Douglas Husak, R. A. Duff, Jeffrie Murphy, Larry Alexander, and Kimberly Ferzan, among others. Even H. L. A. Hart and John Rawls (together with other mixed theorists) are, insofar as they tried to somehow combine it with consequentialism, not completely unfriendly to retributivism.

Thomas Nagel concerning moral luck.[8] And I conclude the section by suggesting that their gesturing does not go far enough and that these forms of retributivism fail to capture the importance of those moral emotions with which they are rightly but insufficiently concerned. In the third section, I begin to delineate the ways in which these forms of retributivism are also inimical to the existence and importance of moral conflicts – themes that will become central to my aims in the later parts of the book. The backdrop to this section is Jonathan Bennett's famous "The Conscience of Huckleberry Finn."[9] The main upshot of this section is that traditional forms of retributivism, in their misguided lack of flexibility and nuance, resemble those characters whose morality Bennett argued is particularly despicable.

In light of their timid engagement with moral emotions and moral conflicts, these traditional forms of retributivism are particularly ill-suited vis-à-vis two important problems, which I discuss in the last two sections of the chapter. In Section 4.4, I focus on the common charge of barbarism against retributivism. While this charge is often exaggerated and misguided, these traditional versions of retributivism are, in a way, at least susceptible to a version of this criticism. For, as I shall show, in eschewing the importance of moral conflicts, these traditional retributivists fail to distinguish retributive punishment from revenge, and revenge is much more susceptible to the charge of barbarism than retributive punishment should be. Finally, in the fifth section, I discuss retributivism in connection to the idea of differentiated wrongdoing; in particular, to the idea that there is a qualitative difference between evil actions and merely bad actions. Clearly, utilitarianism cannot even countenance qualitative differences between types of wrongdoing. It is a point in favor of retributivism that, unshackled from the quantitative ethos of utilitarianism, at least it is capable of saying something meaningful vis-à-vis different forms of wrongdoing. But I shall show how easy it is, even for retributivists (particularly when they eschew the consideration of moral emotions and moral conflicts), to succumb to reductive and simpleminded moves.

### 4.1 HOLISTIC RETRIBUTIVISM AND SHARING STAGES

Perhaps the most famous presentation of retributivism in the history of philosophy is found in Kant's oft-quoted passage:

> Even if a Civil Society resolved to dissolve itself with the consent of all its members – as might be supposed in the case of a People inhabiting an island resolving to separate and scatter themselves throughout the whole world – the last Murderer lying in the prison ought to be executed before the resolution was carried out.[10]

---

[8] B. A. O. Williams and T. Nagel "Moral Luck," *Proceedings of the Aristotelian Society, Supplementary Volumes* 50 (1976): 115–135, 137–151.

[9] Jonathan Bennett, "The Conscience of Huckleberry Finn," *Philosophy* 49 (1974): 123–13.

[10] Immanuel Kant, *The Philosophy of Law* (W. Hastie, trans.), Edinburgh: T. & T. Clark (1887): 198.

The passage is not just famous, but it is also in many ways problematic. Probably the most obvious problem with the passage is that not all of Kant's reasons for endorsing these mass executions are retributive. For while Kant does say that this "ought to be done in order that every one may realize the desert of his deeds," he immediately adds that this ought to be done so that "bloodguiltiness may not remain upon the people."[11] Understandably, some have thought that while the first of these reasons is retributive, the second reason is evidently consequentialist.[12] But I will ignore this particular problem: if (as seems to be the case) the second reason is not retributive, then I will proceed as if this reason had not been offered.

For my purposes here, it is more important to highlight a set of problems that arise form Kant's failure to distinguish between the axiological and the deontic, even if we restrict our analysis to the first, properly retributive reason supporting these mass executions. Kant's position is roughly this: since deserved punishment is intrinsically good, then we ought to inflict it – independently of any consequentialist considerations. In another oft-quoted passage, Kant puts it eloquently:

> The Penal Law is a Categorical Imperative; and woe to him who creeps through the serpent-windings of Utilitarianism to discover some advantage that may discharge him from the Justice of Punishment, or even from the due measure of it, according to the Pharisaic maxim: "It is better that one man should die than that the whole people should perish." For if Justice and Righteousness perish, human life would no longer have *any value* in the world.[13]

It is easy to see the sharp contrast between Kant's position and the utilitarian positions we have discussed earlier. Where those utilitarian doctrines value suffering reduction, Kant values justice. And it is on this obvious difference that the specialized literature has almost invariably focused.

However, in light of the framework I am here recommending, a remarkable – and hitherto insufficiently explored – commonality between the utilitarian and the Kantian approaches also becomes visible. The axiological structure of both approaches is similar: the role that suffering reduction plays within the axiology of utilitarian approaches is quite like the role that justice plays within the axiology of the Kantian approaches. In each case we have a privileged value that downright *excludes* all other values. When a given infliction of punishment maximally reduces suffering, then it is, for the utilitarian, justified – and whether such infliction were deserved would be irrelevant. Similarly, when a given infliction of punishment inflicts on the wrongdoer exactly what he deserves, then it is, for the Kantian retributivist, justified – and whether such infliction were to reduce (or augment) suffering in the world would be irrelevant. In each case, there is a monistic axiology

---

[11]   *Ibid.*
[12]   See, for example, John Cottingham, "Varieties of Retribution," *Philosophical Quarterly* 29 (1979): 238–246, especially at 243–244.
[13]   Kant, *The Philosophy of Law*, 195–196. Emphasis added.

containing one supreme, predatory value that precludes the existence of any other values.

In this regard, and despite its obvious and often discussed differences vis-à-vis classical utilitarianism, Kantian retributivism is revealed as incapable of dealing, at the axiological level, with conflicts between justice and empathy. In fact, it is revealed as incapable of doing so as is the utilitarianism from which Kant so vehemently sought to distinguish his own theory. Moreover, there are problems at the deontic level too. Like classical utilitarianism, Kant embraces a rather flat-footed deontic stance: for he sees the "Right of Retaliation (*jus talionis*)" as "the only Principle which in regulating a Public Court ... can definitely assign both the quality and the quantity of a just penalty."[14] So, whereas the only consideration which classical utilitarians allow when it comes to "regulating a public court" is suffering reduction, the only consideration Kantian retributivists allow is this "right of retaliation (*jus talionis*)."

This flat-footed stance is in a sense more disappointing within the context of Kantian retributivism than within the context of classical utilitarianism. For only in the Kantian context does the stance flow from a simple confusion. *Jus* (or *lex*) *talionis* is after all not necessarily connected to retributivism: any retributivist can recognize value in people getting what they deserve without specifying what it is that they actually deserve. No retributivist need endorse the view that the actual punishment that murderers deserve is death and that the actual punishment rapists deserve is rape and so on. Retributivists merely believe that there is value in deserved punishing being inflicted – whatever this punishment turns out to be. Admittedly, deontic retributivists believe that this value generates a duty to punish, whereas axiological retributivists need not believe so – but even this belief on the part of deontic retributivists does not entail *lex talionis*.[15]

Kant's retributivism, then, is a combination of retributivism both with an unattractive rejection of the difference between the deontic and the axiological and with an endorsement of *lex talionis*. As he combines retributivism with other doctrines, Kant inaugurates what has been a very widespread – and very problematic – tendency among retributivists. The tendency is in prominent display in today's most ambitious and sophisticated champion of retributivism: Moore. In what constitutes a major improvement over Kant's views, Moore rejects linking retributivism to *lex talionis*. But he nonetheless explicitly defends, for example, a very intimate "connection between retributivism and legal moralism."[16] Legal moralism, however, is not a theory of punishment but a theory of *criminalization* according to which it is the immorality of an action, rather than its potential to cause harm, that constitutes

---

[14]  *Ibid.*, 196.
[15]  In Chapter 7, I will argue that Martha Nussbaum misunderstands the relationship between retributivism and *lex talionis*.
[16]  Michael S. Moore, *Placing Blame: A General Theory of the Criminal Law*, Oxford: Clarendon Press (1997): 72.

the best reason for criminalizing it. In terms of the history of ideas, legal moralism is fundamentally opposed to liberalism. The classical debate is that opposing James Fitzjames Stephen and John Stuart Mill, though the conflict plays out perhaps more poignantly in the more recent Hart-Devlin debate.[17] Both debates reveal that legal moralism is essentially about what a legal system ought to recognize as a crime, and thus a matter of political philosophy from which retributivism should be kept separate – more separate than Moore keeps it.

Like Kant, Moore fails to distinguish the axiological from the deontic. In some ways, Moore's failure is more remarkable than Kant's, at least in the sense that Moore is keenly aware of the distinction and that he in fact repeatedly claims that his view of retributivism *is* to be understood as an axiological doctrine. So, Moore admits that "what *is* distinctively retributivist is the [axiological] view that the guilty receiving their just deserts is an intrinsic good."[18] However, Moore also (repeatedly) asserts that retributivism ought to be admitted to be "truly a theory of justice such that, if it is true, we have an *obligation* to set up institutions so that retribution is achieved"[19] and that "the distinctive aspect of retributivism is that the moral desert of an offender is a *sufficient* reason to punish him or her."[20]

Moore thus appears to contradict himself: it cannot be that "the" distinctive aspect of retributivism is axiological (and therefore not deontic) and that its very point is wholly deontic (and therefore not axiological). The contradiction is of course dissipated if it turns out that there is no difference between the axiological and the deontic, in such a way that my parentheticals in the previous sentence are somehow inapposite. But, as I have been urging, there does exist a very important difference between the axiological view that deserved punishment is intrinsically good and the deontic view that therefore we should always inflict deserved punishment. Kant and Moore, impervious to this difference, have to baldly posit punishment's (or the criminal law's) purpose to be "the achievement of retributive justice"[21] or that retributive justice is "*the* intrinsic good that is the function of Anglo-American criminal law [to bring about]."[22]

This disregard of the distinction between the axiological and the deontic explains too the intimate connection between axiological monism and Kant's and Moore's retributivism. As we have just seen, Kant believes that to refuse to insist on retributive justice at all costs is to thereby deprive the world of *any and all* value. Slightly less scandalously, Moore admits that retributivism evinces a certain "inability to share the stage with any other punishment goal"[23] and a certain "intolerance for

---

[17]   See John Stuart Mill, *On Liberty and Other Essays* (John Gray, ed.), Oxford: Oxford University Press (1991); James Fitzjames Stephen, *Liberty, Equality, Fraternity*, Indianapolis, IN: Liberty Fund (1993); Patrick Devlin, *The Enforcement of Morals*, Oxford: Oxford University Press (1959); H. L. A. Hart, *Law, Liberty, and Morality*, Oxford: Oxford University Press (1963). In "The Moralist Strikes Back," *New Criminal Law Review* 14 (2011): 139–161, I criticize efforts by some retributivists to rehabilitate legal moralism.

[18]   Moore, *Placing Blame*, 157.     [19]   *Ibid.*, 91. Emphasis added.     [20]   *Ibid.*, 88. Emphasis added.
[21]   *Ibid.*, 28.     [22]   *Ibid.*, 29. Emphasis in the original.     [23]   *Ibid.*, 28.

partners."[24] Moore does not see the intolerance of (his) retributivism as a shortcoming – even though it is, one would imagine, precisely this structural intolerance as it plays out in classical utilitarianism that spearheaded the retributivist revival of recent years. Moore is in fact proud of the intolerance and of the axiological monism that it helps establish. Still, it is this intolerance that gets Moore – and in fact any deontic retributivist – into trouble.

For example, Moore cannot – on pain of sheer absurdity, like Kant – deny that things other than desert can be of value (intrinsically or otherwise). So he appeals to peculiar strategies in order to persevere in isolating desert as the only thing of value within the context of punishment. Moore claims:

> Punishment may deter future crime, incapacitate dangerous persons, educate citizens in the behaviour required for a civilized society, reinforce social cohesion, prevent vigilante behaviour, make victims of crime feel better, or satisfy the vengeful desires of citizens who are not themselves crime victims. Yet for a retributivist these are a happy surplus that punishment produces and form no part of what makes punishment just; for a retributivist, deserving offenders should be punished even if the punishment produces none of these other, surplus good effects.[25]

Moore's introduction of this peculiar talk of "surpluses" is repeated elsewhere: "[T]hat future crime might also be prevented by punishment is a happy surplus for a retributivist, but no part of the justification for punishing,"[26] and this is of course meant to bolster his monism: "[R]etributivism has no room for such [non-desert related] additional reasons."[27]

It is hard to interpret Moore's talk of surpluses as anything but an effort to at the very least *downgrade* these other values. Self-servingly, Moore partitions the axiological space in such a way that he does not quite have to formally agree with Kant's extreme view that there is only value in desert-based justice. Surely Moore admits that there is value elsewhere. It is just that these other values are *merely* happy surpluses. These other values do not, in Moore's estimation, belong to the problem of the justification of punishment, which in his view, just like in Kant's, is *entirely* a matter of justice, and justice, in turn, is *entirely* a matter of giving people what they deserve. Thus, regarding the justification of punishment, Moore, like Kant, cares only about desert.[28]

## 4.2 EMOTIONS, MORAL LUCK, AND ARROGANCE

After he describes the harrowing murder of Bonnie Garland by her jilted boyfriend, and intimating perhaps a much more serious engagement with emotions than Kant's, Moore urges us to imagine how we would *feel* if it were we who committed the horrible deed:

[24] *Ibid.*, 29.    [25] *Ibid.*, 153.    [26] *Ibid.*, 89.    [27] *Ibid.*, 88–89.
[28] In the last section of this chapter, I will discuss Moore's recent restatements of his view.

Then ask yourself: What would you feel like if it was you who had intentionally smashed open the skull of a 23-year-old woman with a claw hammer while she was asleep, a woman whose fatal defect was a desire to free herself from your too clinging embrace? My own response, I hope, would be that I would feel guilty unto death. I could not imagine any suffering that could be imposed upon me that would be unfair because it exceeded what I deserved. Is that virtuous? Such deep feelings of guilt seem to me to be the only tolerable response of a moral being.[29]

There are at least two independent problems with Moore's position. The first problem concerns the amount of suffering that may be meted out in this case, and it concerns Moore's claim that he cannot imagine *any* suffering that could exceed what this murderer deserves. I do not think that Moore's remark here is to be taken seriously. Anyone can easily imagine amounts of suffering that would clearly exceed what this murderer deserves. I propose putting aside this first problem (though I will return to it, in passing, in the next section), insofar as it is more charitable to read Moore here as if he is speaking figuratively, as if he is presenting this literally untenable view more metaphorically, in order to indirectly bolster a different claim. This different claim is the suggestion that certain emotions – and in particular certain feelings of guilt – are important elements in the justification of punishment.

As I mentioned in Chapter 1, and as I will articulate more fully in later chapters, I think that Moore is very importantly right about the connection between having certain emotions and both one's respectability as a moral being and having a rich and plausible justification of punishment. But I think that Moore is problematically simpleminded regarding the way in which he engages with these emotions. There are two aspects of this simplemindedness that ought to be discussed separately. The first of these aspects has to do with a certain flat-footed transitivity between the first-person and the third-person perspectives that Moore's approach clearly evinces.

Imagine that you indeed consider that what you have done is so very gravely wrong that your guilt actually leads you not merely to blame yourself but to actually punish yourself. The fact that there may be value in the organic whole in which, after you have wronged me, realizing the wrongness of what you did and as a genuine act of contrition, you punish yourself does not entail that the organic whole in which *I* punish you (*ex hypothesi* to the same extent that you would have punished yourself) for what you did has the same value. Pertinent examples are legion, and they range from the banal to the very serious.

On the banal side: imagine that you are playing, say, a friendly squash game (without a referee), and you realize that you have unintentionally badly interfered with your opponent's ability to hit the ball and that as a result you then say "stroke": that is, you award the point to your friend (rather than merely saying "let," which would mean that the point is to be replayed). This is very different from your

[29]   Moore, *Placing Blame*, 145.

opponent awarding *himself* the point – even if all else remains identically the same in the two scenarios. It *is* gracious of you to award the point to him, but it is *not* gracious of him to award himself the point – even if he deserves it all the same.

As for a much more serious example: consider seppuku, the Japanese practice of honorable suicide. We need not endorse this practice in order to see that there is a world of difference between a samurai slashing his own abdomen in recognition that he has done something dishonorable and someone else slashing it for him. In an article that, for different reasons, shall greatly occupy my attention in the next chapter, Duff has put the point eloquently:

> [T]here is too wide a moral gap between a first person judgement that I cannot be restored to human community (except through my death) and a formal third person judgement to that effect, and so between a suicide motivated by that first person thought and an execution justified by its third person analogue.[30]

Moore disagrees. According to him, in order to be consistent and in order to avoid being *condescending* toward others, whatever it is appropriate for you to think must happen to yourself (because you deserve it) is appropriate for you to think must happen to others (because they deserve it).

> To grant that you would be guilty and deserving of punishment, but that others who do the exact same wrong with the exact same culpability would not be, is to arrogate to yourself a godlike position. Only you have those attributes of moral agency making you alone a creature capable of being morally guilty; others are simply lesser beings, to be pitied perhaps, but not to be blamed as you would blame yourself. This is not moral generosity. Rather, it is an elitist arrogance that denies one's common humanity with those who do wrong. Such elitist condescension is no virtue.[31]

Even putting aside the ease with which Moore imagines cases to be "exactly" alike, he surely exaggerates in this passage. There is nothing *necessarily* condescending, elitist, or arrogant about someone not awarding herself a stroke in squash but awarding it to her opponent nor in our perhaps even admiring someone who kills himself (in seppuku or otherwise) as deserved self-punishment without being in the least inclined to admire someone who decides to kill someone else as deserved punishment. Being alive to this asymmetry is not to arrogate a godlike position. It is simply to recognize the difference between first-person and third-person perspectives and to thus reject a flat-footed transitivity between these perspectives.

---

[30]   R. A. Duff, "The Intrusion of Mercy," *Ohio State Journal of Criminal Law* 4 (2007): 360–387, at 383. For similar views, albeit divorced from Duff's talk of restoring wrongdoers' ties to communities, see Jeffrey Reiman; "Justice, Civilization, and the Death Penalty: Answering van den Haag," *Philosophy and Public Affairs* 14.2 (1985): 115–148; David Dolinko, "Retributivism, Consequentialism, and the Intrinsic Goodness of Punishment," *Law and Philosophy* 16 (1991): 537–559; and Leo Zaibert, *Punishment and Retribution*, Aldershot: Ashgate (2006), 193 ff.

[31]   Moore, *Placing Blame*, 165.

The second aspect of Moore's simplemindedness that deserves our attention is subtler. The emotions that an admirable moral being should experience are actually quite complicated. Moore appears to believe that the guilt one would feel upon doing something wrong, itself quite similar to the blame one would pass upon someone else who did the same wrong, smoothly points toward either self-punishment or punishment of that someone else. Moore does not entertain the possibility that just as an admirable moral agent ought to be affected by coming to understand the wrong she has committed, an admirable moral agent ought to be affected (albeit not identically) by the suffering she causes, even if she is "justified" in causing it. As a matter of fact, this complexity applies across the board: not only to punishment but to killing in self-defense and to many cases in which we choose the lesser of two evils. Being alive to these conflicts has little to do with arrogating godlike positions to oneself but instead has to do with appreciating the full import of our emotions and the complexity of moral life. Furthermore, being alive to these conflicts suggests caution before inflicting suffering: just as we do not want, say, trigger-happy police officers, we do not want trigger-happy punishers. In cabining moral emotions so facilely, Moore reveals a certain trigger-happiness about punishment.

Contrast Moore's position to Bernard Williams's, as he presented it within the context of discussing moral luck. In that context, Williams offered what has by now become an almost obligatory reference for any discussion regarding the complexity of moral emotions in the sorts of cases we are considering – the lorry driver case.

> [E]ven at deeply accidental or non-voluntary levels of agency, sentiments of agent-regret are different from regret in general, such as might be felt by a spectator, and are acknowledged in our practice as being different. The lorry driver who, through no fault of his, runs over a child, will feel differently from any spectator, even a spectator next to him in the cab, except perhaps to the extent that the spectator takes on the thought that he might have prevented it, an agent's thought. Doubtless, and rightly, people will try, in comforting him, to move the driver from this state of feeling, move him indeed from where he is to something more like the place of a spectator; but it is important that this is seen as something that should need to be done, and indeed some doubt would be felt about a driver who too blandly or readily moved to that position.[32]

Part of the reason why this example is so famous is that through it Williams introduced the idea of agent regret. Agent regret is a peculiar type of moral feeling: not quite full-blown guilt (or remorse) but also not quite generic sadness or regret (e.g., the regret that we can experience when we witness or learn about sad things with which we have absolutely nothing to do, say, like the acts of complete strangers or natural events) either. Part of what Williams wishes to capture by the expression "moral luck" is precisely cases in which someone can be morally responsible for

[32]  Williams and Nagel, "Moral Luck," 124.

things he did that were not wrong.[33] Even Nagel, who disagrees with aspects of Williams's interpretation of the lorry driver case, admits that with some (for our purposes here) minor modifications, cases similar to Williams's can give rise to peculiar and complicated moral feelings.

Nagel claims that, as Williams presents it, this case is not really one of moral luck because, in his opinion, while the driver will surely "feel terrible," since he is *ex hypothesi* "entirely without fault," he will "not have to reproach himself" at all.[34] Nagel suggests that moral luck would obtain if we imagined instead that the driver had in fact been guilty of "a minor degree of negligence." For then the agent would sensibly blame himself, but he would blame himself extraordinarily more severely than if the child had not been killed – "even though the negligence is the same in both cases, and the driver has no control over whether a child will run into his path."[35] I think that this admittedly slight amendment in a way misses Williams's central point, which is, precisely, that feelings such as agent regret (which, again, are different from ordinary, spectator regret) can be appropriate even in cases in which we really have no reason to reproach or blame ourselves.

Independently of their disagreement regarding the extent to which moral luck may allow for moral feelings of this sort in complete absence of any culpability (Williams's view) or may only function as an augmenter of such feelings in cases of relatively minor culpability (Nagel's view), Williams and Nagel agree on something crucial for my purposes. Moral reality is complicated, and moral agents like us do experience complicated emotions like these. It is only by recognizing this complexity, and by engaging with it, that we could make some progress in understanding – without hastily committing to the realm of the pathological – familiar but perplexing phenomena such as collective guilt, survivor's guilt, and guilt for the "sins of the father."[36] While in principle guilt is not transferable and while in principle the absence of guilt is wholly absolutory, we know, from introspection and by contemplating our own moral experience, that these principles admit of exceptions.

So let us return to Moore's murderous jilted boyfriend case but with Williams's lorry driver case in mind. If I imagine that I was the lorry driver in Williams's example, I, like Moore, would hope that I should feel agent regret – and thus that I would *suffer*, in a complicatedly moral way – after I blamelessly killed that child. Moreover, the contemplation of a lorry driver who in identical circumstances would feel nothing of the sort may strike us as a despicable, chilling sight. And yet this

---

[33] In Chapter 6, I will argue that there is much more to moral luck.

[34] Williams and Nagel, "Moral Luck," 140–141.    [35] *Ibid.*, 141.

[36] The possibility of experiencing moral emotions such as guilt for someone else's actions are explored in Herbert Morris (ed.) *Guilt and Shame*, Belmont, CA: Wadsworth (1971), particularly by Karl Jaspers in his "Differentiation of German Guilt." See also Bernhard Schlink, *Guilt about the Past*, Toronto: House of Anansi (2010); Bernhard Schlink, *The Reader*, New York, NY: Vintage (1997); Nancy Sherman, *Stoic Warriors: The Ancient Philosophy behind the Military Mind*, Oxford: Oxford University Press (2005); John Deigh, *Emotion, Values, and the Law*, Oxford: Oxford University Press (2008); and references in Chapter 8.

would not warrant concluding that we ought to make the indolent lorry driver suffer (via our doing something that may lead him to feel agent regret). Neither would it warrant concluding that a refusal to make sure that the indolent lorry driver suffers (via the experience of agent regret) evinces godlike "arrogance" or "elitist condescension" on our part.

Similarly, and now turning our attention to Kant, it is not true that any refusal to mete out the suffering that someone may deserve is to thereby "creep through the serpent-windings of utilitarianism." There exist perfectly non-utilitarian reasons for so doing. Either to refuse to execute every condemned murderer in the soon-to-disband society or to feel agent regret after having so executed them can be explained in a variety of ways. It could be explained by appeals, for example, to conceptions of human decency or virtue, as a result of considerations related to standing or legitimacy, or as a result of views concerning the reach of state power, among others. And Kant is as dismissive of any of these other reasons as is Moore.

As we saw in earlier chapters, this discussion concerning the complexity of our moral emotions and our moral life has to strike the classical utilitarian as, if not incoherent, then at least entirely misguided; for her, the only point to any of these emotions is their potential medicinal contribution to further reductions of suffering. The retributivist turn that Fletcher and others both championed and celebrated was in part a reaction to what he and others saw as the excessive instrumentalism of classical utilitarianism. But we can now see that both Kant's and Moore's retributivism (again, in turn the most historically influential and the most sophisticated contemporary versions of retributivism) appear as ill-equipped as utilitarianism to deal with these emotions. Surely there are various reasons explaining this shortcoming in these retributivists, but one important such reason is that these retributivists share with classical utilitarians an impoverished, monistic axiology. In the remaining sections of this chapter, I explore further ways in which the monistic axiology of retributivism is as uninspiring as that of classical utilitarianism.

### 4.3 CUTTING ONESELF OFF FROM THE HUMAN CONDITION

In what has rightly become a contemporary classic, Bennett provocatively compared the "moralities" of Huckleberry Finn (the character in Mark Twain's novel), of Heinrich Himmler (the infamous high-ranking Nazi), and of Jonathan Edwards (the eighteenth-century American theologian). Scandalously, Bennett found Edwards's morality to be much worse than either Finn's or Himmler's. The scandal results from the fact that Huck is uncertain of the immorality of slavery and Himmler was a devout Nazi, ultimately responsible for the murder of millions of innocent human beings: How, against such backdrop, could Edwards's morality possibly be worse?

Bennett discusses the famous passage from Twain's novel in which Huck is conflicted between, on the one hand, what he sees as his duty not to free Jim (whom, in Huck's view, properly belongs to Miss Watson) and sympathy for poor

Jim: "Huck's morality conflicts with his sympathy, that is, with his unargued, natural feeling for his friend."[37] Of course, what is odd about the passage is that Huck himself thinks that he is weak-willed (or *akratic*) when he saves Jim: in his mind, the right thing to do is to betray Jim and return him to his rightful owner. But Huck thinks of himself as having failed, and he thus describes his encounter with the bounty hunters who asked him about the skin color of his passenger in the following terms:

> I didn't answer up prompt. I tried to, but the words wouldn't come. I tried, for a second or two, to brace up and out with it, but I warn't man enough – hadn't the spunk of a rabbit. I see I was weakening; so I just give up trying, and up and says: "He's white."[38]

According to Bennett, Huck experienced a conflict between morality and sympathy – and he resolved it in favor of sympathy.

Similarly, Bennett sees Himmler as conflicted between his allegiances to Nazi "morality," which of course Bennett recognizes as a "sick, bad, wicked morality," and some feelings of sympathy (however defective) toward the suffering of others. Bennett begins, however, by quoting from a speech by Himmler in which he appears to boast about the fact that he is *not* conflicted:

> What happens to a Russian, to a Czech, does not interest me in the slightest. What the nations can offer in the way of good blood of our type, we will take, if necessary by kidnapping their children and raising them here with us. Whether nations live in prosperity or starve to death like cattle interests me only in so far as we need them as slaves to our *Kultur*; otherwise it is of no interest to me. Whether 10,000 Russian females fall down from exhaustion while digging an antitank ditch interests me only in so far as the antitank ditch for Germany is finished.[39]

Immediately after quoting these words, Bennett quotes from the same speech by Himmler in which Himmler does appear to be somehow conflicted:

> I also want to talk to you quite frankly on a very grave matter ... I mean ... the extermination of the Jewish race ... Most of you must know what it means when 100 corpses are laying side by side, or 500, or 1,000. To have stuck it out and at the same time – apart from exceptions caused by human weakness – to have remained decent fellows, that is what has made us hard. This is a page of glory in our history which has never been written and is never to be written.[40]

Bennett concludes that while he is "sure that many of Himmler's killers did extinguish their sympathies, becoming 'heartless ruffians' rather than 'decent fellows,'" this was not true of "Himmler himself."[41] Bennett believes that, unlike his more beastly fellows, Himmler "did, after all, bear his hideous burden, and even

---

[37] Bennett, "The Conscience of . . .," 126.     [38] *Ibid.*, 125.     [39] *Ibid.*, 127.     [40] *Ibid.*, 128.
[41] *Ibid.*

paid a price for it. He suffered a variety of nervous and physical disabilities, including nausea and stomach-convulsions."[42] Whether or not Bennett is right about what he takes to be Himmler's psychological profile, he believes that Himmler, like Huck, was conflicted. The important difference between the two cases is that Huck allegedly resolves the conflict in favor of his "sympathy" (at the expense of his "(bad) morality"), whereas Himmler resolves the conflict in favor of his "(bad) morality" (at the expense of his sympathy).

After he has presented these analyses of Huck and Himmler, Bennett quotes the following rather harrowing passage from Edwards:

> Natural men are held in the hand of God over the pit of hell; they have deserved the fiery pit, and are already sentenced to it; and God is dreadfully provoked, his anger is as great towards them as to those that are actually suffering the executions of the fierceness of his wrath in hell . . .; the devil is waiting for them, hell is gaping for them, the flames gather and flash about them, and would fain lay hold on them . . .; and . . . there are no means within reach that can be any security to them . . . All that preserves them is the mere arbitrary will, and un-covenanted unobliged forebearance of an incensed God.[43]

A superficial reading of Bennett's insightful article is that he finds Edwards so deplorable simply because Bennett may be seen as endorsing the (misguidedly) benevolent views I criticized in the previous chapter and thus as horrified by the ease with which Edwards endorses divine punishment. While this may perhaps be part of the story, I think it is at best a small part. To focus on this point is to misinterpret Bennett's main aims in this article, which are considerably more complicated. Another, much larger part of the story is that we are here talking about of an extremely severe punishment: of *eternal* punishment, of eternal *torture* in fiery pits, to be perfectly precise. Bennett sardonically quips that Edwards took care to insist that such truly unfathomable amount of suffering is justified because "it is not more than infinite."[44] And another large part is the fact that Bennett quotes Edwards suggesting that "all" humans deserve this eternal punishment, although God gets to "arbitrarily" choose whom among us to spare.[45] These odd ways in which Edwards thought of desert – seemingly disconnected from any semblance of proportionality, reasonableness, and even rationality – evidently help explain Bennett's position regarding Edwards much better than a bald aversion to any and all punishment.

That Bennett does not belong in the camp of the misguidedly benevolent positions I have already criticized is most decisively highlighted by the way in which he chose to end his article. Bennett admits, for example, that "it was right to take part in

---

[42]   *Ibid.*, 129. Similar afflictions in Himmler are reported by Hannah Arendt too. See Hannah Arendt, *Eichmann in Jerusalem: A Report on the Banality of Evil*, New York, NY: Penguin (1992), 106. In order to make his point, perhaps Bennett does not need to engage with the actual evidence for the allegedly conflicted Himmler. Since Arendt's work was a report, with an obvious historical dimension, her lack of engagement with the evidence is more problematic.

[43]   Bennett, "The Conscience of . . .," 129.     [44]  *Ibid.*, 130.     [45]  *Ibid.*, 129.

the Second World War on the allied side" – and he explicitly rejects pacifism.[46] This is not to say that Bennett necessarily believes that punishing deserving Nazis for their crimes is good in itself – since Bennett's support of the allies could be partly based on purely suffering-reducing or other medicinal rationales – but, I believe, Bennett's admission leaves several possibilities open.

Warrant for my view derives from Bennett's mobilization of Wilfred Owen, the celebrated English poet of the First World War. In Owen's moving "Insensibility," he contrasts those "happy" soldiers, who either have not yet seen the horrors of war or who although familiar with those horrors somehow manage not to suffer as a result, against the "wise," who suffer deeply. Bennett correctly points out that "the poem's verdict goes against the 'happy' ones" – not because Owen thinks that "they will act worse" than the wise ones and not because, absurdly, Owen may be seen as himself indifferent to human suffering – but because "they have cut themselves off from the human condition." In Owen's famous own words, the "happy" ones are to be pitied because "they made themselves immune" to "whatever shares the eternal reciprocity of tears."[47]

Bennett rightly concludes that for Owen "feelings and sympathies are vital even when they can do nothing but bring pain and distress."[48] Wars sometimes ought to be fought, and punishment sometimes ought to be inflicted – even if they cause pain and distress uncompensated by utilitarian calculations. To think that this is only so in cases in which we thereby prevent greater human suffering is a way of cutting oneself off from the human condition. Admitting that sometimes wars and punishments ought to occur for reasons other than the reduction of suffering is not to become a warmonger or a barbarian sadist – and it is not to fail to recognize the moral and emotional dilemmas to which these inflictions of suffering do give rise. It is rather to abandon the dispiriting simplemindedness of the ways in which many contemporary authors – including many punishment theorists – think about punishment.

By far the most important part of the story is that, independently of the problem of wrapping our minds around the notion of anyone possibly deserving *eternal* punishment (fortunately, not an issue for contemporary punishment theorists),[49] Bennett finds Edwards so deplorable because he appears incapable of being *conflicted* by the complexities of human life. By using the expression "complexities of human life," I do not mean to suggest that the rejection of slavery or of genocide (the other issues at stake in Bennett's article) should be seen as complicated matters. They are not. But, in Bennett's presentation, Edwards stands out for the extraordinary *simplemindedness* with which he forestalls any possible conflict between values.

---

[46]   *Ibid.*, 133.    [47]   *Ibid.*, 134.    [48]   *Ibid.*, 133.
[49]   Notice, however, that if we read Moore literally when he asserts that no amount of suffering would be excessive (because undeserved) in the case of the jilted boyfriend, he may be taken to endorse views according to which eternal suffering may be appropriate. This is one reason for my suggestion in the previous section that we better not take Moore at his word on this. But as I will show in the remainder of this section, Moore's retributivism is to be rejected anyhow.

So, Bennett sees Edwards as a worse character than both Huck and Himmler because, (allegedly) unlike them, he is not conflicted, either because he never had "those sympathies which might interfere with one's [moral] principles" or because he gave them up.[50] It is clear that Bennett's main preoccupation concerns Edwards's inability to be conflicted and that, thus, Bennett seems motivated by some form of moderate holism. But, while I am evidently sympathetic to Bennett's attack on the simpleminded moralities that eschew complex moral conflicts, I wish to register one worry and one criticism about his position.

The worry is that Bennett's position may (perhaps too uncharitably) be seen as *conflict fetishism*. Even if Bennett is right about all the facts as he presents them in his article, is Edwards's morality really worse than Himmler's (or Huck's) just because he is not conflicted? I am not sure that his alleged simplemindedness really renders Edwards's morality worse than, say, Himmler's. After all, Edwards was not an actual murderer, nor was he actually involved in large-scale genocide: he merely endorsed a certain theoretical position that many (including Bennett and me) find mistaken. Despite this theoretical position, I, for one, find it hard to imagine Edwards, á la Himmler, murdering or participating in genocide. It remains unclear whether Edwards would have ever acquiesced in *actually* sending anyone to a real fiery pit for any time at all, let alone for eternity.

Moreover, it is not only Edwards who is non-conflicted by the contemplation of eternal suffering. Importantly, God himself would not be conflicted either as he sends people into fiery pits for eternity. Some of us may find such a conception of God problematic or dispiriting, insofar as we may think that being conflicted in these ways is not a sign of weakness or a limitation but a sign of integrity and virtue. Perhaps a being like God, who is supposed to be omniscient, omnipotent, and all good in ways that escape our understanding, could be completely non-conflicted about these matters without thereby losing his "humanity." After all, being supernatural, he may not have any "humanity" to lose. But the fact of the matter is that "humanness" means something that even God could have: in this context, it means to be alive both to considerations related to justice and to considerations related to empathy.

Insofar as God is assumed to be free from conflicts, it is indeed hard to understand how he can be seen as *merciful*. For whatever else is involved in mercy (a point to which I will return in later chapters), being alive to considerations having to do with empathic concern for others' suffering (whether deserved or not) strikes me as part of it. (It would also be hard to understand how God would not be conflicted either in these cases in which he graciously forgives, for why should he not be alive, in those cases, to the considerations of justice that he chooses to disregard?) A being "whose every action is as morally good as possible" and "who is as morally worthy as can be" is what Susan Wolf called a moral saint.[51] And as she insightfully argued, we should

[50]   Bennett, "The Conscience of . . . ," 129.
[51]   Susan Wolf, *The Variety of Values: Essays on Morality, Meaning, and Love*, Oxford: Oxford University Press (2015), 11.

be glad that we are not one of these beings. Part of Wolf's reasoning is that these beings seem immune to the moral conflicts that decent beings, aware of the complex world we inhabit, would experience.

Is God, thus conceptualized, really worse than Himmler (or Huck)? I do not think so. Or, leaving the theological context behind, is it not possible to be a simpleton – at least in the sense of not being conflicted in these ways – but somehow (by luck, even) ending up *doing* the right thing? I cannot help thinking that this is possible. Would this very human simpleton really be worse than Himmler (or Huck) simply because he is not conflicted? Again, I cannot help thinking that this is not so. If these answers are correct, it could then be argued that perhaps Bennett's view that Edwards's morality is *worse* than Huck's and Himmler's allowed for his article to gain fame at the expense of plausibility.

To an extent, however, it could be argued that the worry I have just registered may come back to haunt my own views, since my thesis is that punishment theory would benefit from paying closer attention to the moral conflicts to which punishment gives rise. In other words, it could be argued that if Bennett may perhaps be seen as guilty of conflict fetishism, so could I. I think that the worry loses much of its appeal in the case of my own views, for several reasons.

First, the worry arises in Bennett's case precisely as a result of his self-consciously scandalous ranking of moralities whereby a theologian who never committed a crime somehow turns out to be a worse person (insofar as his morality is worse) than a Nazi mass murderer and than someone who does not clearly see the evils of slavery. In contrast, I am not interested in rankings, let alone deliberately scandalous rankings. Second, and closely related, unlike Bennett, I pay attention to these conflicts in order to evaluate different organic wholes in which people decide to punish others, not in order to compare agents themselves or their "moralities." Of course, the evaluation of an entire organic whole may involve the evaluation of the agents (or their moralities) who are part of that whole, but I am concerned with the entire whole. Moreover, I admit that sometimes – say, in cases such as Ohlendorf's – the conflict between justice and empathy is of very little intensity.

Imagine three organic wholes in which Ohlendorf is punished and everything else is stipulated to remain identical, except that in one the punisher is not conflicted at all, in another the punisher is conflicted (to the appropriate degree, however small), and in a third one the punisher is terribly conflicted (much more than the case seems to warrant). Probably the most valuable organic whole is the second, even though it is not the one that presents us with the most intensely felt conflict. It is arguably the third case – which contains the most intensely felt dilemma – that is the least valuable. What is important to underscore is that not all instances of punishment are like Ohlendorf's – and within the context of contemporary criminal justice systems, for example, *most* are not. Finally, Bennett's attention to these moral conflicts is more or less freestanding. There is of course nothing wrong with that – but, in contrast, I emphasize the existence and importance of moral conflicts in the context of illustrating a certain poverty in traditional justifications of punishment.

Let us then leave my worry behind and focus instead on my criticism. Bennett describes the conflicts that he thinks Huck and Himmler experience (and that Edwards does not) as opposing "sympathy" and "morality." And he insists on portraying sympathy, unlike morality, as somehow devoid of reasons, as a matter of sheer feelings. As he analyzes Huck's conflict, Bennett is emphatic in that this conflict opposes moral *reasons* against mere sympathetic *feelings*: "reasons ... all occur on one side of the conflict: on the side of conscience [where we find] principles, arguments, considerations." "On the other side, the side of feeling," Bennett adds, "we get nothing like that."[52]

Bennett specifically denies that the fact that Huck made a promise to Jim gives him any reason because "in his [Huck's] morality promises to slaves probably don't count."[53] This strikes me as too facile. As Jenny Teichman has perceptively put it, "imagine how foolish Huck's talk ... would be, if Jim were not Miss Watson's slave, but her pony."[54] Even if promises to slaves may mean very little in slave societies, promises to ponies are, as Teichman suggests, indeed different – they are foolish, absurd. Huck could not have the "feelings" that he has for Jim were he not aware that Jim *is* a fellow human being, capable of the same sorts of experiences as he is and thereby entitled, in some way, to something to which ponies are not entitled.

At bottom, it is the very crude opposition between the rational and the emotional that leads Bennett astray. And once again Teichman identifies the shortcoming: "Mr Bennett says that a feeling is not the same as a moral judgment, and he is surely right, for a feeling is not the same thing as any judgment. All the same a feeling may involve a judgment."[55] Thus, while it is possible that the considerations that lead Huck toward helping Jim are "more emotional" than those that that lead him to protect Miss Watson's rights, he must be able to articulate reasons for both sorts of considerations. In fact, Bennett himself appears to be (contradictorily) committed to this view. As he emphasizes how bad Huck's morality was (at least as opposed to "ours"), he claims that, "for us, morality and sympathy would both dictate helping Jim to escape."[56] And I assume that these dictates presuppose some propositional content that both morality and sympathy have, for mere feelings do not "dictate" in the same ways that considered judgments do. Otherwise, Bennett would owe us an explanation as to how these two allegedly different ways of influencing us are in fact different.

In other words, Bennett appears to be suggesting that at least in some cases (such as slavery and genocide) we should, in the end, not be too conflicted after all. And this appears correct. Slavery and genocide are so obviously and so greatly wrong that the normative significance of, say, Miss Watson's suffering for losing her "property"

---

[52] Bennett, "The Conscience of ...," 127.   [53] *Ibid.*
[54] Jenny Teichman, "Mr Bennett and Huckleberry Finn," *Philosophy* 50 (1975): 358–359, at 359.
[55] *Ibid.*, 358.   [56] Bennett, "The Conscience of ...," 126.

seems minuscule. It seems as minuscule as the significance of Himmler's alleged "nausea and stomach convulsions" vis-à-vis his actions and as minuscule as Ohlendorf's imagined suffering in the face of his deserved punishment. But this is consistent with Bennett's central view, which I endorse, that in a *large number* of cases moral conflicts of serious intensity do and ought to arise.

Call the conflict what you will – a conflict between different sets of moral reasons or between empathy and morality, etc. – Bennett and I agree that these conflicts often obtain. Bennett sees these complications as instancing conflicts between moral and non-moral considerations, whereas I explicitly suggest that these complications can include conflicts among moral considerations. The reason I wish to emphasize what may appear to be perhaps only a terminological or otherwise minor point is that the recognition that there are infra-morality conflicts may help foreclose the maneuver whereby some considerations are seen as mere "serpent-windings" and some values are seen as merely "happy surpluses."

For surely Moore's and Kant's retributivisms presuppose a contrast between the value of desert (a moral value) and any other moral value – a contrast that is much more radical than Bennett's contrast between morality and sympathy. While Bennett may perhaps be guilty of framing the conflict in infelicitous terms, Moore and Kant are undoubtedly guilty of plainly rejecting the conflict. For whether punishment may prevent further crime and further suffering or help rebuild (or ruin) a nation, in these retributivists' eyes, is utterly irrelevant vis-à-vis the justification of punishment: the only thing that matters is making people suffer to the extent that they deserve to suffer. These other considerations are, at best, an afterthought: these retributivists may not lament their occurrence, but they would not, in fact, be at all interested in bringing them about when discussing punishment's justification. And just as these retributivists summarily dismiss these other considerations, they also eschew the considerations that have to do with the purely theoretical conflict between justice and empathy, between punishment and forgiveness.

Regarding these theoretical conflicts (and their emotional dimension), these retributivists seem alarmingly similar to Edwards. Admittedly, unlike Kant and Edwards, Moore is neither interested in divine punishment nor unaware of the excesses of contemporary criminal justice systems. But, like Kant and Edwards, he does not strike me as a likely candidate to be conflicted in these cases: if someone receives the punishment she deserves (whatever that punishment may turn out to be), then justice has been done, and then, precisely because justice was done, there simply is no room for emotions such as agent regret. We do not need to agree with Bennett in that this inability to be conflicted makes Edwards's morality (or Kant's or Moore's) worse than that of true monsters like Himmler in order to see that there is something simpleminded about this position – in ways similar to classical utilitarianism. Just as, for example, Bentham and Tadros are not conflicted by the tension between justice and empathy that punishment generates (insofar as they care only about empathy), Edwards, Moore, and Kant are similarly not conflicted (insofar as they care only about justice). In our current context, to espouse a theory that guarantees that we are free from these emotional conflicts is not a point in favor of such theory – quite the contrary.

I must postpone the continuation of the general discussion of moral conflicts and their emotional dimension until the last chapter of the book. Since this chapter is about retributivism in particular, in what remains of it, I will consider how this *no-conflict* version of (deontic) retributivism, premised on the monistic axiology of desert, plays out within the context of distinguishing punishment from revenge and of our responses to evil.

### 4.4 PUNISHMENT, REVENGE, AND THE PALE CAST OF THOUGHT

Famously, punishment and revenge have been seen as very different phenomena. The most famous arguments supporting a distinction have been usefully summarized by Robert Nozick:

(1) Retribution is done for a wrong, while revenge may be done for an injury or harm or slight and need not be for a wrong.

(2) Retribution sets an internal limit to the amount of the punishment, according to the seriousness of the wrong, whereas revenge internally need set no limit to what is inflicted.

(3) Revenge is personal ... whereas the agent of retribution need have no special or personal tie to the victim of the wrong for which he exacts retribution.

(4) Revenge involves a particular emotional tone, pleasure at the suffering of another, while retribution either need involve no emotional tone or involves another one, namely pleasure at justice being done.

(5) There need be no generality in revenge ... whereas the imposer of retribution, inflicting deserved punishment for a wrong, is committed to (the existence of some) general principles (prima facie) mandating punishment in other similar circumstances.[57]

Since I have elsewhere taken issue with all of these arguments, I will here reject them in only the briefest of fashions: these claims are false. There is no revenge for mere slights; revenge also involves limits (even if they are looser than those of punishment); revenge need not be personal (even if it often is); revenge need not mean enjoyment of someone else's suffering *simpliciter*; and revenge can indeed involve appeal to general principles.[58] But I wish here to revisit the fourth claim, to which I will henceforth refer as the emotional claim. This is because I have come to

---

[57]  Robert Nozick, *Philosophical Explanations*, Cambridge, MA: Harvard University Press, (1981), 366–368. We can safely assume that Nozick treats "retribution," "retributive punishment," and "punishment" as synonyms: see Leo Zaibert, "Punishment and Revenge," *Law and Philosophy* 25 (2004): 81–118, particularly 88–91.

[58]  For the substantiation of these claims, see Zaibert, "Punishment and Revenge."

believe that a certain focus on emotions is in fact likelier than I once thought to allow us to establish a difference between punishment and revenge. As may by now be anticipated, it is not the traditional emotions themselves to which I have become attracted or even any particular emotions but some forms of emotional *conflicts*.

Earlier I resisted the way in which the emotional claim is typically mobilized because I thought that to describe the avenger as experiencing "pleasure at the suffering of another" is too crude. Rarely a fictional avenger is portrayed in this way. In fiction, avengers are typically portrayed as obviously interested in *justice*, even if they often appear perhaps obsessed with it or somehow mistaken about what they take justice to demand. In and out of fiction, however, someone who simply finds other people's suffering – even if deserved – *pleasant* resembles a sadist rather than an avenger. The fact that we can easily imagine a sadistic avenger in no way refutes the fact that we can also imagine an avenger who is not sadistic: the connection between vindictiveness and sadism is neither necessary nor common. But it is the very emphasis placed on "pleasure" that I find problematic. For I do not think that even the punisher (as distinguished from the avenger) feels "pleasure" *simpliciter* as she contemplates justice being done. To describe these things in terms of pleasures is to leave much out and to flatten the much more complicated emotional and normative landscape in which punishment and revenge take place. I am willing to grant that the sight of justice being done is not unpleasant, though I would insist that to conclude that thereby it is an unproblematically pleasant sight might be too quick.

I still disagree with the typical mobilization of the emotional claim, but I now think that a *different* take on the emotional claim can indeed be helpful in allowing us to understand these phenomena better and helping us better understand what is involved in the justification of punishment. Independently of the particular details of any of the arguments seeking to distinguish punishment from revenge, they all seem to be in the service of a grander aim. This grander aim is to somehow sanitize punishment at revenge's expense. For the assumption that appears to undergird these different arguments, as summarized by Nozick, is that revenge is bad (unciv-ilized, barbaric, etc.), whereas punishment is at least in principle justifiable. And its justifiability is, albeit indirectly, premised on its alleged difference from revenge. Of course, as we have seen in earlier chapters, classical utilitarians are wont to see retributive punishment (and not merely revenge) as barbaric. But excepting classical utilitarians, many people believe that punishment need not be barbaric whereas revenge perforce must be.

While the stereotypical image of an avenger may not be that of a downright sadist, it *is* nonetheless the image of someone who is not at all conflicted: she is on a mission to give the person whom she believes wronged her the punishment that she thinks she deserves, and she has time neither for meditations nor for conflicts. From her perspective, carrying out her revenge is simplemindedly good: there is nothing to regret (let alone to feel agent regret or remorse or guilt) about making the person she perceives to be a wrongdoer suffer. And then it becomes easier to see why the avenger may seem barbaric, at least when she is contrasted to an imagined punisher who may be afflicted by the moral conflict that obtains whenever she makes someone suffer (even if deservedly).

I am not sure that the word I would use to describe the avenger is "barbaric," but it is clear that there is something unsavory, disagreeable, uninspiring, and indeed frightening about too much resoluteness in making other people suffer, even if the suffering is deserved. A certain diffidence, particularly if it flows from experiencing the right kind of moral conflict, can be seen as virtuous and, at any rate, as civilized. Consider Peter French's discussion of some interesting reactions to *Hamlet*.

> According to [Susan] Jacoby, "The real greatness of Hamlet lies in its depiction of a man undone by the responsibility of carrying out a vengeful assignment unsuited to his nature." Goethe sees Hamlet, as we should see him, as overwhelmed with astonishment and trouble rather than as ready to take on the important task to which he has been assigned. He is not "a young hero, panting for revenge . . . who feels himself fortunate in being called out against the usurper of his crown." The pressure of the responsibility of vengeance drives him to avoidance rather than action. Unlike Achilles, who immediately faces up to the fact that the cost of avenging Patroclus will be his own early death and carries out the task, Hamlet seems to find every way under the sun to put off the job. The differences between Achilles and Hamlet, of course, are great, and perhaps the most important is that Achilles does not face the religious prohibition against private revenge that might play on Hamlet's mind and slow his vengeful reflexes. It does, however, remain something of a mystery to me that Hamlet might think that his assignment flies in the face of the prohibition against private revenge. I am more inclined to side with Goethe who writes, "Shakespeare wished to describe the effects of a great action laid upon a soul that was unequal to it." One of the important things we learn about vengeance from Hamlet is that the responsibility of performing it can overwhelm a person unsuited to the task.[59]

But surely Hamlet is no mere procrastinator. The famous "to be or not to be" soliloquy is much more about the moral conflicts I have been here discussing than about cowardice or laziness. Hamlet's own view:

> Thus conscience does make cowards of us all,
> And thus the native hue of resolution
> Is sicklied o'er with the pale cast of thought,
> And enterprises of great pith and moment
> With this regard their currents turn awry,
> And lose the name of action.[60]

---

[59] Peter French, *The Virtues of Vengeance*, Lawrence, KS: University of Kansas Press (2001), 32. For more on French's views, see Leo Zaibert, "The Ethics of Hostility," in *Reflections on Ethics and Responsibility: Essays in Honor of Peter French* (Zachary J. Goldberg, ed.), Dordrecht: Springer (2017): 185–200.

[60] William Shakespeare, *Hamlet*, in *William Shakespeare: The Complete Works* (Stanley Wells and Gary Taylor, eds.), Oxford: Oxford University Press, 670.

In other words, it is above all because he has a *conscience* that Hamlet is paralyzed. It is not quite that he is simply "unsuited to the task" – it is, rather, that he understands deeply what the task means. For this reason Hamlet is the antithesis of the stereotypical avenger. He is a moving example of a person of *integrity*, to use Williams's understanding of this term.[61] Integrity need not preclude action, but it *shapes* action in important ways. A punisher with integrity may inflict the punishment that is deserved (or that is otherwise called for), but she will still feel a certain type of moral emotion about having had to make someone suffer – something like agent regret. In other words, a punisher who has integrity is, in the majority of cases, not *happy* about punishing; rather, she is *conflicted*. As adumbrated earlier, it is possible that the outward appearance of the punisher with integrity may on this or that occasion be identical to that of the punisher who lacks integrity – say, in cases like Ohlendorf's. But these two punishers are importantly different nonetheless.

Thus, it is tempting to suggest that a crucial – and overlooked – difference between the punisher and the avenger is that the latter is simpleminded whereas the former is not. I do believe that something along these lines is correct.[62] But notice, however, how unlike Hamlet are the *punishers* (not the avengers) that emerge from Kant's and Moore's retributivism. Unlike Hamlet, but like Edwards, these punishers exhibit a certain simpleminded tranquility of spirit as they inflict suffering on the deserving. Unlike Hamlet, but again like Edwards, they seem as preoccupied with discharging their duty to inflict deserved suffering (or to acquiesce with said discharging) as the avenger is preoccupied with her revenge. I would like to suggest that it is in part because of this similarity that retributivism, like revenge, is often taken to be barbaric. But if this is so, it may appear as if that simplemindedness is after all unhelpful in distinguishing punishment from revenge.

This is, however, a very limited and circumscribed worry. In order to assuage its force, all that is needed is to underscore that the simplemindedness is unhelpful in allowing us to distinguish between revenge and punishment, when we embrace the view of punishment based on Kantian or Moorean *deontic* retributivism. This, of course, should not be a surprise, since after all I have criticized these versions of retributivism precisely because they are, like the dogmatic Edwards and like typical avengers, simpleminded. *Axiological* retributivism, in contrast, is not at all simpleminded and thus it does clearly differ from revenge (and from the versions of deontic retributivism Kant and Moore champion) along these emotional lines.

I would like to end this section by noting once again how easy it is to lose sight of the way forward. The problem is not retributivism as such. After all, classical utilitarianism is hardly a promising alternative: for although it does potentially reject retributive or vindictive simplemindedness, it does so at the high price of imposing

---

[61]  Bernard Williams, "A Critique of Utilitarianism," in J. J. C. Smart and B. A. O. Williams, *Utilitarianism: For and Against*, Cambridge: Cambridge University Press (1973): 108, ff., and *passim*.

[62]  Colin McGinn, in his *Ethics, Evil and Fiction*, Oxford: Clarendon Press (2003), 69–71, says something similar.

its own simplemindedness, which refuses to even recognize some of the most essential aspects of the human condition. As we saw in the previous chapter, classical utilitarianism is necessarily simpleminded; as we now see, some forms of retributivism – above all the deontic versions, such as Kant's and Moore's – are simpleminded too, just as are some vindictive impulses. The way forward, then, is to seek a justification of punishment that would be sicklied o'er by the pale cast of thought.

### 4.5 TALKING TO ONESELF

The concluding two chapters of *Problems at the Root of Law*,[63] the last book in Feinberg's long and illustrious career, are about the problem of evil. Feinberg confesses that his original interest in crime was stimulated by the "reported frequency with which cruel and apparently senseless crimes are committed."[64] On some interpretation, these senseless crimes are *evil*, understood as a form of wrongdoing qualitatively different from the merely bad. Rather than presenting his own analysis of "evil," Feinberg suggests that, "in our effort to understand pure evil, we naturally begin by analyzing Adolf Eichmann."[65] And in analyzing Eichmann, Feinberg understandably turns to Hannah Arendt's famous *Eichmann in Jerusalem*.[66]

Arendt has admitted that "probably the most powerful motive" behind her decision to report on Eichmann's trial was "the wish to expose [herself] – not to the deeds, which, after all, were well known, but to the evildoer himself."[67] In anticipation of her face-to-face encounter with a high-ranking Nazi official such as Eichmann, Arendt expected to see the devil personified – a really malevolent and cruel monster. Instead, however, what she thought she found was a mediocre and drab parvenu – a mindless, cliché-ridden bureaucrat. In a word, Arendt found Eichmann to be above all *banal*, and it was this "banality of evil" that she found to be "word-and-thought-defying."[68] In a famous letter to her friend Karl Jaspers, Arendt admits that she found it very difficult to understand Nazi crimes because they

> explode the limits of the law; and that is precisely what constitutes their monstrousness ... this guilt, in contrast to all criminal guilt, oversteps and shatters any and all legal systems ... We are simply not equipped to deal, on a human, political level, with a guilt that is beyond crime ... and an innocence that is beyond goodness or

---

[63] Joel Feinberg, *Problems at the Roots of Law: Essays in Legal and Political Theory*, Oxford: Oxford University Press (2003).

[64] *Ibid.*, viii.    [65] *Ibid.*, 184.

[66] Hannah Arendt, *Eichmann in Jerusalem: A Study in the Banality of Evil*, New York, NY: Penguin (1994).

[67] Hannah Arendt, *The Jewish Writings* (Jerome Kohn and Ron F. Feldman, eds.), New York, NY: Schocken (2007), 475.

[68] Hannah Arendt, *Eichmann in Jerusalem* ..., 252.

virtue. This is the abyss that opened before us as early as 1933 (much earlier, actually, with the onset of imperialistic politics).[69]

The talk of the abyss seems to have started as soon as Arendt began thinking about the Nazis; as Steven Aschheim points out, upon learning of the existence of Auschwitz, Arendt affirmed that

> it was really as if an abyss had opened ... This ought not to have happened. And I don't mean just the number of victims. I mean the method, the fabrication of corpses and so on. Something happened there to which we cannot reconcile ourselves. None of us ever can.[70]

It is not immediately clear what exactly Arendt found so perplexing about Eichmann (or about the Nazis in general). Banal wrongdoers are utterly common; they are tried daily in courtrooms all over the world. Their existence hardly seems "word-and-thought-defying." Ordinary people regularly do awful things – and this is as true of the Nazis as of anyone else. Was Arendt wedded to a romanticized – if not downright kitsch – version of a Nazi? Was she expecting Eichmann to have horns? Why did she believe that being a boring, unimaginative bureaucrat was in any way at odds with doing bad things?[71]

Arendt's bewilderment comes into sharper focus, I think, if we admit to a *qualitative* difference between the merely bad (which could doubtless be very, very bad) and the evil. It is not important for my purposes to defend this distinction in any detail here, although I am sympathetic to the existence of something like this distinction.[72] I introduce it here merely in order, first, to explain why Arendt may have been so bewildered and, second, because it will allow me to show a further shortcoming of the type of retributivism that, like classical utilitarianism, is built upon a monistic simple-minded axiology. Consider this example, useful in shedding light on the nature of this distinction: "[A] tyrannical state executes by firing-squad a young dissident; and then bills the grieving relatives for the cost of the bullet."[73] As Eve Garrard points out, "clearly the main disvalue produced in this case is the killing of the young man. But it is the charging of the bullet that is more likely to strike us as evil."[74]

I would like to argue that it was because Arendt thought that what Eichmann (and the Nazis) did was evil (and not merely bad) that she found his (and their) "banality"

---

[69] Quotation taken (including ellipsis), from Steven E. Aschheim's illuminating "Nazism, Culture and the Origins of Totalitarianism: Hannah Arendt and the Discourse of Evil," *New German Critique* 70 (1997): 117–39, at 131.

[70] *Ibid.*, 126.

[71] Compare Arendt's take to Leonard Cohen's "All There Is to Know about Adolph [sic] Eichmann" (in Leonard Cohen, *Stranger Music: Selected Poems and Songs*, New York, NY: Vintage [1993], 53), where Cohen emphasizes Eichmann's normalness.

[72] Steps in that direction are offered in Leo Zaibert, "Beyond Bad: Punishment Theory Meets the Problem of Evil," *Midwest Studies in Philosophy* 36 (2012): 93–111.

[73] Eve Garrard, "The Nature of Evil," *Philosophical Explorations* 1 (1998): 43–60, at 45.

[74] *Ibid.*, 45.

so "word-and-thought-defying." Had Eichmann (and the Nazis) committed merely bad deeds, then she would not have been bewildered. Indeed, Arendt thought that it was a "misunderstanding" to think "that a direct line existed from the early anti-Semitism of the Nazi Party to the Nuremberg Laws and from there to the expulsion of Jews from the Reich and, finally, to the gas chamber." It was a mistake to think that the "horror of Auschwitz" was "not much more than the most horrible pogrom in Jewish history." This misunderstanding, she thought, was "actually at the root of all the failures and shortcomings of the Jerusalem trial."[75] "None of the participants [in Eichmann's trial] ever arrived at a clear understanding of the actual horror of Auschwitz, which is of a different nature from all the atrocities of the past." The wrongs of the Nazis were unique: "[P]olitically and legally ... these were 'crimes' different not only in degree of seriousness but in essence."[76]

This alleged distinction between the merely bad and the evil is as interesting as it is problematic. One immediately obvious problem with it is that it may unwittingly endow evil acts with some grandiosity – perverse grandiosity indeed, but still grandiosity. A series of letters attest to a preoccupation that both Arendt and Jaspers (among others) shared, whereby Arendt's epic talk may be seen as unwittingly sublimating Nazi evil, turning it into some "satanic greatness."[77] In other words, evil could turn out to be so special that it may in fact be argued that this distinction aggrandizes it. Aschheim, for example, insightfully discusses some ways in which Arendt's treatment of the evil that Eichmann and the Nazis carried out could be perceived as "operatic," "metaphysical," "biblical," and "ecstatic," and he understandably fears that at times her treatment may lead to "overblown analysis."[78]

But for current purposes, the main problem with the distinction lies elsewhere. If the distinction is admitted, then something needs to be said regarding the way in which evil actions (as opposed to merely bad actions) ought to be punished. It should by now be scarcely necessary to repeat that classical utilitarianism is a nonstarter here: for its adherents will only admit of *quantitative* differences between the bad and the evil. They must see "evil" as, at most, meaning "extremely bad." They may concede that it may be useful to pretend that the distinction obtains, but they cannot, on pain of contradiction, admit to its existence in earnest. Neither Arendt nor Feinberg is a classical utilitarian. And yet I shall suggest that their reaction to Eichmann's evil deeds is disappointingly similar to the classical utilitarian reaction.

Arendt distanced herself from the position (somewhat popular at the time) according to which insofar as "Eichmann's deeds defied the possibility of human punishment," this would entail that "it was pointless to impose the death sentence for crimes of such magnitude." Arendt insisted that however bewildering she took Eichmann's combination of evil and banality to be, this "could not conceivably mean that he who had murdered millions should for this very reason escape

---

[75]   Arendt, *Eichmann in Jerusalem*, 267.   [76]   *Ibid.*   [77]   Aschheim, "Nazism, Culture ...," 132.
[78]   *Ibid.*, 129–130.

punishment."[79] So, Arendt agreed with the court's judgment: Eichmann should hang. She, however, disagreed with the court's rationale. Arendt suggested that the court should have "dared" to address Eichmann in the following terms:

> just as you supported and carried out a policy of not wanting to share the earth with the Jewish people and the people of a number of other nations – as though you and your superiors had any right to determine who should and who should not inhabit the world – we find that no one, that is, no member of the human race, can be expected to want to share the earth with you. This is the reason, and the only reason, you must hang.[80]

The problem is that since Arendt admits both that Eichmann did horrible things and that we do not fully grasp the meaning of these things, it is hard to understand why, or at least how, we should punish him. Whether treating Eichmann justly entails giving him what he deserves remains an open question: What does justice demand in the case of evil (so construed)? The fact that no one can be expected to want to share the earth with Eichmann does not strike me as a particularly good reason, let alone the *only* reason, for his execution or even for the fact that he should be punished at all. Needless to say, I am not suggesting that he should not have been punished – only that the fact that people "could not be expected to want to share the earth with him" is not a very good reason.

In an important sense, Arendt's position constitutes an abdication. For the "only" reason she finds for executing Eichmann appears to have very little to do with desert. Rather, it seems to be a concession to a form of desire satisfaction rather at home in a classical utilitarian worldview. Interestingly, Feinberg, a much less "operatic" author and surely one much less prone to "over-blown analyses" than Arendt, appears to abdicate in this context in strikingly similar ways. Apropos his discussion of Arendt's views on the Eichmann trial, Feinberg tells us: "[G]enuinely evil persons are like wild beasts or mad dogs."[81] While Feinberg is of course aware that this position is "not popular with philosophers," he nonetheless believes that "there is surprisingly much to be said" for it.[82] And Feinberg then adds that when dealing with evil people, we should forget about desert and justice and instead treat them like wild beasts:

> [W]e need not hate the wild bear, nor waste our moral judgment on her. There is just one thing to do. Shoot her and get it over with, in the same spirit as that in which we would cope with other natural calamities – fires, storms, slides, quakes, and floods.[83]

Just like people are not expected to want to share the earth with Eichmann, they are not expected to want to experience quakes and floods. Eichmann, other Nazis, and

[79]   Arendt, *Eichmann in Jerusalem*, 250.     [80]   *Ibid.*, 279.
[81]   Joel Feinberg, *Problems at the Root of Law*, Oxford: Oxford University Press (2003), 190.     [82]   *Ibid.*
[83]   *Ibid.*

in general evil agents are equated by Feinberg to wild beasts and to natural calamities. And these things ought to be eliminated in as simple and straightforward a way as possible. No one, I think, would be seriously emotionally conflicted about putting out a fire or putting down a rabid dog. So, this way of "coping" with evil is in fact a way of not punishing it at all. Killing someone because the rest of humanity cannot be expected to want to share the world with him is – unless the idea of this being a deserved response to his wrongdoing is somehow smuggled – *not* to punish him. Killing a rabid dog is not to punish it, and much less is putting out fires to somehow "punish" nature.

Arendt believes that to punish Eichmann on "retributive" grounds is "barbaric."[84] But by "retributivism" Arendt had in mind the blunt and vindictive Kantian version of it that I too have criticized. The axiological retributivism, along the lines I have described, is neither blunt nor vindictive. This axiological retributivism seems both to escape Arendt's and Feinberg's (and Kant's and Moore's) purview and, more importantly, to offer a better framework to think through cases such as Eichmann's. For, in the end, what Arendt and Feinberg suggest we do with evildoers – either to defer to what people want us to do with them or to "cope" with them as we would with natural calamities – seems more at home within the classical utilitarian view than anywhere else. It is not obvious that Kant and Moore reject qualitative differences between the bad and the evil, but to the extent that they are wedded to axiological monism, it is hard to see how they could possibly countenance these differences.

The Jerusalem court, of course, did not need to focus on the alleged *evil* of Eichmann's actions. After all, he also engaged in enough serious garden-variety bad actions (crimes) that warranted whatever the court's maximum punishment happened to be. The pressing question – which none of the authors discussed in this section addresses satisfactorily – is that if a qualitative difference between an "ordinary" murderer and an evil murderer is admitted, it is not at all clear why our response to each of them should be identical. And it seems that Eichmann was punished in the same way a non-evil murderer may have been punished.

The way forward is to seriously embrace axiological pluralism and the framework of organic wholes. Punishment is not the only element of a valuable response to wrongdoing (whether ordinary wrongdoing or evil). Even if the exact words that Arendt recommended the court use to address Eichmann are debatable and even more her reasons for uttering them, that a court in some way or another addresses wrongdoers (whether ordinary or evil) may add extraordinary value to the organic whole in which they appear (and even if they cause more suffering). There is, often, great value in expressing certain things (as we will discuss in full detail in the next chapter).

---

[84]  Arendt, *Eichmann in Jerusalem*, 277.

Even if Feinberg were right that we would "waste" our moral judgment on the truly evil agent, we would not be thereby wasting it on everyone else. Moreover, even if Eichmann *and everyone else* were incapable of understanding the message that justice demanded, to call evil by its name, to condemn it, is not a "waste." This calling, this condemnation, is, rather, a manifestation of integrity – a virtue that only the axiological retributivist is in a position to integrate into a justification of punishment.

It is the very talk of "wastefulness," with all its utilitarian undertones, that we should abandon. The organic whole in which correct moral judgments are expressed is better than that in which they are not. Perhaps the axiological retributivist will never be able to perfectly articulate the words that justice demands; perhaps the words of justice in the face of grave wrongdoing are inherently inadequate; or perhaps the full meaning of justice is downright ineffable. This could be true both of evil actions (as construed herein) and of garden-variety bad actions, and it can render somehow inadequate the punishment meted out by the Jerusalem court and by any other court. But at least axiological retributivists – unlike both classical utilitarians and deontic retributivists – *could* value the mere saying of *something*, something that, even if necessarily incomplete and uncertain, would affirm some of our constitutive convictions. More than anyone else, axiological retributivists are likely to see that sometimes there is value in saying some things, even if no one is listening.

## 4.6 CONCLUSION

In spite of their potential to transcend the monism of utilitarianism, some influential forms of retributivism – again, its most famous historical version and its most sophisticated contemporary defense – fail, as we have seen, to overcome such monism. A particularly poignant bit of evidence regarding the inadequacy of this axiologically monistic retributivism is the way in which Moore himself has recently eschewed his early views, as I shall discuss in closing. (Of course, Moore does not admit that he is *eschewing* any of his earlier positions, but only that he is *clarifying* them.)

Although, as we have seen, Moore has been emphatic in that desert is sufficient to justify punishment – i.e., that it provides us with a "sufficient" reason for punishment, with a duty to punish – he now distances himself from this position. The distancing is the result of his postulating a distinction between what he calls an "internal" (i.e., "vis-à-vis other goods proposed as justificatory of punishment") and what he calls an "external" justification of punishment (i.e., "vis-à-vis all costs and benefits of punishment").[85] So, Moore now explicitly admits that

---

[85]  Michael S. Moore, "Responses and Appreciations," in *Legal, Moral, and Metaphysical Truths: The Philosophy of Michael S. Moore* (Kimberly Kessler Ferzan and Stephen J. Morse, eds.), Oxford: Oxford University Press (2016): 343–426, at 346.

[a]chieving retributive justice is an intrinsically good state of affairs, but in the budget room its attainment is no more of a categorical obligation than is the attainment of distributive justice, corrective justice, rights-preservation, etc. Trade-offs in terms of how much of these goods we can afford are not only inevitable but desirable.[86]

This admission contradicts Moore's thunderous talk about retributivism not being able to "share the stage with any other punishment goal" that we encountered before, and it also contradicts his systematic and thoroughgoing rejection of the mixed justifications of punishment.[87] When confronting the objection[88] that this recent admission renders him "a 'mixed theorist' of punishment rather than the 'pure retributivist' that [he] bill[s] [himself] as," Moore replies: "[M]y 'purity' is at the level of internal justification solely," and he further adds that "in the budget room where trade-offs must be made, I let the kitchen sink in like everyone else."[89] I leave aside whether Moore does indeed have a coherent position here.[90] What I would like to emphasize is that Moore's "purity" is only intelligible if we accept the woefully inchoate distinction between "internal" and "external" justification that Moore now has introduced. Whatever else may be true of such distinction, it strikes me as a textbook example of self-serving gerrymandering. First, Moore continues to refer to *any* consideration that may defeat judgments of desert "externally," in the "budget room," as a "pleasant bonus,"[91] just as much earlier in his career he claimed that it was a "happy surplus."[92] Second, while he sees that desert is "internally" sufficient to justify punishment, he appears to unhelpfully define the "internal" as "that universe of discourse in which desert is sufficient to justify punishment." And this is just too problematically circular.

I have elsewhere suggested that Moore's views are marred by his simultaneous (and problematic) understanding of retributivism in axiological and in deontic terms.[93] His recent appeal to the distinction between internal and external justifica-tion, like his previous invocations of the context dependence of the term "sufficient,"[94] really "obfuscates as much as it illuminates."[95] Moreover, the appeal prevents Moore from endorsing the much more intelligible and capacious distinc-tion between the axiological and the deontic. Moore claims to have been interested in opposing thinkers "who found it morally unintelligible to think . . . that requiting

---

[86]   *Ibid.*, 347.        [87]   Moore, *Placing Blame*, 28.
[88]   Raised by Douglas Husak in "What Do Criminals Deserve?," *Legal, Moral, and Metaphysical Truths*, 49–62.
[89]   Moore, "Responses . . .," 348.
[90]   Contrast Moore here to Mitchell Berman, who in "Punishment and Justification," *Ethics* 188 (2008): 258–290, distinguishes, like Moore, between "tailored" and "all-things-considered" justifications but who, unlike Moore, does not talk about retributivism not sharing the stage with other punishment goals.
[91]   Moore, "Responses . . .," 348.        [92]   Moore, *Placing Blame*, 153.
[93]   Zaibert, *Punishment and Retribution*, 161 ff.        [94]   Moore, *Placing Blame* . . ., 172 ff.
[95]   To echo Husak's way of putting it in "What Do Criminals Deserve?," 50.

wrongdoing with suffering was good at all."[96] Moore, however, continues to define a retributivist as someone who believes that deserved suffering is "intrinsically right, good, and just."[97] In previous chapters, I, too, have tried to show (in different ways) that these thinkers Moore opposes are indeed mistaken. But, unlike Moore, I have urged a separation between the elements that Moore continues to run together. Deserved suffering is intrinsically good (in the sense that its goodness need not depend on medicinal considerations, in the sense that it can by itself add value to an organic whole). Full stop. Whether it is also right and just, as Moore claims, is a different matter.

Even if Moore's appeal to the distinction between internal and external justification were to survive the charge of circular gerrymandering and were it to be shown to be intelligible and convenient, it would not save his version of retributivism.[98] For the trade-offs and conflicts, Moore admits, all take place within the "budget room." The budget room, however, is scarcely the place for *theoretical* conflicts. Whatever the consideration of this alleged "external" justification of punishment may add to his (confessedly limited) "internal" retributivism, Moore's recent move will not help us with the theoretical problem of punishment. It will not show how his version of retributivism could possibly countenance theoretical *moral* conflict. It will not show how his retributivism could possibly say something meaningful about differentiated forms of wrongdoing. And it will not show how his retributivism could avoid relying on a retributive punisher as callously indifferent to the human condition as is the classical utilitarian. Things do not, then, look up for deontic retributivism.

---

[96] Moore, "Responses . . .," 347. Oddly, Moore refers to these thinkers as "liberals"; they should be called (classical) *utilitarians*.

[97] Moore, "Responses . . .," 344.

[98] Confidence in Moore's distinction between "internal" and "external" justification is weakened by the fact that in an article published *after* "Responses . . .," Moore seems to forget about it and to revert to his earlier views. In this recent article ("Liberty and the Constitution," *Legal Theory* 21 [2015]: 156–241), Moore sees retributivism as so extraordinarily capacious that it grounds nothing less than political *liberty*. This remarkable view presupposes Moore's traditional linkage between retributivism and legal moralism and in fact introduces a further linkage between retributivism and autonomy. Independently of the success of these linkages, their spirit strikes me as inconsistent with the spirit of his remarks on "internal"/ "external" justifications in "Responses . . .".

# 5

## Communication, Forgiveness, and Topography

For the past few decades, the communicative approach to punishment has been extraordinarily popular.[1] The popularity is understandable, not only given its apparent superior articulacy concerning differentiated forms of wrongdoing that we have just discussed (in the context of addressing the differences between the merely wrong and the evil) but also given the many obstacles facing the traditional justifications of punishment that we have been discussing throughout. The communicative approach emphasizes the presumably noble idea that punishment should above all seek to get wrongdoers to understand the wrongness of what they have done rather than the apparently cruder idea that punishment should simply seek to make wrongdoers suffer. Consider the gist of this approach, as formulated by R. A. Duff, arguably its most influential contemporary champion:

> Criminal punishment, I argue, should communicate to offenders the censure they deserve for their crimes and should aim through that communicative process to persuade them to repent those crimes, to try to reform themselves, and thus to reconcile themselves with those whom they wronged.[2]

This truly is a lovely set of desiderata. This is also to expect punishment to accomplish quite a lot – a point to which I will return in due course. But I want to note at the outset that the communicative approach is immediately revealed as attractive for at least three reasons. First, it appears to be a rather humane approach, well poised to avoid, for example, the many excesses of contemporary criminal justice systems. Second, it appears well equipped to harmoniously achieve several of punishment's goals: when the suffering that is constitutive of punishment is the

---

[1] See Joel Feinberg, "The Expressive Function of Punishment," in *Doing and Deserving: Essays in the Theory of Responsibility*, Princeton, NJ: Princeton University Press (1970): 95–118; R. A. Duff, *Punishment, Communication, and Community*, Oxford: Oxford University Press (2001); Andrew von Hirsch, *Censure and Sanctions*, Oxford: Clarendon Press (2003). Thomas Scanlon (as we saw in Chapter 2) and Derek Parfit (as we shall see in the appendix) are also attracted to the communicative approach.

[2] Duff, *Punishment, Communication* . . ., xvii.

result of understanding the wrongness of what one has done and when this understanding is, in turn, the result of having been told what the wrongness was (and what its significance was, etc.), then some other worthy goals of punishment – such as those R. A. Duff mentions in the passage just quoted – are likely to be met as well. And third, insofar as the means to get wrongdoers to understand the wrongness of what they have done are potentially very richly variegated and may involve the consideration of many different values, the communicative approach seems particularly well equipped to underwrite a pluralistic approach to punishment of the sort I have defended here.

While I am sympathetic to the *idee mere* of the communicative approach, in this chapter I wish to nonetheless problematize its alleged attractiveness. To a large extent the chapter is centered on the discussion of the three reasons just presented. Thus, in Section 5.1, I will explore whether there is something in the communicative approach that renders it necessarily more humane than its alternatives and whether there is something in it that allows it to harmoniously combine different punishment goals. I will suggest that the communicative approach fails on both counts. In the second section, I turn to the question of whether the communicative approach is amenable to the pluralism that transcends simplemindedness. Again, I will suggest that it is not.

In these first two sections, the emphasis will be on Duff's extraordinarily influential version of the communicative theory of punishment. But in Section 5.3, I turn my attention to another communicative theorist, John Tasioulas, who objects to Duff's position because he finds it insufficiently pluralistic. I think that Tasioulas's position represents an important improvement over Duff's. And yet I will suggest that, in ever more subtle ways, the exact nature of his disagreement with Duff turns out to be elusive. Moreover, I will suggest that in spite of his earnest commitment to non-simpleminded pluralism, Tasioulas does not quite embrace the axiological turn I here recommend as earnestly as he should, to the detriment of his pluralism.

Before proceeding any further, I wish to expand on a terminological clarification I offered already in Chapter 1. By and large, the background for this chapter is a debate between Duff and Tasioulas regarding the notion of *mercy*. Given the title of the chapter and given that I have said very little about mercy in the book thus far, this may seem odd. But the oddity is easily dispelled. In general, there are obvious differences between mercy and forgiveness. But, and as noted, in the present contexts – both regarding the role that mercy may play as a response to wrongdoing and regarding the debate between Duff and Tasioulas – "mercy" and "forgiveness" can indeed be treated as synonyms. For what Duff and Tasioulas (and other punishment theorists) mean by "mercy" is what I mean by "forgiveness."

For example, Duff tells us that "[a] bank robber who loosens the ropes with which he tied up a bank employee to relieve her suffering"[3] should not be seen as exhibiting

---

[3] R. A. Duff, "The Intrusion of Mercy," *Ohio Journal of Criminal Law* 4 (2007): 360–387, at 364.

mercy. This is mostly because for Duff mercy, in this context, is a matter "of remitting or mitigating a burden of penalty to which the recipient would otherwise be liable."[4] Tasioulas puts it similarly: the mercy that interests him is different "from most other variants of charity, such as giving relief to the destitute and the sick."[5] Of course one can offer succor to wrongdoers too, and in some contexts, these actions can be described as merciful, but, like Duff, Tasioulas is uninterested in those cases. The mercy these authors care about displays an "inherent concern with the punishment of wrongdoers."[6] And I agree that in this particular context this is the mercy worth our attention. Very roughly, the mercy that punishment theorists care about is that which would unburden agents who would otherwise have been deservedly punished: the subjects of mercy for Duff and Tasioulas are the exact same subjects of forgiveness for me.

I believe that it is better to refer to this phenomenon as *forgiveness* and not as *mercy*. Admittedly, there is at least one advantage in using the term "mercy," as Duff and Tasioulas do, over my use of the term "forgiveness," for mercy is more amenable to the sorts of gradational diminishments of punishment that I do not wish to deny, whereas forgiveness often (though not always) is taken to mean a *complete* refusal to punish.[7] But there is also at least one important disadvantage to their use of "mercy" instead of "forgiveness": Duff and Tasioulas need to expend energy explaining how restricted their sense of mercy really is vis-à-vis the ordinary understanding of the term.[8] In contrast, I only need to emphasize that when I talk about forgiveness I include partial forgiveness, and this strikes me as more straightforward and less at odds with ordinary language. So, although I prefer the term "forgiveness," I will sometimes use "mercy" when deviating from other authors' own words risks needless confusion.

Independently of terminological preferences, however, the substantive question concerns the central conflict of values around which any plausible pluralistic axiology of punishment should be built. This is the conflict that already in Chapter 1 I suggested is captured by expressions such as "justice and charity," "justice and equity," "justice and mercy," "justice and sympathy," "punishment and forgiveness," "punishment and mercy," and so on. This deep conflict, which has been referred to as the "paradox of

---

[4]   Duff, "The Intrusion . . .," 363.
[5]   John Tasioulas, "Mercy," *Proceedings of the Aristotelian Society, New Series* 103 (2003): 101–132, at 104.
[6]   Tasioulas, "Mercy," 104.
[7]   The first sentence of Duff's article reads: "Mercy is, of course, a virtue, and to act mercifully is to act rightly" (Duff, "The Intrusion . . .," 361). It may be then thought that this reveals yet another advantage of the term "mercy" over the term "forgiveness." But nothing prevents us from seeing forgiveness, or, as Charles Griswold has suggested, "forgivingness," as a virtue too. See Charles L. Griswold, *Forgiveness: A Philosophical Exploration*, Cambridge: Cambridge University Press (2007), 17 ff., 67 ff.
[8]   Tasioulas usefully reminds us that this "specific interpretation" of mercy "goes back to Seneca." See, e.g., John Tasioulas, "Where Is the Love: The Topography of Mercy" in *Crime, Punishment, and Responsibility: The Jurisprudence of Antony Duff* (Rowan Cruft et al., eds.), Oxford: Oxford University Press (2011): 37–53, at 40. See also *Seneca: Moral and Political Essays* (John M. Cooper and J. F. Procopé, eds.), Cambridge: Cambridge University Press (1995), at 120 and ff.

forgiveness"[9] (and which could of course also be called the "paradox of mercy")[10] is the following: if someone can be a beneficiary of forgiveness, then she is perforce a wrongdoer who deserves to be punished, not forgiven, and then forgiveness is not what justice demands, and it is not the right thing to do. If, on the other hand, a given wrongdoer does not (in spite of initial appearances) deserve to be punished, then to refrain to punish her is not to forgive her (rather, it is to excuse or justify or absolve her). Moreover, and for our purposes more poignantly, how does the *value* of sparing someone's (deserved) suffering stack up against the *value* of giving her the suffering that she deserves? How do we resolve this conflict?

## 5.1 THE LIMITS OF COMMUNICATION

The suggestion that someone deserves *censure*, which lies at the center of the communicative approach, admits of at least two importantly different interpretations. The expression can mean either that someone deserves to receive a certain message (paradigmatically via words) somehow *simpliciter* but decidedly *instead of* a punishment or that someone deserves to receive a certain message (paradigmatically via words) *because* that message will make her suffer and she deserves that suffering. The first interpretation strikes me as problematically inchoate: How could wrongdoers deserve simply to *hear* a certain message and nothing else? It seems to me that communicative theorists of punishment should adopt the second interpretation, lest their view be revealed as but a new (perhaps unwitting) instance of the misguided piety I discussed in Chapter 3. They better want the communicative process to generate a certain understanding – an understanding that causes suffering – and sometimes even extreme suffering.[11]

Once this point is underscored, however, then it ceases to be clear how exactly the emblematic and supposedly noble idea of the communicative approach differs from the supposedly cruder idea of other approaches. If, as is likely, the relationship between the expected understanding and the suffering it is supposed to generate is intimate (as I suggested in Chapter 3), then the contrast between the noble and the cruder idea presented at the outset is attenuated. Even if this attenuation is granted, however, the defender of the communicative approach may retort that an important difference between expecting punishment to produce understanding (however suffering-inducing such understanding may be) and expecting punishment to inflict suffering *simpliciter* must nonetheless be admitted. Suffering, in other words, needs to be *differentiated* (as, for example, our earlier discussion of Strawson and Scanlon

---

[9]　See Leo Zaibert, "The Paradox of Forgiveness," *Journal of Moral Philosophy* 6 (2003): 365–393, *passim*.

[10]　Tasioulas, "Mercy," *passim*, but especially 107 ff.

[11]　For a contrasting view see, e.g., Klaus Günther, "Crime and Punishment as Communication," in *Liberal Criminal Theory: Essays for Andreas von Hirsch* (A. P. Simester et al., eds.) Oxford: Hart (2014), 123–140, who claims that the message and the suffering are "in a certain way mutually exclusive" (at 134).

made clear). While the sheer suffering of the deserving wrongdoer may, as we have seen, add value to an organic whole, the value appears to be greater if this suffering is of a particular *type*. For example, just as suffering that is the result of punishment seems *ceteris paribus* to add more value to a given organic whole than suffering that is the result of an act of nature, suffering that is the result of understanding (coming to terms, owning up, etc.) the wrong one has done seems *ceteris paribus* to add even more value than the suffering of punishment without understanding.

I think that this defense of the communicative approach is on the right track. Still, the fact that the communicative approach is not really opposed to inflicting suffering, even if the differentiated suffering it seeks to inflict is somehow more valuable (or more civilized) than other forms of suffering, does call into question the alleged humaneness of the communicative approach. The hypothetical retort just discussed does not affect the fundamental fact that punishment without suffering is not punishment. To the extent that the communicative theory remains a theory *of punishment*, it perforce must seek to inflict deserved suffering, even if it inflicts it by means of conveying certain messages. Differentiation as such does not quite show the communicative theory to be more humane.

Perhaps, however, the communicative approach can be seen as more humane in the sense that the actual suffering it assumes wrongdoers deserve (whatever its origin) is in fact *lesser* than the suffering other punishment theories assume wrongdoers deserve. After all, while words can no doubt hurt, even the most hurtful words imaginable cannot match the suffering that physical torture can produce. Most human beings would prefer to hear any words whatsoever (no matter how hurtful) rather than being burned alive or having their fingernails pulled. That is why physical torture – rather than hurtful speech – has been the method of choice when attempting to break people's wills and why torture chambers are made up of instruments that cause sheer physical pain quite independently of words. But this is not to deny, however, that words can be very painful indeed and that great suffering can be brought about by means of words alone. Communication can cause suffering, and sometimes brutally and nastily so.[12]

Since no one in the contemporary debate is in favor of denailing, flailing, or hamstringing wrongdoers, the comparison of communicative suffering with these sorts of extreme torments may seem somewhat otiose. My goal is simply to highlight that even if never as painful as extreme tortures, communication *can* be very painful. There are realistic scenarios in which communicating something to a wrongdoer appears more painful than, say, incarceration. For example, recall the French women who in the aftermath of World War II were suspected of *collaboration horizontale* with occupying Nazi forces. Their humiliating public shaving arguably caused them (and was intended to cause them) more suffering than a variety of other

---

[12]    Even against the backdrop of the unspeakably awful physical afflictions inflicted upon Job, he at times seems more affected by words than by physical afflictions. See, e.g., *Job* 19:2, when he implores, "How long will you torment me and crush me with your words?"

punishments, such as incarceration (even if, admittedly, not more than every conceivably physical punishment). Although the shavers surely were brusque and unkind, it was not the physical pain that hurt these women the most: it rather was the shame and humiliation that the message of their public parade communicated. Humiliation and shame are essentially matters that involve communicating meanings (with words or otherwise), not matters of physical force. Sadists need not at all be limited to the physical. And there is nothing in the communicative approach, qua communicative, that would preclude the possibility of humiliating, shaming, or sadistic punishments.

Moreover, a punisher *may* wish to communicate certain things to a punishee not *instead* of inflicting the suffering typically associated to physical punishment but rather precisely in order to *surpass* the suffering that the mere physical punishment would cause. For example, and as Peter French notes, "exquisitely devised punishments" often involve sending messages, precisely in order to make these punishments more, not less, severe. This is why "Achilles tells Hector why he is killing him, and, presumably, Hector has a moment or two to reflect on how he came to such an end."[13] Achilles wants Hector to reflect on his own end in order to make him suffer more, not less. And many a physical torture can be made all the more tormenting by accompanying it with certain communications – as well-worn literary tropes attest.

To be sure, contemporary communicative theorists do not wish to send messages in order to make punishments particularly nasty. Rather, they wish that these messages be sent so as to avoid making wrongdoers suffer *simpliciter*. Even if hearing these messages may (or ought to or will) make wrongdoers suffer, what these theorists care about is the communication of these messages, not the suffering they may (or ought to or will) generate. But then it becomes clear that what may perhaps be humane about the communicative approach is not really connected to communication as such, since communication can be very painful indeed. What occurs is that contemporary communicative theorists combine their emphasis on communication with other, independent humanitarian or civilized principles. And these additional principles – whatever they turn out to be – can be embraced by communicative and non-communicative theorists alike.

Of course, if it turns out that no punishment that goes beyond communication is ever civilized or humane, then this humanitarian emphasis – again, whatever it turns out to be – would only be available to communicative theorists. But, in light of the discussion in Chapter 3, without further explanation this looks like a new iteration of the misguidedly pious position discussed therein. In order to see how this would be so, I turn to the discussion of the second reason explaining the attractiveness of the communicative approach: its alleged ability to combine different desirable punishment goals.

---

[13]  Peter French, *The Virtues of Vengeance*, Lawrence, KS: University Press of Kansas (2001), 30.

Duff presents his account of communicative punishment (quoted at the outset) immediately after discussing a certain skepticism regarding the plausibility of a "unitary 'theory of punishment.'" Duff identifies two reasons for the skepticism: the existence of a "sheer variety of crimes and of punishments" and the existence of an "untidy collection of indissolubly conflicting values."[14] It is against this variegated and pluralistic backdrop that he "nonetheless" offers his view, which he declares to be "unitary."[15]

Duff's desire to avoid this skepticism is well taken. What is not clear, however, is how exactly his communicative theory is supposed to be an antidote to it – above all, because it is not clear what exactly is "unitary" about his theory. Of course, the communicative approach could be seen as unitary in the sense of being presumably applicable to all crimes (to all wrongs?), independently of their differences and independently of moral conflicts. But this sense of "unitary" strikes me not as merely idiosyncratic but as rather useless: "unitary" would then simply (and somewhat vacuously) mean something along the lines of "not skeptical" or "not defeatist." So understood, "unitary" would not convey the much more fundamental senses of something being a unit or of forming a coherent whole (organic or otherwise). And it would not differentiate the communicative approach from any of the traditional justifications of punishment, since those are as "unitary" (in this odd sense) as Duff's own.

In more fundamental senses, Duff's communicative approach does not strike me as unitary. There are, after all, several moving parts to Duff's "unitary" theory of punishment. In Duff's communicative theory, punishment is supposed to produce a concoction of goals, and this concoction involves appeals to desert (though, again, the operative connection is between desert and *censure*, not between desert and punishment *per se*) and appeals to repentance, reform, and reconciliation (what Duff calls the "three R's of Punishment").[16] Evidently these admittedly worthy goals can conflict with each other. And not only can the three Rs conflict among themselves, but, more poignantly, any or several of them, on the one hand, can conflict with *deserved suffering*, on the other.

At this point, the crucial question suggests itself: How would Duff's communicative theory resolve these potential conflicts? I have trouble finding a satisfactory answer to this question in Duff's writings. As long as a satisfactory answer is not found, then the alleged ability of the communicative approach to combine different punishment goals remains elusive. I will assume that Duff would, in principle, reject causing a wrongdoer to repent, reform, and eventually reconcile with her victims, if this involved communicating to her *more* (or perhaps even *less*) censure than she deserved. Similarly, I will assume that Duff would, in principle, insist on communicating deserved censure, even in cases in which doing so may in fact *preclude* repentance, or reconciliation, or reform.

---

[14]  Duff, *Punishment, Communication . . .*, xvii.   [15]  *Ibid.*   [16]  *Ibid.*, 107.

These assumptions are necessary if we are to interpret Duff's communicative theory in the most charitable way: without them, his theory would risk structurally reducing to a simpleminded utilitarianism in which "suffering avoidance" is simply replaced with "communication of the messages conducive to the three Rs." The assumptions, moreover, offer what could perhaps be a *clue* as to how the conflicts could be resolved within the communicative framework. The idea would be to arrange deserved censure and the other goals (taken as a group) lexicographically: first give people the censure that they deserve, and then try to bring about the three Rs. Admittedly, this is not much – and it certainly is of no help regarding potential conflicts among the three Rs themselves. But it is better than nothing.

In light of these assumptions, however, it turns out that for the communicative approach to avoid being but a new version of the flat-footed utilitarianism we have discussed, it needs to privilege desert in ways that may deemphasize the importance of the three Rs or of communication itself. So, while Duff's three Rs are medicinal, I think that it would be mistaken (and unproductive) to conclude that his communicative theory is fully medicinal, since the medicine is circumscribed by the fact that the messages cannot involve more (or less, one imagines) than the "censure" that is deserved. Duff's communicative theory is thus best seen as a new mixed justification of punishment in which medicinal considerations are combined with considerations of desert.[17] His pursuit of the three Rs is constrained by considerations relating to deserved censure. As such, however, Duff's communicative theory stands to inherit some of the traditional problems faced by the mixed justification of punishment: above all, their infamous inability to offer guidance regarding the trade-offs between the different goals they seek to attain.

It should come as no surprise that I do not think that the fact that a proposed justification of punishment faces these dilemmas and conflicts should be seen as a point against it. On the contrary, I think that recognizing the reality of these problems is a step in the right direction. I agree with Duff in that a concern with the messages that punishment communicates "deserves a central place, even if not the only place, in our normative understanding of punishment."[18] As noted in the previous chapter, for example, the proper reaction to evil deeds may be different from the proper reaction to bad but not evil deeds – and sometimes this difference can best (or only) be articulated *in words*. Still, these dilemmas and conflicts do not necessitate the communicative theory of punishment, and the mere fact that a punishment theory is in this sense communicative does not help solve them either.

Duff admits that a "unitary" justification of punishment need not quite posit "a single goal or value," provided it posits "at least a coherent set of goals and values."[19] Evidently, his communicative theory cannot be seen as unitary in the first sense. But, insofar as his theory does not explain how coherence may ensue from the

---

[17] This eclecticism is also visible in Duff's efforts to combine liberalism and communitarianism, see, e.g., his *Punishment, Communication* . . ., 35–74.

[18] *Ibid.*, xviii.  [19] *Ibid.*, xvii.

complicated interactions among its many moving parts, it does not seem unitary in Duff's second sense either. So, Duff's communicative theory appears as *not* unitary in any of Duff's own two senses. Like the mixed theories of old, Duff's own communicative theory enjoys a certain attractiveness that stems from its laudable attempt to realize multiple punishment goals. The multiplicity of these goals is in part the result of the complexity of human life – a complexity that Duff's communicative theory to an extent registers but to which, sadly, it does not do justice. Like the mixed theorists of old, Duff fails to take the next step after registering these complexities: to take the distinction between axiology and deontology seriously. The goals that Duff's communicative theory seeks to attain – the three Rs – are indeed *valuable*, independently of their deontic force. But other goals are valuable too, and it is not at all clear why Duff's communicative theory would privilege some valuable goals and exclude others, particularly when he does include so many.

At this stage, the peculiar way in which Duff's communicative theory can be seen as monistic begins to emerge. For in spite of the fact that it has many moving parts (and putting aside that therefore Duff appears to be wrong when he suggests that his theory is "unitary"), he narrowly restricts what belongs to the justification of punishment. Nowhere does this narrowness come across more vividly than in Duff's famous discussion of mercy – a context in which Duff admits that his communicative theory is shallow and in which he defends this shallowness.

## 5.2 GAMES PEOPLE PLAY

Duff believes that there is a connection between the communicative theory of punishment and mercy. His "The Intrusion of Mercy" even includes a section called "Communicative Mercy,"[20] and he in fact begins the article by telling us that "on the basis of a communicative theory of criminal punishment, [he will] show how mercy has a significant but limited role to play in the criminal law."[21] Unfortunately, however, nowhere does Duff tell us what he means by the tantalizing idea of "communicative mercy" or what exactly it is about the communicative approach that allows for mercy to play a role in the criminal law. What appears clear is that this role must be very limited indeed, since, as the very title of this important article indicates, Duff thinks that mercy is an "intrusion." In Duff's estimation, "mercy involves an intrusion into the criminal law of values and concerns that are not themselves part of the perspective of criminal law."[22]

Duff repeatedly tells us that he is interested in the relation (or lack thereof) between mercy and the *criminal law*. Remarks of the following tenor appear often in the opening pages of Duff's article: "I will first ... need to identify the kind of mercy that seems both morally and philosophically most puzzling, at least in relation to criminal law,"[23] "[i]n the context of criminal law and punishment,

---

[20] Duff, "The Intrusion . . .," 366.   [21] *Ibid.*, 361.   [22] *Ibid.*   [23] *Ibid.*, 362.

mercy at least involves remitting or mitigating a burden of penalty ...,"[24] "my focus, like that of most theorists who discuss mercy in the criminal law, will be on sentencing ...,"[25] on "how could mercy ... have any proper role to play in a system of criminal law and punishment?"[26] In spite of these remarks, I think that what Duff has in mind is in fact the relationship between mercy and punishment *in general* and not just that between mercy and criminal punishment. As we shall see immediately, his article to a very large extent actually revolves around what Duff admits is "an extra legal example,"[27] which, he thinks, "offers a moral analogue of mercy in the criminal law."[28] Duff's starting point in this article is the following example:

> [A] friend has done me some moderately serious wrong: perhaps he has betrayed my trust in quite a serious way, or used something that I told him in confidence to his own advantage, in a way that causes me serious embarrassment or loss. I go to his home to confront him – to "have it out with him." I might not know whether our friendship can survive – much depends on how he responds to me; but my immediate aim is to confront him forcefully with what he has done, to make clear how wrong it was, to communicate my hurt and my anger. I intend, that is, to criticize and censure him: my aim is to get him to understand, and ideally to accept, the moral condemnation that is appropriate to the wrong he has done. But when I reach his house, he greets me with the news that his wife has just died. At once (or so we might hope) my anger is replaced by sympathy: even if I did not know his wife myself, I share in his grief, and feel for him in his loss. As for my complaint against him, my determination to call him to account for the wrong he did me, of course I do not pursue it; indeed, one might hope that a true friend would simply forget about it – it would be pushed from her mind by the friend's plight.[29]

Duff believes that it would be "obviously inappropriate for [him] to insist on talking about the wrong [done to him]."[30] I agree. The problem is that Duff appears to believe that the (best? only?) way in which this inappropriateness could be explained is through the mobilization of his communicative theory of punishment. In other words, Duff believes that the inappropriateness flows from the fact that the point of criticizing the wrongdoer is "to get him to focus on, to attend carefully to, the wrong [that he committed]."[31] But "given what he has now suffered," Duff continues, "it would be callously inhuman to expect him to do so,"[32] for "his attention will be quite understandably, perhaps quite properly, focused on what he has now suffered."[33]

To the extent that Duff bases the inappropriateness of insisting on talking about the wrong committed on the wrongdoer's sheer *inability* to focus on the wrong he committed, the communicative approach runs into difficulties. First, this move appears to give too much importance to the efforts to get the wrongdoer to focus on the wrong he did to the detriment of treating him in the way he deserves. After all, *ex hypothesi* he deserves the censure whether or not he is able to attend to it, so not

---

[24] *Ibid.*, 363.   [25] *Ibid.*   [26] *Ibid.*, 365.   [27] *Ibid.*, 366.   [28] *Ibid.*   [29] *Ibid.*
[30] *Ibid.*, 367.   [31] *Ibid.*   [32] *Ibid.*   [33] *Ibid.*, 369.

censuring him simply because he may be unable to focus seems to give short shrift indeed to the notion of desert. And if desert plays such a humble role in Duff's communicative theory, then the conclusion that the theory would in fact reduce to the wholly medicinal (and that it would thus be revealed as simpleminded in the ways characteristic of purely medicinal approaches) gains in plausibility.[34] Still, I think it best if we (perhaps stubbornly) avoid such a conclusion and instead continue to assume that Duff's position is not purely medicinal. Even in that case, his communicative approach would also run into difficulties.

Imagine that everything in Duff's example remained the same, except for the fact that when Duff arrives at the wrongdoer's house, he learns not that the wrongdoer's wife has just died but that the wrongdoer has just won hundreds of millions in the lottery. Here, too, it would be unreasonable to expect the wrongdoer to (be able to) focus his attention away from the millions he just won. So, if what matters is whether the wrongdoer *can* indeed focus on or effectively turn his attention to the wrong that he has committed, the communicative theory faces at least the following difficulty: this ability can be impaired both by sad events (such as the death of a wife) and by happy events (such as winning the lottery). So, "inhuman" may not be the best word to capture what goes on in these variations: to expect the grieving or the celebrating friend to attend to a moderately serious complaint that has nonetheless been dwarfed by circumstances is, rather, "impractical," "unrealistic," or downright "silly."

If, however, it is only the inability to focus that flows *specifically* from sad events that renders the insistence on pressing wrongdoers to talk about their wrongdoing "obviously inappropriate," then Duff should have told us about why he thinks this is so. I do believe that there is something that renders the inability to focus produced by sad events significantly different from the inability to focus produced by happy events, but I think that the explanation for this difference involves precisely that discussion of *values* that Duff avoids. The organic whole in which someone who initially seeks to have a conversation with a friend about a moderately serious wrong gives up on the plan upon learning that said friend has lost his wife is probably more valuable than one in which all remains the same except that the conversations is not even attempted. Either of these two organic wholes strikes me as more valuable as one in which the conversation is attempted. This ranking, however, does not seem to hold if the friend has just won the lottery. And these differences are not necessarily connected to anything communicative.

---

[34] Duff conspicuously avoids the word "punishment": all the wronged friend in his example wishes to do is variously described as "communicating," "criticizing," "censuring," "calling to account," "complaining," and even "confronting forcefully" – but never *punishing* the wrongdoer. (Duff once uses the term "castigate" (368), which is the closest he comes to "punishment.") Duff's avoidance of the word "punishment" makes it harder to understand how this is truly "a moral analogue" (366) to anything relevant happening in the context of actual criminal law, since surely actual criminal law *punishes* wrongdoers. Had Duff more explicitly said that he wanted to visit his friend in order to *punish* him, the analogue between this example and the criminal law would have been much clearer (and the specter of the sort of misguided piety discussed earlier less worrisome).

Assume, for example, that the wronged Duff may have wanted not merely to have a conversation but to *punish* the friend who did him wrong, that is, that he wished to inflict on him the suffering that he thought he deserved. Surely the wronged Duff could have done this without any desire to communicate anything: he may have gone to his friend's house only with a desire to slap his friend, without uttering a word; or he could simply have gone there in order to secretly slash the tires of his friend's car.[35] Even in these explicitly non-communicative scenarios, the wronged Duff, upon learning that the wrongdoer's wife has just died, may have refrained from slapping his friend, or from secretly slashing the tires of his car. Why? Because punishing this particular wrongdoer, given the richer organic whole that includes also the fact that his wife just died, is *ugly*. It is also petty, churlish, smug, self-centered, undignified, tasteless, tactless, and, in some ways, downright repugnant. And these features have no necessary connection with any communicative enterprise whatsoever: the organic whole in which a scheming tire slasher (who never wanted to communicate anything) abandons his plan upon learning about his friend's grief is arguably more valuable than one in which he carries on with his plan despite his knowledge of the death of the wrongdoer's wife.

Since Duff believes that this case is analogous to some criminal law cases, he believes that when criminal defendants may be unable to focus on the wrong they have committed (say, because a major tragedy has befallen them – *not*, we must assume, because they have won the lottery), then the value of things like mercy could somehow "intrude" into the logic of criminal law. Even in such cases, however, Duff is intent on emphasizing that "mercy marks, not an application of penal justice, but rather an intrusion into the sphere of penal justice by moral values and concerns that are not matters of justice."[36]

In circumscribing the "justice" of the criminal law, of punishment, to the confines of the purely deontic, to the detriment of the axiological considerations whose importance I have been here emphasizing, Duff, as we have seen, is no different from myriad other authors. But he surely is more explicit (and arguably more self-conscious) than most others: "the criminal courtroom, in which trial, conviction, and sentencing take place, is a formal forum in which the various people involved have their role to play." These people are not just unencumbered, free "citizens who happen to have come together" and who may be seen as engaged in an "unconstrained moral discussion" as to the defendant's guilt. They are, instead, "players in this game – a game that defines their roles for them."[37]

In a footnote, Duff offers the obligatory qualification whereby his claim that the criminal courtroom is to be seen as a game "is not to imply that it is either unimportant or detached from reality."[38] Be that as it may, Duff's position does

---

[35]  These are descriptions of *possible* punishments, not endorsements or justifications of them. See Leo Zaibert, *Punishment and Retribution*, Aldershot: Ashgate (2006), 59 ff.

[36]  Duff, "The Intrusion . . .," 381.      [37]  *Ibid.*, 370.      [38]  *Ibid.*, 370, fn. 24.

reduce the normativity of the courtroom to the normativity of the constitutive rules of games – and such normativity is conspicuously humble and conspicuously inimical to axiological considerations.[39] Just like in chess, for example, you ought not to move the rooks diagonally, a participant in a criminal trial ought not consider matters "extraneous" to the trial – the defendant's life, the fuller context in which her actions have taken place, the standing of the state or of this specific court to inflict suffering, and the very nature of that suffering itself, for example, may not really belong in the courtroom. Like thoroughbreds that can only run with blinkers on, jurors and judges alike ought to be limited in their field of vision.

Duff is of course aware that he is defending an "avowedly limited, and in an important sense shallow, institution [of criminal law]."[40] But he thinks that these limits and this shallowness are nonetheless necessary, for "[t]hese kinds of constraints have a particular significance and shape in a liberal polity that seeks to limit the reach and scope of the criminal law."[41] Duff's worry appears to be that to broaden the types of values with which the criminal law is concerned would threaten "a liberal system of criminal law," which, in his view, "should forbid" a judge from basing "her sentencing decisions on an all-embracing consideration of the offender's whole life and character."[42] This entails that, for Duff, judges – those charged with making people suffer – should treat those about to potentially be made to suffer as *abstractions*. And Duff thinks that this is not merely tolerable but right and good: "[A] liberal system of criminal law that is to respect its citizens' privacy will need to abstract agents quite drastically, if it is to avoid intruding improperly into the deeper, more personal, aspects of citizens' characters and lives."[43]

I cannot help thinking that Duff's worry about overstepping reasonable liberal limits is misplaced. Even if a correct understanding of liberalism includes respecting people's privacy roughly along the ways Duff assumes, it surely includes also a particular view of the criminal law. *Part* of the rationale for many a procedural matter in the criminal law, after all, is to protect alleged (or real) wrongdoers from possible abuses by the state concerning the ways in which it wields its immense punitive power. As Ronald Dworkin eloquently put it:

[I]t would be a mistake to suppose that the liberal thinks that ... procedural rights will improve the *accuracy* of the criminal process, that is, the probability that any particular decision about guilt or innocence will be the right one. Procedural rights intervene in the process, even at the cost of inaccuracy, to compensate in a rough way for the antecedent risk that a criminal process, especially if it is largely

39 See Zaibert, *Punishment and Retribution*, 144–154, and Leo Zaibert and Barry Smith, "The Varieties of Normativity: An Essay on Social Ontology," in *Intentional Acts and Institutional Facts: Essays in John Searle's Social Ontology* (Savas Tsohatzidis, ed.), Dordrecht: Springer (2007): 157–174. See also Leo Zaibert, "Rules, Games, and the Axiological Foundations of (International) Criminal Law," *International Criminal Law Review* 16.2 (2016): 346–360.
40 Duff, "The Intrusion ...," 376. 41 Ibid., 371. 42 Ibid., 371–372. 43 Ibid., 371.

administered by one class against another, will be corrupted by the impact of external preferences that cannot be eliminated directly.[44]

Duff's desire for the state not to probe too deeply into the individuals' "motives, attitudes, or character"[45] should be reexamined in the cases at hand – in cases of mercy, in which the probing would seek to *protect* the individual from the state's exercise of its punitive power. This would admittedly constitute an asymmetrical treatment: encroachment into privacy should be permitted in cases in which this may redound in the individual's benefit and not in cases in which it may hurt her. But this asymmetry is neither uncommon nor problematic. There are many instances in the criminal law in which we make exceptions in favor of the defendant, such as the defenses associated to the *res judicata* or the *in dubio pro reo* principles, among many others. Given the enormous power differential between the state and the typical criminal defendant, these asymmetries seem not only not problematic but downright convenient.

Crucially, the main reason why, as a matter of *political* philosophy, we may decide not to look too closely into the defendant's whole life or to consider a wider variety of values than typically considered in criminal trials is that they may further *harm* the individual. We wish to *protect* individuals from an overzealous and over-powerful punisher. Contra Duff, I think that it is inaccurate to say that these considerations do not belong in the "game" of criminal law. For example, no one can seriously doubt that a defendant who although acquitted of a crime is later revealed to have actually committed it is to be assessed differently from one who was acquitted and was in fact innocent. The reason we recognize the "defense" of *res judicata* is not that we think that the fact that the acquitted defendant actually committed the crime "does not belong" in the criminal law or does not matter for our normative assessment of her conduct. Rather, the explanation is that this is a (liberal) way of protecting individuals from the state's punitive power. And, in general, individuals should be protected from the awesome punitive power of the state, even if, in this or that particular case, this or that guilty defendant may "get away with it."

I would thus suggest that what explains Duff's modeling state punishment on games is not, in spite of what he says, an alleged commitment to liberalism.[46] Rather, his game model is the result of his (perhaps unwitting) aversion to engage with precisely those deep and sometimes very difficult conflicts of values that a pluralistic axiology of punishment generates and reveals. Games, after all, must have clearly

---

[44] Ronald Dworkin, *A Matter of Principle*, Cambridge, MA: Harvard University Press (1985): 197–198. For more on this see Leo Zaibert, "The Moralist Strikes Back," *New Criminal Law Review* 14.1 (2011): 139–161. I emphasize that Dworkin's insightful remark captures *part* of the rationale behind procedural safeguards because I believe that considerations related to what people deserve play a role too.

[45] Duff, "The Intrusion . . . ," 371.

[46] In fact, sometimes Duff appears to take his communicative approach in ostensibly illiberal ways. As von Hirsch points out, Duff's view "is meant to elicit certain *internal* states" in wrongdoers; and he reminds us, too, that "when censuring, we [should] act more as judges than as abbots" – see Andrew von Hirsch, *Censure and Sanctions*, 72, and 73.

specified constitutive rules, and these rules are inimical to real, deep conflicts of values. So, while Duff admits that, in general, "we face a world of diverse and irreconcilable values which make ineluctably conflicting demands on us,"[47] he also is quick to add: "[W]e must of course be careful not to embrace conflict too readily: it can be exciting, or at least easier than careful thought, to leap to the conclusion that what we face in this or that situation is an irremediable conflict of values."[48] It is hard to ascertain what exactly Duff has in mind when he claims that to be alive to difficult moral conflicts is "exciting" or when he asserts that recognizing these conflicts is somehow an abdication of "careful thought."[49] But what is beyond doubt is that Duff finds these conflicts bothersome and that he wishes to isolate the "logic" of "our practices"[50] or the "logic of punishment"[51] or "the logic" of mercy from exposure to them.[52]

This is why Duff sees the conflict between justice and mercy not as a conflict between two values that are on a par. For Duff, this conflict is not "*within* the perspective of one institution, but rather between that perspective (the perspective of the criminal law, within which sentencers function, and within which offenders appear to be judged and sentenced as offenders) and others which also claim our allegiance."[53] In cabining justice so neatly and in eschewing precisely those conflicts that are intrinsic to the moral complexity of punishment – the problem of the need to impart justice by means of making people suffer – Duff's communicative approach is revealed as simplemindedly monistic too. This may not be the same exact simpleminded monism we encountered before, but it is simpleminded monism nonetheless.

It may be thought that my case against the alleged attractiveness of the communicative theory of punishment is now complete. To the extent that Duff's version of this theory is authoritative and influential and to the extent I am right in my preceding arguments, the theory does not really meet the three reasons I suggested at the outset explain its alleged attractiveness. In other words, it is not clear what is necessarily humane about the communicative theory, it is not clear how the theory may combine various laudable punishment goals, and it is not clear how it may support the type of pluralism that ought to be supported. Recall that a *properly* pluralistic justification will centrally value the infliction of deserved suffering *and* its merciful remission. Since Duff explicitly rejects the latter, he evidently is not a proper pluralist. Still, I think it is worth considering another, in my opinion more promising, communicative theory of punishment. Despite its many and profound merits, this other theory is to be ultimately rejected too, but it is useful for my purposes to discuss it at length, in light of the way in which it contrasts with

47  Duff, "The Intrusion . . .," 379–380.    48  *Ibid.*, 380.
49  Perhaps Duff is afraid of the sort of "conflict fetishism" I mentioned when discussing Bennett's views in Chapter 4. Still, recognizing conflicts need not be fetishistic at all.
50  Duff, "The Intrusion . . .," 373.    51  Echoing Tasioulas's position on "Mercy," 362, fn. 2.
52  Duff, "The Intrusion . . .," 377.    53  *Ibid.*, 380.

Duff's theory in particular and in light of the problems it reveals about the communicative approach in general.

## 5.3 A VARIETY OF SKEPTICISMS

On first approximation, it may appear that the story about the debate between Duff and Tasioulas is straightforward: Duff believes that mercy is an "intrusion" (in the sense just discussed), and Tasioulas does not. Things are, however, considerably more complicated. The first thing that needs to be underscored is that this debate is none other than the debate between (Duff's) monism and (Tasioulas's) pluralism. It is precisely in virtue of the fact that Duff sees mercy as an intrusion that Tasioulas rightly sees him as a monist (and precisely in virtue of the fact that he does not himself see mercy as an intrusion – and that he values desert *too* – that Tasioulas is rightly seen as a pluralist). While I think that Tasioulas is correct in seeing a strong connection between Duff's jaundiced view of mercy's role within punishment theory and monism, this needs further explanation.

In light of the fact that Duff's communicative theory of punishment seeks to combine so many different goals – deserved censure and the three Rs – how could it still be considered monistic?[54] A plausible answer should include the point just made: a punishment theory that does not value mercy is not *properly* pluralistic, even if it may (as does Duff's) value a variety of punishment goals. It is in not being properly pluralistic that Duff's position can be seen as monistic. Now, Tasioulas admits that Duff is "the contemporary philosopher to whose writings on crime and punishment [he is] most indebted."[55] But what Tasioulas admires the most in Duff's work is his *general* endorsement of value pluralism. As we have seen repeatedly throughout the book, a certain disconnect between individual thinkers' general views and their views on punishment in particular is a very common phenomenon: Scanlon, Nussbaum, and Tadros, among many others, are pluralists in general yet not pluralists in the right ways when it comes to punishment. Duff is no exception: his general pluralism coexists with his monism regarding punishment. Whether or not Tasioulas realizes how common this phenomenon is, he rightly sees a "deep tension" between Duff's general pluralism and his "reductionism" regarding punishment.[56]

It is crucial at this point to clear up two terminological obscurities. Investigating why Tasioulas would choose to use "reductionism" rather than "monism" (or "nonpluralism") to refer to the opposite of "pluralism" is unimportant for my purposes. What is important is to clarify, in the first instance, that by "reductionism" Tasioulas evidently can be taken to mean "monism" (or "non-pluralism"). Secondly, there is a general obscurity as to what exactly the term "unity" means when it comes to

---

[54] The question is pertinent independently of whether Duff's theory ultimately succeeds.

[55] Tasioulas, "Where Is . . .," 37.

[56] See John Tasioulas, "Punishment and Repentance" *Philosophy* 81 (2006): 279–322, *passim*, but explicitly at 286.

punishment theories. Contra Duff, I have argued that vis-à-vis any ordinary (or indeed any useful) sense of the term, his theory (in light of the multiplicity of goals that it explicitly seeks to realize) is not sufficiently "unified." Tasioulas, in contrast, believes that Duff's theory is *too* unified – unified, that is, "under the *aegis* of retributive desert" – and that it is precisely because of its being "unduly dominated by the idea of retributive desert" that the theory fails.[57] This appears to reveal a fundamental disagreement between Tasioulas and myself. Things are, however, otherwise.

It would be absurd to suppose that Tasioulas is not aware of the multiplicity of goals officially at play in Duff's communicative theory of punishment. How, in light of these, can Tasioulas criticize Duff's theory for being *too* unified? The explanation is that what Tasioulas gathers together under the heading "retributive desert" is not really anything particularly retributive, but rather a collection of values whose main commonality is just their opposition to the value of mercy. When Tasioulas refers to "the *aegis* of retributive desert," he does not have in mind the axiological retributivism I defend here, since this type of retributivism is happy sharing the stage with other values – including the value of mercy. And Tasioulas does not have in mind, either, traditionally, deontic retributivism. For Tasioulas recognizes that "the exclusion of mercy is not peculiar to retributive theories." Instead the exclusion is the result of a tendency "at the most abstract level" to "regard norms of justice ... as exhausting the considerations bearing on justified punishment."[58] Since Tasioulas recognizes that this tendency is widespread in these ways, it becomes even clearer that what he means by "retributive desert" is really *justice*, not only as it plays out in retributivism but as it in fact plays out in many a normative ethical theory and in many a justification of punishment. Duff's view is, in Tasioulas's mind, unduly dominated by the *aegis* of justice (not of retributivism), in the sense that Duff sees justice as opposed to and as, in a way, excluding mercy.

As it turns out, then, there is no fundamental disagreement between Tasioulas and me here: the reasons why Tasioulas refers to Duff's communicative theory of punishment as *unitary* are quite similar to my reasons for referring to Duff's theory as *monistic*. Tasioulas here uses "unitary" either as a synonym or as a proxy for "monistic." The spirit of our positions vis-à-vis this aspect of Duff's communicative theory is, I take it, much more similar than the letter of our positions may suggest. Unlike Duff, Tasioulas and I are both proper pluralists about punishment theory; we both agree that Duff fails to capture the central importance of the value of remitting (deserved) punishment, the value of mercy.[59]

---

57  Tasioulas, "Mercy," 286. For another "unified" theory of punishment (not too different from Duff's, though more self-consciously Hegelian), see Thom Brooks, *Punishment*, London: Routledge (2012).
58  Tasioulas, "Mercy," 114.
59  Tasioulas raises a number of other criticisms against Duff's theory with which I will not here engage. Importantly, Tasioulas believes that Duff also "fails to capture the full significance of repentance," see John Tasioulas, "Punishment and ...," 286.

Thus, there is a sense in which Duff can be seen as a *skeptic* regarding mercy or, more specifically, a skeptic regarding the view that mercy has an integral place to play within a punishment theory. Interestingly, the sense in which Duff is a skeptic about mercy is different from any of the multiple forms of mercy skepticism Tasioulas illuminatingly discusses. Tasioulas discusses three forms of mercy skepticism: "transcendence, elimination and reduction,"[60] and in one way or another all these skeptical variations revolve around the idea that mercy, if it really existed, would be *opposed* to justice. The organizing idea is that it can never be morally correct to behave mercifully toward a wrongdoer, insofar as to show mercy is precisely to refuse to treat this wrongdoer in the way that justice demands she be treated. The transcendence strategy consists in positing mercy as a prerogative only belonging to the deity, whose reasons are beyond our capacity to understand. The elimination strategy suggests that what looks like mercy is in fact something else. Finally, the reductionist strategy, in its most popular version, "contends that mercy is equity," whereby mercy is simply a matter of perfecting justice in the concrete case.[61]

The first of these strategies can, I think, be dismissed rather summarily, for this is a version of the type of theological theodicy that we encountered before, which explains problems away by *deus ex machina* suggesting that mere humans cannot understand the deity's reasons. Understandably, Tasioulas finds this strategy unattractive. I do too – and I can scarcely add to his observation that sometimes *humans* forgive (or show mercy) and that the transcendence strategy has to either remain silent on these cases or else seek to (dogmatically) explain them away by suggesting that they are somehow not genuine instances of forgiveness (or mercy).[62] Luckily, neither Duff nor any important participant in the contemporary secular discussion of punishment pays much attention to this strategy.

The second skeptical strategy is also easily dismissed, even if not as easily as the first one. It should suffice to note that while it is true that often what appears as an instance of mercy (or forgiveness) is in fact something else (say, an excuse, or a justification), the fact that this confusion is *possible* – or even widespread – does not show that there are no genuine cases of mercy.[63] Defenders of this form of skepticism need to show that *all* there is to mercy is a confusion, and not merely that they can *sometimes* theoretically account for mercy in different ways. Otherwise this strategy amounts to nothing more than the eliminativism that is conspicuous in classical utilitarian approaches: just as robust notions of blame or desert, for example, could be "eliminated" in favor or medicinal mechanisms

---

[60] Tasioulas, "Mercy," 109.    [61] Tasioulas, "Mercy," 111.
[62] See, however, David Konstan's thesis that in antiquity forgiveness was indeed seen as an exclusive prerogative of the deity. David Konstan, *Before Forgiveness: The Origins of a Moral Idea*, Cambridge: Cambridge University Press (2012).
[63] See examples in my "The Paradox of Forgiveness."

seeking to steer humans toward the diminution of suffering, so could be a robust notion of mercy.[64]

Finally, Tasioulas is unquestionably correct in that an obstacle facing the third skeptical strategy, which seeks to reduce mercy to equity, is that "equitable judgment can both aggravate as well as mitigate strict legal justice."[65] But, as Tasioulas also admits, it is possible to further refine and qualify the reductionist strategy so as to account for the asymmetry between aggravation and mitigation and to somehow isolate "mitigating equity" as the operative notion. Still, Tasioulas opposes this strategy because in such cases "reduction 'saves' mercy only at the price of sacrificing its irreducible distinctiveness."[66]

While I again agree with Tasioulas here, an uncharitable reading of Tasioulas's opposition to the reductive strategy would view it as viciously circular. For he could be interpreted as claiming that the strategy seeking to deny mercy's distinctiveness fails in that it denies mercy's distinctiveness. Seeking to stave off this reading, a safer way of dealing with this form of skepticism is to note that *in extremis* the reduction strategy just boils down to the elimination strategy. And one could then deploy the arguments against the elimination strategy against the "improved" version of the reduction strategy ("improved" merely in the sense of restricting itself to "mitigating equity"). This suggested amendment may reveal that Tasioulas is in fact discussing two, not three, skeptical versions of mercy skepticism.

Independently of how many specific versions of skepticism there are, however, Tasioulas believes that it is (some version of) the communicative theory of punishment that allows us to incorporate mercy into the discussion of punishment. Thus, after insightfully discussing – and, in my opinion, convincingly rejecting – these various skeptical positions, Tasioulas concludes: "[W]e can make room for mercy only by putting retributive justice in its proper, if still central, place as one value among others in an account of justified punishment." To which he immediately adds: "[T]he so-called communicative theory of punishment is ... best understood as enabling us to do precisely this."[67] There exists, then, a certain structural, or strategic, similarity between Tasioulas and Duff. Where Duff turns to the communicative theory as an antidote to skepticism about a "unitary" justification of punishment, Tasioulas turns to the communicative theory of punishment as an antidote to skepticism about mercy (and eventually to that very monism he rightly detects in Duff's theory of punishment).

At this stage, two interrelated and important questions suggest themselves. First, to what extent do these rejections of skepticism affect Duff's communicative theory of punishment? After all, Duff does not appear to be a skeptic about mercy in any of these three ways: he expressly admits that mercy is a virtue, he does not chalk up the talk of mercy to the inscrutable workings of deities, and he does not appear to

---

[64]  See Smart's endorsement of this strategy in his "An Outline of a System of Utilitarian Ethics," in
       Smart and Williams, *Utilitarianism: For and Against*, 46 ff.
[65]  Tasioulas, "Mercy," 112.   [66] *Ibid.*, 114.   [67] *Ibid.*

eliminate or reduce the notion in the ways Tasioulas discusses (even though Tasioulas does dub Duff's position "reductionist"). Second, to what extent is the communicative theory of punishment of help in refuting mercy skepticism? After all, Duff is unquestionably a communicative theorist, and he nonetheless, by Tasioulas's own admission, fails to recognize the significance of mercy. Moreover, and even more importantly, none of the arguments Tasioulas has presented against mercy skepticism – convincing as they are – turns on anything communicative: transcendence is rejected for his obscurantism, and elimination and reduction are rejected after they are shown to be woefully inchoate.

Perhaps the first question can be answered in what appears to be a quick, straightforward way. Although it is odd that Tasioulas would not register quite the exact way in which Duff is a mercy skeptic, he clearly is a mercy skeptic. Insofar as Duff believes that mercy does not belong in the game of punishment, the fact that he is not a skeptic in the ways Tasioulas considers does not at all show that he is not a skeptic in yet another way. We are better off assuming that Tasioulas's list of mercy skepticisms is not exhaustive. In order to describe Duff's own variety of mercy skepticism, a term I introduced in the previous chapter seems fitting again: gerry-mandering. How exactly are the boundaries between "the game of punishment" and other "games" drawn? Duff's stipulation that mercy has no "place" within the context of punishment is reminiscent of the Moorean gambit whereas this or that consideration does not have a place within the "internal" justification of punishment but only in "the budget room." What good does it do to admit that mercy is virtuous (and that to act mercifully is to act rightly, etc.), as Duff does, if one *also* maintains – as Duff also maintains – that mercy has no place within the game of punishment? So, in order to account for Duff's own variety of mercy skepticism, in addition to "transcendence," "elimination," and "reduction," we need to recognize a form of mercy skepticism that is predicated on the gerrymandering of normative spaces.

The answer to the second question, in contrast, is more complicated. Of course, Tasioulas suggests that in addition to Duff's "three Rs," "a further type of considera-tion, that of mercy," ought to be recognized.[68] But it is plain that, unlike any of the three Rs, mercy is not a goal of punishment in the sense that any of Duff's three Rs can be seen as a *goal* of punishment. So, without at least some guidance as to a different sense of "goal," this suggestion by itself is not terribly helpful. More significant, however, is the fact that none of Tasioulas's other arguments for taking mercy seriously (most of which are quite compelling) seem to me to be connected to anything particularly communicative.

Tasioulas asks us to consider four kinds of cases that allegedly highlight the value of mercy: cases in which a wrongdoer's upbringing was truly terrible, cases in which reasons for leniency (different from those typically relevant in a court of law) obtain, cases in which the wrongdoer has already suffered enough (though not as a result of

---

[68]    *Ibid.*, 115.

previous punishment), and cases in which the wrongdoer has already repented (and reformed, apologized, etc.). About these cases he tells us that

> the facts brought into view *qua* grounds for mercy favour leniency but not by revising downwards the level of punishment judged to be deserved. Instead, the general idea underlying such grounds is that the imposition of the sentence warranted by the retributive norm is an excessive hardship.[69]

Assume Tasioulas's view is correct. Still, it is hard to see what is necessarily *communicative* about it. Furthermore, when Tasioulas does foreground a communicative element, he does so in ways strikingly similar to Duff's own example discussed earlier. Thus, Tasioulas asks us to imagine a "bereaved father" who also deserves some punishment and whose nonpunitive suffering, if added to his deserved (punitive) suffering, would render his overall suffering excessive. And he tells us that "to force him to attend to his wrongdoing in a way that takes no account of the fact that he is already consumed by suffering and remorse" would be "harsh, and at the limit, *cruel*."[70] Again, assume Tasioulas is correct. The communicative theory still does not add much. As I argued when discussing Duff's example of deciding not to have a conversation with a wrongdoer friend when we learn that the friend is bereaved, one could also, for the same reasons, refuse to slash the tires of his car – a perfectly non-communicative punishment. The alleged harshness or cruelty would be the result *not* of forcing him to attend to this or that message but of the fact that his suffering would be excessive independently of any communication.

As it turns out, then, despite loudly trumpeting an allegedly great importance of the communicative approach in explaining the importance of the unique and irreducible value of mercy, important aspects of Tasioulas's position, just like in Duff's, are revealed as not really relying on communication after all. As I will show next, the similarities between Duff and Tasioulas in fact go much deeper.

## 5.4 TALES FROM TOPOGRAPHIC OCEANS

I will conclude this chapter discussing why Tasioulas's arguments showing how his views differ from Duff's are unsuccessful and why, in the end, Tasioulas is closer to Duff than he may realize. (In the next chapter, I explain the root error in Tasioulas's approach in greater detail.)

The first of Tasioulas's arguments involves problematizing the notion of "unity." Tasioulas suggests that there are in fact two senses of unity: "substantive" and "formal." Tasioulas does not really define these terms too rigorously, but he is explicit in that he wishes to replace the "substantive unity" of Duff's communicative theory, with a certain "formal unity." It is not entirely clear how, if the conceptual proximity between his sense of "unity" and "monism" I have suggested is correct, this

---

[69]   *Ibid.*, 119.    [70]   *Ibid.*

could possibly be a helpful way of putting it for a pluralist. Is Tasioulas in favor, then, of "formal monism"? It seems to me that Tasioulas thinks that he has to accept some form of "unity" in order to avoid his theory "issuing in a mere colocation of disparate evaluative concerns."[71] In other words, Tasioulas thinks that he needs to fasten to some form of "unity" (even if just "formal") in order to preserve a certain "coherence" to his theory of punishment: properly construed "the desideratum of unity" in theories such as Duff's is one that "even a pluralistic theory must respect."[72]

Tasioulas's worry is very serious and very important. One of the goals of this book is to show how one can indeed have a properly pluralistic justification of punishment that *coherently* combines a variety of values (even if I, like Tasioulas, focus on *two* of those values). But regarding the problem at hand, I cannot escape concluding that Tasioulas simply equivocates, in effect using two senses of "unity": one in which "unity" means "monism" and another one in which "unity" means "coherence." When Tasioulas talks about "formal unity," he is to be understood as meaning "formal coherence," not "formal monism." Needless to say, any theory better seek to be coherent. And the coherence of Duff's theory, despite all its moving parts, does not seem to me to be jeopardized by its alleged subservience to "retributive desert."

The distinction between substantive and formal unity seems to be related, in Tasioulas's estimation, to another distinction he makes: one between what he calls "top-down," or "theory-driven," approaches, on the one hand,[73] and an unnamed, but presumably not top-down, or not theory-driven, approach, on the other. Someone instantiates what Tasioulas calls a "top-down" approach to punishment when she begins, as it were, by embracing a comprehensive moral doctrine (or some other general starting point) – typically, either deontology or utilitarianism – and then applies it to the specific case of punishment – thus becoming either a retributivist or a consequentialist as if by default. I reject this strategy as much as Tasioulas does. I have, however, insisted on the fact that endorsing one of these comprehensive moral doctrines does not *entail* anything in particular within the realm of punishment theory as such: endorsing deontology does not entail that one must endorse retributivism; endorsing comprehensive consequentialism does not entail endorsing consequentialism about punishment.[74]

Tasioulas believes that both deontology and (classical) utilitarianism presuppose a certain monism and that if either of these comprehensive moral doctrines is our starting point, then their generic monism will infect, too, our approach to punishment. Thus, he suggests that starting our thinking about punishment from either of the classical comprehensive moral doctrines would promote a "regimentation that leads to a reduction in both the number of values or principles relevant to the justification of punishment and also the potential for conflicts among them."[75] As we

---

[71] Tasioulas, "Punishment and ...," 286.    [72] *Ibid.*
[73] *Ibid.*, 279–283. I assume that Tasioulas uses these two expressions as synonyms. I will use them as synonyms.
[74] See Chapter 1.    [75] Tasioulas, "Punishment and ...," 280.

have seen already (above all in Chapter 2) the relationship between the top and the bottom is complicated. *Ideal* utilitarianism is a "top" comprehensive moral doctrine in which the right type of pluralism (regarding a variety of phenomena, including punishment) can nonetheless thrive. And as we have just seen in this chapter, and as Tasioulas in effect recognizes, Duff is neither a full-blown deontologist nor a full-blown utilitarian, though he denies pluralism when it comes to punishment. This underscores that the real problem is monism – and monism can come in the top-down variety or in any other. Thus, while I am not unsympathetic to the rejection of top-down approaches (as, say, my endorsement of particularism in Chapter 2 evinces), I do not think that this consideration helps us to sufficiently distinguish between Tasioulas's and Duff's theory of punishment.

One is to assume that Tasioulas thinks that Duff's theory is somehow top-down and that his own is not. But, construed so generally, it is not clear how this "top-down" description does not apply, too, to Tasioulas's own approach. Rather than proceeding from either deontology or consequentialism toward a certain view of the justification of punishment, Tasioulas could be seen as proceeding "from a commitment to ethical pluralism" (or from a "skepticism about the claims of top-down theory").[76] The "down" remains constant in all cases: the justification of punishment; but Tasioulas merely replaces the "top." Admittedly, "ethical pluralism" is not a comprehensive moral doctrine – but it is, if anything, an even more general metaethical position than these comprehensive moral doctrines. So, the structure of his position could thus be seen as top-down as well.

Even if I am right in thinking that Tasioulas's position is more like Duff's than he realizes, there appears to remain the unquestionable difference between the two authors. Duff believes that mercy is an intrusion, and Tasioulas does not. But even this can be questioned. The questioning is necessarily circuitous, but not for that any less instructive. Let us begin by considering Tasioulas's discussion of one effort to reduce mercy to justice: H. S. Hestevold's disjunctive theory of justice.[77] According to this position, justice "issues in a disjunction of penalties of varying degrees of severity, each disjunct representing adequate 'deserved' punishment for the wrong in question." The merciful person would be "characterized by the disposition to select one of the less severe disjuncts."[78] Perceptively, Tasioulas rejects this strategy, calling it "ultimately artificial" given that its "reliance on the disjuncts of deserved punishment ranging in practically every instance from whatever maximum penalty is stipulated by justice to a disjunct imposing no penalty" ends up "emptying retributive justice of its normative content."[79] Not only do I agree with Tasioulas's rejection, but his argument against disjunctive theories can be further strengthened.

---

[76]  *Ibid.*, 283.

[77]  H. S. Hestevold, "Justice to Mercy," *Philosophy and Phenomenological Research* 46 (1985): 281–291. For a similar recent version of this sort of argument, see G. Duus-Otterström, "Why Retributivism Should Endorse Leniency in Punishment," *Law and Philosophy* 32 (2014): 459–483.

[78]  Tasioulas, "Mercy," 125.    [79]  *Ibid.*

After all, according to this strategy, acting on *any* of the permissible choices – potentially ranging *widely* from whatever is the maximum punishment for the act to no punishment whatsoever – would be to discharge one's duty (of justice), and this would cast doubt not only on the normative content of the notion of duty but on its very *cogency*. In other words, if for any given action, one has many, perhaps infinite, different "just" responses, then it becomes hard to understand what exactly "justice" may mean.

Crucially, Tasioulas points out that this strategy fails to take account of the fact that supererogatory action, such as merciful action, "is not only permissible but also *valuable*." And he adds: "[T]his *axiological* point is independent of, and partly accounts for, mercy's deontic implications."[80] Tasioulas's position *here* is utterly disconnected from anything communicative. Furthermore, it appears to involve precisely the axiological turn in punishment theory that I recommend. Unfortunately, immediately after registering the singular axiological significance of mercy, and in fact immediately after admitting that he wishes to avoid "straight-jacketing it into a particular deontic shape,"[81] Tasioulas, it appears to me, does exactly that: he straightjackets the value of mercy into a particular deontic shape.

Bernard Williams famously argued that it is a mistake "to try to make everything into obligations [or duties]."[82] On first approximation, it may appear that Tasioulas agrees with Williams, not only given his general position vis-à-vis the limits of theory and his general suspicion of top-down approaches but also specifically given the fact that he thinks that the view that "only a duty can defeat a duty" is an "illusory idea."[83] But when Tasioulas discusses the role of mercy in the courtroom, however, things get very confusing very quickly. Immediately after distancing himself from the "illusory idea," Tasioulas describes the view that he favors as follows:

> [D]uties are particularly stringent sorts of reasons for action: their applicability to their subjects is non-optional, their force is in some degree exclusionary of otherwise applicable reasons, they are typically grounded in a due sensitivity to the interests of others and failure to comply with them is regarded as a basis for criticism. When mercy rightly tempers justice it requires us to depart from the obligation to comply with justice that would otherwise apply.[84]

And then Tasioulas unequivocally asserts: "Only a duty of mercy, I think, could have that effect."[85]

I am unsure, then, about how Tasioulas's position here really differs from what he himself terms an illusory idea. For he explicitly admits that, in the courtroom, the only way in which mercy could play a real and effective role is for it to be conceived of as a duty (or as an obligation). At least within the specific context of the behavior of

---

[80] *Ibid.*, 126. Emphases added.   [81] *Ibid.*
[82] Bernard Williams, *Ethics and the Limits of Philosophy*, London: Routledge (2006), 180. I will return to Williams's point in the next chapter.
[83] Tasioulas, "Mercy," 126.   [84] *Ibid.*   [85] *Ibid.*

a "criminal court judge," Tasioulas believes that "only a *duty* to grant mercy could possess the normative force needed to justify deviation from his duty to implement justice."[86] And this seems to be nothing less than (an instantiation of) the illusory view whereby only a duty can defeat a duty, even if it is perhaps supposed to hold only in the case of punishment or in the case of state punishment.

In light of this, Tasioulas's disagreement with Duff regarding mercy begins to get blurry. For I argued previously that Duff's reason for excluding mercy from the "game of punishment" is not really a liberal concern for privacy but rather a concern with "the logic of punishment" and the proper functioning of the criminal law. Duff explicitly excludes mercy from the logic of punishment in order for this logic to play itself out. But this, too, is what leads Tasioulas to accept a "deeply counterintuitive" idea of mercy.[87] This counterintuitive idea of mercy, moreover, seems to force us to recognize not only a duty of mercy but the no less counterintuitive idea of a "right" to mercy, features that, Tasioulas also admits, "stretch credulity."[88] Just like Duff, Tasioulas embraces this self-consciously counterintuitive apparatus in order to let the logic of punishment play itself out.

Admittedly, Tasioulas's worry as to the proper functioning of the criminal law is not baseless. For example, it is not merely that Tasioulas thinks that if mercy were not a duty (or a duty-like entity of some sort), it would be limp and thus unable to defeat the judge's duties of justice. Tasioulas is also concerned with issues of comparative and procedural fairness: if mercy did not issue in duties and rights, then like cases may not be treated quite alike, and procedural fairness would be violated. Tasioulas, however, assuages his own worry:

> [E]ven if procedural fairness is violated in [some] cases, it is but one value among others, and it may be judged worth the cost of introducing an element of inconstancy into the penal system if it is thereby rendered more humane. Indeed, the offender himself potentially stood to gain from a merciful judgment. The fact that he has not simply puts him in the position he would have occupied were the system concerned exclusively with retributive justice.[89]

I, for one, find Tasioulas's reaction to the worries about procedural justice effective and compelling (perhaps because it shares a spirit with my own reaction to Duff's worries about the fact that to allow mercy into the courtroom would entail the violation of liberal principles concerning privacy). Oddly, however, immediately after presenting it, Tasioulas distances himself from this reaction. While he admits that this response has some effectiveness vis-à-vis the worries related to procedural fairness, he thinks that it nonetheless fails to "overcome a deeper point." The deeper point relates

not to the fact that others similarly situated stand to benefit from mercy whereas the offender has not, but rather [to the fact] that what is determining something as important as an offender's sentence is the personality of the judge who happens to decide his case.[90]

I do not see how this "deeper" worry cannot be assuaged too with a similar argument to the one Tasioulas offered before. To paraphrase him: this offender would not be worse off than he would have been had we not admitted mercy into the criminal law, and even some inconstancy (allegedly based exclusively on judges' personalities) may be worth admitting if it ushers in more humanness. Humanness strikes me as a rather important value, and thus it can be mobilized both regarding worries related to procedural justice and worries related to an alleged expansion of the impact that mere differences in judges' personalities may have on offenders' fates.

Even if I am missing the depth of Tasioulas's worry about judges' personalities or if I am wrong in thinking that his own response to the "superficial" problem of procedural fairness can effectively be deployed regarding it, Tasioulas is aware of at least another, independent, complication facing his position. Tasioulas seems forced to recognize "a radical asymmetry between personal and judicial decision-making." After all, the worry does not seem very serious in the personal realm, where "we find it unobjectionable that when reason underdetermines the outcome it is an individual's tastes and inclinations [i.e., her personality] that take over."[91] In contradistinction to what happens in the personal context, Tasioulas believes that in the institutional context this phenomenon of personality playing too impor-tant a role (even though only when the case is underdetermined) would be objec-tionable. Unfortunately, Tasioulas does not tell us how to avoid this state of affairs that he rejects, except for swinging away from axiology and back toward not even the communicative approach but the very deontic straitjacketing he is otherwise trying to avoid. Moreover, Tasioulas concludes his article with what strikes me as a beautiful but nonetheless enigmatic abdication: "[I]n some cases, the proper response to the problem [of the role of mercy within institutions such as the criminal law] may itself be underdetermined by reason."[92]

Once the dust settles, then, the apparently straightforward difference between Tasioulas and Duff – again: Duff believes that mercy is an intrusion and Tasioulas does not – turns out to be much more complicated. For Duff sees mercy as an intrusion because, *given an intuitive understanding* of mercy (whereby it is not deontically straitjacketed), it has no obvious place within the logic of punishment. Tasioulas's position is to welcome mercy within the logic of punishment, but only a counterintuitive, deontically straitjacketed understanding of mercy. Startlingly, then, it is likely that the mercy that Duff believes is an intrusion is one that Tasioulas also believes is an intrusion and, conversely, that the mercy that Tasioulas believes is not an intrusion is one Duff may agree is not an intrusion. Surely this makes it

[90] *Ibid.*   [91] *Ibid.*   [92] *Ibid.*, 132.

surprisingly difficult to ascertain what exactly their disagreement is supposed to be about.

Perhaps this possibility also helps explain the fact that in a matter of only a few years Tasioulas's understanding of his debate with Duff seems to have undergone a remarkable transformation. As we have seen, in early writings Tasioulas claimed that his disagreement with Duff centered on the fact that Tasioulas is a pluralist regarding the justification of punishment whereas Duff is a monist (or, again, a "reductionist"). More recently, however, Tasioulas has described the debate rather differently, claiming that what he and Duff "disagree about is a question of moral *topography*, as it were, concerning the *location* of mercy in relation to the institution of legal punishment."[93] The topographical motif then allows Tasioulas to describe the debate not in terms of pluralism versus monism but in terms of (his) "internalism" versus (Duff's) "externalism": Duff has to see mercy as "an intruder that subverts the logic of punishment" and as necessarily opposed to the "more internally differentiated and potentially conflictual account of the logic of punishment" that Tasioulas favors.[94] To repeat, insofar as Tasioulas relies on an idiosyncratic understanding of mercy, whereby it issues in counterintuitively precise rights and duties, it is not very clear how his logic of punishment is more potentially conflictual than Duff's. After all, whatever conflicts Tasioulas's position may encounter, they will presumably be easily resolvable, in that it will be clear when the duties of mercy defeat the duties of justice and when they do not. They will be at least as "easily" resolvable as the conflicts that arise in matters of punishment even if mercy would be considered an intrusion.

Tasioulas's invocation of spatial imagery is reminiscent of Moore's own invocation of internal and external realms (discussed in last chapter). The moves are evidently not identical: Moore mobilized the spatial imagery (concerning internal and external justifications) in order to defend his retributivism from pointed objections, whereas Tasioulas mobilizes it merely in order to describe the nature of a debate he has with Duff. But I think that there is at least one crucially important similarity between the two mobilizations: they allow these authors to avoid taking the axiological turn seriously. Tasioulas's most recent way of describing his debate with Duff effectively dilutes its importance.

Contra Tasioulas himself, his debate with Duff should not be seen as merely about moral topography; properly understood, the debate ought to be seen as concerning the tension between monism and pluralism. Duff is not an axiological pluralist about punishment, whereas Tasioulas is (or at least wants to be). As such, Tasioulas is indeed alive to the fact that the problem of the justification of problem is much more complicated than the comfortable and convenient monistic axiology of Duff (and of deontic retributivism and classical utilitarianism) can possibly take it to be.

---

[93]  Tasioulas, "Where Is . . .," 38. Emphasis added.    [94]  *Ibid.,* 39.

As we have just seen, Tasioulas flirts with the axiological turn but does not quite commit to it. His endorsing what he admits is an idiosyncratic understanding of mercy whereby it issues in rights and duties and his redescription of his debate with Duff in topographical terms are but symptoms of that lack of commitment. And then, notwithstanding the fact that Tasioulas's position regarding the justification of punishment is, to my knowledge, the one position that has come closest to embracing the type of axiological pluralism about punishment I am here recommending, this lack of commitment is to be lamented.

### 5.5 CONCLUSION

This chapter has been devoted to the consideration of the fashionable communicative justifications of punishment because they appeared to offer a promising framework both for understanding the complexity in the justification of punishment and for humanizing the institutional infliction of punishment. Despite appearances, however, there is nothing necessarily humane about the communicative approach, it does not offer sufficient guidance as to how to realize different punishment goals, and it does not really support the type of proper pluralism worth supporting.

For roughly the first half of this chapter, my emphasis was on Duff's version of the communicative theory – again, arguably its most influential contemporary version. On some plausible interpretations, however, the communicative approach can be revealed as, structurally, a new version of classical utilitarianism, in which "suffering avoidance" is replaced by "communicating correct messages." Although I resist interpreting Duff's position in these ways, even when his position is interpreted in more charitable ways that do not reduce it to utilitarianism, Duff's communicative justification of punishment appears to face a variety of obstacles. Chief among these is that the most valuable aspects of Duff's communicative theory do not really have much to do with communication.

In the second half of the chapter, I turned to Tasioulas's version of the communicative justification of punishment. Tasioulas's approach is particularly attractive in that he explicitly offers a version of the communicative theory of punishment that is properly pluralistic. Although officially billed as offering a contrast to Duff's "reductionist" version of the communicative theory, in the final analysis, however, Tasioulas's pluralistic version turns out to be, in important respects, remarkably similar to that reductionist position from which it sought to differentiate itself. While Tasioulas's version of the communicative theory is, in my opinion, the most attractive on offer, it too fails to take the axiological turn seriously enough.

At the outset of one of his excellent articles, Tasioulas tells us:

> I believe we should be sceptical about the ambitions of theory in ethics and that, in abandoning the idea of a master-criterion, we should instead embrace a form of pluralism that recognizes an irreducible plurality of ethical values that are prone to

conflict in individual cases. Moreover, the conflicts among these values are not always rationally resolvable and, even where they are, they are not always resolvable by appeal to a pre-given principle nor always resolvable without remainder.[95]

It should by now be obvious that I wholeheartedly agree with the spirit of these remarks, emphasizing as they do exactly that type of pluralism I have been defending throughout the book. If a given theory were to be dominated by a single value (as Tasioulas thinks retributive desert dominates Duff's position but also as suffering avoidance evidently dominates classical utilitarianism), then it will be unduly monistic (or "unified," in one of Tasioulas's senses of the term). As such, it would eschew the richness and depth of the conflicts that a plausible theory of punishment must countenance. Unfortunately, Tasioulas's own understanding of mercy – which he admits is deeply counterintuitive – strikes me as somehow at odds with the spirit of the passage just quoted. For if mercy really gave rise to rights and duties in the deontically straitjacketed and counterintuitive way Tasioulas claims it does, it is hard to see how it could then generate the deep conflicts that sometimes may not be "rationally resolvable" and that do not resolve "without remainder," of which Tasioulas speaks in the passage just quoted.

[95]  Tasioulas, "Punishment and . . .," 279.

# 6

# The Allure of the Ledger: Better Than a Dog Anyhow

Despite the many important differences among the justifications of punishment discussed thus far, they all share one common shortcoming. Their adherents do not take the axiological turn I recommend seriously enough. This is a shortcoming insofar as it is precisely by taking this axiological turn that we can then take pluralism seriously, in ways likely to advance the debate over punishment and its justification. Of all the authors we have discussed, John Tasioulas comes closest to embracing this pluralism. He comes so close because he believes that forgiveness (or "mercy," as we have seen)[1] should, in hitherto insufficiently recognized ways, be part of any effort to offer a robust justification of punishment. Tasioulas understands that the attempt to justify punishment without considering the value of inflicting deserved punishment *in concert* with the value of mercifully remitting it is importantly incomplete.

Tasioulas ultimately falls short because he defines "mercy" in ways that undermine his own otherwise illuminating criticism of the (exaggerated and naïve) ambitions of (moral) theory that I discussed at the end of the previous chapter. Tasioulas's criticism of the usual expectations vis-à-vis moral theory – regardless of whether we take "theory" to mean a comprehensive moral doctrine or, more specifically, a particular approach to the justification of punishment – is, like Bernard Williams's, illuminating above all because it highlights that these expectations betray a failure to take seriously the complexity of moral life. Moral dilemmas – again, whether at the level of comprehensive moral doctrines or, more specifically, at the level of justifications of punishment – often do not resolve neatly: they often generate deep conflicts, not always resolvable and, when resolvable, often not without remainders. Despite his laudable recognition of the limits of theory, Tasioulas in the end succumbs to the temptation to "normalize" punishment theory via the mobilization of a peculiar understanding of mercy that is in the final analysis not likely to admit complex moral dilemmas.

---

[1] John Tasioulas "Mercy," *Proceedings of the Aristotelian Society* 103 (2003): 101–132.

The way forward is to acknowledge that for a justification of punishment to succeed where others have failed is to take the interplay between punishment and forgiveness seriously, more seriously than even Tasioulas has. This is the first, and foremost, step of a properly pluralistic justification of punishment. A corollary to this first step is that the forgiveness worth our attention is precisely that which gives rise to precisely the complex moral dilemmas that Tasioulas's "normalized" sense of mercy actually avoids. My recommendation as to what is the way forward may appear paradoxical, for to incorporate into one's justification of punishment forgiveness in the sense I defend it – a sense that, unlike Tasioulas's, does not issue in *duties* to forgive – seems to render the justification of punishment too unmanageably messy. How can *that* be the way forward?

It would no doubt be wonderful if one's theories always had something perfectly precise to say about what people ought to value or do. This would not be quite so wonderful, however, if such precision is bought at the price of oversimplifications of the world in which we live. And I think that all extant justifications of punishment are guilty, albeit in different ways and degrees, of trafficking in these convenient over-simplifications. The way forward *does* involve advancing a justification of punishment displaying more complexity than its traditional alternatives but because this is to more meaningfully engage with the complexity of the underlying moral universe.

Before delving directly into the interplay between the values of punishment and forgiveness (something I will undertake in earnest in the next chapter), I wish to discuss in this chapter the ways in which my approach to punishment and its justification fits within the framework of moral philosophy in general. I would like to further clarify the ways in which my approach fits within the context of some general debates in moral philosophy, from which the specialized punishment literature has remained largely isolated. The consideration of these general debates may help explain the origins of some pernicious tendencies within punishment theory in particular.

But this examination of the tradition in moral philosophy in general highlights, too, how remarkably different the state of play is in moral philosophy in general and in punishment theory in particular. As I shall show, some of what I deem pernicious tendencies in criminal law theory have correlates in – and in fact are at times traceable to – tendencies in moral philosophy in general. But within the context of moral philosophy in general, these tendencies coexist with other famous and influential positions that seek to criticize and challenge them. In contrast, at the specific level of punishment theory itself, in vain we look for something resembling, even if only in spirit, these critical positions. In this more specific context, there is virtually nothing like a criticism of these received tendencies.

Part of what we find within the general context of moral philosophy but not within the specific context of punishment theory concerns the nature (and extent) of the guidance that we should expect from theory. It is of course natural to hope – and indeed to try to make sure – that our favored moral philosophy provides us with the tools necessary to actually resolve problems. Thus, a certain disappointment regarding any theory that may be comparatively less able to provide such tools is to a point understandable. It seems potentially too self-serving, and too unproductive, to rest content with one's theory being less able to resolve the problems it was meant to resolve by perhaps too facilely claiming that those problems are too complex and to leave it at that.

The disappointed critic of complex and pluralistic theories may object to them along the following lines: well, if the problems really are so complex that your theory cannot solve them, we then need a better theory. As we saw in the previous chapter, the disappointment that these potential problems may cause may have led Duff to actually "exclude" mercy from the logic of punishment. Even Tasioulas seemed so disappointed that, although he is very much aware of the unique deficiencies in standard approaches to the justification of punishment, he ends up championing a counterintuitive account of mercy anyhow because in his estimation this account averts the disarray that those potentially very complex problems may generate.

By reflecting on our expectations of moral philosophy in the first place, I shall try to keep this disappointment under control. So, in the first section in this chapter, I will offer an interpretation of the perplexing notion of moral luck, whereby it is best understood as questioning a certain too ambitious set of expectations vis-à-vis moral philosophy that are related to a certain imagined *neatness*. This neatness is embodied in the very supposition that there exists a "moral mathematics" that will yield unambiguous solutions to all manner of moral problems. I will suggest that this supposition faces considerable obstacles. In the second and third sections, I engage with Williams's criticisms of some of the central presuppositions of moral philosophy in general. And I will show how these presuppositions have in fact contributed to keeping punishment theory isolated, mostly out of a fear that abandoning these presuppositions would produce a woefully unmanageable approach. Finally, in the fourth section, I will argue that, while the abandonment of these presuppositions may indeed bring about increasing complexity in our theories, such complexity is not only much more manageable than it may be feared, but the avoidance of this complexity is in fact a hindrance to the development of punishment theory.

## 6.1 MORAL LUCK AND MORAL MATHEMATICS

Both expressions in the title of this section must strike the uninitiated as very strange. Nothing, perhaps, comes more naturally to the ordinary person's mind when asked to contrast morality and mathematics than to see the two disciplines as *obviously* antithetical. Mathematics is ordinarily taken to be "objective," precise, and not a matter of opinion, whereas ethics is ordinarily taken to be "subjective," imprecise, and indeed very much a matter of opinion.[2] As for the oddity surrounding the idea of

---

[2]    I am not here endorsing any of these naïve views of morality (or of mathematics) – I am merely pointing to their prevalence among nonspecialists.

"moral luck," it was recognized by the very person who coined the expression in the first place. Almost two decades after he first used the term, Williams told us "when I introduced the expression moral luck, I expected it to suggest an oxymoron."[3] After all, "there is something in our conception of morality . . . that arouses opposition to the idea that moral responsibility or moral merit or moral blame should be subject to luck."[4] The assumption animating "our conception of morality" goes even beyond the problem of moral responsibility and moral merit, covering the whole of morality. We assume that the *whole* of morality must be perfectly immune from luck, in the sense that moral matters are "up to us." The assumption is that moral matters are never arbitrary. As John Rawls, waxing Kantian motifs, has famously put it, "a rational individual is always to act so that he never need blame himself no matter how his plans finally work out."[5]

Williams's example of moral luck that we encountered before, concerning the lorry driver who through no fault of his own runs over a child, does not fit well within this widespread view of morality so neatly captured in Rawls's statement.[6] The standard view suggests that sad as he may be, the driver has nothing to blame himself for, since, *ex hypothesi*, he did not do anything wrong. Williams's point is that there better be *theoretical* room for the driver to feel something more robustly moral than mere (non-moral) sadness when he runs over the child, even if through no fault of his own. And it is in this that moral luck consists: though it was a matter of sheer luck that the child would find himself in front of the lorry, this admittedly fortuitous event does have moral consequences for the morally blameless driver. On my interpretation, Williams's mobilization of the idea of moral luck seeks, at its core, to subvert nothing less than the standard way of understanding morality.

An obligatory presupposition of the widespread view of morality that Rawls expresses in the quotation above is that it is *possible* to plan one's life so as to never have to blame oneself. If Williams is right, however, Rawls is wrong. Accepting something like the idea of moral luck is to *thereby* disrupt the apparent simplicity of the widespread view of morality that Rawls so succinctly captured. My suggestion here is not that, absent the possibility of moral luck, to plan one's life so as to never have to blame oneself would be particularly easy (and I do not think that Rawls, or any other thinker, ever held that). Rather, the suggestion is that it would be *easier* than if, in addition to the inherent complications of the planning itself, one would have to contend with the complexities introduced by accepting the existence of moral luck.

---

[3]  Bernard Williams, "Postscript," in Daniel Statman (ed.), *Moral Luck*, Albany, NY: State University of New York Press (1993): 251–258, at 251.

[4]  *Ibid.*

[5]  John Rawls, *A Theory of Justice* (revised edn.), Cambridge, MA: Harvard University Press (1999), 370–371.

[6]  See Section 4.2 in Chapter 4.

In those rare occasions in which moral philosophers have considered the impact that moral luck may have on punishment theory, they have limited their field of vision to the admittedly very interesting way in which it plays out within the context of criminal attempts.[7] Typically, we are asked to imagine a pair of cases in which two equally blameworthy agents, each attempting to commit an *ex hypothesi* identically reprehensible murder but in which only one of the agents succeeds – the other agent failing as a result of a totally fortuitous, "lucky" occurrence (say, because a bird flew in the trajectory of the bullet, thus saving the otherwise certain victim).[8] Again, I do not wish to deny that this is indeed an important and interesting context in which to discuss (an aspect of) the moral luck problem. But I believe that the problem of moral luck cuts much more deeply, casting doubt on the otherwise overly tidy connection between moral theory *as a whole* and the moral universe that it purports to regulate.

Whether consciously or (much more frequently) unconsciously, in avoiding these extra, inconvenient complexities, moral theorists have gravitated toward much simpler, and indeed simpleminded, positions. Classical utilitarianism (together with its descendants within punishment theory in particular) and deontological ethics (together with its descendants within punishment theory in particular) are instructive examples of this cavalier disregard of the variety of problems the idea of moral luck generates. Just as the view of morality that supports the Rawlsian view whereby it is possible to avoid *ever* having to blame oneself makes matters much easier for him, these views make matter much easier for punishment theorists.

One conspicuous way in which traditional moral theories immunize themselves from the complexities of moral luck is by seeking to emulate mathematical methods or by assuming that mathematics has itself a protagonist role to play within moral theory. This is to be expected, since the notion of "mathematical luck" really is very close to sheer, irredeemable absurdity: the actual solution of a mathematical problem (the solution *itself*, as opposed to the fact that this or that mathematician may *find* or *hit upon* it) cannot really be a matter of luck at all. Whether or not it existed before, this ethos of connecting ethics with mathematics has been particularly popular since the enlightenment. Locke, for example, expressly championed it, say, when he asserted that "moral knowledge is as capable of real certainty as is mathematics," since, in his view, mathematical ideas and moral ideas are the only true "archetypes."[9] Locke's position evidently influenced Bentham's famous

---

7   A noteworthy exception is Gary Watson, "Responsibility and the Limits of Evil: Variations on a Strawsonian Theme" in his *Agency and Answerability*, Oxford: Clarendon Press (2004), 219–259. Although, as noted in Chapter 3, Watson strikes me as too facilely anti-retributivist, there are similarities between his take on moral luck and mine.

8   See, for example, the authoritative Dana K. Nelkin, "Moral Luck," *The Stanford Encyclopedia of Philosophy* (Winter 2013 edn., Edward N. Zalta, ed.), http://plato.stanford.edu/archives/win2013/entries/moral-luck/.

9   John Locke, *An Essay Concerning Human Understanding*, Oxford: Clarendon Press (1975), 565. Contrast Locke's "enlightenment" position against Aristotle's famous admonition at the beginning of the *Nicomachean Ethics*: "Our discussion will be adequate if it has as much clearness as the subject-matter admits of, for precision is not to be sought for alike in all discussions, any more than in all the

"felicific calculus," itself preceded by a wide variety of works on moral theory which either assumed or sought to show (and sometimes both) an intimate connection between morality and mathematics.[10] But it is in its contemporary incarnation that the term "moral mathematics" highlights the approach upon which I wish to shine a light.

In its contemporary incarnation of interest to me, the idea of "moral mathematics" is particularly prominent in Derek Parfit's *Reasons and Persons*, which contains a section titled "Five Mistakes in Moral Mathematics."[11] Unfortunately, Parfit did not really explain what exactly he meant by this expression. Although unlike many of his predecessors, Parfit did not turn to mathematics in order to advance either utilitarianism or egoism, important aspects of his moral theory are devoted to the analysis of a wide variety of moral problems in whose solutions mathematical calculations figure prominently. The section on "moral mathematics" (like much of the rest of his undoubtedly deep and thought-provoking philosophy) contains a seemingly inexhaustible variety of examples of moral situations in which we face the choice of harming (or saving) X number of persons by saving (or harming) Y number of persons.

It is not just because these examples involve numbers that they are to be seen as cases of "moral mathematics." It is also the very supposition on which they rely whereby moral problems are resolvable by "ledgering" (as in mathematics) the pros and cons for each alternative course of action so as to find an unequivocal right answer (again, as in mathematics). It is the combination of the concern with numbers *and* this underlying methodological assumption that deserves the name of "moral mathematics." As Parfit discusses what he takes to be the "mistakes" of moral mathematics, the number of examples he devises increases, as does their degree of (at times openly baroque) sophistication. Whatever mistakes Parfit finds in other approaches to the problems of moral mathematics he concocts, he never questions the moral mathematics approach itself. In other words, Parfit never questions the extent to which the number crunching that is necessary to engage with his ingenious thought experiments may perhaps itself be a hindrance to real progress in moral philosophy. Of course, the very existence of organic wholes puts

products of the crafts," in Aristotle, "Nicomachean Ethics," in *The Complete Works of Aristotle* (Jonathan Barnes, ed., W. D. Ross, trans.), Princeton: Princeton University Press (1991): 1094b12–1094b26. Contra Locke, Aristotle leaves open the possibility that ethics is *not* quite as precise as mathematics. Williams believes that some of the problems with contemporary moral theory stem from its peculiar understanding of enlightenment principles and ideals. As far as I am concerned, the effort to link morality and mathematics may indeed be a product of the enlightenment. I wish to steer clear of these historical meta-narratives: whatever its precise genealogy, much of contemporary moral theory (and much more of contemporary punishment theory) unconsciously assumes this link.

10   Bentham's "felicific calculus" informs much of his work. For earlier instantiations of this *"furor mathematicus,"* see Luis I. Bredvold, "The Invention of Ethical Calculus," in Richard Foster Jones, *The Seventeenth Century: Studies in the History of English Thought and Literature by Richard Foster Jones and Other Writings in His Honor*, Stanford, CA: Stanford University Press (1951), 165–180.

11   Derek Parfit, *Reasons and Persons*, Oxford: Clarendon Press (1984), 67–86.

limits on moral mathematics; after all, by definition, where there is an organic whole, its value cannot be a simple or weighed sum of the value of its parts.

Parfit's approach to (moral) philosophy, based on these sorts of thought experiments, has become extraordinarily influential in contemporary moral theory.[12] In highlighting some of the shortcomings of this approach, a real-life story, as told in another book by Parfit (though not told by Parfit himself), is particularly helpful. Parfit's *On What Matters* includes a series of "commentaries" on his views by four prominent philosophers. In one of these, Allen Wood "frankly admit[ted]" as to his main motivation in writing his commentary: he wished to "to get off [his] chest some complaints about what many moral philosophers do nowadays" and to "challenge some fashionable ways" of doing moral philosophy.[13] Interestingly, while Parfit responded to many of the points these philosophers made, he did not respond to these specific remarks by Wood. And these remarks by Wood are very important for my purposes, for while his complaints are not aimed at punishment theory in particular, I will suggest that they can be profitably applied to this subfield of moral theory. Not only do I find myself in profound agreement with Wood on these complaints, but I will further suggest that they allow us to reassess which values should be seen as properly belonging (i.e., not as "intrusions") to the justification of punishment.

Wood begins his criticism of the fashionable way in which much contemporary moral philosophy is done by relating the following event:

> In May of 2001, the Tanner lecturer at Stanford University was Dorothy Allison, author of the novel *Bastard Out of Carolina*. Allison didn't talk much about moral philosophy as such, but she did discuss a "lifeboat problem" that she had heard about from a philosopher. Her reaction was to reject the problem – to refuse to answer it at all – on the ground that we should refuse on principle to choose between one life and five lives. Even to pose the question in those terms, she said, is already immoral. The only real moral issue raised by such examples, she thought, is why provision had not been made for more or larger lifeboats.

Wood then points out:

> To many philosophers her remarks would no doubt seem naive or even unreasonable. Yet I think Allison's reaction to the lifeboat problem is far more sensible and

---

[12]  Parfit certainly did not invent these thought experiments. The usual "birthplace" of "trolley" problems tends to be located in Philippa Foot, "The Problem of Abortion and the Doctrine of Double Effect," *Oxford Review* 5 (1967): 5–15. See also, among many others: Judith Jarvis Thomson, "The Trolley Problem," *Yale Law Journal* 94.6 (1985): 1395–1415; David Edmonds, *Would You Kill the Fat Man? The Trolley Problem and What Your Answer Tells Us about Right and Wrong*, Princeton, NJ: Princeton University Press (2015); Frances Kamm, *The Trolley Problem Mysteries* (Eric Rakowski, ed.), Oxford: Oxford University Press (2015).

[13]  Allen Wood, "Humanity as an End in Itself," in Derek Parfit, *On What Matters*, Vol. 2, Oxford: Oxford University Press (2011), 66.

right-minded than what we usually get from most of the philosophers who make use of such examples.[14]

Wood's grievances concern not only "lifeboat problems" but "trolley problems" and, in general, the overly schematic thought experiments that abound in contemporary (moral) philosophy, whose framing – and whose "solution" – is taken to be a matter of mathematics (in the sense sketched previously).

Wood admits that he has "long thought that trolley problems provide misleading ways of thinking about moral philosophy."[15] I agree. The main problem with these thought experiments is that they *oversimplify* moral phenomena and that they both presuppose and generate *reductive* versions of morality. Consider the paradigmatic case: a trolley heads down a track leading it to kill five people; the trolley cannot be stopped, but it can be diverted in such a way that it goes onto a track that leads it to kill only one person (and thus to not killing the initial five people). Standardly, we, respondents, are not supposed to know anything about the six people facing death (or about ourselves as machinists), and neither are we supposed to have had anything to do with the creation of this regrettable state of affairs: all we are supposed and allowed to do is to decide whether we kill the one or the five. (Countless variations are possible: one versus one hundred or versus one thousand; loops can be added to the tracks so as to invite discussions of probabilities; and so on and on.)

There is no denying that there are some contexts in which thought experiments of this sort can be very useful – above all, pedagogical contexts. These thought experiments are often helpful teaching devices. Moreover, sometimes they can help us discover what exactly our own view about a case is by allowing us to discover what some of our moral intuitions are (these thought experiments are often amusingly called "intuition pumps") or how some of our intuitions conflict among themselves or how they relate to general principles we believe we hold. I do not think that Wood's antipathy toward these thought experiments is an antipathy to them *per se* – certainly *mine* is not. Not even Williams – whose skepticism about the powers of morality are second to none (and to which I will return in the next section) was flatly opposed to using these devices. As it turns out, in the context of arguing for the importance of the notion of *integrity* (a notion that classical utilitarians simply cannot, in Williams's view, countenance – and that in any case has *no* place within the trolley problem universe), he offered two famous thought experiments. While the discussion of Williams's thought experiments themselves does not concern me here, it is important for my purposes to point out that while they were remarkably richer than typical trolley problems, Williams nonetheless admitted that they were "inevitably schematized, and [that] they are open to the objection that they beg as many questions as they illuminate."[16] But then, with characteristic insight, Williams added:

---

[14]  *Ibid.*, 66–67.   [15]   *Ibid.*, 69.
[16]  Bernard Williams "A Critique of Utilitarianism," in J. J. C. Smart and B. A. O. Williams, *Utilitarianism: For and Against*, Cambridge: Cambridge University Press (1973), 96.

These difficulties, however, just have to be accepted, and if anyone finds these examples cripplingly defective in this sort of respect, then he must in his own thought rework them in richer and less question-begging form. If he feels that no presentation of any imagined situation can ever be other than misleading in morality, and that there can never be any substitute for the concrete experienced complexity of actual moral situations, then this discussion, with him, must certainly grind to a halt: but then one may legitimately wonder whether every discussion with him about conduct will not grind to a halt, including any discussion about the actual situations, since discussion about how one would think and feel about situations somewhat different from the actual (that is to say, situations to that extent imaginary) plays an important role in discussion of the actual.[17]

It would indeed be very difficult to do philosophy without ever using thought experiments – whether they involve trolleys, dark caves, evil geniuses, soon-to-be-deserted islands, veils of ignorance, virtual-reality machines, twin earths, demons who manipulate gas molecules, or cats who are simultaneously dead and alive, among many others. I am as guilty as anyone else of appealing to them – in this book and elsewhere. But problems with thought experiments can nonetheless arise quickly, particularly within the context of *moral* philosophy. One family of problems arises when they gain so much in prominence that philosophers seemingly forget that there is more to moral philosophy than whatever the thought experiments are devised to highlight. A second family of problems arises when philosophers set up these thought experiments in, to borrow Wood's term, particularly "cartoonish" ways – that is, in ways that do render them "cripplingly defective."[18] Like Wood (and others), I believe that these two families of potential problems are conspicuous in contemporary moral philosophy.

The connection I wish to draw between these potential pitfalls in the appeal to thought experiments and the specialized literature on the justification of punishment is not quite that punishment theorists necessarily employ these thought experiments in exactly these potentially flawed ways. (To be sure, punishment theorists sometimes do appeal to these thought experiments, and sometimes in very systematic ways.)[19] Rather, I wish to underscore the fact that punishment theorists – whether or not they rely on thought experiments – do approach the justification of punishment in reductive ways that resemble the reductionism of the thought experiments that we have just mentioned.

So, just as "trolley problem philosophers" (to yet again borrow Wood's label) reduce moral phenomena in such a way that lives can be "added" and "deducted" simplemindedly, as in a ledger, punishment theorists reduce the justification of

---

[17]  *Ibid.*, 97.     [18]  Wood, "Humanity as an End in Itself," 69, 70.

[19]  Perhaps the two most famous examples are Immanuel Kant, *The Metaphysical Elements of Justice: Part I of the Metaphysics of Morals* (John Ladd, trans.), New York, NY: Macmillan (1965), 102 ff., and H. J. McCloskey "A Note on Utilitarian Punishment," *Mind* 72 (1963), 599 – further elaborated by J. J. C. Smart in his "An Outline of a System of Utilitarian Ethics," in *Utilitarianism: For and Against*, 69 ff.

punishment to a matter of ledgers. Either wrongdoing and deserved suffering (in the case of deontic retributivism) or the suffering caused by punishment and the suffering prevented by punishment (in the case of classical utilitarianism) can be simplemindedly added and deducted from each other. At least some moral dilemmas resist this treatment, and they are utterly out of place in the world of the contemporary trolley problem philosopher and in the world of the typical contemporary punishment theorist.

Both the trolley problem philosopher and the typical contemporary punishment theorist eschew the axiological turn that I am here recommending. And this eschewing contributes as much to the cartoonishness of the typical deployment of these thought experiments as it hinders progress in punishment theory. Wood perceptively points out:

> Trolley problem philosophers would regard us as missing the whole point of the problem if we even bothered to express any of the moral intuitions that don't directly involve saying what the agent should *do*. These philosophers are focusing our attention shortsightedly, even compulsively, solely on the question about what you should *do* in the immediate situation, as if that were the only thing moral philosophy has any reason to care about.[20]

Similarly, the whole point of contemporary punishment theory tends to be to tell us when punishment is (or is not) justified, in the thin deontic sense of whether it should (or should not) be *inflicted*. And I suspect that contemporary punishment theorists' reaction to my suggestion that we take the axiological turn is likely to be similar to Wood's imagined trolley problem philosophers' reaction to his insistence on the importance of non-action-guiding values. They will say that I am somehow "missing the whole point" of punishment theory. Admittedly, this is just a suspicion. But the similarity between what Wood deems "shortsighted, even compulsive" tendencies in trolley problem philosophers and what I deem "simpleminded" tendencies in the contemporary punishment theorist is not just a suspicion.

Perhaps there is no better-known, or at any rate more eloquent, example of the cartoonishness of which Wood speaks or of the simplemindedness of which I speak than Charles Darwin's famous ledger of pros and cons concerning reasons for and against his own marriage. On the "Not Marry" side of the ledger, Darwin included considerations such as the time children and a family would waste, the financial costs of maintaining a wife, the visits from the in-laws, and "fatness and idleness." On the "Marry" side of the ledger, Darwin included considerations such as companionship, the "charms of music & female chit-chat," and the acquiring of an "object to be beloved & played with – better than a dog anyhow."[21] More than the considerations themselves – some of which are admittedly repellent – what seems above

---

[20]  Wood, "Humanity as an End in Itself," 72. Emphasis added.
[21]  The text is found online in www.darwinproject.ac.uk/tags/about-darwin/family-life/darwin-marriage, curated by Cambridge University Library.

all off about Darwin's way of considering the question of marriage is the very project of deciding something as important as one's partner on the basis of this sort of ledger. Even if every single one of Darwin's considerations were to be perfectly sensible or irreproachably admirable, to base this decision entirely on this sort of ledger would seem to leave something important out, something not quite ledgerable.[22] In other words, there is something deeply troubling about Darwin's *method*.

The extent to which Darwin's example belongs to moral philosophy is of course debatable. But the example is helpful for my purposes in that it illustrates a certain misguidedness in the very way in which one approaches one's topic. A great deal of the cartoonishness of which Wood speaks is related to a misguided way of approaching moral philosophy: either as if it were mostly a matter of mathematics or as if mathematics played some especially prominent role in moral theory. A similarly misguided approach pervades contemporary punishment theory. Of course this has nothing to do with the way punishment theorists think about marriage but instead deals with their assumption that something like Darwin's ledger ought to be the right method vis-à-vis the justification of punishment.

This points to an interesting connection between the two expressions in the title of this section: moral luck and moral mathematics. For we now see that moral luck can be understood as a radical and far-reaching effort to challenge some central presuppositions of moral philosophy, and moral mathematics can be understood (albeit perhaps more loosely) as that approach to moral philosophy most clearly inspired by those very presuppositions that the idea of moral luck enjoins us to rethink. Exploring how moral luck, thus understood, may affect the way we think specifically about punishment theory, as I do here, has hitherto been truly uncharted territory.

## 6.2 THE CRITIQUE OF THE MORALITY SYSTEM

I briefly noted in Chapter 5 that Williams thinks that it is a mistake "to try to make everything into obligations."[23] This view is the result of Williams's overall guarded attitude regarding the powers of theory. Williams believes that theory has many limits, many more than typically acknowledged. And I have in the previous section suggested that the effort to account for putative moral considerations by means of a ledger very much at home in the world of moral mathematics is closely related to the effort "to make everything into obligations." We thus are in a position to connect Williams's mobilization of the problem of moral luck and his overall attitude concerning the limits of theory.

---

22   See Robert Nozick's (opposing) view about why one may decide to stay with one's partner even if one discovers another person who surpasses one's partner in each of a group of "ledgered" considerations. At the very least, one shares with one's partner a *history*, a life lived together, which is not itself amenable to this ledgering. (Nozick, however, finds this "historical" character of love "puzzling.") Robert Nozick, *Anarchy, State, and Utopia*, Oxford: Blackwell (1999), 167–168.

23   Bernard Williams, *Ethics and the Limits of Philosophy*, London: Routledge (2006), 180.

Probing this connection requires paying attention to Williams's lucid and penetrating – and difficult – *Ethics and the Limits of Philosophy*.[24] Interestingly, while Williams openly attests to a connection between his early views on moral luck and his much more systematic efforts in *Ethics and the Limits of Philosophy*, the latter is rarely read as expounding on the former. This is surprising, if for no other reason simply because Williams himself suggested the connection. In his "Postscript" to Daniel Statman's useful volume on moral luck, Williams admits that his way of saying things in his original "Moral Luck" may have given rise to some misunderstandings – and he expressly directs the reader to his views in *Ethics and the Limits of Philosophy* for clarification, at least regarding one of these possible misunderstandings.[25] Still, the connection between Williams's early views in "Moral Luck" and his more mature views in *Ethics and the Limits of Philosophy* remains regrettably underexplored.

From a certain perspective, the misunderstanding Williams discusses may appear to be purely terminological: in his later work, Williams makes a distinction between "ethics" and "morality." In Williams's opinion, "morality" is but one "particular variety" of the broader realm of the ethical. "Ethics," in Williams's opinion, has many shortcomings, but "morality" (or, even more precisely, what he calls the "morality system") he finds downright pathological, both the cause and the effect of (comforting) illusions.[26] But it is not just terminology that is at stake here. As I shall try to further elaborate in this section, Williams's objections to the "morality system" (both those directly linked to the idea of moral luck and those even remotely linked to it) do not seek to "bring down" moral theory as such – but only to criticize one particular way of doing moral theory. Surely Williams is not a moral relativist; famously, Williams has referred to relativism as "the anthropologist's heresy, possibly the most absurd view to have been advanced even in moral philosophy."[27] And he is not a nihilist either: in the "Postscript," he is emphatic about the fact that his view should not "be taken to mean that the difficulty [that his notion of moral luck seeks to highlight] must arise with (any) morality; that is to say, with any scheme for regulating the relations between people that works through informal sanctions and internalized dispositions."[28]

It is thus useful to see Williams's distinction between ethics and the morality system as (in part) allowing him to emphasize that his criticisms of the latter are not meant to amount to a thoroughgoing skepticism of moral philosophy in general

---

[24] *Ibid.*    [25] Williams, "Postscript," 251.    [26] Williams, *Ethics and the Limits of Philosophy*, 174.

[27] Bernard Williams, *Morality: An Introduction to Ethics*, Cambridge: Cambridge University Press (1993), 20.

[28] Williams, "Postscript," 251. Interestingly, Williams admits that the difficulties posed by the consideration of moral luck may not affect Aristotelian ethics. *Ibid.*, 252. I am unsure virtue ethics can avoid all these difficulties.

(such as relativism or nihilism).[29] While, unlike Williams, I do not distinguish between ethics and morality,[30] I nonetheless wholeheartedly agree with the spirit of his critics (applicable, from my perspective, to what he calls "morality" or "the morality system," to what he calls "ethics," and above all to "punishment theory"). The spirit of Williams's criticism is none other than that "morality" (or the "morality system") fails to do justice to the complexity of human life and it is thus simpleminded. An important part of this simplemindedness is related to its dismissal of axiology.

Williams discusses the ways in which two interrelated notions play out in the context of morality: first, the notion of an *action*, and second, a particularly "moral" notion of *obligation*. (In the same vein as before, it is important to emphasize that in Williams's view it is specifically *moral* obligation – that is, the notion of obligation that belongs within the morality system – that is a problem, not the notion of obligation in general.)[31] One of the aspects that Williams finds problematic about moral obligation is that it is often taken to be "a kind of practical conclusion," customarily articulated "in terms of the output or conclusion of moral deliberation."[32] In other words, Williams thinks that the focus on moral obligation is problematic in part because it too closely links moral thinking to *acting* and, moreover, to acting in an axiologically tidy world.

Insightfully, Williams suggests that

> there are actions (also policies, attitudes, and so on) that are either more or less than obligations. They may be heroic or very fine actions, which go beyond what is obligatory or demanded. Or they may be actions that from an ethical point of view it would be agreeable or worthwhile or a good idea to do, without one's being required to do them.[33]

Ethical phenomena, in contrast, are not in Williams's view necessarily tied to action in this way. For example, and focusing on the "attitudes, and so on" that Williams mentions in this passage: to have a cooperative or a generous or a grateful *attitude* or *disposition* may be praiseworthy and valuable even if, at the very moment in which one is praised for possessing attitudes or dispositions of these sorts, one is not manifesting them in action. There are many cases in which we are under no

---

[29]  Martha Nussbaum claims that Williams (and others) have "assailed ethical theorizing, especially in its Enlightenment forms, as both useless and pernicious, as distorting practice and contributing nothing that could not be gained through more informal types of ethical reflection," in her "Why Practice Needs Ethical Theory: Particularism, Principle, and Bad Behaviour," in *Moral Particularism* (Brad Hooker and Margaret Olivia Little, eds.) Oxford: Oxford University Press (2000): 227–255, at 230. I think Nussbaum's harsh indictment fails to capture the spirit of Williams's criticism of the morality system.

[30]  Traces of the famous Hegelian distinction between *Sittlichkeit* and *Moralität* are obvious, though this does not render Williams a Hegelian. See, for example, his "Pluralism, Community and Left Wittgensteinianism" in *In the Beginning Was the Deed: Realism and Moralism in Political Argument*, Princeton, NJ: Princeton University Press (2005), 29–39.

[31]  Williams, *Ethics and the Limits of Philosophy*, 174.    [32]  Ibid., 175.    [33]  Ibid., 179.

*obligation* to behave in a grateful, generous, or cooperative way. And the same, of course, holds for just or merciful attitudes: they can be valuable even if not manifested in action.

In Williams's opinion, a typical way in which morality (at least in its "central, deontological [deontic], version")[34] deals with these actions that are either more or less than obligations, or with those other ethical phenomena that are not even actions, is to problematically try "to make as many as possible into obligations."[35] This applies as much to Kant's "deontological" ethics as it does to classical utilitarianism: in the Kantian universe these actions would become moral insofar as they are rationally universalizable, and in the classical utilitarian universe insofar as they are utility-maximizing.

Williams offers three reasons why this way of conceiving morality is mistaken. First, he suggests that this notion of moral obligation may conflict with the way in which "obligation" is often used in ordinary language. Second, and much more interestingly, Williams suggests that this notion of moral obligation may have difficulty "finding room for morally indifferent action"[36], and it may eventually come to "dominate life altogether."[37] For example, imagine you break the "moral obligation" to keep a promise to a friend concerning a relatively minor issue in order to devote yourself to the advancement of a noble cause. The morality system, relying on its sense of moral obligation, will tend to analyze this situation in terms of your having a more stringent (albeit less obvious, perhaps) moral obligation to advance this noble cause than to keep your promise – and it is this former obligation that defeats the latter obligation. But if this is so, every single action that we could possibly perform must inescapably – and hence problematically – fall within the scope of one obligation or another. Oppressively, it would turn out to be effectively impossible to act in such a way that was *not* governed by one moral obligation or another. Perhaps this is more conspicuous in the case of classical utilitarianism (given its straightforward maximizing ethos), but it is in Williams's view equally true of deontological (Kantian) ethics.

For current purposes, however, by far the most important reason why I think Williams is right in stressing that it is a mistake to try to turn all normative concerns about which we may deliberate into moral obligations is that, thirdly, this strategy inescapably generates an "economy of morality,"[38] which is also linked to certain "administrative ideas of rationality."[39] Pointedly, Williams suggests that the morality system wants to operate with what "may be called the *obligations-out, obligations-in* principle."[40] As we saw in the previous chapter, it is precisely something resembling this principle that leads Tasioulas, after insightfully emphasizing the importance of mercy in punishment theory, to give the game away (by introducing what he himself admits is a counterintuitive notion of mercy). After all, it was precisely because this

---

[34] *Ibid.*   [35] *Ibid.*   [36] *Ibid.*, 181.   [37] *Ibid.*, 182.   [38] *Ibid.*, 180.   [39] *Ibid.*, 197.
[40] *Ibid.*, 181.

odd sense of mercy is able to generate these moral obligations that Tasioulas felt compelled to adopt it. And as we saw in the previous section, something like this obligations-out, obligations-in principle relates to the allure of the ledger, to the desire (conscious or otherwise) to mathematize and economize morality. Williams wisely objects to this ethos whereby obligations can add and detract from each other this neatly. This ethos, too quantitative for its own good, seems much more at home in the world of accounting and bookkeeping than in the world of (moral) philosophy and much more appropriate for dealing with monetary transactions than with complex and often unquantifiable moral phenomena.

With Darwin's scandalous marriage ledger in the background, consider the sense in which acquiring a new dog (as a pet) may help us deal with the sorrow that the death of our old dog may have caused. While we are likely to remember the old dog and its special characteristics (such as they were), there is a sense in which a new dog will relatively quickly replace the old dog and its role in our lives. Contrast how this fungibility of dogs differs from how it must feel to lose a loved spouse. One of course may want to avoid loneliness and may wish to find a new spouse. But the sense in which the new spouse will *replace* the old one is extraordinarily more complicated than the replacement of dogs, if the idea of replacing spouses is meaningful at all. However problematic the "dog-out, dog-in" principle may turn out to be, the "spouse-out, spouse-in" principle is downright abominable. Just as a "spouse-out, spouse-in" principle would betray a terribly impoverished appreciation of others, Williams believes that the ethos of the traditional "morality system," predicated upon the "obligations-out, obligations-in" principle, robs moral life of some of its most important constitutive elements.

And it is precisely something resembling this ethos of the morality system that has dominated punishment theory, encouraging relatively facile conclusions regarding the fact that if, after deliberation, a given instance of punishment is seen as "justified" (in a narrow sense of "justification" very much at home within what Williams calls the "morality system"), then some action (say, inflicting it) simply obtains, and nothing remains to be discussed or lamented. After this action is carried out, all important normative and philosophical problems regarding the imposition of said punishment allegedly come to an end. This ethos can, as we have seen, superimpose itself on any of the classical justifications of punishment: whether consequentialist or (deontic) retributivist. Therein, in fact, lies a great deal of their simplemindedness. Williams's journey away from morality is a journey away from its inapposite economicist simplemindedness – a simplemindedness in particularly conspicuous display regarding the justifications of punishment we have discussed.

If you are a classical utilitarian, you will think that once you can confidently conclude that this particular instance of punishment will generate less suffering than any other course of action, then it will be justified – and, then, the problem of the justification of punishment would have run its course. Something similar would hold if your preferred justification of punishment is based on (deontic) retributivism:

once you determine that a given punishment is deserved, then you are justified in inflicting it, and, again, the problems would end. Something similar will also hold even in the potentially richer communicative justification of punishment: once you determine what is the correct message, or the correct message-*cum*-hard-treatment to which a certain wrongdoer is liable, then you ought to communicate it, or communicate-*cum*-inflict it, and problems would cease. As we have seen, even Tasioulas, who does defend a properly pluralistic justification of punishment, seems to fall prey to this ethos: once you determine that someone is *owed* the "duty of mercy" (to whatever extent it is owed), then this is somehow neatly deducted from the punishment that was due to her, and then moral problems are supposed to end.

As I have been arguing, the values that should matter for the justification of punishment are richer and much more varied than typically assumed. They extend far beyond the usual elements that adherents to the traditional justifications of punishment have assumed (again: suffering reduction for classical utilitarians, desert for retributivists, and a combination of these mixed with transmissions of messages for communicative theorists). In other words, there are plenty of *important* elements involved in justifying punishment that have been summarily excluded from the traditional justifications of punishment. I do not mean merely the important aspects of the justification of punishment that, say, a deontic retributivist is wont to exclude insofar as they will strike her as too utilitarian or the important aspects that a classical utilitarian is wont to exclude as they will strike her as too (barbarically) retributivist. The values that I suggest matter for the justification of punishment go beyond *all* the values that these traditional justifications are capable of including.

Before zeroing in on these aspects, I would like to expand on the notion of "importance" that I have emphasized in the previous paragraph, insofar as it is a somewhat (but only somewhat) technical notion. By and large, I follow Williams in his use of "importance," even though Williams admits that he has left the notion "poorly understood."[41] The importance of "importance" for Williams is that he thinks that it is precisely this notion that allows us to "see around the intimidating structure that morality has made out of the idea of obligation," to stave off the model of simpleminded accountancy.[42]

Williams believes that he can draw three interrelated conclusions about this admittedly poorly understood sense of importance. First, the notion exists, i.e., some things are important, *period*. What he means by this is that some things really are, in a nonrelativistic sense, important in themselves, or "important *überhaupt*, as others might put it, or important period."[43] Second, people can, in principle, distinguish things they find important in a relativistic sense from those they find

[41] *Ibid.*, 182.   [42] *Ibid.*

[43] *Ibid.* While this sense of important is not relativistic, it is not to be taken to mean that what is important period is somehow "important to the universe," for, according to Williams, "in that sense, nothing is important," *ibid.*

important, period. Third, the discussion of importance is to be distinguished from the discussion of "deliberative priority," i.e., the fact that you find something important, or even "important, period," does not necessarily entail that, all things considered, you should *act* so as to bring it about or to preserve it, etc. In other words: despite the fact that some things may be nonrelativistically important, they still need not issue in action.

One valuable way of seeing the interconnection between Williams's three conclusions is to again attend to the distinction between the deontic and the axiological. To say that a thing is "important, period" is to say that that thing is *valuable*, and in fact *intrinsically* so: valuable in a way that is not medicinal and that it does not need to issue in action. In my own terms: something can be important not because of its alleged propensity to cause good things but because it forms part of an organic whole that is good in itself and that is made better by its presence. Williams's talk of importance is to a large extent axiological, and that is why it serves him to see past the "intimidating structure" of the morality system or, in my terms, past the pernicious conflation of the axiological and the deontic. Part of its intimidation is connected to the way in which the morality system tends to turn everything into a deontic matter. Although there better be some connection between the axiological point about something being important (or valuable) and the deontic point of its issuing or recommending a certain course of action, the connection is much more complex than punishment theorists have traditionally assumed. For they have in fact operated wholly within the intimidating structure Williams describes: they have seen the problem of the justification of punishment through the lens of the "obligations-out, obligations-in" principle.

Both some deserved punishments and some merciful remissions of said deserved punishments are important in this sense – important, period. As we have seen, only (axiological) retributivists can even *see* this point – for consequentialists cannot possibly countenance it. But both (deontic) retributivists and consequentialists have failed to see that the remission of punishment that constitutes *forgiveness* can also be important, period. While in this book I focus on the tension between these two important values, an axiologically pluralistic approach will recognize many such values. Taking these other values seriously generates combinations that have traditionally been overlooked by punishment theorists. "Justified" punishment could be ugly (or repugnant, petty, etc.). Famous literary examples include Sophocles's *Antigone* or Melville's *Billy Budd*.[44] Conversely, "unjustified" punishment can be beautiful (or admirable, dignified, etc.): typical examples here involve extrajudicial justice, say, like the Sholom Schwartzbard case (in which in broad daylight Paris Schwartzbard assassinated Simon Petliura, avenging the latter's role in

---

[44] Sophocles "Antigone," in *Antigone, The Women of Trachis, Philoctetes Oedipus at Colonus* (Hugh Lloyd-Jones, ed., trans.) Cambridge, MA: Harvard University Press (1994): 1–127; Herman Melville, "Billy Budd, Sailor (an Inside Narrative)" in *Billy Budd and Other Stories*, New York, NY: Penguin Books (1986): 287–385. I will discuss *Billy Budd* at length in Chapter 8.

many pogroms in Ukraine) that Hannah Arendt mentions in her *Eichmann in Jerusalem*.[45]

The existence of these combinations suggests at least two important conclusions. First, a more robust approach to the justification of punishment involves paying attention to what Williams called "thick" ethical concepts. Famously, Williams broke down moral concepts into thick and thin.[46] The latter are very general terms, like "right" and "wrong," "good" and "bad," "permissible" and "impermissible" – and "justified" and "unjustified"; the former are much more specific, like "treacherous," "courageous," "ungrateful," "spineless," and so on.[47] Within the context of the specialized literature on punishment theory, however, "justified" and "unjustified" have – in spite of their evident thinness – crowded out the universe of discourse in such a way that the analysis of any thick concepts whatsoever has been essentially ignored. Second, and closely related, in addition to the thin sense of "justification" that has monopolized the attention of punishment theorists, we may need a richer way of evaluating punishment. From this richer perspective, the justification of punishment is not a matter of a binary distinction between the justified and the unjustified, but it is a matter of taking into account other important (i.e., valuable) elements.

Evidently, these two conclusions do not sit well within the context of the morality system. In spite of these conclusions, I would like to end this section indicating why punishment has been so particularly amenable to be treated in the ways characteristic of the morality system. The main reason is that punishment is as much at home in moral philosophy as it is in law; or, as stated in Chapter 1, punishment generates both theoretical and practical problems. And the law is, necessarily, much more a legal *system* than moral philosophy is a morality *system*. Had Williams criticized the "legal system" along the lines he criticized the "morality system," his position would have verged on the absurd. Even if not particularly inspiring, the view that the law sometimes needs to draw bright lines and to simplify matters, that it just *cannot* afford to take the many elements that could perhaps be valuable and relevant for a robust and not simpleminded justification of punishment, is perfectly sensible, if not downright inescapable.[48]

---

[45]   Hannah Arendt, *Eichmann in Jerusalem: A Study in the Banality of Evil*, New York, NY: Viking (1963): 265–267. For an excellent discussion of Schwartzbard's case see Anna Schur, "Shades of Justice: The Trial of Sholom Schwartzbard and Dovid Bergelson's *Among Refugees*," *Law and Literature* 19 (2007): 15–43. The idea that an "unjustified" punishment could be in some other ways admirable was already present in Max Horkheimer's "The Arrest of Eichmann" in his *Critique of Instrumental Reason*, New York, NY: Continuum (1996): 119–123, at 122.

[46]   Williams, *Ethics and the Limits of Philosophy*, 129 ff.

[47]   Williams deployed the distinction between thick and thin for a variety of purposes – including a reexamination of the alleged is/ought gap and some problems of liberalism (a tradition to which, in my opinion, he belongs). These other purposes do not concern me here.

[48]   I have myself mobilized a version of this view in the context of discussing Vera Bergelson's excellent *Victims' Rights and Victims' Wrongs*, where she has compellingly argued against the simplifications that the criminal law imposes on the cases it studies. Prominent among these simplifications is what Bergelson calls "the penal couple," comprised of a flat and non-nuanced perpetrator and a flat and

And yet to expect moral *philosophy* to avoid all the theoretical difficulties that a legal system sometimes must avoid is to fall prey to the allure of the ledger, to be under the spell of moral mathematics. Punishment theory, I think, has been to an extent stunted in its development by the fact that although punishment generates both philosophical and practical problems, the latter tend to monopolize attention. If progress is to be attained, however, paying attention to Williams's theoretical criticisms of the morality system seems to me to be crucial.

## 6.3 PUNISHMENT, THE PECULIAR INSTITUTION

Even though, as I emphasized at the beginning of the previous section, Williams is neither an ethical relativist nor an ethical nihilist, the shape of the moral philosophy that flows from his views may be met with resistance. Independently of whether my interpretation whereby Williams's axiological pluralism can be traced back to his concern with moral luck is correct, it cannot be denied that Williams's view of ethics is complicated, perhaps *too* complicated. As a result of his emphasis on the fact that some things may be important (i.e., valuable) even if they do not issue in action, Williams fails to provide direct guidance as to how these different important axiological elements ultimately affect the deontic. As Susan Wolf notes, moral philosophers are likely to find Williams's position "depressing and disturbing," and many may fear that if a philosophical system is denied the (deontic) "power to advise," this may be to deny also "all intelligent and sensible reflection."[49]

The axiological pluralism I defend within the context of punishment theory is similarly susceptible to a certain skepticism arising from the fact that it does not always generate direct guidelines – either in particular cases or in general. As we have seen, this is in part the result of the fact that axiological pluralists recognize that life is not as simple as to always allow precise general guidelines. To that extent the pluralist is not very worried about this skepticism, for she sees it as at home within the (mistaken) worldview whereby life is simpler than it really is. She would admit that sometimes there are no easy (or algorithmic, mathematic, ledgerable, etc.) solutions to certain moral dilemmas, even though in other occasions there may exist very precise and straightforward guidelines for action. The skeptic position presupposes a belief in the existence of precise and straightforward guidelines in *all* cases, not only in some.

I think that a recent exchange between Alon Harel and myself captures the spirit of this sort of skepticism about axiological pluralism well. While there is a lot to like in Harel's *Why Law Matters*[50] – including his very decision to focus on moral

non-nuanced victim. While evidently very sympathetic to her approach, I have suggested that perhaps there are *some* cases in which the criminal law must keep things very simple and non-nuanced. See Vera Bergelson, *Victims' Rights and Victims' Wrongs*, Stanford, CA: Stanford University Press (2009). For discussion, see my review in *New Criminal Law Review* 14.4 (2011): 671–680.

[49] Susan Wolf, "The Deflation of Moral Philosophy," *Ethics* 97.4 (1987): 821–833, at 822.

[50] Alon Harel, *Why Law Matters*, Oxford: Oxford University Press (2014).

dilemmas (and their connection with, among other phenomena, punishment) –
I have criticized him for overly simplifying the nature and import of those moral
dilemmas.[51] Part of Harel's response to my criticism has been to suggest that there
exists "a fundamental gap" between our approaches – a gap that "reflects a different
intellectual disposition" in each of us.[52] The approach I recommend, Harel believes,
"is often satisfied pointing out that under some circumstances whatever we do, we
are both wrong and right." Moreover, Harel continues, this approach often "exempts
itself from making an unambiguous statement concerning what ultimately ought to
be done."[53] In contrast, Harel's own approach seeks to provide "an answer to the
question as to what we ought to do and when."[54]

By way of registering Harel's dismissal of the axiological in favor of the
deontic, I would like to focus in some detail on the ways in which Harel's
position shows how the reticence to recognize the truly complex nature of some
moral conflicts may tend to generate caricatures. Harel uncharitably presents
views that recognize this complexity as somehow self-indulgently "exempting
themselves" from doing their (deontic) homework. It is hard to resist the
thought that something like this caricaturizing ethos may partly explain why
Duff, as we saw in the previous chapter, believes that to discuss moral dilemmas is "exciting, or at least easier than careful thought."[55] And this caricaturizing ethos may shed light, too, on why, despite recognizing the importance of
mercy for punishment theory, in the end Tasioulas mollifies that importance by
favoring a counterintuitive account of mercy that downplays the very moral
dilemmas that it would have otherwise countenanced. While there surely are
plenty of situations in which there exist obvious, non-ambiguous answers to
some moral choices – say, the choice as to whether to punish someone like
Ohlendorf – I think that it is also plain that there are situations in which this is
not the case. To assume that all cases are as crisp as Ohlendorf's is, I think,
a nonstarter. In other words, to massage the facts so as to have them yield
unambiguous answers, even when these facts do not admit of such unambiguous answers, is not the way forward.

Harel's diagnosis of our disagreement – the "gap" separating our different "intellectual dispositions" – concerns not just our particular views on the justification of
punishment. Rather, the disagreement concerns moral philosophy in general.
Indeed, Harel's talk of different intellectual dispositions is reminiscent of
a famous – and insightful – reaction to Williams's own work. Commenting on
Williams's *Ethics and the Limits of Philosophy*, Thomas Nagel claims that, although
it is "a superior book, glittering with intelligence and style," it nonetheless is a form

---

[51]   See Leo Zaibert, "Tragic Choices and the Law," *Critical Analysis of Law* 2.2 (2015): 257–267.
[52]   Alon Harel, "Facing Up: A Response to Critiques of *Why Law Matters*," *Critical Analysis of Law* 2.2
       (2015): 294–313, at 305.
[53]   *Ibid.*, 305–306.    [54]   *Ibid.*, 305.
[55]   R. A. Duff, "The Intrusion of Mercy," *Ohio Journal of Criminal Law* 4 (2007): 360–387, at 380.

of "new romanticism."[56] The invocation of "romanticism" evidently conjures up the usual indictment of irrationalism (anti-Enlightenment, etc.) often leveled against that movement, and it goes, I think, hand in hand with the dismissal of the "intellectual disposition" that Harel thinks undergirds my approach.

I do not think it is fair – or useful – to assume that those philosophers who recognize the *limits* of theory and the fact that moral experience is suffused with deep and complicated moral dilemmas – as Williams does for morality in general and I do for the justification of punishment in particular – are necessarily guilty of what Harel sees as a somewhat dilettantish "intellectual disposition." I do not think, either, that recognizing the complexity of life necessitates that one dabbles in unintelligibility or in unscientific, loose (if not downright irrational) "romanticism." And I am not sure that whatever limitations my intellectual disposition may have vis-à-vis action-guidance are really a *defect*. After all, it is not clear that unambiguous answers – Harel's or anyone else's – do not sometimes come at the price of artificially oversimplifying the situations to which they are responsive.

Without adjudicating the merits of the "romantic" objection to the general (Williams's) questioning of the limits of theory, we could turn to what appears to be a particularly powerful objection aimed specifically against *my* approach in this book. Even if I share a certain "intellectual disposition" with Williams and other moral philosophers, their general questioning of the limits of theory may be seen as less problematic than my questioning the limits of punishment theory. After all, theorizing about moral philosophy in general need not be action-oriented. In that general context, meta-theory, indeed metaethics, are perfectly respectable approaches. But what, it may be protested, would it be to do meta-punishment theory? What is punishment theory *for* if not for telling us when punishment is (and is not) justified? When, in other words, should we (or should we not) inflict it? Even if I am right in my criticisms of extant justifications of punishment, and independently of whatever problems the romantic approach to moral philosophy in general may face, what could a "non-deontic," "romantic" punishment theory possibly have to offer?

My first reaction to the criticism that seems to me to underwrite these questions is to push back against the supposition that punishment theory needs to be *exclusively* concerned with action-guiding considerations. Even if my reflections in this book do not amount to a complete set of concrete guidelines as to when and how much we should punish, they may reveal errors to be avoided, and to evoke the very title of the book, these reflections may thereby suggest different ways of *thinking* about punishment. Just as it may be valuable to identify shortcomings in the ways in which moral philosophers approach their field and propound their theories, it may be equally legitimate to examine the shortcomings in the ways that punishment theorists

---

[56]  Thomas Nagel, "Review of *Ethics and the Limits of Philosophy*," *Journal of Philosophy* 83.6 (1986): 351–360, at 352.

approach the subject matter of their concern and the way they propound their theories. And just as problems can be identified at the general level of moral philosophy as such, they can be identified at the particular level of punishment theory itself as well.

But I have yet another reaction, which I think highlights the sense in which, rather than it being somehow particularly problematic, to subject punishment theory to this meta-level analysis can be particularly helpful and timely. Far and beyond Nagel's charge of "new romanticism," Scheffler, too, resists Williams's attack on the morality system along the following lines:

> [I]f modern ethical thought, for all its faults, has helped to produce many of the features of the modern world that most deserve our support and allegiance, we would do well not to repudiate it unless we absolutely have to, or else unless we are very sure that we have something better to put in its place.[57]

As a general propaedeutic matter, Scheffler's cautionary note is of course well taken. But its force within the context of Williams's *Ethics and the Limits of Philosophy* is more limited. First, as we have seen, Williams's target is not quite "modern ethical thought" as such but, explicitly, one particular way of engaging in ethical thinking – one particular province of modern ethical thought – which he calls "the morality system" (and which I have linked to a certain way of privileging the methods of mathematics and economics).[58] Second, it is not clear whether those specific aspects of the morality system Williams has criticized have helped support specifically those features of the modern world that, as Scheffler correctly points out, indeed deserve support and allegiance. And third, just like my goals in this book, Williams's goals in *Ethics and the Limits of Philosophy* above all concern *theoretical* problems. "Rethinking Morality" would have been as pertinent a title for Williams's book as "Punishment Theory and the Limits of Philosophy" would have been for mine. This of course is not to suggest that because a certain project is theoretical, then its practical consequences cannot be invoked in order to criticize it. But I do wish to suggest that it is possible that Williams's criticisms of the morality system are consistent with a comprehensive moral position that would underwrite those features of the modern world that Scheffler (rightly) suggests deserve support.

As it turns out, however, the case of punishment theory is surprisingly strong vis-à-vis the type of worry Scheffler invokes when he reminds us of those features of the modern world that indeed deserve our support and allegiance. In an undeniable display of progress, the actual punishments inflicted nowadays upon criminal wrongdoers are, at least in theory, much more civilized, than, say, those of medieval torture chambers. But it is unclear how exactly punishment theory itself has helped bring about this progress. As I argued in the previous chapter, the attractive

---

[57]  Samuel Scheffler, "Morality through Thick and Thin: A Critical Notice of *Ethics and the Limits of Philosophy*," *The Philosophical Review* 96 (1986): 411–434, at 434.

[58]  This is reminiscent of Nussbaum's position. See footnote 29 above.

humanness of the communicative approach to punishment, for example, is not really part of the communicative approach as such – rather, it is something external to it. Similarly, there seems to be little in those justifications of punishment based on either classical utilitarianism or (to a lesser extent) on deontic retributivism, in themselves, that would ensure particularly humane institutions. After all, certain extraordinarily severe punishments could turn out to be utility-maximizing, and certain extraordinarily awful acts may deserve extraordinarily severe punishments. The reasons why we may decide not to inflict these very severe punishments may, in a sense, lie outside punishment theory proper – or at least outside punishment theory as it has been traditionally understood. So the progress that can be discerned regarding *some* punishment practices, positive as it undoubtedly is, is not necessarily linked to punishment theory as such.

Moreover, the fact that the debate between the two central schools of thought regarding the justification of punishment has remained similarly intractable for millennia invites skepticism regarding the supposition that punishment theory, as such, has given rise to specific punishment practices that deserve our support and allegiance.[59] The statistics mentioned in Chapter 1 speak for themselves: millions of people punished by the state, most of them for actions whose alleged immorality is very questionable. The complaints with overcriminalization that worried Tacitus almost two millennia ago have reached exorbitant levels nowadays – particularly in otherwise more or less well-functioning liberal democracies. Beyond those statistics, however, one (admittedly scandalous) concrete contemporary example from the United States may show just how much some of our specific punishment institutions do *not* deserve our support and allegiance.

It is well known that the Thirteenth Amendment to the *United States Constitution* abolished slavery and involuntary servitude. Much less known is the fact that this abolition was never *tout court*, for it prominently includes a scandalous exception: slavery was abolished "except as punishment for a crime." In other words, someone could – strictly speaking – still be turned into a slave in the United States, provided this is done as punishment for a crime. The fact that the United States' abolition of slavery has never been complete and that the United States continues to explicitly permit slavery as a punishment, even if only "in the books" and not in terms of real practice is, of course, a scandal. And it speaks volumes as to the United States' anachronistic and harsh understanding of wrongdoers and of their rights – and of punishment theory itself. The United States recognizes that committing some crimes may render their perpetrators not merely liable to undergo considerable suffering but liable to forego the *totality* of their rights, including, a fortiori, all of their human rights.

---

[59] See, e.g., Plato, *Protagoras*, W. K. C. Guthrie (trans.), in Edith Hamilton and Huntington Cairns (eds.), *The Collected Dialogues of Plato*, Princeton, NJ: Princeton University Press (1989): 308–352 (especially at 324a–b).

In *Slavery by Another Name*, Douglas A. Blackmon points out how

> [b]eginning in the late 1860s [on the wake of the passing of the Thirteenth
> Amendment], and accelerating after the return of white political control in 1877,
> every southern state enacted an array of interlocking laws essentially intended to
> criminalize black life. Many such laws were struck down in court appeals or
> through federal interventions, but new statutes embracing the same strictures on
> black life quickly appeared to replace them.[60]

Blackmon's Pulitzer-winning book amply – and depressingly – documents how
these despicable efforts to enslave African Americans continued with remarkable
"success," long after slavery was "abolished." While, as the title of his book suggests,
Blackmon's book documents matters until the Second World War, it is not that
repugnant practices ended then.[61] The sheer demographic composition of the
United States' bloated prison population – where African Americans are extraordinarily overrepresented – serves as a shameful reminder of the continuation of the
problem.[62]

The fact that in the United States slavery-as-a-punishment is – in the second
decade of the twenty-first century – still permitted is not a frequent topic of discussion among contemporary punishment theorists. This is of course not to suggest that
contemporary punishment theorists are not (or would not be) as appalled by this
reality as I am. Neither it is to suggest that any justification of punishment must
perforce take this specific horrific aspect of the United States' peculiar take on the
nature of punishment into consideration. Conceptual work is not really possible if
we do not sometimes bracket out some things. My mentioning these facts is meant to
capture the way in which the standard monistic way of approaching the justification
of punishment brackets out, with great ease, *important* considerations. The fact that
slavery-as-a-punishment is still permitted in the United States should at least be *part*
of the conversation among specialists. And even if in this or that context this fact
could – or even should, as I will explain later – be bracketed out, at some point it
should receive the attention it deserves. Properly pluralistic approaches to punishment, unshackled from the strictures of the illusions of tidiness engendered by the

---

[60]  Douglas A. Blackmon, *Slavery by Another Name: The Re-Enslavement of Black Americans from the
      Civil War to World War II*, New York, NY: Anchor Books (2008), 53.

[61]  See Michelle Alexander, *The New Jim Crow: Mass Incarceration in the Age of Colorblindness*,
      New York, NY: The New Press (2012).

[62]  For a depressing example of the United States' criminal justice system, consider how Blackmon's
      book was banned in a prison in Alabama after an inmate (incidentally, himself serving a life sentence
      for a murder committed when he was fourteen) wanted to read it: authorities alleged the book was an
      incitement to violence. See Campbell Robertson, "Alabama Inmate Sues to Read Southern History
      Book," *The New York Times*, September 26, 2011, A14, and "A Book Ban Overreaction,"
      *The Washington Post*, October 3, 2011, A16. About convict lease more generally, see Milfred
      C. Fierce, *Slavery Revisited: Blacks and the Southern Convict Lease System 1865–1933*, New York,
      NY: Africana Studies Research Center (1994). In the preface, Fierce points out how "the widespread
      and merciless mistreatment of leased Black convicts was, more than anything else, the element that
      characterized the convict lease system and made it infamous," *ibid.*, viii.

moral mathematics approach I have sketched previously, are better equipped to bring the more technical aspects of the justification of punishment in conversation with those other aspects of life whose consideration is also *important*. To do this is neither to fail to support those features of our moral world that do deserve support and allegiance nor to succumb to romanticism, dilettantism, or obscurantism.

## 6.4 PLURALISM, THE VALUE OF FORGIVENESS, AND THE MESSINESS OF THE WORLD

I do not believe that Harel's attitude regarding my take on moral conflicts is *identical* to Scheffler's attitude regarding Williams's take on the morality system. But I do believe that, at bottom, they are both (even if only partially) motivated by a similar worry. This is a worry that we have encountered before: when we were confronted with Tasioulas's endorsement of an odd account of forgiveness or with Duff's privileging of the normativity of games or with Arendt's and Feinberg's remarks as to the inability of the law to respond to evil. The worry is that positions such as Williams's regarding morality or mine regarding the justification of punishment may be just too unmanageably *messy*.

Admittedly, the axiological pluralism I defend in this book does entail that a wide variety (in fact, an infinity) of factors – including, as we just saw, the fact that slavery (as a punishment) is still permitted in the United States – can enter into play when seeking to non-simplemindedly justify punishment. If the sheer number of factors were not by itself enough of a problem, I believe that many of those factors cannot be ledgerable and do not lend themselves to anything like the ordering that the economicist "morality system" would impose upon them. Yet, warts and all, the morality system's ledgers at least allow us to bring some order into an otherwise too messy and undifferentiated universe. And thus, even if I succeeded in the previous section in showing why my approach is not susceptible to the criticisms that Scheffler levels against Williams's views or that Harel levels against my own (dilettantish) "intellectual disposition," my approach may nonetheless appear to be too messy and unmanageable.

I have insisted throughout the book that this feared messiness is not a flaw of my axiologically pluralist approach but rather a feature of the messy world we inhabit. My axiological pluralism simply registers more faithfully than its alternatives the underlying (brute) fact that the world *is* messy – a fact that ordinary, everyday experience reveals to us.[63] Thus, I think the burden of proof falls on those who wish to deny what ordinary, everyday experience reveals to us. But in this last section I wish to highlight some ways in which, independently of this general point, my

---

[63] Williams tells the following anecdote: "I recall a remark made to me by Stefan Körner, which I found a complement, after a paper on moral conflict: 'You said it's all a mess and it is all a mess.'" See his "The Liberalism of Fear," in *In the Beginning Was the Deed: Realism and Moralism in Political Argument*, Princeton, NJ: Princeton University Press (2005), 52.

approach is perhaps less messy – and more manageable – than it may be feared and
ways in which, even if ultimately messier than its alternatives, this is not a point
against it.

The first point I wish to make is that the attractiveness of something *resembling* the
axiological pluralism I advocate, and often as a result of a similar disappointment
with the most unsavory aspects of monism, has not been lost on *all* contemporary
punishment theorists. Some of the mixed theorists in the second half of the twen-
tieth century, for example, were attracted to something like the axiological pluralism
I recommend here (even if unconsciously and at any rate without noticing its full
implications). An overture toward axiological pluralism was noticeable already in
the work of H. L. A. Hart. In the first sentence of Hart's famous "Prolegomenon to
the Principles of Punishment," he openly admitted that his main goal was to show
that "any morally tolerable account of this institution [criminal punishment] must
exhibit it as a compromise between distinct and partly conflicting principles."[64] And
he was expressly motivated by "the suspicion that the view that there is just one
supreme value or objective (e.g. Deterrence, Retribution, or Reform) in terms of
which *all* questions about the justification of punishment are to be answered, is
somehow wrong."[65]

Needless to say, I believe that Hart was right in that traditional justifications of
punishment were narrowly focused on one single value (either the indiscriminate
diminution of suffering or the infliction of deserved suffering). "Manageable" as the
traditional justifications may have thereby been, they were, in Hart's view, nonetheless defective. Whatever problems can be detected in Hart's position, I know of
no one who may have suggested that these are the result of it somehow being
too messy or too unmanageable. So, whatever additional messiness Hart's strategy
vis-à-vis the axiological monism he criticized may have generated, this messiness has
not been seen as particularly problematic at all. The consideration of Hart's position
allows us to see that there is really nothing about "messiness" as such that is to be
feared – particularly, of course, when this messiness is justified.

The comparison to Hart's position, however, helps me only to a point. It helps in
the sense that my strategy to expand the number of values with which punishment
theory must contend – a strategy that, in some form, I share with Hart – need not
involve any particularly *worrying* messiness. But the comparison does not help in the
sense that I in fact think that Hart went wrong precisely because, although he
expanded the number of values that matter to punishment theory, his approach
remained too narrow nonetheless – not messy enough. Insofar as the spirit of Hart's
position was that justifications of punishment focused on just one value were overly
narrow, one would have thought that the natural next step would have been to
embrace a pluralism that admits a much greater number of values. Yet, when Hart

[64] In H. L. A. Hart, *Punishment and Responsibility* (2nd edn.), Oxford: Oxford University Press (2008), 1.
    Hart's use of the word "principle" (instead of "rule") is irrelevant in this context.
[65] *Ibid.*, 2.

listed the values that he thought stood in need of combination, he enumerated only three: "Deterrence, Retribution, or Reform." Moreover, these "three" values are really two, since after all deterrence and reform can be grouped together under the heading of "medicinal" values. Hart's position was in a sense a real baby step: rather than considering just *one* value when trying to justify punishment, he suggested considering *two* values: the value of desert and medicinal value.

The deeper reason why Hart's position remained problematically narrow – even if not quite as narrow as those positions he was criticizing – goes beyond a numerical point (in fact, I too focus on just two values). The deeper reason relates to the fact that one of the two types of value Hart cared about – medicinal as it was – was not an intrinsic value at all, not a type of value that was in itself *important* (in Williams's sense of this term). Thus, in spite of his gesturing toward a pluralist axiology, Hart remains too firmly anchored in the morality system, with its neat moral mathematics and its narrowness. Hart's failure to more decisively engage with a properly pluralist axiology is much more pronounced than Tasioulas's, since Hart never engaged with the value of forgiveness, understood, to repeat, as a particular way of remitting deserved suffering that is valuable in itself (or that it adds value to an organic whole that is made better by its presence, absent any medicinal considerations).

So, I can only find limited support in the fact that other punishment theorists have also gestured toward axiological pluralism, since I believe that they erred precisely because their gesturing did not go far enough. In other words, these other approaches were, from my perspective, not messy enough. By failing to engage with the intrinsic value of forgiveness, Hart avoided the discussion of precisely the deep – and seemingly intractable – moral conflicts that I believe are part and parcel of a properly pluralistic justification of punishment. In yet another version of the gerrymandering gambit, Hart famously placed each of the two values about which he cared under a different heading, which he called "general justifying aim" and "distribution," and in so doing he essentially thwarted any serious examination of the real conflicts that can arise between the values with which a properly pluralistic justification of punishment should be concerned.[66] Even Tasioulas, who, unlike Hart, does meaningfully engage with the value of forgiveness, in the end succumbs to the allure of the ledger and embraces a counterintuitive understanding of the term that is at home in the neat world of the morality system.

And then the fear, even if in somewhat of an attenuated form, remains: How can I explain the messiness of my approach? Other than reiterating the general point whereby insofar as what is messy is the world itself, then theories that seriously engage with such messy world will be messy as well, I would like to say the following. Contra Hart (and in a way, perhaps also contra Tasioulas), I have suggested that the values that a properly axiological justification of punishment needs to countenance

---

[66] *Ibid.*, 1–13. For more on the peculiar ways in which Hart divides up the territory of punishment (and for Hart's views on punishment generally), see John Gardner's excellent "Introduction" to H. L. A. Hart, *Punishment and Responsibility*, xiii–liii.

are indeed innumerable. Punishment theory needs to have something to say about, for example, the fact that a given country permits slavery as a punishment. Like Hart, however, I have argued that *two* of those many values are especially central: the administration of justice and the merciful diminution of suffering. As just noted, these are not quite Hart's two values – though they are in essence Tasioulas's two values. So, in the end, just like these proto-pluralists, I too focus on the tension between a pair of values. Given the way I have defined these two values, it is clear that my approach is messier than these proto-pluralist approaches (and much messier than the simplemindedly monistic approaches that both the proto pluralists and myself reject). Still, centered around the tension between two values, my approach in this book is, I think, considerably less messy than if I were to attempt to engage with an open-ended – or even a large – number of values.

In wishing to seriously engage with the moral conflict that punishment necessarily generates (again, insofar as when we realize the value that punishment realizes, we necessarily fail to realize the value that forgiveness would have realized), I do not need to get tangled up in the complicated problems of determining whether there is one value that overrides all the others or even in the more restricted case of the two values of justice and sympathy, whether one always overrides the other. This has been a central preoccupation of the philosophical discussion of pluralism, in part because it has been assumed that not to have a neat hierarchy of values specifying which ones defeat which others is to leave matters somehow "underdetermined by reason." But for my purposes in this book this is not an important endeavor. I agree with Berlin and Williams, when, responding to a criticism of this tenor by George Crowder, they assert:

> In his talk of "underdetermination by reason," Crowder seems unsure which of two quite different views about potentially conflicting values he is ascribing to the pluralist: that it is not a requirement of reason that there should be one value which in all cases prevails over the other; or that in each particular case, reason has nothing to say (that is there is nothing reasonable to be said) about which should prevail over the other. Pluralists – we pluralists, at any rate – see the first of these views as obviously true, and the second as obviously false.[67]

In other words, one can be a pluralist without taking a stand on the question as to which values defeat which other values in this or that occasion, and this in no way entails that thereby the position is incoherent or otherwise unmanageable. In fact, these remarks by Berlin and Williams are offered in the context of defending a certain affinity between pluralism and liberalism. And turning to this venerable and overabundant school of thought in political philosophy illustrates my stance well.

---

[67] Isaiah Berlin and Bernard Williams, "Pluralism and Liberalism: A Reply," in Isaiah Berlin, *Concepts and Categories*, Princeton, NJ: Princeton University Press (2013): 325–330, at 328.

While liberalism is undoubtedly a Protean concept, one central theme in liberal theory is that liberty and equality are both valuable and that they may conflict with each other in profound ways.[68] Different theories may privilege liberty over equality or vice versa, but it is often assumed that these two values can indeed coexist and that diminutions in one of them need not be fully expressible in terms of the other. Liberal pluralists need not have a view (though they may) as to whether one of these values always trumps the other one – and they need not (though they may) have a single scale, or a supra-value, in terms of which conflicts between liberty and equality are to be expressed.

This is a useful model for understanding my approach in this book. Just as the tension between liberty and equality is at the core of many a liberal theory (a tension that does not render them unmanageably messy), the tension between the incompatible values that punishment and forgiveness may realize is at the core of any properly pluralistic justification of punishment, like mine (without thereby rendering the ensuing justification of punishment unmanageably messy). As it turns out, moreover, the justification of punishment is a particularly crisp example of pluralism in the sense that it is *impossible* for punishment to exist without generating a conflict between the value of justice (achieved via the infliction of deserved suffering) and the value of sympathy (achieved via the merciful remission of said deserved suffering).

It may look as if this necessarily dilemmatic structure of punishment reveals a disanalogy between punishment theory and pluralistic political theories. And it may seem that this disanalogy may then render my comparison between punishment theory and political theories such as liberalism not too helpful – after all, the tension between liberty and equality is, arguably, *not* conceptually necessary. But I do not think that even if the disanalogy is admitted, this would undermine the pertinence of my mobilization of Berlin's and Williams's general point. One can be a pluralist about punishment (in the sense of seeing value in both the infliction of deserved suffering and in its merciful remission) without having to provide a precise rule as to when and why one of these values defeats the other and without one's approach thereby becoming incoherent or otherwise unmanageable.

## 6.5 CONCLUSION

I have tried in this chapter to highlight how the ways in which punishment theorists approach their own field may be related to the way in which *some* moral philosophers more generally approach the larger field of moral philosophy as such. As my

---

[68] See e.g., Isaiah Berlin "Two Concepts of Liberty," in *Liberty* (Henry Hardy, ed.), Oxford: Oxford University Press (2002): 166–217; John Rawls, A *Theory of Justice* (revised edn.), Cambridge, MA: Harvard University Press (1999); Ronald Dworkin, *Justice for Hedgehogs*, Cambridge, MA: Harvard University Press (2011).

emphasis on the word "some" in the previous sentence suggests, there is a remarkable difference between these two arenas. It is only at the general level that this perspective is ever questioned. Punishment theorists do not question it, and in fact they operate in remarkable isolation from these discussions at the general level. The common perspective eschews the notion of moral luck and too uncritically embraces a view of moral philosophy that is too economicist and too mathematical for its own good.

It may be feared that in rejecting this approach, a certain theoretical looseness or even a certain obscurantism becomes unavoidable. But I have tried to show how this is not true of the view of punishment theory I defend. Still, even if neither obscurantist nor loose, it may still be argued that my view of punishment theory is hopelessly messy, at least in the sense that it allows a multiplicity of factors to be relevant in evaluating whether a particular infliction of punishment or punishment in general is justified. And my response to this last worry is that while I am unapologetically invested in defending a broad pluralistic approach – one that is indeed capable of taking into account a very large number of considerations – I do not in this book work out how those multiple considerations would actually play out. Instead, I focus on two elements: the value of the infliction of deserved suffering and the value of the merciful remission of said deserved suffering (i.e., the value of forgiveness). Dealing with just two values is much less messy than dealing with many and very diverse values.

Even limited to the consideration of these two values, however, my view of punishment theory is not utterly immune from the skepticism that would see it as too messy. After all, I have rejected views of forgiveness that see it as neat and tidy – say, Tasioulas's view, in which forgiveness generates duties. My view of forgiveness sees it as a very complicated – indeed paradoxical – phenomenon. Echoing the spirit of Williams's criticism of the morality system, my view of forgiveness sees it as explicitly noneconomic, nonmathematical, and not duty-generating. The next chapter is devoted to showing both how a properly pluralistic justification of punishment can greatly benefit from taking a look at the specialized literature on forgiveness and how, even when we turn to forgiveness, it is easy to go astray.

# 7

## The Right Kind of Complexity

While the inescapably dilemmatic structure I have sketched previously plays out very similarly whether we are in the presence of punishment or of forgiveness, it is, oddly, mainly authors contributing to the specialized literature on forgiveness who typically discuss this structure. Punishment theorists, in contrast, hardly ever discuss these moral dilemmas. Chiefly two interrelated reasons explain this asymmetry. First, punishment theorists have been much more closely tied to both monistic axiologies and to overly mechanistic views of morality. Second, the sense of conflict, of doing something that is somehow simultaneously right and wrong, seems to attach more naturally to forgiveness than to punishment. I have in fact elsewhere used the expression "the paradox of forgiveness" to characterize a common view among forgiveness theorists as to the nature of forgiveness.[1] There is nothing original in my use of this term: specters of deep predicaments, quagmires, quandaries, and paradoxes (etc.) are perfectly commonplace in the specialized literature on forgiveness. This is quite unlike what occurs within the context of the specialized literature on punishment, where the expression "the problem of punishment," to take the closest analog, although evidently registering a difficulty, does not conjure up quite the same degree of bewilderment.

Much theoretical housecleaning is necessary in order to distinguish bona fide instances of forgiveness from a variety of other phenomena with which it is frequently confused. For example, to "forgive" because one realizes that the wrongdoer has already suffered enough or because one realizes that, when she acted wrongly, the wrongdoer was undergoing a personal tragedy (say, the death of a loved one) or indeed because one realizes that this would bring about negative consequences is not to forgive. These cases involve realizing that the person has *already* suffered in the way that punishment was supposed to make her suffer (thus rendering any further infliction of suffering excessive and unjust) or involve *excusing* the agent or involve *justifying* her action or involve garden-variety utilitarian number-crunching.

[1] Leo Zaibert, "The Paradox of Forgiveness," *The Journal of Moral Philosophy* 6, (2009): 365–393.

Once we exclude those spurious cases, then we are confronted with genuine cases of forgiveness: cases in which although it would be just – and *valuable* – to punish someone who deserves punishment (and who has no excuses, mitigations, or justifications), we nonetheless conclude that it is all-things-considered better – i.e., *more valuable* – if we remit this punishment.

The paradox of forgiveness obtains because to forgive means to refuse (or, as I have sketched previously and will explain further later, to *deliberately* refuse) to do what *justice* demands: to forgive appears to be to refuse to do the right thing. And, again, there seems to be no equivalent phenomenon in the case of punishment: when punishment is justified (whatever one's justification of punishment might be), then one is *eo ipso* doing the right thing. While I will argue that both of these positions are to be rejected, I will in this chapter explain why the first of them is less simpleminded than the second and, thus, why the specialized literature on forgiveness has embraced the complexity of our responses to wrongdoing in more illuminating ways than the specialized literature on punishment.

What should be already obvious is that there exists a purely analytic connection between punishment and forgiveness: only what is punishable is forgivable, and only what is forgivable is punishable. Culpable wrongdoing is a logical precondition of both punishment and forgiveness. As Hannah Arendt has put it: we "are unable to forgive what [we] cannot punish."[2] This connection does not entail that punishment and forgiveness are jointly exhaustive (for there are other possible responses to culpable wrongdoing, including doing nothing at all). The connection does not deny, either, that punishment and forgiveness are (simultaneously) mutually exclusive: one cannot at one and the same time both punish and forgive one and the same wrongdoer for the one and the same transgression. For, as we have been insisting, to punish is to let the value of administering justice "defeat" the value of diminishing suffering; to forgive is to let the value of diminishing suffering "defeat" the value of administering justice. But the connection does highlight the insufficiently explored theoretical proximity between punishment and forgiveness.

Despite this patent proximity, punishment theorists (with very few exceptions) have not shown any great interest in forgiveness. Few would deny that punishment and forgiveness are somehow related, but even those who notice a relationship do not probe its depth, instead limiting themselves to registering a few generalities – such as that both punishment and forgiveness are responses to (perceived) wrongdoing. Typically, when contemporary punishment theorists encounter the topic of forgiveness and when they do not chalk it up as an "intrusion" into the rarified air of punishment theory proper, they condescendingly see it as, at best, a charming but subsidiary topic and leave it at that. For example, none of the authors discussing "the problem of punishment" listed in the first footnote of this book has anything to say about forgiveness. John Tasioulas, as we have seen earlier, is a welcome exception.

---

[2]    Hannah Arendt, *The Human Condition*, Chicago, IL: University of Chicago Press (1958), 241.

In light of her influential work on forgiveness, which I will discuss at length in this chapter, Martha Nussbaum can perhaps be seen as another exception. Unfortunately, she belongs to a group of philosophers who frame the connection between punishment and forgiveness in such a jaundiced way that one is tempted to think that it would have been better had they not seen it in the first place. These moral philosophers – Nussbaum included – have, perhaps unwittingly, perpetuated two flawed views, which have degenerated into veritable myths: first, that forgiveness is at odds with retributivism, and second, that forgiveness is particularly at home within utilitarian worldviews.

In the first section of the chapter, I will discuss the first myth, paying particular attention to how Nussbaum's influential work has contributed to perpetuating it. The perpetuation is related to a certain cartoonish demonization of retributivism and to a confused tendency to equate it to *lex talionis*, to a flat-footed and insensitive form of strict liability writ large, and to what Nussbaum all too glibly deems "magical thinking." In the second section, I discuss the second myth, and there I endeavor to show that despite superficial affinities, classical utilitarianism has in fact no theoretical place for forgiveness. This is above all because forgiveness needs to be motivated by a very specific kind of moral reason, a reason that simply has no room among the maximally limited number of reasons available to classical utilitarians. In the third section, I critically explore different suggestions as to what might be that right kind of reason that should undergird forgiveness. This exploration leads me, in the fourth section, to a discussion of the useful ways in which the well-known debate among forgiveness theorists concerning conditional and unconditional forgiveness could be extended to punishment theory as well.

## 7.1 RETRIBUTIVISM AND MAGICAL THINKING

More than a century ago, Hastings Rashdall began his famous article on forgiveness by asserting: "The duty of forgiveness is a subject which obviously could not be thoroughly discussed without a previous investigation of the theory of punishment. The rationale of forgiveness must depend on the rationale of punishment."[3] For reasons that should by now be obvious, I reject Rashdall's talk of the *duty* of forgiveness (an issue I discussed in Chapter 5 and to which I will return later). Putting this point aside for the moment, however, Rashdall's overture should be music to my ears. Unfortunately, discordant notes are in the offing. In the immediately following paragraph – the second paragraph in the article – Rashdall finds it necessary to tell us that his

> paper is written from the point of view of one who regards the retributive theory of punishment as irrational, immoral, and ... wholly unchristian. The idea that

---

[3] Hastings Rashdall, "The Ethics of Forgiveness," *International Journal of Ethics* 10.2 (1900): 193–206, at 193.

punishment can be an end in itself apart from the effect which it is to produce upon some spiritual being is to my mind inconsistent with the very idea of rational morality.[4]

Views of this tenor have been popular for quite a long time, and as one could glean from remarks I have made previously (mainly in Chapter 3), they continue to hold sway among contemporary philosophers – albeit often without the overt Christian panegyrics.

I would like to pay special attention to the way in which one of today's most inspiring moral philosophers has painted an even more harrowing view of retributivism. Since Nussbaum's oeuvre is so vast and wide-ranging, I will try to limit myself to some main themes in her seminal and influential "Equity and Mercy," which are further developed in her much more recent work.[5] And I will argue that notwithstanding the many merits of Nussbaum's views, throughout this long span of her career (roughly twenty-five years), her views in this matter have been predicated on an inadequate opposition between mercy (both in the general sense and in the restricted sense in which I use it here, in which it is a synonym of forgiveness)[6] and retributivism.

Famously, Nussbaum begins "Equity and Mercy" focusing on Andrea Dworkin's novel *Mercy* and by describing the horrible abuses to which its protagonist, Andrea, was subjected.[7] This repeated abuse led Andrea to an "angry refusal of mercy" and toward a "determination to exact retribution without concern for the identity of the particulars."[8] While Nussbaum admits that it would be reasonable to assume that one point of the novel is to highlight how her "terrible experiences have corrupted Andrea's perception [and her judgment]," Nussbaum does not sufficiently distance herself from Andrea's perspective. Nussbaum tells us that Dworkin's

> novel does not read like a traditional novel, because its form expresses the retributive idea that its message preaches. That is, it refuses to perceive any of the male offenders – or any other male – as a particular individual, and it refuses to invite the reader into the story of their lives.[9]

[4] *Ibid.*, 193–194.
[5] Martha Nussbaum, "Equity and Mercy," *Philosophy and Public Affairs* 22.2 (1993): 83–125; Martha Nussbaum "Transitional Anger," *Journal of the American Philosophical Association* 1.1 (2015): 41–56; Martha Nussbaum, *Anger and Forgiveness: Resentment, Generosity, Justice*, Oxford: Oxford University Press (2016).
[6] Unlike Tasioulas and Duff (and myself), Nussbaum does not see forgiveness as mercy-in-the-case-of-punishment. She understands mercy as something broader than forgiveness, something linked to sympathetic understanding more generally. Still, the Greek term she translates as "sympathetic understanding" – *suggnômê* – is often translated as "forgiveness." Although Nussbaum thinks that this is a mistake (*ibid.*, 267, fn. 29), she herself has made it. My criticism of Nussbaum's demonization of retributivism is independent from the difference between mercy and forgiveness.
[7] Andrea Dworkin, *Mercy*, New York, NY: Four Walls Eight Windows (1990).
[8] Nussbaum, "Equity and Mercy," 84.   [9] *Ibid.*

Andrea's "retributive idea" appears to be that it is acceptable to ignore the differences between individuals and to harm innocent men, whom she knows to be innocent. And Nussbaum appears to acquiesce with Andrea's (and Dworkin's) view that "[retributive] justice is cruel and hard," although this is often asserted indirectly, by way of asserting that mercy is intimately connected to a certain "vision of the particular" that is absent from retributivism.[10] But there really can be no doubts as to how close Nussbaum's views on retributivism and mercy are to Dworkin's: she sees the former as "rigid," "harsh," "strict," "stubborn," and "inflexible"; whereas the latter she sees as "mild" and "gentle."[11] Nussbaum even tells us that nothing less than full-blown "cruelty" can be seen as "a frequent outgrowth of retributive anger."[12] Unequivocally, Nussbaum asserts her own view whereby "Dworkin's novel provid[es] us with a striking modern example of the strict retributivist position."[13]

Perhaps these may have been accurate descriptors of retributivism in antiquity, and perhaps some of them may – embarrassingly – apply in some contexts to someone like Kant. But the picture that emerges from Nussbaum's remarks really is an anachronistic caricature of contemporary retributivism – even of those deontic versions of retributivism I have criticized.[14] For example, no contemporary retributivist, qua retributivist, would refuse to look at the particulars; no contemporary retributivist would ever justify punishing someone she knows is innocent. In fact, she should very much want to look at those particulars insofar as this is *necessary* for determining what it is that wrongdoers deserve. Contemporary retributivism is not a matter of seeing every instance of wrongdoing as a strict liability offense (e.g., those in which "the particulars" Nussbaum has in mind are indeed bracketed out). Andrea not attending to the "detail" that her victims were wholly innocent has, in this day and age, absolutely nothing to do with retributivism, in *any* of its varieties. It seems to me that this particular "detail" should have mattered to any retributivist throughout history, no matter how primitive.

Furthermore, attending to the "detail" that a man one is about to kill is wholly innocent, and to therefore desist of one's original plan, does not strike me as a case of *merciful* behavior either. Imagine you were once harmed by someone named Mike; you are not going about "punishing" each and every other Mike you may afterward encounter does not render you merciful – just as your "punishing" each and every Mike does not render you a retributivist. These behaviors render you mad, or at least wildly confused. Even if you were harmed not by a single Mike but instead by various members of a certain group, say, by Germans during Second World War, there would be absolutely nothing retributive in your "punishing" other Germans whom you know to be wholly innocent. And there

---

[10]  *Ibid.*, 85.   [11]  *Ibid.*, 86.   [12]  *Ibid.*, 102.   [13]  *Ibid.*, 122.

[14]  This is a caricature. For the differences between retributivism and other views with which it is commonly confused, see Michael Moore, *Placing Blame: A Theory of the Criminal Law*, Oxford: Clarendon Press (1997) 88–91, 153–159, and *passim*. I will return to this issue later in the chapter.

would be nothing "forgiving" or "merciful" in your refusing to "punish" those innocent Germans either.

As much here as anywhere else, of course, these cartoons are best avoided. But I would like to underscore how odd it is for Nussbaum to fall prey to these cartoons, given some of her other views – views with which I wholeheartedly agree. First, Nussbaum rejects a certain attitude by (criminal) judges according to which "the offender should be treated as a thing with no insides to be scrutinized from the internal viewpoint, but simply as a machine whose likely behavior, as a result of a given judgment or punishment, we attempt, as judges, to predict."[15] Nussbaum correctly places this type of attitude within positivistic or quasi-positivistic world-views (such as those of Oliver Wendell Holmes and Richard Posner). The similarities between these attitudes and the mechanistic views we have examined previously – above all utilitarianism but also the views put forth by authors who are not full-blown utilitarians or positivists (think of Duff and his game imagery) – are also remarkable. So, it should be obvious the extent to which I agree with Nussbaum's rejection of these attitudes. Second, Nussbaum correctly rejects a myopic – and insensitive – position as to the significance of a *perfect* structural symmetry between mitigation and aggravation, á la Antonin Scalia and Plato.[16] Roughly, this position asserts that if we expand the lens through which we look at wrongdoers, this may turn out to lead to harsher, not milder, punishments, since some of the details we may discover may be aggravating rather than mitigating. While in a sense this may be true, views of this sort too glibly ignore the reality of suffering – a reality I have sought to emphasize throughout this book. Third, Nussbaum has misgivings about the way in which typical efforts to engage with the "justification of punishment" have been reductive and have tended to over-simplify the phenomena under investigation. Thus, Nussbaum claims, "a rational lawgiver will reject the entire way in which the debate over the management of wrongdoing is typically cast, as a debate about the 'justification of punishment'."[17] Once again, my agreement with Nussbaum on this point should be obvious.

Yet my reasons for rejecting typical discussions of the "justification of punishment" are importantly different from Nussbaum's. In the preceding chapters I have sought to complicate the justification of punishment. Part of this complication has to do with giving the distinction between the axiological and the deontic its proper due and with seeing how it is at bottom a certain axiological impasse (i.e., whether suffering is invariably bad) that allows us to understand what the debate concerning the justification of punishment really is about. Nussbaum's "official" position may be that she is not opposed to complicating matters, but in reality she does simplify too much. The impetus animating her project is to somehow go beyond the "archaic" (if not inflexible, harsh, cruel, etc.) worldview of justice and punishment (emblematized by retributivism) and to embrace a more nuanced, mature, and

---

[15] Nussbaum, "Equity and Mercy," 111.   [16] *Ibid.*, 87.   [17] Nussbaum, *Anger and Forgiveness*, 179.

civilized worldview of mercy and forgiveness. Even if the specialized literature on forgiveness is more complex than the specialized literature on punishment in exactly the terms Nussbaum thinks it is, by altogether dismissing any and all considerations in favor of punishment as a possible, legitimate response to wrongdoing, Nussbaum is in effect employing a major simplifying gambit.

In contrast, I do not think that the worldview of forgiveness should *replace* the worldview of punishment. I do not believe that punishment is necessarily barbaric or that forgiveness is necessarily admirable. Deserved suffering sometimes has value (in the sense that it can add value to the organic wholes in which it appears) independently of any further consequence, and the same is true of forgiveness. Rather than replacing one worldview with another – as does Nussbaum – I wish to put two specialized literatures (that of punishment and that of forgiveness) in more fruitful contact with each other.

Nussbaum's bald aversion to (her cartoonish version of) retributivism prevents her from fruitfully connecting these two specialized literatures. In a section of "Equity and Mercy" titled "A Model of Judicial Reasoning," Nussbaum explicitly dismisses retributivism *tout court*:

> [I]n order to depart from a retributivism that is brutal in its neglect of human complexity, we do not need to embrace a deterrence-only view that treats people as means to society's ends, aggregating their good and ill without regard to what is appropriate for each. The deterrence view is all too close to the retributive view it opposes, in its resolute refusal to examine the particularities of motive, intention, and story, in its treatment of people as place-holders in a larger social or cosmic calculus. A merciful judge need not neglect issues of deterrence, but she is above all committed to an empathetic scrutiny of the "insides" of the individual life.[18]

The reason I quote this passage in full is not so much to flog the dead horse that Nussbaum is not a friend of retributivism. Rather, I wish to highlight that back when she wrote "Equity and Mercy," she at least thought it necessary to underscore that the rejection of retributivism she urged did not quite entail thereby endorsing "deterrence." She was then, at least in this passage, aware of a certain proximity between what she calls "the deterrence view" (which, for our purposes here, can be equated with "utilitarianism") and "the retributive view." But Nussbaum's views have changed.

Insofar as, following Aristotle, Nussbaum understands *anger* as including a certain "desire for retribution," and she finds this desire unqualifiedly and invariantly wrong, Nussbaum now tells us (as we noted in Chapter 3) that her current view on punishment

> seems, and is, very Utilitarian, and this may be surprising. But sympathy with the Utilitarian idea of punishment arises as the more or less inexorable conclusion of

18 Nussbaum, "Equity and Mercy," 115.

some thoughts about why anger is problematic – irrational in some cases, morally objectionable (because hooked on one's own status) in others. I began working on anger with little sympathy with Utilitarian views of punishment, having criticized them in print numerous times. I find it hard to avoid the conclusion that Bentham had a deep insight about the defects of his society, suffused as it was with status-consciousness and a virulent payback mentality.[19]

In other words, her early desire to find a way to transcend both retributivism and the utilitarianism of what she called "the deterrence view" has now given way to a much more decisive – and in my opinion regrettable – rapprochement with classical utilitarianism.

Only a year after publishing the article from which I have just quoted, Nussbaum absorbed it into Chapter 2 of her *Anger and Forgiveness: Resentment, Generosity, Justice*. One of the most significant differences between the original and the recycled texts concerns precisely this endorsement of classical utilitarianism. The paragraph from "Transitional Anger" I have just quoted is transformed in *Anger and Forgiveness*. In the recycled version, Nussbaum tells us that her current view on punishment

> seems, and is, welfarist, and this may be surprising to readers, given my criticisms of some forms of Utilitarianism elsewhere. But the errors that I have elsewhere imputed to Utilitarianism need not be made by the person who takes this road: she does not need to hold that all goods are commensurable; she does not need to ignore the boundaries between persons; and she does not need to deny that some good things are so much more important than others that they should enjoy a special protected status. She can, that is to say, be Mill rather than Bentham.[20]

I must admit that I am not persuaded by the replacement of "very Utilitarian" with "welfarist." It strikes me as facile, evoking as it does the euphemistic maneuvers discussed in Chapter 3 whereby philosophers deny that they are utilitarians by claiming that they are instead "instrumentalists" or "consequentialists." I have rejected these maneuvers above all by insisting that the *idee mere* of utilitarianism (about punishment) is that suffering is invariably bad and that, therefore, the fact that suffering may be deserved in no way changes its badness. It seems to me that Nussbaum agrees with this essential axiological point: she does believe that suffering is invariably and unqualifiedly bad. If this is so, her replacing "very Utilitarian" with "welfarist" remains rather unconvincing, and I will henceforth refer to her view as "utilitarian" and not as "welfarist."

Perhaps more promising is Nussbaum's replacement of "Bentham" with "Mill," which seeks to qualify the type of utilitarianism that she now supports. As I pointed out in Chapter 3, there really is nothing very "deep" about Bentham's point that suffering is prima facie bad. As noted then, Mill surely is less simpleminded than Bentham. But why stop at Mill? While Mill is surely a step forward over the crudity

---

[19] Nussbaum, "Transitional Anger," 51.  [20] Nussbaum, *Anger and Forgiveness*, 30.

of Benthamite (classical) utilitarianism, his views are fraught with difficulties. After all, Mill sought to humanize Bentham's utilitarianism but without fully embracing the axiological turn that was necessary in order to unshackle himself from Benthamite constraints. In other words, Mill's utilitarianism remains a somewhat improved version (at least in the sense of being more well-meaning, more humane) of *Benthamite* utilitarianism – and it did not effect a sufficient break with it. Famously, as much as one may want to like Mill's distinction between higher and lower pleasures or his view concerning the preferability of being "Socrates dissatisfied" rather than "a pig satisfied," straitjacketed as he was by the utilitarian credo, *Mill* did not really have theoretical space for these qualitative differences among pleasures.[21] Nussbaum's replacing Bentham with Mill is just not sufficient, for some important problems in Bentham's crude utilitarianism persist – even if in attenuated forms – in Mill's.

Of course, I believe that Nussbaum would have been much better served had she paid more attention to the ways in which many of the problems of classical utilitarianism (still present in Mill's utilitarianism) do disappear in Moore's ideal utilitarianism. Ideal utilitarianism is, as we have seen, not wedded to the allegedly invariant badness of suffering. And it is much better equipped to deal with the axiological structure exhibited by both punishment and forgiveness. It is, moreover, much better equipped than both Benthamite and Millian utilitarianism for incorporating the kinds of considerations that Nussbaum championed early in her career, as she sought to find a way of avoiding both retributivism and utilitarianism.[22] For Moore's ideal utilitarianism and its emphasis on organic wholes are very well equipped to understand the complexity of human life and phenomena that so often eludes the traditional justifications of punishment. It is, moreover, particularly well suited to accommodate the "reasoning of the concerned reader" that Nussbaum has so powerfully and eloquently defended.[23]

To be sure, this is not to say that I agree with Nussbaum's wholesale rejection of retributivism. It has always seemed to me that Nussbaum's aversion toward retributivism is neither well thought out nor well informed. Already by the time she published "Equity and Mercy," Nussbaum's anti-retributivism, expounded via the consideration of Andrea Dworkin's *Mercy*, was, vis-à-vis contemporary versions of retributivism – including those versions of retributivism that I, too, have criticized (albeit for different reasons) – a rather grotesque caricature. Despite the otherwise profound erudition on display in that rightly influential article, Nussbaum's anti-retributivism (vis-à-vis contemporary versions of retributivism) was utterly unsupported by an engagement with any of those views she hastily rejected. It was not until her most recent book – more than twenty years later – that Nussbaum finally

---

[21]   See references in Chapter 1.
[22]   Above all in her extraordinary *The Fragility of Goodness: Luck and Ethics in Greek Tragedy and Philosophy*, Cambridge: Cambridge University Press (1986).
[23]   Nussbaum, "Equity and Mercy," 110.

engaged (albeit breezily) with some contemporary versions of retributivism. While I cannot but welcome this engagement, I do not think Nussbaum has yet fully appreciated the philosophical import of retributivism.

Toward the end of *Anger and Forgiveness*, Nussbaum recognizes that up to that point (we must assume she means this point in the book, though this is true also of this point in her career), she has "simply assumed, on the basis of my prior arguments, that the right approach [to punishment] is forward-looking [i.e., 'welfarist' or, as she had it only a year before, 'very Utilitarian']" and that she has "not fully confronted the strongest retributivist arguments."[24] But her confronting retributivism is, I think, insufficient – an insufficiency that she, to an extent, recognizes:

> So I need to say more at this point about how my argument so far relates to the subtler forms of retributivism. Because there is a vast literature on this topic and this is not a book about punishment, I must be highly selective, omitting many worthy contributions to the debate and treating others with compression; I do not hope to satisfy all readers.[25]

Nussbaum's declaration that her book "is not about punishment" is too self-indulgent. To a very large extent – much larger than Nussbaum appears to recognize – her book *is* a book about punishment. And this is so independently of the general conceptual and axiological proximity between forgiveness and punishment for which I have been arguing throughout the book. Nussbaum's book is after all a book that elaborates on the themes already present in her seminal "Equity and Mercy," which was itself to a large extent a sprawling article *conspicuously* about punishment. The article gets going by considering Andrea's "punishing" men, and roughly the second half of the article is devoted to punishment, including important sections titled "A Model of Judicial Reasoning" and "Mercy and the Criminal Law." Similarly, the recent book explicitly deals – from cover to cover – with punishment and related topics. Arguably *the* central thesis of the recent book is of the same spirit as *the* central thesis of the early article: that we should temper the irascible, brute, barbaric impulses (of retributivism) in favor of more civilized, rational, and forward-looking utilitarian impulses (of forgiveness). Nussbaum does suggest that retributive punishment, at least, is to be replaced by a different, utilitarian response – preferably not punitive at all. Thus, I think that it was incumbent upon Nussbaum to more systematically engage with the richness of that retributivist tradition that she – in my opinion too summarily – wishes to reject.

Be that as it may, Nussbaum's main gripe with retributivism turns out to be an alleged connection between it and *lex talionis*, which she defines as the "idea that a wrongful act is somehow balanced out or paid back by *similar* suffering" – and which she summarily dismisses as a "fantasy of payback" that "is simply not rational" and that constitutes "mere magical thinking."[26] Like Nussbaum, I reject classical formulations of *lex talionis*, although not quite for Nussbaum's reasons and certainly

---

[24] Nussbaum, *Anger and Forgiveness*, 183.    [25] *Ibid.*    [26] *Ibid.* Emphasis added.

not because they involve "magical thinking."[27] Nussbaum's charge of "magical thinking" strikes me as overdone, establishing a veritable leitmotif in the book, not sufficiently supported by arguments, but rather invoked as a mantra.[28]

When thinking about retributivism, Nussbaum appears to have in mind strict liability, sprinkled with a certain relish for the cruel and the sadistic. Independently of the general inaccuracy of this view, Nussbaum's approach to *lex talionis* is internally problematic in that she equivocates between two versions of the doctrine. The first version goes as follows. Immediately after the passage just quoted, Nussbaum offers a pair of examples allegedly showing the moral bankruptcy of *lex talionis*: "[W]e never think," Nussbaum confidently tells us, "that the right response to having your wallet stolen is to steal someone else's wallet, or that the right response to a rape would be to arrange for the rapist to get raped. What good would that do?"[29] It would appear that these examples clarify the otherwise somewhat loose usage of the word "similar" in her account of *lex talionis*, which I highlighted previously. And that would accord with standard, classical versions of *lex talionis*: "an eye for an eye, a tooth for a tooth." The problem is that when Nussbaum discusses the two contemporary "subtler" retributivist positions – Herbert Morris's and Michael Moore's[30] – she ends up rejecting them, to a large extent, because they either "collapse" into *lex talionis* (Morris) or rely on certain intuitions that are themselves ultimately "based" on *lex talionis* (Moore).[31] This is, however, incorrect.

The version of *lex talionis* that may perhaps be linked to Morris's and Moore's retributive views is *not* the "eye for an eye" version but a different one whereby there is value in deserved suffering that is *proportional* to the harm done. Surely neither Morris nor Moore ever recommended raping rapists and so on, though each saw value in meting out deserved punishment. It clearly is extraordinarily different to see value in, say, (1) Nazis being sent to gas chambers after having cruelly sent their victims to gas chambers and (2) Nazi murderers suffering *in proportion* to the magnitude of their crimes (whatever that proportional suffering may turn out to be). And yet the equivocation leads Nussbaum's to reject Morris's and Moore's retributivism as if they were somehow committed to (1), when at most they are committed only to (2).

Closely connected to this equivocation is another perplexing aspect of Nussbaum's rejection of retributivism. Nussbaum claims that Gandhi "equated a violent response to Hitler with "Hitlerism" and that he further claimed that

---

[27]  See, e.g., Leo Zaibert, *Punishment and Retribution*, Aldershot: Ashgate (2006): 105 ff., and Leo Zaibert, *Five Ways Patricia Can Kill Her Husband: A Theory of Intentionality and Blame*, Chicago, IL: Open Court (2005): 35 ff.

[28]  Nussbaum invokes the alleged "magical thinking" of retributivism in many other places. See, Nussbaum, *Anger and Forgiveness*, 24, 25, 29, 33, 36, 38, 54, 127, 136, 161, 184, 185, and 187.

[29]  Nussbaum, *Anger and Forgiveness*, 183.

[30]  Nussbaum also discusses the views of R. A. Duff and of the late Dan Markel, but she considers these "borderline retributivism," Martha Nussbaum, *Anger and Forgiveness*, 188.

[31]  *Ibid.*, 185, 187.

"Hitlerism will never be defeated by counter-Hitlerism."[32] With terse confidence, Nussbaum claims that "Gandhi's views about war are not sensible," and she further adds that the suggestion that we ought to approach Hitler "through nonviolence and love was simply absurd, and would have been profoundly damaging had anyone taken it seriously."[33] One of Nussbaum's reasons for this indictment is this: "[S]elf-defense is not morally equivalent to aggression, nor is the defense of decent political institutions equivalent to their subversion."[34]

I cannot help but agree with the substance of Nussbaum's rejection of Ghandi's reputed position and of its woefully undifferentiated understanding of violence. But I cannot help wishing, too, that Nussbaum would have extrapolated and explored the resonances of her response to Gandhi within the context of punishment theory. In order to oppose the death penalty, for example, one need not avail oneself of the "not sensible" and "simply absurd" position whereby the death penalty is murder by the state. Evidently, the state need not act with malice aforethought when it executes. One does not need to claim that the state *murders* in order to oppose capital punishment. Similarly, Nussbaum is obviously correct that a killing in self-defense is importantly different from an aggressive criminal killing. But the parallel point – which Nussbaum glibly ignores – is also obvious: the suffering that is inflicted because it is the deserved response to a certain wrongdoing is "not morally equivalent" to the suffering that a wrongdoer gratuitously (or sadistically, etc.) causes in the first place. And this, I think, highlights the oddity of Nussbaum's suggestion that retributivism is somehow a matter of approximating as much as possible the *exact* characteristics of the act being punished: stealing the wallet of the pickpocket, having the rapist raped, and so on.

In contrast to her nuanced views regarding war and self-defense, Nussbaum's views on punishment in particular do appear to be inspired by a certain flat-footed Benthamism (even if she sometimes calls it "welfarism") whereby the suffering constitutive of punishment is somehow equivalent to the suffering maliciously caused by a wrongdoer: all punishment is in itself evil. Moreover, once the shortcomings of Nussbaum's linking of retributivism and *lex talionis* are exposed, it becomes clear that what Nussbaum sees as "magical thinking" is, in fact, the axiological thesis whereby the default disvalue of suffering is not invariant. But this is a position that Nussbaum has *not* shown to be mistaken, since, as it turns out, she has yet to even engage with it.

## 7.2 UTILITARIANISM, FORGIVENESS, AND MORAL REASONS

Even if Nussbaum's (and Rashdall's and many others') jaundiced take on retributivism is to be rejected, a problem does remain for deontic retributivists. There really is disappointingly little in deontic retributivism – say, such as Kant's

---

[32] *Ibid.*, 219.    [33] *Ibid.*    [34] *Ibid.*

or Moore's – that may open up theoretical space for forgiveness.[35] And even "revisionist" retributivists who want to recognize the value of forgiveness seem ill at ease in the attempt. Consider Heidi Hurd:

> It is commonplace amongst retributivists to believe that mercy [forgiveness] cannot be morally justified, and that it is a confusion on the part of religion, literature, opera, and the movie industry to portray acts of mercy as laudable instances of institutional justice, moral goodness, or personal virtue. Indeed, many retributivists measure others' commitment to retributivism by whether they have mastered what is thought to be a sophomoric lesson about retributivism – the need to reject mercy as an institutional ideal, and perhaps as a personal one, as well.[36]

Despite this remarkably harsh indictment of forgiveness (mercy), Hurd is in fact gesturing toward a certain rapprochement between retributivism and forgiveness. Unlike other deontic retributivists (such as Kant and Moore), Hurd believes that forgiveness could be morally legitimate. But Hurd still believes that "the arena in which mercy is moral is incredibly circumscribed" and that "retributivists are right to insist that, as a general matter, mercy is an unjustified gesture and a dubious moral virtue."[37] This "incredibly circumscribed" arena of which Hurd speaks is the arena of relationships of love and friendship. I do not think that this arena is as small as Hurd thinks, but my arguments in favor of the central importance of forgiveness are not based on expanding it.

Rather, my view that retributivism and forgiveness are both potentially valuable is based, first and foremost, on my axiological understanding of retributivism. As we have seen, all the axiological retributivist claims is that deserved suffering is not invariably bad and that it can indeed add value to the organic wholes of which it is part. And this claim in no way denies that certain organic wholes can gain in value, too, when they include forgiveness rather than deserved suffering. The axiological retributivist can perfectly well recognize that there could be more value in an organic whole either because it includes forgiving wrongdoers or because it includes making deserving wrongdoers suffer. What is more, the axiological retributivist is particularly well positioned to recognize that both punishment and forgiveness are *structurally* dilemmatic. To punish is to conclude (fallibly, of course) that administering justice adds more value to an organic whole than forgiveness would have added and to forgive is to conclude (again, fallibly) that diminishing suffering adds more value to an organic whole than punishment would have added.[38]

I would like to suggest that, properly understood, forgiveness ought to verge on the *unintelligible* for the classical utilitarian (or for the "welfarist," the "instrumentalist," etc.). I take it that it is obvious that there are forms of diminishing suffering that have

---

[35] See, for example, David Sussman "Kantian Forgiveness," *Kant-Studien* 96.1 (2005): 85–107.
[36] Heidi Hurd, "The Morality of Mercy," *Ohio State Journal of Criminal Law* 4 (2007): 389–421, at 390.
[37] *Ibid.*, 392.
[38] As we have seen, in some particularly harrowing cases the dilemma may have very little intensity. But in a majority of cases these dilemmas cut deeply indeed. I return to this issue in the next chapter.

nothing do to with forgiveness, such as, paradigmatically, cases not involving culpable wrongdoing. When one feeds the hungry or shelters the needy or consoles a bereaved friend, one is (*ex hypothesi*) diminishing suffering but not thereby "forgiving" the hungry, the needy, or the grieving. But even in the cases that do involve culpable wrongdoing, matters can be more complicated than the uninitiated may think.

Despite its much-touted benevolence, classical utilitarianism, on pain of incoherence, cannot possibly justify forgiveness. This is a remarkable result, in that forgiveness is after all a matter of sparing suffering and utilitarianism, as we have seen, is a doctrine monomaniacally devoted to reducing suffering in the world. So remarkable is this result that it is likely to meet great resistance. Yet the explanation as to why the utilitarian cannot countenance forgiveness is, I think, straightforwardly convincing. As we have seen, from the utilitarian perspective, punishment could only be justified if it maximizes (or is reasonably expected to maximize) utility; and if in a given case, punishment maximizes utility, then "forgiveness" would not maximize utility, and it would be simply wrong, and that is that.

Of course, if punishment did not maximize utility, then the utilitarian would oppose its infliction, but *this* refusal to punish would not be forgiveness at all: forgiveness involves the suspension of a punishment that *is* justified – if the punishment to be potentially spared was not in fact justified, then this sparing is not an instance of forgiveness. The utilitarian is simplemindedly invested in maximizing utility (or reducing suffering), and this would dictate that she should "punish" whenever expedient and "forgive" whenever expedient – always simplemindedly. These terms, however, are mere placeholders for faux punishment and faux forgiveness: just like this simplemindedness cannot countenance the axiological complexity of punishment, it cannot countenance the axiological complexity of forgiveness either.

In other words, a classical utilitarian *must* refrain from inflicting deserved suffering (or in fact suffering *simpliciter*) on a wrongdoer when she believes that this is conducive to the reduction of overall suffering. This is exactly what the utilitarian credo *enjoins* her to do. But to "forgive" simply because one wishes to reduce overall suffering is not quite to forgive.[39] After all, forgiveness is typically taken to be optional, elective, gracious. This is precisely why Tasioulas correctly admits that his non-optional account of mercy (forgiveness) *is* counterintuitive. Utilitarian forgiveness (if the expression is even admitted) is as obligatory as utilitarian punishment and indeed as any action dictated by the sacrosanct utilitarian calculus. This may be part of the reason why despite his aversion to retributivism, Rashdall nonetheless confessed that "if by 'utilitarian' theory is meant a view resting upon a

---

[39]   See Ingvar Johansson, "A Little Treatise on Forgiveness and Human Nature" *The Monist* 92.4 (2009): 537–555, particularly on fn. 9, where Johansson claims "it is as logically impossible to punish retributively by means of utilitarian reasons as it is to love for such reasons."

hedonistic theory of ethics, I have nothing to say in its favor."[40] Admittedly, the consequences of the utilitarian withholding of suffering we are now considering may, particularly from the perspective of its beneficiary, be no different from the consequences of genuine forgiveness. But, again, there is more to life than consequences.

An insightful point made by Claudia Card further highlights the problems facing utilitarian approaches to forgiveness.

> When . . . a deserved penalty is withheld only to protect the rights or welfare of others – as when a notorious and powerful gangster is not punished solely for fear of the revenge of his colleagues – it does not seem that mercy is being shown [or forgiveness being granted], although the consequence for the offender may be the same.[41]

In other words, to "forgive" a wrongdoer because we have a train to catch (even if catching this train allows us to greatly alleviate suffering elsewhere) is not really to forgive him – even if somehow some salient consequences for the wrongdoer may turn out to appear identical. As Williams pointed out, a serious problem for utilitarianism is that in its obsession with consequences, it is "basically indifferent to whether a state of affairs consists in what I do or is produced by what I do."[42] There does appear to exist something special that genuine forgiveness must include. While this something special is remarkably elusive for anyone, it is necessarily nonexistent for the utilitarian.

The standard move in the specialized literature on forgiveness is to try to distinguish genuine cases of forgiveness from spurious cases (such as Card's gangster) by insisting that the diminution of suffering that is constitutive of genuine forgiveness (or the forswearing of resentment or the forswearing of revenge, in other formulations) must be the result of acting "for a moral reason."[43] In other words, the suggestion is that we need to take a look at the "peculiar grounds" on which forgiveness is based.[44] I think that this move is sensible and promising. Unfortunately, however, the move does not go far enough.

The results of my admittedly unscientific – but not for that entirely worthless – poll among students, colleagues, and friends are remarkably uniform. I have never

---

[40] Rashdall, "The Ethics of . . .," 196. Rashdall embraced ideal utilitarianism. Unfortunately, however, vis-à-vis his views on forgiveness and punishment, Rashdall did not take the axiological turn that so neatly fits within ideal utilitarianism seriously enough.

[41] Claudia Card, "On Mercy," *The Philosophical Review* 81.2 (1972): 182–207, at 187. As explained, "mercy" and "forgiveness" can be in this context used interchangeably.

[42] Bernard Williams, "A Critique of Utilitarianism," in J. J. C. Smart and B. A. O. Williams, *Utilitarianism: For and Against*, Cambridge: Cambridge University Press (1973), 93.

[43] Jeffrie G. Murphy, "Forgiveness and Resentment," in Jeffrie G. Murphy and Jean Hampton, *Forgiveness and Mercy*, Cambridge: Cambridge University Press (1988), 24. For some interesting modifications (which do not affect the substance of my concerns here) of Murphy's views see his "Remorse, Apology, and Mercy," *Ohio State Journal of Criminal Law* 4.2 (2007): 423–453, and his *American Philosophical Association* "Presidential Address," published as "Legal Moralism and Retribution Revisited," *Criminal Law and Philosophy* 1.1 (2007): 5–20.

[44] Card, "On Mercy," 187.

encountered *anyone* willing to defend the view that to release the gangster out of fear of reprisals in Card's example is to forgive him. So far so good. But the obvious problem immediately suggests itself. It seems hard to deny that the desire to protect innocent people from the wrath of the gangster's colleagues *is* a moral reason. This is in fact *the type* of moral reason that constitutes the entirety of the utilitarian arsenal of reasons. If the release of Card's gangster is indeed *not* forgiveness, even though it *is* done for a moral reason, then it becomes evident that the invocation of moral reasons is not *by itself* sufficiently illuminating as to what is supposed to be unique about forgiveness.

More, it seems, needs to be done in order to specify what *type* of moral reason is invoked when it is claimed that forgiveness must be done "for a moral reason." This is particularly urgent if something like Williams's criticisms of the morality system is on the right track (as I think it is). By the lights of Williams's criticisms, it is easier to see that examples such as Card's are not carefully constructed exceptions; rather, they are in fact the norm when life becomes "dominated" by the morality system's oppressive idea of obligation.

Since the utilitarian's life must be (entirely) devoted to diminishing suffering (or maximizing utility), she can hardly *avoid* acting for a moral reason. She could of course be wrong on this or that occasion about the reasons for her action or about the relative weights she assigns to different reasons, but provided she is trying to follow the utilitarian credo, she cannot help to be acting on "a moral reason." Surely in adhering to the credo the utilitarian could be failing to act for a *better* moral reason, but the mere fact that the utilitarian seeks to reduce suffering *already* shows that she is acting for a moral reason. This further highlights the sense in which the relationship between forgiveness and utilitarianism is more complicated than it appears at first glance. Utilitarianism is indeed concerned with the reduction of suffering *simpliciter*, but forgiveness is *not* a matter of reducing suffering *simpliciter*. Consider the utilitarian who "forgives" a wrongdoer because he knows that this wrongdoer is generally well liked, and thus she realizes that there will be more suffering in the world if this popular wrongdoer is punished. Just like in Card's example, it seems to me that this utilitarian would not be really forgiving this wrongdoer.

It is instructive at this point to compare the invocation of moral reasons within the context of the specialized literature on forgiveness (where it occurs frequently) and what we could speculate it would be within the context of the specialized literature on punishment (where it occurs rarely). Formally, the structure of Card's example is this: you do something (release the gangster and thus spare him suffering), some of whose consequences (no suffering for the gangster, etc.) are identical to the consequences of forgiving the gangster. Yet what you do is not forgiveness because your reason (to avoid the widespread suffering the gangster colleagues would generate) was not the right kind of reason. A parallel in the case of punishment would be this: you do something (imprison a gangster and thus make him suffer), some of whose consequences (the suffering of the gangster, etc.) are identical to the consequences of punishing the gangster. Yet what you do is not punishment because your reason (say, to let your sadism play out or your hatred of this particular gangster run free or to take advantage that people dislike him very much or to show off how powerful you are or because its consequences would be good) was not the right kind of reason.

This comparison highlights the fact that despite punishment theorists' relative silence on this point, there is no reason why it should be denied that punishment, too, must be done for (a certain type of) a moral reason. Furthermore, the inadequacy of limiting the moral reasons available to bald suffering reduction should be admitted to be as problematic within the context of punishment as it is within the context of forgiveness. "Forgiving" the gangster in order to appease his associates (as in Card's example) is as spurious as "punishing" a wrongdoer because we actually hate him (in ways independent from his wrongdoing) or because we know the population hates him (in ways similarly independent from his wrongdoing) or because of its good consequences.

We are taking for granted that in both cases the gangster has done something wrong, something that renders punishment or forgiveness at least pertinent. In other words, both cases are taken to be *responsive* to wrongdoing (the opportunistic sadist in the case of punishment, for example, would not have unleashed her sadism on an innocent; she is just enjoying the opportunity to be a sadist that the wrongdoing of the gangster affords her, etc.). Put in different terms, the problem is that evidently there are different senses of "responsive," and some actions are not responsive in the right ways.

What is needed here is a basic distinction between a generic kind of responsiveness and a more fine-tuned kind of responsiveness: the opportunistic sadist is, in a general sense, responsive to wrongdoing; had wrongdoing not occurred, she would not (let us stipulate) have inflicted any suffering. It is precisely in the fact that she piggybacks on the wrongdoing that her opportunism consists. But, beyond the fact that she (again, opportunistically) takes wrongdoing as a necessary condition for unleashing her *sadism*, she is not responsive in the right ways. These ways of being responsive are surely part of what acting from the right moral reason means.

The inadequate reason in Card's gangster example may in the end be admitted to be "moral," although it certainly is *not moral in the right way*. This reason is none other than an instantiation of the general utilitarian injunction in favor of decreasing as much suffering (or increasing as much utility) as possible. Yet it is exactly this very reason – which is insufficient to undergird genuine forgiveness – that undergirds all consequentialist justifications of punishment, based as they ultimately are (or to the extent that they are) on the classical utilitarian view whereby the only justification of punishment is its tendency to reduce further suffering. This constitutes a startling asymmetry: the very reason that is taken by punishment theorists to underwrite the many consequentialist justifications of punishment is expressly denied a role by forgiveness theorists in underwriting justified forgiveness.

It is important to underscore that the asymmetry can hardly be explained by appealing to the widespread – and not unreasonable – view that to alleviate suffering stands in less need of a justification than to inflict it. After all, what is rejected as being a sufficiently moral reason in the case of forgiveness is precisely the desire to alleviate overall suffering. Thus, for example, Card is not to be taken as *opposing* the release of the gangster (she is silent on that matter): what she opposes is viewing such a release as an instance of forgiveness.

This may make it look as if the problem here is merely a matter of semantics, merely concerning what to call "forgiveness" or "punishment." I do not think that this is so. What is at stake is the crucial question as to what exactly forgiveness and punishment are supposed to *be*. The suggestion is that the utilitarian framework is simply unable to account for features – *real* features, not linguistic features – of these phenomena. This inability allows me to raise the following objection against utilitarianism. The impoverished monistic axiology of utilitarianism forces upon its adherents a similarly impoverished *ontology*, unable to distinguish between forgiveness and other forms of suffering alleviation and between punishment and other forms of suffering infliction. Again, I find it remarkable that this inability seems to be well understood among forgiveness theorists (insofar as the fact that the moral reason that turns a given sparing of suffering into genuine forgiveness goes beyond the mere desire to diminish suffering *simpliciter* is widely recognized). But it seems to be not very well appreciated among punishment theorists (insofar as many justifications of punishment are built precisely upon the goal of diminishing suffer-ing *simpliciter*).[45]

The utilitarian may try to defend herself from the objection by limiting its scope. She may, for example, suggest that Card's gangster thought experiment does (against all appearances and good sense) constitute an instance of forgiveness but that this says nothing whatsoever about punishment. However, presupposing even a modest isomorphism between the structure of punishment and the structure of forgiveness would militate against this odd restriction of scope. If the gangster was indeed forgiven, why is the opportunistic "punisher" of my example not really punishing? If deeper moral reasons (deeper than reducing suffering simpliciter) do not matter in one context, why do they matter in the other? Perhaps the utilitarian could reject even this modest isomorphism and then suggest that while the case of Card's gangster is indeed not an instance of forgiveness, my allegedly isomorphic case of the opportunistic sadist is indeed an instance of punishment (or vice versa). But I do not know what argument could possibly be adduced for denying the isomorphism: for the denial of the isomorphism would very implausibly entail that while forgivers are expected to act for a robust moral reason (that goes beyond the desire to reduce suffering *simpliciter*), punishers are not so expected (or vice versa).

---

[45]   See, e.g., Jeffrie Murphy, "Forgiveness and Resentment"; Claudia Card, "On Mercy"; Aurel Kolnai, "Forgiveness," *Proceedings of the Aristotelian Society* 74 (1973): 91–106.

For these reasons, I think that in the end the likeliest response by the utilitarian is to reject the "for a moral reason" strategy *altogether*. Provided my actions effectively diminish suffering (or maximize utility) in the world, the utilitarian may ask, "Who cares about my moral reasons?" There is in the utilitarian universe but *one* moral reason: to reduce suffering, *simpliciter*. This seems to me, moreover, to cohere well with the "forward-looking" essence of utilitarianism; being *responsive* is necessarily "backward-looking," in ways that seem to be if not quite foreclosed to at least fraught with difficulties for utilitarians. But this reveals yet another manifestation of the uninspiring simplemindedness of utilitarianism that Williams – and Strawson and Berlin and Elster, among many others – have so compellingly discredited. The combination of a monistic axiology and its ensuing impoverished ontology paint the utilitarian into yet another theoretical corner. To put it in terms of the contemporary axiological debate: to the extent that she has access to only one kind of reason, the utilitarian is simply immune to the famed "wrong kind of reason" problem.[46] This immunity shows yet another dimension of utilitarianism's unacceptable way of flattening moral life.

### 7.3 MICROMANAGING LIFE

The discussion in the previous section has, I hope, helped dispel the myth of an allegedly tight connection between utilitarianism and forgiveness. Utilitarianism is too simpleminded to deal with the complexity of punishment *and*, we have just seen, with the complexity of forgiveness. But this discussion has not shed sufficient light on the problem of determining what exactly is the moral reason that, beyond an overly general sense of "responsive" to wrongdoing (such as would apply to the opportunistic sadist), would transform otherwise spurious instances of forgiveness into genuine instances. In trying to elucidate what this reason is, I would like to consider a widespread strategy among forgiveness theorists that seeks to specify the moral reason that may be singularly important for forgiveness: repentance.

The idea has been that when we spare suffering because we realize that the wrongdoer has repented (or has repented-and-apologized or has repented-apologized-and-offered-compensation, etc. – possibilities I will cover under the single heading of "repentance"), then this sparing of suffering is genuine forgiveness (and morally admirable). It is often hard to determine the exact import of this view because it is not clear whether what is meant by it is that, as a matter of logic, it is impossible to forgive the unrepentant or that, as a normative matter, forgiving the unrepentant is objectionable. Murphy, for example, has actually defended the

---

[46] Perhaps the most famous version of this problem is to be found in Pascal's wager: to believe in God as a result of the cost-benefit analysis he sketches seems to believe in him for the wrong kind of reason. The contemporary debate began as a result of objections to Scanlon's "buck-passing account of value," in T. M. Scanlon, *What We Owe to Each Other*, Cambridge, MA: Harvard University Press (1998), 96 ff.

view that the definitional and the justificatory enterprises cannot be neatly sepa-
rated in the case of forgiveness: "'What is forgiveness?' cannot after all be sharply
distinguished from the question 'How is forgiveness justified?' ... We cannot
define forgiveness and then ask what moral reasons make it appropriate."[47]

Repentance is taken to symbolize the wrongdoer's repudiation of his action, and it
is in its being responsive to this repudiation that forgiveness is rendered genuine and
respectable. But why should this repudiation have these effects? If, in a given
situation, punishment is taken to be valuable, why should the fact that the wrongdoer repents render said punishment less valuable (or militate against inflicting it)?
Pointing out, for example, that by repenting the wrongdoer has already punished
herself will not do – for refusing to punish a wrongdoer because she has already been
punished (even if by herself) is, as we have seen, simply not forgiveness. Evidently,
inmates who are released because they have served their sentences are not thereby
being forgiven.

It seems hard to disagree with the view that it is generally a good thing when
wrongdoers understand the wrong they have done and thereby repent. One could
then easily imagine that this repentance could potentially add value to the organic
whole of which it may be part. But deserved punishment can of course add value to
an organic whole as well. So, without falling into the trap of the simple arithmetic I
have criticized previously (which is, as we have seen, particularly out of place within
the framework of organic wholes), it is not clear why it is not best to have an organic
whole containing *both* the potentially valuable repentance and the potentially
valuable punishment than one in which the repentance, via forgiveness, *replaces*
the punishment. Repentance and punishment are, after all, not mutually exclusive.
Imagine that, for example, Ohlendorf had repented. Would the value of his punishment have been then preempted by the (stipulated) value of his repentance? Why
not have both?

Although we *cannot* punish and forgive the same wrongdoer for the same action
simultaneously, we *can* punish a repentant wrongdoer just like we can punish an
unrepentant wrongdoer. Punishment and forgiveness are *contradictories*, but punishment and repentance are not. Yet the widespread strategy of linking forgiveness
too closely to repentance risks subverting these basic points. For if forgiveness is tied
too closely to repentance, then punishment and repentance (like punishment and
forgiveness) could be seen as properly contradictory. What is more, since the close
connection between forgiveness and repentance that is so frequently on display in
the specialized literature is not merely conceptual but normative – that is, since the
amalgam of repentance and forgiveness is often taken to do both conceptual and
normative work – then this move risks preempting the question as to what justifies
forgiveness, since forgiveness-because-repentance could be taken to be a (circularly)
self-justifying notion.

[47]  Murphy, "Forgiveness and Resentment," 23.

A famous example of an allegedly self-justifying notion is a white lie. A white lie can be (partly) defined as a lie that is told for a good reason (typically, to spare pointless suffering). The reason why the lie is told is built into the very definition of a white lie. In a sense, then, white lies can be seen as self-justifying. Perhaps, however, the charge of circular self-justification can be resisted: just as one could perfectly intelligibly wonder whether to tell a white lie is in this or that occasion the right thing to do (all things considered), one could do the same with forgiveness predicated upon repentance. This resistance would be to insist that the self-justification is only partial, which is to tacitly admit that the worry about circular self-justification is *partially* correct.

Whether the linkage between forgiveness and repentance is supposed to be purely conceptual or normative or both (and if, in the latter two cases, it can survive the charge of circular self-justification), the main danger in seeing repentance as the specific reason that renders forgiveness genuine (or genuine-and-admirable) remains pressing. That danger is none other than turning the forgiving of a (repentant) person into precisely the type of mechanistic process I (and others) have criticized. It risks rendering forgiveness into the counterintuitive duty-generating practice that Tasioulas nonetheless endorsed. It risks, in short, placing forgiveness too neatly within the morality system. Pointing to his repentance, a wrongdoer may then *demand* forgiveness – and this seems to be different from the more intuitive view, whereby forgiveness, by its very nature, could be neither owed nor demanded; whereby forgiveness, by its very nature, is always the gracious, supererogatory prerogative of the forgiver. To be sure, one could perhaps rightly criticize a potential forgiver for not acting on her prerogative – but this does not entail that she has a *duty* to forgive or that repentant wrongdoers have a right to be forgiven.

The fashionable privileging of repentance is often associated with yet another, alleged ultimate goal of forgiveness: reconciliation. It is often assumed that reconciliation – both at the personal and at the political levels – is invariantly good. Just as I am not at all invested in the view that repentance lacks value, I am not invested in the view that reconciliation lacks value. On the contrary, I readily admit that both repentance and reconciliation are often very valuable indeed. But I do wish to underscore that the problem I have just described related to linking forgiveness and repentance too closely applies just as well to linking forgiveness and reconciliation too closely. The problem arises because the potential goodness of either repentance or reconciliation, even if it is admitted to be *default* goodness, is not *invariant* goodness. While in general it may be downright impossible for society or for individuals to function without sometimes seeking reconciliation, there may be particular wrongs regarding which a person (or, perhaps, a society) should not be expected to wish to seek reconciliation because in those cases reconciliation is not good.[48] Perhaps there is value in forgiving, say, a repentant Ohlendorf in order to

---

[48] The case of societies may be harder at least in the sense that collective agency is more fluid.

then reconcile with him – but perhaps there is not. The very unqualified sanctification of reconciliation seems to be yet another effect of the alleged benevolence often associated with utilitarianism. Reconciliation is, after all, but a forward-looking mechanism aiming to reduce suffering. And while the reduction of suffering is a default good, it is not an invariant good.

The problem we are facing is deep. If we leave the moral reason that must motivate forgiveness too unspecified, then the notion of forgiveness loses its uniqueness: utterly counterintuitively, "forgiveness" then becomes a synonym for "suffering reduction." We thus need to further specify the type of moral reason that must motivate forgiveness. But if we specify it too much, then we run the risk of mechanizing (institutionalizing, ledgering, etc.) forgiveness to such an extent that it becomes susceptible to the challenges to the morality system based on the "obligations-out, obligations-in" approach we discussed in the previous chapter. It seems to me that, just like punishment, forgiveness does not sit comfortably within the overly neat morality system.

A rather interesting illustration of the problems that this mechanization can create is found in the *Talmud*. Underwritten by the general goal of reconciliation – without which communal life would be difficult, if not downright impossible – Jewish law and tradition contain remarkable regulations concerning forgiveness. There are rules governing the cases and the ways in which wrongdoers should apologize to those they have wronged, as well as the ways in which the victims of wrongdoing are expected to accept apologies. There are even rules governing the ways in which victims of wrongdoing are expected to help create conducive conditions so that wrongdoers may more easily apologize. Moshe Halbertal calls attention to three *Talmudic* stories dealing with repentance, apologies, and forgiveness. Of particular importance for my purposes is the following story:

> A certain animal slaughterer injured Rav. [The slaughterer] did not come [to Rav] on the eve of the Day of Atonement. Said [Rav], I will go and appease him. R. Huna met him. He said, "Where is my master going?" He said, "To appease so-and-so." [R. Huna] said [to himself] Abba [that is, Rav] is going to kill a man. Rav went and stood over him. The slaughterer was seated, cleaning the head [of an animal]. He raised his eyes and saw him [Rav]. He said to him, "Abba, go; I have no dealings with you." While he was still cleaning the animal's head, a bone let fly from it, struck the slaughterer's neck, and killed him.[49]

Two aspects of this story strike me as particularly odd: the very presence of R. Huna in it and the crucial bit about the bone freakishly flying off the animal and killing the slaughterer. If the story did not include these aspects, one essential point

---

[49]  Moshe Halbertal, "At the Threshold of Forgiveness: On Law and Narrative in the Talmud," manuscript in author's possession. A shorter version of this article appears in the fall 2011 issue of *The Jewish Review of Books*, available online: https://jewishreviewofbooks.com/articles/74/at-the-threshold-of-for giveness-a-study-of-law-and-narrative-in-the-talmud/.

would have been made anyhow. Rav was wronged by the slaughterer; the slaughterer persevered in his abusive behavior by not appeasing Rav, even though Rav, in a formidable display of largesse, sought to create (force?) the conditions for the slaughterer to do the right thing. Of course, if creating the conditions for the slaughterer to do the right thing is actually *mandated* by Jewish law, then the largesse could be called into question. Either way (whether Rav was *required* to behave as he did or not), the slaughterer, in effect adding insult to injury, spat in Rav's face (metaphorically speaking). This would have been enough, I think, to convey the point that life is complicated and that the law cannot really seek to foresee and regulate all possible complications: Rav's (and Judaism's) desire to promote reconciliation would have backfired just the same.

The presence of R. Huna in the story seems to serve the purpose of offering us a glimpse into Rav's state of mind: in R. Huna's estimation Rav was not really in the proper mood to facilitate reconciliation; rather, he was seething. But regardless of Rav's state of mind – whether he was really seething or in the most conciliatory of spirits – the slaughterer's reaction would have been awful. Similarly, even if the story had ended without the bone incident, the essential point about the way in which the slaughterer added insult to injury would have been conveyed anyhow. In other words, if the story ended without the slaughterer actually dying this freakish death, the slaughterer's nastiness toward Rav still would have been awful (even if perhaps then the story would not have been sufficiently disastrous). The ratcheting of disastrousness in the story appears to serve mostly a didactic purpose. Thus, I would like to suggest that these two aspects of the story are there in order to highlight (perhaps heavy-handedly) the shortcomings of the idea that the law (or morality) should seek to micromanage life, in this case by overregulating the complex processes of forgiveness and reconciliation.

There is, I think, a reading of the story that allows us to connect it to punishment. Although we are not told what the (initial) injury to Rav was, we are to assume that the death of the slaughterer, as a punishment for it, would have been excessive. So, the ratcheted disastrousness in the story – via the freakish death of the slaughterer – also evokes (albeit indirectly) a reflection on the sense of proportion inseparable from the idea of justified punishment. Needless to say, Rav is not himself punishing the slaughterer in the story (and I would prefer not to read the story in a way that God could be seen as punishing him), but had someone punished the slaughterer by death, that would have been excessive – and this adds a layer to the disastrousness of the story. Had the story ended, say, by having the bone merely scratch the slaughterer's face, this would have been a much more proportional outcome, although the didactic message of the story may have been diluted.

I agree with Nussbaum's interpretation whereby the main point of the Talmudic stories Halbertal discusses is to "short-circuit the formalistic process of supplication" (an interpretation that, I think, Halbertal himself shares).[50] But I wish to underscore that the formalization "short-circuited" in these Talmudic stories should not be seen as limited to the legal context – a point that should get some immediate traction given the difficulties, within Jewish tradition in particular, attendant to the efforts to separate normative realms. The main point of the story, it seems to me, is none other than to expose (even if heavy-handedly) the foibles of the formalization ethos that Williams suggests affects modern moral philosophy in general. The morality system tends to micromanage matters in ways similar to those on display in the Talmudic story we have just discussed. But I would like to call attention to how easy it is to lose track as to what exactly the problem worth our attention really is.

Nussbaum's view, for example, appears to be not quite that the essential point of the story is that the overly formalistic process it depicts is to be abandoned but rather that it should be abandoned in favor of "a forward-looking and generous relationship."[51] Interestingly, Nussbaum takes her interpretive cues precisely from the presence of R. Huna in the story – a presence that I have suggested can be seen as superfluous. And it seems to me that Halbertal, too, attaches more importance than I do to R. Huna's role in the story. After all, Nussbaum approvingly cites Halbertal's felicitous remark: "[T]he story forces us to confront squarely the ambivalence between sanctity and narcissism that inheres in any act of grace."[52] I agree with Nussbaum that Halbertal is onto something really important in this remark. It is an important truth that the motivation with which we do things – or, to put in in the terms we have been using, the specific moral reason with which one acts – *matters*. And it is also an important truth that even forgiveness, so often seen as an unqualifiedly virtuous act, can be non-virtuous. Had Rav really been in the state of mind R. Huna thought he was, his visiting the slaughterer would not have been virtuous but "narcissistic" or worse.

And yet, while I do not wish to deny that the inscrutability of human motivation is a real and deep problem, I want to underscore that *if* we are to read this story as being fundamentally about the problems of micromanaging life, *then* the problem of human motivation is a red herring. The criticism of the legal system's – *and* of the morality system's – efforts to micromanage complex phenomena via "formalistic processes" remains essentially intact whether we are supposed to trust or even know R. Huna's evaluation of Rav's motivation. The wrongness of the slaughterer's behavior is independent of Rav's motivation. Focusing too much in the admittedly real and deep problem of the opacity of human motivation in this context risks intimating that the problem facing the law (and the morality system) relates crucially to such opacity. And this is a mistake: repentance, forgiveness, and reconciliation (indeed, just like punishment) would resist being so neatly

---

[50] Nussbaum, *Anger and Forgiveness* . . ., 86. Nussbaum says this about the first two of the Talmudic stories Halbertal discusses (which I am not here discussing), but her point extends to the third story too.

[51] Nussbaum, *Anger and Forgiveness* . . ., 86.     [52] *Ibid.*, 87.

micromanaged even if people were not ambivalent about their motivation. In other words, even had the story stipulated that Rav went to the slaughterer in perfectly good faith, it would still be unwise to try to regulate complicated phenomena such as repentance, forgiveness, and reconciliation *ex ante*. An obdurate nasty slaughterer, for example, would short-circuit the formalistic process we are considering even if the complexities of human motivation were stipulated away.

## 7.4 FROM UNCONDITIONAL FORGIVENESS TO UNCONDITIONAL PUNISHMENT

Needless to say, I do not mean the consideration of the Talmudic story in the previous section to be a contribution to Talmudic scholarship or to the study of Judaism. Rather, it is meant as an illustration of a very common phenomenon – in religious traditions, in philosophical and psychological theories, and even in pop psychology and self-help approaches to forgiveness. The phenomenon consists in overregulating, and thereby oversimplifying, forgiveness – as if forgiveness were amenable to be neatly cabined and then mobilized in the advancement of these or those goals. (By discussing aspects of Nussbaum's and Halbertal's remarks as to the opacity of human motivation, I also meant to illustrate how easy it is to lose sight of what exactly the problematic phenomenon in question is.)

I find it illuminating to connect the phenomenon we have discussed in the previous section to a debate within the specialized contemporary literature on forgiveness: the debate between defenders of conditional and defenders of unconditional forgiveness. Conditional forgiveness is the most widespread approach to forgiveness. It is visible in perhaps the most influential contemporary account of forgiveness, Charles Griswold's.[53] Although rather than "conditional," she calls it "transactional," Nussbaum has endorsed the spirit of this account, and she has, rightly, deemed it the "classical account."[54] The central idea of the approach can be easily gleaned from its very name: forgiveness is given (or at least *admirably* given) on condition that something else obtains, in *exchange* for that something else or at least as a *response* to it. As we have just seen, this something else typically is repentance (a heading under which, as noted, I mean to include a variety of related conditions: apologies, reconciliation, reparation, etc.).

---

[53] Charles Griswold, *Forgiveness: A Philosophical Investigation*, Cambridge: Cambridge University Press (2007), 62 ff., and *passim*.

[54] Nussbaum, *Anger and Forgiveness* . . ., 58 ff. As Nussbaum correctly points out, another influential account of forgiveness, David Konstan's (in David Konstan, *Before Forgiveness: The Origins of a Moral Idea*, Cambridge: Cambridge University Press [2010]) is "basically the same" as Griswold's. Konstan, too, sees conditional forgiveness as the standard, default account of forgiveness.

The other approach, although admittedly less widespread, has been defended by a number of contemporary authors,[55] including myself.[56] Proponents of this other approach prefer not to see forgiveness as mechanistically conditioned, by repentance, apologies, reconciliation, overall happiness, or anything else. Jacques Derrida has eloquently (if too grandiloquently) defended the view that forgiveness is "unconditional, gracious, infinite, aneconomic . . ., granted to the guilty as guilty, without counterpart, even to those who do not repent or ask forgiveness."[57] Derrida further claims that "forgiveness is thus mad. It must plunge, but lucidly, into the night of the unintelligible."[58] If this was not enigmatic enough, Mary-Jane Rubinstein reports that in the "last meeting of a seminar he [Derrida] taught with Avital Ronell at New York University in October, 2001," after having spent several weeks discussing the many difficulties surrounding the notion of forgiveness, Derrida "finally offered his audience a sketch of what he called an 'authentic scene of forgiveness.'"[59] According to Rubinstein, Derrida suggested that "pure, unconditional, forgiveness . . . would look something like this: one criminal would continually commit the same crime against one victim, and the victim would continually forgive him, knowing he would never apologize and never change."[60]

Derrida's penchant for histrionics aside, the stark difference between unconditional forgiveness and the forms of conditional forgiveness we have been considering should be obvious. Unconditional forgiveness appears to be interestingly antithetical to all these (conditional) versions of forgiveness in which certain exchanges generate duties to forgive (including even Tasioulas's). The very exorbitance of Derrida's example is helpful for my purposes: for it suggests that we *can* forgive even the most recalcitrant and unrepentant wrongdoer and that such forgiveness *can* be valuable. This is not to suggest that Derrida – or any other defender of unconditional forgiveness – must have anything against apologies, repentance, reconciliation, or harmonious communal life. One need not deny that reconciliation, harmonious coexistence, and so on, are noble goals in order to object to the instrumentalization of forgiveness as a mere vehicle for achieving them. Defenders of unconditional forgiveness merely insist on the fact that forgiveness is both theoretically possible and potentially valuable even in the absence of any transactional elements

[55]  Eve Garrard and David McNaughton, "A Defense of Unconditional Forgiveness," *Proceedings of the Aristotelian Society* (2003): 39–60; Cheshire Calhoun, "Changing One's Heart," *Ethics* 103.1 (1992): 76–96; and Glen Pettigrove, *Forgiveness and Love*, Oxford: Oxford University Press (2012).

[56]  Leo Zaibert, "The Paradox of Forgiveness".

[57]  Jacques Derrida, *Cosmopolitanism and Forgiveness*, London: Routledge (2005), 34.

[58]  Derrida, *Cosmopolitanism and Forgiveness*, 49. I have discussed Derrida's views on forgiveness in Leo Zaibert "The Paradox of Forgiveness," See also Vladimir Jankélévitch, *Forgiveness* (Andrew Kelley, trans.), Chicago, IL: University of Chicago Press (2005); and Aaron T. Looney, *The Time of Forgiveness*, New York, NY: Fordham University Press (2015).

[59]  Mary-Jane Rubinstein, "Of Ghosts and Angels: Derrida, Kushner, and the Impossibility of Forgiveness," *Journal for Cultural and Religious Theory* 91.3 (2008): 79–95, at 83.

[60]  Rubinstein, "Of Ghosts . . .," 83–84.

and any consideration of further consequences. In their view, this is exactly what renders forgiveness *unconditional*.

Another important difference between defenders of unconditional forgiveness and defenders of conditional forgiveness is that the latter typically assume (or are forced to assume) that whatever the condition they believe legitimizes (or conceptually permits) forgiveness turns out to be, the presence of that condition also makes forgiveness *obligatory*. In their view, repentance, for example, both legitimizes forgiveness and renders it *demandable*: if a wrongdoer shows adequate contrition, then she could demand it, and her victim *ought* to grant it (say, along the lines of the Talmudic stories discussed earlier).[61] These oughts are sometimes expressed as full-blown duties or obligations, sometimes as quasi-obligations.[62] But the inescapable corollary to the conditional approach to forgiveness is that forgiveness is more or less stringently owed to certain wrongdoers. Independently of the fact that this risks engaging in precisely the type of problematic micromanagement the Talmudic stories seek to criticize, this poses an additional problem for defenders of conditional forgiveness.

In a very insightful contribution, Cheshire Calhoun has made a distinction between "minimalist" and "aspirational" forgiveness.[63] For my purposes here, and conscious that I am taking some liberties, I suggest that we read Calhoun's "minimalist" forgiveness as "conditional" forgiveness and her "aspirational" forgiveness as "unconditional" forgiveness. Speaking about the problems of the former, Calhoun remarks "to the extent that repentance is allowed to count in favor of forgiving, to that extent the wrongdoer ceases to be viewed under a damning description, and forgiving ceases to be elective."[64] And Calhoun compellingly argues that many endorsers of conditional forgiveness in effect engage in what she calls "double vision." So, she wonders how, for example, Aurel Kolnai (an influential defender of conditional forgiveness) can hold that forgiving the repentant (because she repents) is "an exquisite act of charity or benevolence," when he also "explicitly states that, because the repentant appear[s] to deserve forgiveness, forgiving them is 'duty-like' and a 'quasi-obligation.'"[65] Understandably, Calhoun then remarks:

> How can something that I am quasi, albeit not strictly, obligated to render be an "exquisite" act of charity? Surely a quasi-obligation to forgive the repentant would make forgiveness at best only a minor act of charity, not an aspirational achievement.[66]

Part of what Calhoun wishes to resist is the assumption that forgiveness can be *deserved*. Her sense of desert here is, however, more general than the sense of desert with which I have been concerned in this book or at play within the context of justification of *punishment*. What Calhoun means by "deserved" forgiveness is

---

[61] Evidently, this sort of view is by no means exclusive to Judaism.
[62] For a variety of these uses, see Calhoun, "Changing One's Heart."
[63] Calhoun, "Changing One's Heart."    [64] *Ibid.*, 81.    [65] *Ibid.*, 82.    [66] *Ibid.*

forgiveness that has been *earned* or to which one has made oneself *entitled* and that can therefore be *demanded* (or quasi-demanded). In Calhoun's sense of "desert," her point is that according to defenders of conditional forgiveness, one could "deserve" to be forgiven because one has repented or apologized or because one is genuinely willing to reconcile with the person one has wronged. In her sense, to say that forgiveness is "deserved" is to say that it follows, more or less mechanically, from the fact that one (or more) of these conditions obtain.

The importance of Calhoun's point can hardly be overestimated. Forgiveness is often touted as a lofty, deeply admirable act. But if forgiveness were really a duty (or a quasi-duty), it would then be hard to see what would be so admirable about granting it. I think that an important aspect of what Calhoun means by "aspirational" in this context is this: we aspire to move beyond the morality system, to engage in "forgiveness for culpable, unrepentant, unpunished, and unrestituted wrongdoing whose existence is not dismissed by refusing to think about it."[67]

Evidently, I agree with Calhoun's rejection of "minimalist," "conditional," or any other version of forgiveness that is too neatly at home within the morality system. But I want to emphasize that endorsing unconditional forgiveness is perfectly consistent with a commitment to the view that for a token instance of suffering diminution (even if "responsive" to wrongdoing) to *count* as an instance of forgiveness, it must be done for a very specific type of moral reason. In other words, it would be a mistake to see my view (or Calhoun's or any other unconditional view of forgiveness) as a disguised form of "conditional" forgiveness, differing from other accounts of conditional forgiveness merely in that my condition is not "repentance," "reconciliation" (etc.) but "being done for the right kind of reason." My point in this context is purely conceptual: it is a mistake to think that one's account of, say, "bachelor" is "conditioned" by "maleness." This conceptual point whereby forgiveness must be done for a reason – so that, for example, not every instance of suffering diminution (even if "responsive" to wrongdoing) counts as forgiveness – in no way forces the defender of unconditional forgiveness into seeing forgiveness as something that can be demanded (or quasi-demanded).

An interesting connection between the consideration of unconditional forgiveness and the discussion of punishment has now emerged. One thing that the defender of unconditional forgiveness has to accept is that there may be value in certain instances of suffering diminution in themselves, even in the presence of unrepentant and unapologetic wrongdoers, and even if they are not meant to lead to reconciliation or to the overall diminution of suffering in the world. Sometimes forgiveness is valuable in and of itself. And this is but a manifestation within the case of forgiveness of what I have suggested is true of punishment: the suffering constitutive of punishment is sometimes good in and of itself, independently of the consequences it may bring about, just as the suffering diminution that is constitutive

---

[67]  *Ibid.*, 80.

of forgiveness is sometimes good in and of itself, independently of the consequences it may bring about. But then unconditional forgiveness is revealed as the type of phenomenon that only the *axiological* retributivist can countenance – and as the type of phenomenon that (deontic) retributivists and (classical) utilitarians (together with defenders of conditional forgiveness) *cannot* even countenance.

Recall my reaction to Tadros's example of Hitler on the deserted island from Chapter 3; I suggested then that there is value in giving Hitler bad weather, even absent any possible medicinal benefit from so doing. One thing that can be said of this reaction is that it evinces my commitment to "unconditional punishment." Just like the value of unconditional forgiveness need not be predicated on repentance, apologies, or reconciliation, the value of unconditional punishment need not be predicated on deterrence, reform, communication, or indeed anything else beyond its intrinsic justice. Of course, this is not to deny that repentance, apologies, and reconciliation (in the case of forgiveness) can be of great value too or to deny that deterrence, reform, or communication (in the case of punishment) can be of great value as well. But it is to affirm that there *can* be value in punishment and in forgiveness independently of any conditions or consequences.

It may appear as if a certain disanalogy between unconditional punishment and unconditional forgiveness, for the value of the former, can be found in its intrinsic justice. Whence the value of unconditional forgiveness? Could there be value in *forgiving* Hitler in the island? (Assume that refusing to give him bad weather is for you to forgive Hitler.)[68] Even if in the particular case of Hitler or of Ohlendorf, it is hard to see how sparing *their* suffering could be too valuable, there could be cases of unconditional forgiveness that are valuable in themselves. This better not be based simplemindedly on the fact that suffering would thereby be reduced. For to succumb to such a view would in fact be, as we have seen, to *evade* engaging with the question. After all, such a reduction of suffering would be as much "forgiveness" as the release of Card's gangster in order to prevent the havoc his associates would otherwise wreak. The potential value of genuinely forgiving Hitler on the island would have to be connected to the fact that by not giving him bad weather the world would be a better place – that is, that one would thereby create an organic whole with more value than otherwise – again, for reasons that go beyond the mere fact that suffering has been diminished.

This may seem unsatisfactory. After all, despite its shortcomings the conditional approach to forgiveness can at least tell us what exactly is the reason that infuses forgiveness with value: typically, as we have seen, repentance. The defender of unconditional forgiveness seems to be at a disadvantage, for she cannot do the same. At best, in my search for that specific type of moral reason that would infuse value into forgiveness, I have merely managed to exclude *some* reasons: those

---

[68] In "The Paradox of Forgiveness," I have suggested that, in essence, forgiveness is the deliberate refusal to punish.

typically invoked by defenders of conditional forgiveness and those linked to classical utilitarianism. But I have not been able to point directly to what that elusive specific reason might be. In closing, I would like to suggest that to see this inability as a real problem is to misunderstand the nature of the question we are trying to answer.

Compare forgiveness with other supererogatory actions, such as giving gifts or behaving heroically. (Evidently, the defender of unconditional forgiveness has to see forgiveness as supererogatory.) These other actions better be done for a specific moral reason too. Thus, for example, if I give you a "gift" because this is the only way to prevent the associates of a mafia don from causing a great deal of undeserved suffering, then this seems not to be a genuine gift. Similarly, if I do something "heroic" but only because I struck a deal with the mafia don's associates, then this does not seem genuinely heroic. Not that my actions in these cases are necessarily not admirable – they may very well be: to spare the suffering of the mafia don (in order to placate his associates) may be morally respectable – but it is not forgiveness. The point is that seemingly supererogatory actions may turn out to be not really supererogatory after all, insofar as they could be done for reasons that, though potentially respectable, are just not the requisite reasons for supererogation.

So, to ask for *the* reason that renders a given instance of sparing suffering a genuine instance of forgiveness, in the way conditional theorists ask it, is in a sense misguided. It is like asking for *the* reason that renders a certain transfer of the property rights over a thing a genuine instance of a gift or the reason that renders a certain going beyond one's duties in a certain context a genuine instance of heroism. This way of asking the question presupposes, I think, precisely the naïve instrumentalism that is essential to the morality system that Williams has so insightfully criticized and that the Talmudic story just discussed attempts to short-circuit.

The specific type of moral reason that renders a given instance of sparing suffering *genuine* changes from context to context – from organic whole to organic whole. This reason is thus connected to the axiological considerations related to moral particularism and moderate holism defended in the earlier chapters (especially in Chapter 2). One's behavior can really count as forgiveness, and it can really be admirable as such, if it is, in itself, *fitting*, independently of the potential value of any of its further consequences. Summarily committing these considerations of fittingness to the wastebasket of "magical thinking," as Nussbaum does (though mainly in the case of retributivism), is to discard huge – and hugely important – portions of our moral lives and of moral philosophy.[69]

---

[69] Nussbaum's insufficiently argued indictment of retributivism along the lines that it is based on magical thinking is odd also in the following sense. Nussbaum insightfully notes the many similarities between gratitude and retributive emotions – similarities that have been studied by a number of thinkers – from Epicurus to Adam Smith. Is the belief in the intrinsic value of gratitude also a matter of magical thinking? It seems to me that Nussbaum can only avoid this conclusion by availing herself of two arguments. First, gratitude does not seek to inflict suffering on anyone. This is of course true, but it does negate the other similarities between gratitude and retributive emotions. Second, she sees the value of gratitude predominantly in its potential contribution to improving relationships. Again, it

When trying to shed light on that elusive specific type of moral reason that makes forgiveness conceptually possible, defenders of unconditional forgiveness have often turned their attention to the process of constructing *narratives*. An emphasis on these narratives was a staple of Nussbaum's earlier work, which is problematically at odds with her "very Utilitarian" or "welfarist" turn of late. Defenders of unconditional forgiveness assert that to forgive is to place the isolated actions that are constitutive of wrongdoing within a much broader context (within a much larger organic whole). As Calhoun admits, these "aspirational stories" (i.e., stories about unconditional forgiveness) often "appear impossible."[70] Be that as it may, these stories, these "integrated biographies," are part of what it means "to treat someone as a person."[71] The "appearance of impossibility" of which Calhoun speaks is related to the necessary dilemmatic structures of *both* punishment and forgiveness – a topic to which I will return in the next chapter.

Interestingly, then, this discussion of the debate between conditional and unconditional forgiveness helps us to understand the central tenet of (axiological) retributivism: the value of "unconditional" punishment can be made less mysterious by looking at the ways the value of unconditional forgiveness has been theorized. There are yet other ways in which punishment theory stands to benefit by paying closer attention to forgiveness theory. And I will devote the last chapter of the book to indicating how some other themes that are very well known among forgiveness theorists would play out in a richer understanding of punishment theory.

### 7.5 CONCLUSION

Nussbaum's *Anger and Forgiveness* is dedicated to Bernard Williams. Williams's influence indeed shines through many aspects of Nussbaum's work – including her latest book. But concerning the aspects I have discussed, Nussbaum takes a relatively easy route, circumventing the complex pluralism for which Williams stood. By way of conclusion to *Anger and Forgiveness*, Nussbaum tells us: "[I]f this book achieves anything, I hope it achieves that sort of square-one reorientation, getting its readers to see clearly the irrationality and stupidity of anger."[72] Since, following Aristotle, Nussbaum thinks that "anger" involves a desire for retribution, she finds retributivism itself "irrational and stupid." This is why she does *not* want to bring punishment theory in conversation with forgiveness theory, for she is

---

is true that expressing gratitude can improve relationships. But this does not address the question as to what makes gratitude *fitting*. Nussbaum does not seem sufficiently interested in exploring the intrinsic value of feeling grateful (even if this gratitude is not expressed, or it does not lead to better relationships).

[70] Calhoun, "Changing One's Heart," 87 ff.
[71] *Ibid.*, 96. Similar themes are to be found in Eve Garrard and David McNaughton, "In Defence of Unconditional Forgiveness," *Proceedings of the Aristotelian Society* 103.1 (2012): 39–60.
[72] Nussbaum, *Anger and Forgiveness* . . ., 249.

inclined to think that the rational course is to refuse for several decades to use the word 'punishment' at all since it narrows the mind, making one think that the only proper way to deal with wrongdoing is through some type of "mischief," as Bentham puts it, inflicted on the wrongdoer.[73]

What Nussbaum wants to do is to *replace* punishment theory with forgiveness theory. I believe that the contemporary philosophical reflection on forgiveness (and mercy, etc.) has been, in some ways, less simpleminded than philosophical reflection on punishment. This does not, however, support Nussbaum's refusal to engage with punishment theory at all. This refusal constitutes a missed opportunity to explore the fruitful ways in which the two specialized literatures can reciprocally enrich each other. And it ends up being too simpleminded for its own good – exactly in Williams's understanding of this term.

This is the reason why despite the many deep, important, and penetrating things Nussbaum has to say about forgiveness (and mercy, etc.) and despite the immensely erudite and valuable historical account as to the ways in which in ancient Greece the rigid discourse of punishment was superseded by a much more nuanced and rich discourse of forgiveness (or mercy), her recent project fails. In a way, Nussbaum's project seeks to *reproduce* the history she has shown us. She wants to *replace* punishment, and its alleged "magical thinking," with a "very utilitarian" attitude that flatly rejects the value of deserved suffering and that is monomaniacally invested in increasing general welfare. But this involves forcibly – and anachronistically – superimposing what she sees as lessons from the history of ancient Greece to current debates in punishment theory, as if two millennia of reflection on these topics had not taken place.

Like Nussbaum, I wish that this book may contribute to a "square-one reorientation." Unlike Nussbaum, however, my goal is to indeed *reorient* punishment theory, not to *abolish* it. Unlike Nussbaum, I do not believe that a world without punishment – in either the personal or the public arenas – is a realistic or a desirable scenario. Nussbaum's recent views strike me as instantiations of the one-eyed utilitarianism (or of one-eyed "welfarism," if one prefers) we have encountered before. The square-one reorientation to which I would like to contribute is, in contrast, a matter of *enriching* – and indeed *complicating* – our thinking about punishment by considering the typically overlooked connections that punishment has with forgiveness.

---

[73]  *Ibid.*, 179.

# 8

## The Jugglery of Circumstances: Dirty Hands and Impossible Stories

The discussion in the previous chapter reveals that Martha Nussbaum's championing of forgiveness fails for a variety of reasons. First, by recurrently claiming that retributivism is "brutal in its neglect of human complexity" and even more so by summarily dismissing retributivism as a matter of "magical thinking," Nussbaum has missed the real enemy.[1] To repeat, the real enemy is axiological monism, a view that is presupposed *both* by deontic retributivism and by the very utilitarianism that she now defends. Second, she is thus mistaken in thinking that the solution to the problems she sees in retributivism is to be found in her latter-day embrace of utilitarianism. There really is very little axiology in Nussbaum's recent writings, but to the extent that there is any, it is of an overwhelming utilitarian flavor. This is an odd and regrettable turn of events for the author of as non-utilitarian and profound a book as *The Fragility of Goodness* – a book to a large extent devoted to exploring precisely some of those problems that utilitarianism cannot even countenance.[2] And third, Nussbaum is mistaken in engaging in what strikes me as too facile a paradigm shift: to *replace* punishment theory with forgiveness theory, to *replace* all justice-related concerns with empathy-related concerns.

As a result of these mistakes, Nussbaum's current position turns out to be as simpleminded as those doctrines she used to criticize. Before her utilitarian turn, Nussbaum was importantly right that a good judge (either in a courtroom or elsewhere) should reject oversimplified and reductive maneuvers and should instead be "above all committed to an empathetic scrutiny of the 'insides' of the individual life [of the wrongdoer]."[3] Nussbaum's early laudable recommendation that we pay more attention to the particulars of situations and to the insides of agents' lives has now

---

[1] Martha Nussbaum, "Equity and Mercy," *Philosophy and Public Affairs* 22.2 (1993): 83–125, at 115.
[2] Martha Nussbaum, *The Fragility of Goodness: Luck and Ethics in Greek Tragedy and Philosophy*, Cambridge: Cambridge University Press (1986).
[3] Nussbaum, "Equity and Mercy," 115.

become merely a part of her overarching agenda to reduce as much suffering as possible.

Given both Nussbaum's recent shift and the many shortcomings of classical utilitarianism, I will ignore her recent utilitarian/welfarist turn and pay attention instead to her early preoccupation with developing an empathetic scrutiny of the insides of wrongdoers' lives. This empathy is greatly benefited if we cultivate a "literary" or "narrative" imagination.[4] This process of cultivation ought eventually to produce a form of judicial reasoning "modeled on the reasoning of the concerned reader of a novel."[5] I agree with Nussbaum. In fact, I think that the process should transcend *legal* reasoning: for it applies just as well – and in fact more fundamentally – to *moral* reasoning. (Bernard Williams's criticisms, after all, concerned the *morality* system, not the *legal* system.) And I think that the process is itself part of an overall effort to acknowledge the complexity of the moral universe: *ceteris paribus*, someone who cultivates her literary and narrative imagination is likely to be much more attuned to nuance and subtlety than someone who does not. And this should bring about more mature judgment.

To a large an extent, unfortunately, Nussbaum's strategy is to consider literary sources that, notwithstanding their merits, are too transparently chosen given their support of her recommended paradigm shift. Nussbaum thus reads novels such as Charles Dickens's *David Copperfield* and Joyce Carol Oates's *Because It Is Bitter and Because It Is My Heart*. These texts revolve around situations in which characters, narrators, or authors choose to appreciate wrongdoers (*ex hypothesi* deserving of punishment) in broader and more charitable lights. Rather than punishing wrongdoers, these characters, narrators, or authors instead choose to forgive them.

As I have insisted earlier, sometimes an organic whole that contains forgiveness instead of punishment is more valuable than one that contains punishment instead of forgiveness, although I do deny that this is *always* the case, as Nussbaum appears to believe. In other words, while I wholeheartedly agree with Nussbaum's plea for more nuanced responses to wrongdoing, I do not think that these responses *exclude* punishment (and I do not think Nussbaum has compellingly argued for this position). Thus, in contrast to Nussbaum's gambit, I will conclude this book by focusing on a famous literary text that is centered *not* around forgiveness but, rather, around punishment – or, better yet, around the problematic tension between punishment and forgiveness. One of my goals is to show that the admittedly very important concern with the "insides" of wrongdoers' lives need not (though of course it may) result in forgiveness. The text around which this entire chapter will unfold is the masterpiece by Herman Melville: *Billy Budd, Sailor (an Inside Narrative)*.[6]

---

4   *Ibid.*, 105, 106. I do not think that Nussbaum now rejects these earlier views, though, to repeat, I do think that her recent rapprochement with utilitarianism undermines them.
5   Nussbaum, "Equity and Mercy," 110.
6   Herman Melville, *Billy Budd, Sailor, and Other Stories*, New York, NY: Penguin Books (1986).

*Billy Budd* is a famously difficult text – and in fact this difficulty partly explains my decision to focus on it. If the rejection of simplemindedness is to mean anything, it has to at the very least mean recognizing that insofar as life is complex, our thinking about, for example, our responses to wrongdoing better be complex too. Unlike Nussbaum, who would like to *replace* "punishment theory" with "forgiveness theory," I will seek to *complicate* and *enrich* punishment theory by taking seriously the "insides" of the lives both punishers and punishees, forgivers and forgivees, and the ways in which these insides relate to an axiological universe that is far richer than both Nussbaum and contemporary punishment theorists in general recognize. *Billy Budd* will help me do that.

In the first section, I lay bare those aspects of *Billy Budd* that are fundamental for concluding that, in ways hitherto insufficiently acknowledged, punishment should be seen as a fundamentally dilemmatic phenomenon. I will in this section advance my own interpretation of *Billy Budd*, according to which Melville's masterpiece is very importantly about the *theoretical* problem of punishment with which I have been concerned in this book. In the second section, I will discuss moral taints and moral emotions – in particular those of the punisher (rather than those of the punishee). I will suggest that inflicting punishment taints us and that these taints have emotional repercussions. With this discussion I seek to shine a light on the specific *type* of moral dilemma that punishment is and on the theoretical avenues that may be fruitful to explore as we try to cope with it. In particular, I will suggest that punishment's dilemmatic nature highlights some important aspects of the very structure of its justification. In the third and final section, I will emphasize how important it is to recognize the essentially axiological nature of the dilemma of punishment. And I will argue that, for my purposes here, the nurturing of literary and narrative imagination that Nussbaum has so forcefully championed is valuable above all because it helps to reveal the full axiological complexity of punishment (and other moral phenomena).

## 8.1 PUNISHING INNOCENCE

Thanks to their captivating simplicity, typical thought experiments in contemporary moral philosophy (say, trolley problems) are very manageable and indeed sometimes very helpful in teasing out specific intuitions or tensions between typically binary conflicts of intuitions. In contrast, complex texts such as *Billy Budd* are not helpful in *those* regards: they do not offer shortcuts and are not pedagogical in watered-down ways. Rather than offering sketchy simulacra, they do much more faithfully capture the complexity and multiplicity of dilemmas real human beings face – and this explains a great deal of their helpfulness. *Billy Budd*, however, is *especially* complicated. As Richard Weisberg has nicely put it, its very title resounds magically within the spirit of anyone who has grappled with the intricacies of Melville's final tale. As with a biblical story, each sentence, even a single word, produces new questions for the interpreter and inspires passionate partisanship among the exegetes ...

And certainly no one who has entered into the studied complexity of Melville's final work would easily swallow any schematic attempt to describe its "plot."[7]

In the same vein, Christopher Gowans tells us that "what is fascinating about Billy Budd is not only the story itself, but the extraordinary diversity of responses it has elicited from its readers."[8] Given *Billy Budd*'s complexity – and in particular Melville's treatment of one of its main characters (Captain Vere, to whom I will turn shortly) – it should not be surprising that so many divergent interpretations of Vere's actions have been hazarded. As Gowans points out,

> [T]wo contrary traditions of interpretation of *Billy Budd* have developed. The dispute between them centers primarily on the moral evaluation of the captain. ... For some, Vere was a hero who did what was morally, albeit tragically, necessary, while for others he was simply an authoritarian ruler lacking compassion and a sense of justice. For example, for Lewis Mumford, Vere was "a man of superior order," while for Lawrence Thompson, the captain was "a sinner and a criminal."[9]

There is a sense, then, in which to do full justice to the depth of a work like *Billy Budd* one would have to write it again in whole. Insofar as that evidently is not a viable option, *some* simplification is in fact unavoidable – although nothing quite like the excessive simplification effected by those typical thought experiments I am expressly seeking to avoid.

Melville's masterpiece takes place in the late eighteen century on board the *HMS Bellipotent*. We are to assume that the specific historical period is of at least some importance because the events narrated in Melville's novel happen to have taken place shortly after two famous mutinies in the British Royal Navy.[10] The novel's eponymous protagonist is painstakingly described as an extraordinarily morally pure – and extraordinarily beautiful – young man. This connection between morality and aesthetics runs through Melville's novel: "[M]oral nature was seldom out of keeping with the physical make."[11] Melville describes Billy as "a foundling, a presumable by-blow" though "evidently, no ignoble one."[12] The "Handsome Sailor," as Billy's fellow seamen often call him, is presented as "essentially good-

7   Richard H. Weisberg, *The Failure of the Word*, New Haven, CT: Yale University Press (1984), 133, 136.
8   Christopher Gowans, *Innocence Lost: An Examination of Inescapable Moral Wrongdoing*, Oxford: Oxford University Press (1994), 6.
9   *Ibid.*, 7. Gowans further points out that the interpretation of Vere's actions "has been something of a litmus test of its readers' political outlooks": conservatives tend to approve of Vere more than liberals do. *Ibid.*
10  These were the *Spithead* and the *Nore* mutinies. See Conrad Gill, *The Naval Mutinies of 1797*, Manchester: Manchester University Press (1913).
11  Melville, *Billy Budd*, 292.   12   *Ibid.*, 300.

natured,"[13] as somehow spontaneously virtuous (if the oxymoron be admitted), and as unassumingly dignified: "[H]is simple nature remained unsophisticated by those moral obliquities which are not in every case incompatible with that manufacturable thing known as respectability."[14]

Except for the fact that he was illiterate (which, tellingly, is not presented as an unqualified deficiency), the only defect that marred the otherwise unblemished Billy was "an occasional liability to a vocal defect," which manifested itself in "more or less of a stutter, or even worse."[15] When relatively early in the novel Melville tells us about this speech impediment, he warns us: "[T]he avowal of such an imperfection in the Handsome Sailor should be evidence not alone that he is not presented as a conventional hero, but also that the story in which he is the main figure is no romance."[16] As we shall see, this imperfection portends the complexity of punishment with which I shall argue Melville so masterfully grappled in this his final work.

Two other characters are of great significance in *Billy Budd*. One is John Claggart, the masters-at-arms (somewhat of a chief of police on board the *Bellipotent*). Also relatively early in the text, of Claggart Melville tells us: "[H]is portrait I essay, but shall never hit it."[17] Claggart is presented as a rather complex man, a fact that explains the wide variety of interpretations that critics have given of him, ranging from comparisons to Iago to comparisons to Jesus Christ.[18] Melville himself describes him as a man of "superior capacity," "constitutional sobriety," and a "certain austere patriotism," on the one hand, but also of "ingratiating deference to superiors" and as possessing a "peculiar ferreting genius," on the other.[19] Whatever holds for Claggart's relationships with others, his relationship with Billy was based on one smallish set of hateful emotions: envy, malice, animosity. The gratuitousness of Claggart's hatred toward the Handsome Sailor is odd in that Melville tells us that with the exception of one other person (to whom I will turn shortly), Claggart was "perhaps the only man in the ship intellectually capable of appreciating the moral phenomenon presented in Billy Budd."[20] In this hostility toward Billy, Claggart was alone, for the Handsome Sailor was otherwise universally well liked. While Claggart was perfectly capable of hiding his most disagreeable feelings and dispositions, he could not really "annul the elemental evil in him [vis-à-vis Billy]."[21] And while Billy had in fact been alerted about Claggart's hostility toward him, he never gave credit to these rumors: part of Billy's purity involved a certain naivety and a certain disarming inability to even comprehend malevolence.

Finally, the other (and perhaps most) important character in *Billy Budd* is the Honorable Edward Fairfax Vere, the ship's captain. Vere is presented as an

---

[13]   *Ibid.*, 331.   [14]   *Ibid.*, 301.   [15]   *Ibid.*, 302.   [16]   *Ibid.*   [17]   *Ibid.*, 313.

[18]   The connection between Claggart and Iago is widespread. For the connection of Claggart to Jesus Christ, see Weisberg, *The Failure of the Word*, 173 ff.

[19]   Melville, *Billy Budd*, 317.

[20]   *Ibid.*, 328. As for the gratuitousness of Claggart's attitude, see Peter Kivy, "Melville's 'Billy' and the Secular Problem of Evil: The Worm in the Bud," *The Monist* 63.4 (1980): 480–493.

[21]   Melville, *Billy Budd*, 328.

eminently just and honest man. Vere is a man of virtue, a man of "exceptional character," with a "marked leaning to everything intellectual."[22] He is "intrepid to the verge of temerity, though never injudiciously."[23] Interestingly, Melville also tells us that while Vere had many "sterling qualities," he "was without any brilliant ones": this suggests that while Vere certainly was not mediocre, he was not admirable in a completely superlative way either.[24]

Partly on account of a certain "dreaminess of mood" that would often find Vere "absently gaz[ing] off at the blank sea," he was nicknamed "Starry Vere."[25] Whether or not we are to assume a deliberate connection between Melville's use of "starry" and Kant's famous linking of the "moral law" to the "starry heavens above," there is no doubt that Melville depicts Vere as a man genuinely and profoundly bound by his sense of duty.[26] Although Vere was always "mindful of the welfare of his men," he nonetheless "never tolerat[ed] an infraction of discipline."[27] Some interpreters have seen Vere as a consummate utilitarian (or at least as attracted by utilitarianism), but I think that such a view is problematic.[28] At best, Vere's alleged utilitarianism would have been side-constrained by deontological considerations, mostly associated with his duties to king and country. (I see no basis for supposing that Vere's allegiance to king and country was itself underwritten by utilitarian principles.) Moreover, it seems hard to explain why Vere would be so taken by Billy's moral beauty if he were just a utilitarian – after all, disconnected from medicinal considerations, the idea of moral beauty clearly belongs to that immense set of ideas the utilitarian cannot, on pain of incoherence, really appreciate. Vere is, of course, that other person whom – in addition to Claggart – Melville credits with the intellectual capacity to appreciate Billy in his full moral splendor – a splendor that is perforce invisible to utilitarianism. This intellectual capacity, however, did not come to Vere's help when he found himself ensnared in that crucial event around which the entire novel revolves.

In ways too complex to capture in a brief summary, Claggart's toxic combination of cunning and hostility toward Billy culminated in his seeking out Vere in order to present a false accusation concerning a certain "dangerous" sailor on board the

---

[22]  *Ibid.*, 311.   [23]  *Ibid.*, 309.

[24]  *Ibid.*, 310. The "sterling but not brilliant" description of Vere can be seen as presaging a central theme that in due course I will suggest helps us discover interesting layers of meaning in *Billy Budd*, concerning the difference between justified action and supererogatory action.

[25]  Melville, *Billy Budd*, 310.

[26]  Immanuel Kant, *Critique of Judgment and Other Works on Ethics* (T. K. Abbott, trans.) London: Longmans (1898), 260. Again, Vere is clearly a man of duty but not very imaginative and certainly quite incapable of true supererogation.

[27]  Melville, *Billy Budd*, 309.

[28]  See Richard A. Hocks, "Melville and the Rise of Realism: The Dilemma on History in *Billy Budd*," *American Literary Realism: 1870–1910* 26.2 (1994): 60–81; Ray B. Browne, "Billy Budd: Gospel of Democracy," *Nineteenth-Century Fiction* 17.4 (1963): 321–337. For a rejection of this view somewhat similar to mine, see Daniel J. Solove, "Melville's *Billy Budd* and Security in Times of Crisis," *Cardozo Law Review* 26 (2005): 2443–2470.

*Bellipotent*. The reader can easily see how Claggart exploits the background information concerning recent mutinies in the British Navy in order to carry out his
malevolent plan – these events would lend gravitas, if not quite credibility, to his
fabrication. The dangerous sailor in Claggart's fib turned out to be Billy. Truly
a good judge of character, however, Vere was not merely incredulous – he was
actually suspicious, and he warned Claggart about the dire consequences of perjury.
Thus, Vere's high opinion of Billy appeared to remain unaffected by Claggart's story.
Almost as if to expose Claggart's perfidy but certainly also because this was the
proper thing for him to do regardless of the veracity of the accusation or the identity
of the allegedly dangerous sailor, Vere summoned Billy to his quarters and ordered
Claggart to repeat his accusation to Billy's face – an order that Claggart diligently
obeyed.

As Claggart retold his story in front of Billy, Vere for the first time realized that
Billy had a speech impediment. Utterly stunned by the slanderous accusation, Billy
became almost paralyzed and could only manage "a strange dumb gesturing and
gurgling."[29] The judicious Vere understood Billy's predicament quite well and tried
to calm Billy down: "[T]here is no hurry, my boy. Take your time, take your time."
And then Melville tells us:

> Contrary to the effect intended, these words so fatherly in tone, doubtless touching
> Billy's heart to the quick, prompted yet more violent efforts at utterance – efforts
> soon ending for the time in confirming the paralysis, and bringing to his face an
> expression which was as a crucifixion to behold. The next instant, quick as the flame
> from a discharged cannon at night, his right arm shot out, and Claggart dropped to
> the deck.[30]

Even after this most extraordinary turn of events, Vere did not quite lash out against
Billy. Instead, he asked Billy to help moving Claggart's inert body, telling him, in
a barely audible but obviously distressed tone: "Fated Boy! What have you done!"[31]
At this point, Vere summoned the ship's surgeon. Immediately after the ship
surgeon's confirmed Claggart's death, Vere uttered the words that have now
acquired a life of their own among Melville's readers: "Struck by an Angel of God!
Yet the Angel must hang!"[32]

Vere summarily set up a tripartite drumhead court on board the *Bellipotent*,
a court in which he served as the only witness. Incapable of behaving any differently,
Billy was perfectly truthful during the trial: he admitted to killing Claggart, though
he denied virtually every other aspect of Claggart's malevolent fabrication. Part of
Billy's forthright testimony involved his allegation that he did not mean to kill
Claggart: "[C]ould I have used my tongue I would not have struck him."[33] Both

---

[29]  Melville, *Billy Budd*, 349.     [30]  *Ibid.*, 350.     [31]  *Ibid.*
[32]  *Ibid.*, 352. While in my view *Billy Budd* is centrally about punishment, this has not been the central
    concern of its interpreters – not even among legal scholars. See, for example, Weisberg, *The Failure of
    the Word* and Richard Posner, *Law and Literature*, Cambridge, MA: Harvard University Press (1988).
[33]  Melville, *Billy Budd*, 357.

the members of the court and Vere himself were deeply affected by these events, above all by the way in which, given "the jugglery of circumstances," as Melville beautifully put it, the "innocence and guilt personified in Claggart and Budd in effect changed places."[34]

The members of the drumhead court pleaded with Vere, so as to find some extenuating circumstance – and even some measure of mercy – for Billy. Although the tragedy of the situation was not in the least lost on Vere, he insisted on downplaying the importance of the "clash of military duty with moral scruple"[35] – even as he was forced to confront the court officers' probing question: "But your scruples: do they move as in a dusk?"[36] Vere soberly concluded that in this martial court matters were perfectly clear: no penalty other than death was appropriate for Billy.

Admittedly, there is some support for supposing that Vere's stern position was in part responsive to the recent mutinies. At least we are explicitly told that Vere set up the summary drumhead court – instead of availing himself of a more nuanced and less rushed courtroom once back in port – in part because acting otherwise may "tend to awaken any slumbering embers" of the recent mutinies.[37] But I think that it is very important to warn against overestimating the importance of this factor. In spite of the wide variety of interpretations of *Billy Budd*, the suggestion that Vere's conflict has to do with the tension between justice and expediency, that is, between treating Billy justly and allowing a mutiny, is quite widespread, indeed orthodox. The underlying idea is that the dictates of expediency suggested trying and executing Billy on board (so as to avoid a mutiny, etc.), whereas the dictates of justice suggested Billy's mainland acquittal (in light of his "angelical" innocence). According to this interpretation, Vere can then be seen as succumbing to the pressures of expediency: he treated Billy unjustly in order to prevent a mutiny. As Richard Posner, for example, has expressed it: Vere's behavior "puts the reader in mind of the most disturbing feature of utilitarianism – that, in principle anyway, it countenances the deliberate sacrifice of an innocent person for the sake of the general good."[38]

And yet this interpretation misses something crucial. As we have seen, Melville made every effort to present Vere as a thoughtful man and one with sophisticated – even literary – sensibility for the nuances of life. In light of this overarching sensibility, it is not easy to cast Vere as a classical utilitarian. *Billy Budd* gives us no reason to believe that Vere would have *ever* "deliberately sacrificed" Billy or that we would have otherwise punished him undeservedly, even if, say, we tinker with the text such as to make it somehow *certain* that this would have been the only way to avert a mutiny.[39] For these reasons, I think that it is a mistake to read *Billy Budd* as a defense of utilitarianism's obsession with mere expediency. If these reflections

---

[34] *Ibid.*, 354.　　[35] *Ibid.*, 361.　　[36] *Ibid.*　　[37] *Ibid.*, 355.　　[38] Posner, *Law and Literature*, 171.

[39] In one of the oddest interpretations of the situation, Weisberg suggests that the reason Vere condemns Billy to death on board the *Bellipotent* (rather than waiting to get to port) is in fact envy. According to Weisberg, it is Vere – and not Claggart – who was moved by envy. See, e.g., his *The Failure of the Word*, 160 ff.

were not enough, further support can be gleaned from the fact that Melville makes no effort to hide his disdain for "martial utilitarians" and for "the Benthamites of war."[40] It would be remarkably strange for Melville to then conceive of Vere – upon whom so much of the novel's poignancy falls – as a mere utilitarian calculator.

Moreover, the sense in which punishing Billy was, or was not, an injustice is precisely what is so masterfully at stake in *Billy Budd*. Many interpreters get Billy's "innocence" wrong. Billy's innocence was, by and large, some sort of "angelical innocence," and this form of innocence does not mean innocence in any standard legal or moral sense whereby its meaning relates to "not guilty." Billy is unequivocally portrayed as innocent only in the sense in which he was pure, uncontaminated, childlike, etc. Doubtless *Billy Budd* deliberately ambiguates the notion of innocence, but Melville repeatedly describes Billy as a "child-man" and "unsophisticated" and as possessing a certain "blank innocence"[41] and "ignorant innocence" – and ignorance that in the end "was his blinder."[42] His was a form of immanent "essential innocence," importantly disconnected from Claggart's death.[43] Fundamentally, the sense in which Billy was innocent flows from an overall assessment of his personality and demeanor: Billy was an innocent *being*, not an innocent *defendant*. Of course, taking those factors into account may be important in his trial, and it is *possible* that this angelical innocence may have rendered him much less culpable than Vere took him to be. Perhaps the angelical innocence rendered Billy fully innocent in the narrow, legalistic sense concerning Claggart's death. But it is also possible that although an innocent being, he was indeed a guilty defendant.

Was Vere's decision regarding Billy's punishment, *all* these things considered, correct? Billy *did* kill Claggart, and this *was* a serious crime – independently of any utilitarian calculus related to possible mutinies. Some interpreters have suggested that Billy's striking at Claggart was inadvertent or accidental.[44] And certainly Billy himself says that he "did not mean to kill" Claggart.[45] But I think that it is a mistake to assume that "not meaning to do it" translates into Billy's action being an accident or inadvertent. Billy acted of his own free will; he was not forced to do what he did. Of course, we can well sympathize with his horror as he listened to Claggart's perfidy. We could, furthermore, perhaps go as far as seeing Claggart's lies as a provocation of sorts, particularly in light of Billy's own peculiar inarticulacy, which surely made him feel even more horrified and vulnerable. But none of this amounts to Billy's action being accidental, even if its result was unquestionably unintended. Although Billy's action was not malicious, much less premeditated or hateful, it was not accidental or inadvertent either. Thus, in punishing Billy, Vere was plausibly doing justice (even if there is ample room for debating whether the

---

[40]  Melville, *Billy Budd*, 306–307.  [41]  *Ibid.*, 336.  [42]  *Ibid.*, 338.  [43]  *Ibid.*, 373.
[44]  See, for example, Barbara Johnson, "Melville's Fist: The Execution of *Billy Budd*," *Studies in Romanticism* 18.4 (1979): 567–599, at 575 and *passim*, and H. Bruce Franklin, "Billy Budd and Capital Punishment: A Tale of Three Centuries" in *American Literature* 69.2 (1997): 337–359, *passim*.
[45]  Melville, *Billy Budd*, 357.

actual punishment Vere inflicted on Billy – death – was *itself* just). It is by no means clear that in punishing Billy, Vere thought that he was allowing the practicalities of life to defeat justice.

Rather, Vere was – in ways not often noticed but crucial for my purposes – dealing with the *theoretical* problem of punishment with which I have been concerned throughout the book. *Billy Budd* tackles this problem, beautifully heightening the pull of its different dimensions. *Billy Budd's mise-en-scene*: Billy's overall "angelical innocence" juxtaposed to Vere's "sterling-but-not-brilliant" judiciousness and, of course, to Claggart's gratuitous hostility, makes the problem all the more poignant, if also all the more difficult. The first of these elements makes us feel compassion for the perpetrating angel's suffering, the second makes us despise his repellent victim, and the third makes us respect the just man's impossible burden. Even if Melville presents this more movingly – and indeed more beautifully – than others, in essence this is the same grand problem that preoccupied a variety of thinkers – from Leibniz to Weber and from Brentano to Strawson – as we saw in earlier chapters. This is the problem of the tension between punishment and forgiveness (or justice and mercy, etc.).

Quoting directly from Melville's text, Wendell Glick has suggested that in *Billy Budd* Melville's

> interest was less in art than in "Truth uncompromisingly told." [Melville] was quite willing . . . to sacrifice "the symmetry of form attainable in pure fiction" and to risk "ragged edges" on his final work if by so doing he could tell a story "having less to do with fable than with fact."[46]

Thus, Melville himself thought of *Billy Budd* as a vehicle through which he could in fact transcend literature. And *Billy Budd* itself gives us every reason to think that at least part of this project that Melville thought transcended literature was the theoretical problem of punishment. Part of this "truth uncompromisingly told" concerns the complexity of moral life and the way that *punishment* generates moral conflicts that the simpleminded monism of both utilitarianism and deontic retributivism just cannot countenance. Reading *Billy Budd* as *merely* showcasing the tension between justice and expedience is to ignore a lot of what Melville was expressly trying to do.

Upon the conclusion of the trial, Vere chose to inform Billy of its outcome personally. Melville describes Vere's expression at the end of his private meeting with Billy as evincing "the agony of the strong" and as revealing that "the condemned one suffered less than he who mainly had effected the condemnation."[47] Melville further describes this final meeting between Vere and Billy as one between "him who never left it alive, and him who when he did leave it left it as one

---

[46]  Wendell Glick, "Expedience and Absolute Morality in *Billy Budd*," *PMLA* 68.1 (1953): 103–110, at 104. See also Melville, *Billy Budd*, 380–381.

[47]  Melville, *Billy Budd*, 367.

condemned to die."[48] In one of the most famous moments in *Billy Budd*, we learn that as Vere lay on his deathbed (long after the incident surrounding Billy's trial and execution), he "was heard to murmur words inexplicable to his attendant: 'Billy Budd, Billy Budd'."[49]

None of this makes much sense if we read Vere as purely (or even mainly) interested in dull cost-benefit analyses or in applying perfunctory maxims. The details of what transpired on board the *Bellipotent* changed Vere to his core. Recall Max Weber's first two obstacles to a meaningful existence discussed in Chapter 1: undeserved suffering and unpunished injustice. These are, I think, on conspicuous display in *Billy Budd* and above all in connection to Vere's predicament. Clearly Vere did not, for a variety of reasons, want to leave an injustice unpunished. But *Billy Budd* problematizes matters so well that we are not clear as to what exactly the injustice – if any – actually was.

Before turning to a deeper exploration of what Vere's predicament tells us about punishment, I want to conclude this section by considering what *Billy Budd* tells us about Nussbaum's suggestion that we should replace the punitive paradigm with the merciful paradigm, insofar as only the latter allows to appreciate the rich complexity of life. Even my unavoidably brief summary of *Billy Budd* reveals that Vere was very much aware of the complexity of life and of the emotional and experiential "insides" of wrongdoers. (If my summary fails in this regard, then reading *Billy Budd* would reveal this.) In fact, Vere was tragically and painfully aware of these insides – and yet he nonetheless chose to punish Billy. And this, I think, should give us pause before agreeing with Nussbaum's suggestion whereby awareness of the complexity of life and of the insides of wrongdoers' inner world necessarily leads to the adoption of the merciful paradigm.

But perhaps the spirit of Nussbaum's position could be defended along the following lines. Even if Vere was *aware* of those emotional and experiential insides that Nussbaum believes necessitate a turn toward mercy, he chose to *ignore* those insides and to punish Billy as if they did not matter. In so ignoring these insides, Vere may be seen as in fact confirming Nussbaum's thesis, since he thereby could be seen as highlighting the poverty of the punitive paradigm. I think that this defense misses the target. The point of reading *Billy Budd* – and indeed of *writing* it – is not to defend Vere's decision. What renders *Billy Budd* a true masterpiece is the way in which it exposes the complexity of moral life (and the way in which this affects the problem of punishment), not the actual decision – or procedures – of the drumhead court Vere convened. As Gowans has put it, rather than focus on whether Vere reached the right overall decision,

> we should read Melville as being interested first and foremost in encouraging our reflection on the complex moral nature of Vere's situation, and as being concerned

[48] *Ibid.*   [49] *Ibid.*, 382.

with inviting us to evaluate Vere's response to that situation only in light of this complexity.[50]

It is likely that Vere was indeed too harsh, and perhaps he ought to have shown Billy more leniency, either on board the *Bellipotent* or after returning to port. But the important point, rather, is to contemplate the *depth* of Vere's predicament. Melville evidently constructed Billy's case as involving "a moral dilemma" containing more than a small amount of the "tragic."[51] Vere was doomed (morally speaking) no matter what he did: there is little reason to think that had Vere actually forgiven Billy, he would not have still been deeply affected by the events on board the *Bellipotent*.

To the extent that *Billy Budd* does not revolve around the bald alleviation of suffering, then it seems to me not to underwrite Nussbaum's recent utilitarian turn. After all, and by her own admission, independently of the practical problems exhibited by many contemporary criminal justice systems, Nussbaum wants a moratorium on punishment *theory*. Refusing to engage with the axiological complexity that the tension between punishment and forgiveness generates – and that *Billy Budd* masterfully explores – is to replace the simplemindedness of either utilitarianism or deontic retributivism with a "simpleminded mercifulness." This refusal will evidently not advance punishment theory, but it is not even likely to yield a good forgiveness theory either. For, as I have been insisting throughout the book, the way forward in either case is to recognize how intimately connected punishment and forgiveness really are.

## 8.2 MORAL TAINTS: FROM AULIS TO THERESIENSTADT

A revealing lens into the complexity of Vere's situation is afforded by a passage in *Billy Budd* that, although not very often discussed, is absolutely crucial for my purposes (and for a proper understanding of Melville's preoccupations during the writing of his last work). This relatively underexplored passage happens to follow immediately after Vere's very famous last words, "Billy Budd, Billy Budd." After telling us that these words were "inexplicable to his attendant,"[52] Melville adds:

> [T]hat these were not the accents of remorse would seem clear from what the attendant said to the *Bellipotent*'s senior officer of marines, who, as the most reluctant to condemn the members of the drumhead court, too well knew, though here he kept the knowledge to himself, who Billy Budd was.[53]

This is as rich as it is enigmatic. We are in the dark as to what Vere's deathbed attendant actually told the senior officer. Regardless, how could *his* words – that is, the words of someone who knew nothing about Billy's trial and execution and who consequently found Vere's words "inexplicable" – give us, or the senior officer whom he addressed, any lens whatsoever as to Vere's state of mind? Moreover, how could the fact that the officer knew very well who Billy Budd was tell us anything about whether Vere's last words, as communicated to the clueless attendant, did not evince remorse? (In any case, if knowing Billy very well suggested anything to him, it should have been that Vere must have felt remorse.) Whatever Melville sought to convey with this mysterious passage, the stated view that Vere had no remorse cannot be considered a narrative fact.

Gowans discusses the passage I have just quoted (or, more precisely, its first portion) and appears to reach a slightly different conclusion. He appears to confer more verisimilitude to the narrator's bald assertion that "these were not the accents of remorse" than I do. Upon citing these very words, Gowans concedes, "Vere did not feel remorse in the sense of feeling that he had made the wrong decision."[54] This, however, appears to contradict what Gowans says in the very next sentence, which in fact contains one of the most insightful theses in Gowans's book. In this sentence, Gowans tells us that by murmuring "Billy Budd, Billy Budd," Vere was "perhaps expressing his anguish that in doing what he confidently believed was morally best he nevertheless did something morally wrong."[55] The tension between the two sentences is plain: in one sentence, Gowans claims that Vere thought he did not make the wrong decision and, in the next, that he did after all think that he did wrong. It is the juxtaposition of these two seemingly contradictory ideas that leads Gowans to conclude: "[I]n the end we are left to speculate about Vere's true state of mind [about whether or not he felt remorse]."[56]

I agree with Gowans that Melville very much wanted to keep us well within the speculative realm. But I would like to more forcefully resist the suggestion that Vere felt no remorse and in fact propose that Melville's oblique circumlocution in this passage actually seeks to subvert what the passage straightforwardly states. I believe that Melville wished to *cast doubt* on the supposition that Vere really had no remorse. As we have seen previously, Melville is emphatic in that Vere's participation in Billy's trial left him, the punisher, "suffering more" than Billy, the punishee; that Vere was in agony ("the agony of the strong"); and that in a sense he was "no longer alive" after the incident. These descriptions do not seem to fit someone allegedly without remorse.

Gowans concedes that even if Vere did not feel *remorse*, he may have nonetheless felt *anguish*. The question as to whether there are important differences between remorse and anguish – and agent regret and guilt, etc. – actually opens up a crucial investigation on the nature and import of these emotions. Gowans does not tell us whether he thinks that there is a difference between these two particular emotions (remorse and anguish), but he introduces a fundamental and very important distinction between two general types of emotions: between those emotions that have a moral dimension and those that do not. As he canvasses the specialized literature on the different terms that have been used to describe the emotions of certain agents in the wake of situations such as Vere faced, Gowans tells us that "rather than engaging in a fruitless debate about whether this feeling is correctly thought of as regret, guilt, remorse, or something else, I will set these terms aside and speak of the feeling I define as being 'morally distressed' or 'morally disturbed.'"[57]

While later in this section I will further specify the moral emotion that inescapable wrongdoing generates, Gowans is, I think, fundamentally correct in thinking that the general distinction between moral emotions and non-moral emotions, by itself, does an immense amount of work regarding our efforts to understand both moral dilemmas and the complexity of moral life in general.[58] When we learn of, say, an earthquake that causes many deaths, we may feel sad, perhaps very sad; we can certainly *regret* that it happened. Furthermore, it may be perfectly fitting to feel this form of non-moral sadness on occasions like these. But this is very different from the emotion that would be fitting to experience after we come to realize that we have behaved, say, disloyally. In this latter type of case, the fitting emotion is a *moral* emotion. And this is an important difference. So, when I insist that Vere felt remorse, I am not invested in *terminology*. What matters is that Vere was not merely (generically, non-morally) sad or regretful. Whatever we may want to call it – remorse, anguish (provided this is understood morally), or agent regret, etc. – Vere was afflicted by a decisively *moral* emotion.

It can scarcely be doubted that Melville portrayed Vere as intensely and deeply distressed by what transpired on board the *Bellipotent*, and it is hardly an exaggeration to say that Melville wanted us to see the sense in which Vere was downright *destroyed*: he was after all "no longer living." This strongly suggests both that Vere's emotions were moral and that he was not simpleminded (either in the utilitarian or in the deontic retributivist version of simplemindedness). But it may not be immediately obvious why simpleminded agents cannot feel very bad – even profoundly bad – about the costs of certain actions. So, I want to explore some reasons to believe that there really exists a certain opposition between certain *moral* emotions and the type of moral simplemindedness that I have criticized in this book and that *Billy Budd* exposes in such a masterful fashion.

Why, for example, would a simpleminded calculator feel as *existentially devastated* as Vere felt? If she did, she would at the very least be failing to live up to the standards of the classical utilitarian credo. After all, according to this credo, if one did the best one could, then there is, as a matter of sheer logic, nothing to be remorseful about what one has done. Again: one could perhaps lament that some of

---

[57]  *Ibid.*, 95–96.
[58]  If Gowans means "anguish" to differ from "remorse" in that it does not have a moral dimension, then this remark as to the possibility that Vere felt anguish instead of remorse contradicts some of the essential theses of his book. And if Gowans thinks that both anguish and remorse have a moral dimension, then this remark does not really do much work for him, since in this crucial respect both anguish and remorse amount to the same thing: both anguish and remorse would be moral emotions.

those costs had to be incurred, but there is no way one could feel as if there was something morally wrong in what one did, since it was, *ex hypothesi*, the best one could have done. Had Vere been a simpleminded calculator and had he thought that he did the best he could, he may have lamented, non-morally, what happened to Billy, but he could not have been affected in quite the ways Melville portrays him. Insofar as deontic retributivism also presupposes a monistic axiology, *mutatis mutandis* the same would hold for its adherents as it does for classical utilitarians – provided they properly fulfilled their duties, there simply would be no rational room for moral distress.[59]

Recall Vere's words upon learning that Billy indeed killed Claggart: "Struck by an Angel of God! Yet the Angel must hang!" Evidently, Vere was immediately aware that he faced a tragic dilemma – a dilemma of the sort that a simpleminded utilitarian or a simpleminded deontic retributivist cannot even countenance. It is not just that Vere's emotions were very intense – though they unquestionably were that – it is that they were *moral* emotions. They were moral because Vere was aware that he could not have escaped doing *wrong*: from his perspective, it would have been wrong not to punish Billy, but it was nonetheless wrong to punish Billy *too*, even if he was *justified* in punishing him.

Here we have, then, an important lesson that the discussion of moral emotions contains vis-à-vis the problem of the justification of punishment: the typical understanding of "justification" may have indeed stunted progress in punishment theory. Even when we are justified in acting in a certain way, there may be room, even ample room, for *moral* distress afterward. Sometimes actions that really are justified (including punishment) can still be in a sense wrong. This possibility forces us to recognize a complexity in the very structure of justification as such that punishment theorists have hitherto ignored. Vere represents an exquisitely well-crafted example of someone who, although perhaps justified in doing what he did, nonetheless did something wrong. To be clear, however, this is not a skeptical position about justification in general at all: some acts that stand in need of justification (including some instances of punishment) can indeed be justified. The lesson concerns the *structure* of justification that punishment theorists typically presuppose: this structure is too much at home in the morality system. And *Billy Budd* can helpfully be read as disentangling the idea of justification from the overly neat mechanisms of the morality system.

Of course, the idea that one may be inescapably doomed to do something wrong no matter what one chooses – and even if one is justified in so choosing – immediately invites a certain skepticism, at least among the uninitiated. As a first step to dispelling these skeptical doubts, it is useful to take a look at the specialized philosophical literature on moral dilemmas. Following Gowans, we can profitably

---

[59] See, for example, Jens Timmermann, "Kantian Dilemmas: Moral Conflict in Kant's Ethical Theory," *Archiv für Geschichte der Philosophie* 951 (2013): 36–64.

approach said literature by dividing it into two subgroups. On the one hand, we have those who believe that these types of moral dilemmas exist, and on the other hand, we have those who deny their existence. Those skeptical of these types of moral dilemmas often base their skepticism on either the simpleminded monism we have discussed before or their (typically concomitant) adherence to "some abstract and purportedly obvious principles of deontic logic."[60] Admittedly, these types of moral dilemmas do on first approximation appear paradoxical: Why, if you have done the right thing (or chosen the best option available), should you nonetheless feel bad, let alone *morally* bad, about having done it? Michael Walzer points out that many believe that to posit the existence of this type of moral dilemma is to "pile confusion upon confusion."[61] Similarly, Williams tells us that the emotions that these moral dilemmas generate "are from a strictly [classical] utilitarian point of view [and also from the strict deontological point of view] irrational."[62] There is something see-mingly irresistibly in the idea that if, in a given situation, one does the best one can, then there is nothing that could possibly warrant a negative *moral* emotion (such as remorse).

Those who grant the existence of these types of moral dilemmas, in contrast, rely "rather heavily on the phenomenological argument."[63] We *know* what it is to face a morally dilemmatic situation, and we *know* the ways in which these feelings are impervious to cost-benefit considerations. There is nothing abstruse here: we know these things because we have experienced them. Williams pithily recounts a conversation he had with another philosopher who, like him, believes in moral dilemmas (Michael Stocker) in which they concluded that their "work consisted largely of reminding moral philosophers of truths about human life which are very well known to virtually all adult human beings except moral philosophers."[64] Given what I have said in this book, it should be obvious that I believe that punishment theorists need to be "reminded" of these truths even more than do moral philosophers in general. After all, something like the debate over moral dilemmas among moral philosophers is virtually nonexistent in punishment theory.

In explaining the nature of the phenomenological argument, Gowans refers us back to "its original formulation by Williams."[65] In the context of classical tragedies, Williams tells us, the very

---

[60] Gowans, *Innocence Lost*, 93.

[61] Michael Walzer, "The Problem of Dirty Hands," *Philosophy and Public Affairs* 2.2 (1973): 160–180, at 162.

[62] Williams, "A Critique of Utilitarianism," 101. Again, I think that from a strictly Kantian point of view, they are irrational as well.

[63] Gowans, *Innocence Lost*, 93. Among the influential philosophers who recognize the existence of moral dilemmas, we find not only Michael Walzer and Bernard Williams but also Thomas Nagel, Jonathan Bennett, Christopher Gowans, Michael Stocker, and the early Martha Nussbaum (the Martha Nussbaum of *The Fragility of Goodness*).

[64] Bernard Williams, "The Liberalism of Fear," in *In the Beginning Was the Deed: Realism and Moralism in Political Argument*, Princeton, NJ: Princeton University Press (2005), 52.

[65] Gowans, *Innocence Lost*, 94.

notion of "acting for the best" may very well lose its content. Agamemnon at Aulis may have said "May it be well." But he is neither convinced nor convincing. The agonies that a man will experience after acting in full consciousness of such a situation are not to be traced to a persistent doubt that he may not have chosen the better thing; but, for instance, to a clear conviction that he has not done the better thing because there was no better thing to be done. It may, on the other hand, even be the case that by some not utterly irrational criteria of "the better thing," he is convinced that he did the better thing: rational men no doubt pointed out to Agamemnon his responsibilities as a commander, the many people involved, the considerations of honor, and so forth. If he accepted all this, and acted accordingly: it would seem a glib moralist who said, as some sort of criticism, that he must be irrational to lie awake at night, having killed his daughter.[66]

Despite his view about the mundaneness of the phenomenological argument, Williams's example of choice may perhaps give the impression that these moral emotions are necessarily related to larger-than-life choices such as Agamemnon's. My focus on *Billy Budd* may unwittingly reinforce this impression. After all, the entire setup of *Billy Budd* is meant to shine a light on the tragic nature of Vere's predicament: he was not merely faced with the choice of punishing someone in a complicated case; he had to punish the "angel of God," no less. Crucially for my purposes, however, the interesting phenomenon that Williams describes via the consideration of Agamemnon – and that Vere's situation may be seen as instantiating – is not restricted to tragic cases. Tragic cases are helpful because they render the problem more conspicuous, since after all tragedies can be seen as partly constituted by the presence of this phenomenon.

What threatens to strip the notion of "the better thing" of its content is the very structure of a pluralistic axiology in which values can conflict as deeply as, for example, the value of deserved suffering and the value of its merciful remission do. It is not, of course, that the notion of "the better thing" is jeopardized by situations in which the choices we face are of identical value: identical options may make it true that there is no "better thing," but not in Williams's sense. Even if, technically speaking, one of these two courses of action is in this or that occasion "better" than the other one, the significance of the "defeated" course of action is such that the very talk of "better" and "worse" somehow rings hollow. Consider, for example, the question as to which, between New York and Philadelphia, is closer to Alpha Centauri. One of the two cities is indeed closer to that star, but, still, the very content of the question seems odd.

I think that moral dilemmas of the sort that exercised Williams and others are perfectly common. We have all found ourselves in situations where whatever we choose to do we will do uneliminable wrong (even if we will also do right). Luckily for us, we rarely need to sacrifice our own daughter or to execute the

---

66   Bernard Williams, "Ethical Consistency," in his *Problems of the Self: Philosophical Papers 1956–1972*, Cambridge: Cambridge University Press (1973), 173.

Angel of God – but, still, ordinary life is rife with conflicts of this type. It is a mistake, then, to think that conflicts, involving "acts that are justified, even obligatory, but none the less wrong and shameful" can only be faced by characters in tragedies (or by politicians, as is also often assumed), even if they are perhaps faced more frequently or more dramatically by characters in tragedies (and by political actors).[67]

A frequent way of referring to these moral dilemmas is to call them "dirty hands" problems. In its contemporary technical sense, the origin of the name "dirty hands" is to be found in an eponymous play by Jean-Paul Sartre centered around the phenomenon: a politician needs to do all sorts of unsavory things, even if for a good purpose.[68] But the dilemma is built upon a very old and very widespread idea: that there is a strong connection between bodily cleanliness and moral purity, itself conspicuously visible in many religions and other belief systems. The Old and New Testaments contain many references to cleanliness and sometimes specifically to clean *hands* as a sign of moral purity: in *Job* 17:9, 22:30; *2 Samuel* 22:21; *Psalm* 18:20, 24:4, 26:6; and perhaps most famously *Matthew* 27:24, the passage that describes Pilate washing his hands as if to remain unpolluted. The theme of moral pollution and its connection to hands have been a common literary trope too; recall Lady Macbeth's famous words:

> Out, damned spot, out. I say ... Hell is murky ... What, will these hands ne'er be clean? No more o' that, my lord, no more o' that. You mar all with this starting ... Here's the smell of the blood still. All the perfumes of Arabia will not sweeten this little hand. O, O, O![69]

And, of course, the theme is central to Greek tragedies, to which Williams paid so much attention.[70] The *idee mere* of the phenomenon of dirty hands is that sometimes we cannot avoid moral pollution, precisely in the sense of inescapably having to do wrong, even if we are simultaneously doing right and even if we are justified in acting as we do.

---

[67]  Michael Stocker, *Plural and Conflicting Values*, Oxford: Clarendon Press (1990), 9. I think it is true that dirty hands can give rise to shame, as Stocker suggests. But I here focus on guilt-like feelings such as remorse rather than on shame. After all, the former group of feelings are more directly linked to morality: one could feel shame for utterly non-moral reasons, say, when one feels shame for one's looks.

[68]  Jean-Paul Sartre, *No Exit and Three Other Plays*, New York, NY: Vintage (1955).

[69]  William Shakespeare, *Macbeth in William Shakespeare: The Complete Works* (Stanley Wells and Gary Taylor, eds.), Oxford: Clarendon Press (1988), 996. The idea has even made it into psychology, where some speak about an alleged "Macbeth effect," whereby subjects react differently to cleanliness depending on whether they have been primed to think of bad deeds or good deeds. See Chen-Bo Zhong and Katie Liljenquist, "Washing Away Your Sins: Threatened Morality and Physical Cleansing," *Science* 313.5792 (2006): 1451–1452.

[70]  It could be argued that the problem of dirty hands is alluded to in the very opening of Plato's *Euthyphro*, when we are presented with the dilemma between the value of justice and the value of loyalty to one's father. See Plato, *Euthyphro*, 3–5, in B. Jowett, *The Dialogues of Plato*, Vol. II, Oxford: Oxford University Press (1931), 77 ff.

In order to show how this type of moral conflict illuminates the discussion of punishment, I will highlight a few of its characteristics in increasing order of importance. First, it would be a mistake to apply the idea of dirty hands to conflicts that Hitler or Ohlendorf or any other more or less uniformly bad person may have faced. In a sense, *they* cannot get their hands dirty – for they are dirty all over already: there is just no polluting what is already polluted to such a high degree. The idea of dirty hands applies only in the cases of *otherwise* more or less "clean" persons. The *contrast* between fundamental cleanliness and the results of the inescapable wrongdoing are often called moral *taints*. Doing wrong in general may in a different sense taint a fundamentally clean person too. But I shall restrict myself to cases in which more or less clean people are tainted as a result of doing wrong within the context of those moral dilemmas in which we inescapably do wrong and even more specifically to cases in which these dilemmas arise as a result of our responses to wrongdoing.

Thus, while both Vere and Claggart did wrong, there was a moral taint (in the sense that interests me) only to what Vere did because there was something *inescapably* wrong in what he did (and he knew it) and because Claggart, unlike Vere, was already dirty. Nothing of what Vere went through applies to Claggart: Claggart did wrong (more serious wrong than Vere, in fact), but his wrong was not inescapable, was not the result of finding himself trapped in a tragic dilemma. I hope it is not necessary to belabor the point that to say that Claggart (or Ohlendorf, Hitler, etc.) is not tainted is in no way to justify, excuse, or mitigate the gravity of what he did. Claggart is, for example, evidently a much worse character than Vere, and this is, in part, precisely because he is not tainted. Claggart is an unalloyed villain, whereas Vere is not. But part of our respect for Vere flows from the fact that he *is* tainted.

Second, moral taints have a way of *sticking* to ourselves, or, in other words, they have a way of *remaining*: they constitute *remainders*. It is in this sense that Williams famously claimed that "moral conflicts are neither systematically avoidable, nor all soluble without remainders."[71] Even more often than the discussion of moral dilemmas, the discussion of moral remainders is met with resistance, as if it were more mysterious than it really is. To a large extent this resistance can be traced back to the looming influence of the morality system. As a result of its quantifying ethos, the morality system simply cannot countenance moral *taints*; all it can countenance are moral *costs* – and, to bring back a term that was important in the early chapters, moral costs are always medicinal. The morality system may of course deal with someone lamenting, say, a certain surgery that decreases her hearing but that is necessary to save her life – but it cannot deal with someone feeling *remorse* for, say, having to punish someone justly. Similarly, to the extent that one embraces the

---

[71] Williams, "Ethical Consistency," 179. As noted in Chapter 1, I treat "moral conflict" and "moral dilemma" as synonyms. Another name for "remainders" is "residues." For a useful contribution in which the latter term is preferred, see Wai Chee Dimock, *Residues of Justice: Literature, Law, Philosophy*, Berkeley, CA: University of California Press (1996).

moral mathematics underwriting the morality system, one simply cannot face the type of moral dilemma that we are considering. From the perspective of the morality system, there always is a non-hollow better option (no matter how difficult it may be to discover or to attain and excepting the uninteresting case of choices between identically valuable options). The defender of the morality system, the skeptic of moral dilemmas, and the denier of moral luck (often the same person) simply cannot, as a matter of sheer logic, admit the existence of moral taints: all they can accept are moral costs.

Paying attention to Williams's original presentation of moral remainders can help dispel some overblown worries. Compare conflicts of beliefs and conflicts of desires. If, having initially been unsure as to whether to believe that the sky is blue or that the sky is not blue, you come to realize that the sky is blue, then this realization *fully* defeats the belief that the sky is not blue. The latter belief (or at least its pull) then in a sense *disappears* – it does not *remain*: this is one of the necessary consequences of coming to realize that the sky is blue. Conflicts of desires are different. Imagine, in contrast, that you have the conflicting desires of, say, keeping to your diet and eating a delicious calorie-rich cake; and imagine that you conclude that it is best to keep to your diet: your desire to keep to your diet defeats the cake desire. But, unlike the case of beliefs, this is not a *full* defeat: the losing desire does not altogether disappear (and neither does its pull). The defeated desire can *remain* in the sense that you still desire the cake (even if you also desire to keep to your diet).[72] There is, I hope, nothing mysterious about the sense in which the desire for the cake remains – and the best evidence for it is to be found in what the phenomenological method amply reveals about our ordinary experiences.[73]

Perceptively, Williams suggests that moral conflicts between potential courses of actions are much more like conflict of desires than like conflict of beliefs. When one potential course of action defeats another one, this need not mean that the attractiveness of the defeated course of action *disappears*. Sometimes the sense of loss attendant to not taking that other course of action can *remain*. Consider this beautiful passage in George Eliot's *Daniel Deronda*:

> For Macbeth's rhetoric about the impossibility of being many opposite things in the same moment, referred to the clumsy necessities of action and not to the subtler possibilities of feeling. We cannot speak a loyal word and be meanly silent; we cannot kill and not kill in the same moment; but a moment is wide enough for the

---

[72]  The example of the diet and the cake does double duty: as an example of a conflict of desires and as an example of a conflict of courses of action. This should not be too surprising. After all, despite important differences, desires are much more like intentions than beliefs are like intentions. And actions can be seen as the condition of satisfaction of intentions. For more on this, see my *Five Ways Patricia Can Kill Her Husband: A Theory of Intentionality and Blame*, Chicago, IL: Open Court (2005).

[73]  For an interesting examination of these sorts of experiences, see Kieran Setiya, "Retrospection," *Philosophers' Imprint* 16 (2016): 1–15.

loyal and mean desire, for the outlash of a murderous thought and the sharp backward stroke of repentance.[74]

While Eliot mentions neither axiology nor the deontic in this passage, her reference to the "clumsy necessities of action" evokes the deontic realm, and her reference to the "subtler possibilities of feeling" evokes the axiological realm. And she alludes to the ways in which opposite things can coexist in the latter realm.

Thus, it really is not that mysterious to say that some moral dilemmas leave remainders, even when the course of action we choose is justified. Punishment constitutes precisely this type of moral dilemma: to say that we were justified in punishing someone is not to say that thereby this justified action leaves no remainders. And it is the possibility of remainders that punishment theorists have typically ignored. When we are justified in punishing someone, this does mean that the course of action involving inflicting deserved suffering has defeated the course of action whereby we could have forgiven this person – but that need not mean that the attractiveness, i.e. the *moral significance*, of the defeated course of action has vanished in thin air.

Punishment theorists have treated the problem of the justification of punishment as if modeled on conflicts of beliefs, although a much more promising strategy is to model the justification of punishment on conflicts of desires and courses of action, so as to recognize the theoretical space needed for remainders. It is because of this typically overlooked structure of justification that Vere, even if we assume that he thought that he was justified, was so morally devastated by what he did. The unrealized value of forgiving Billy remained, even after it was defeated by the realized value of administering justice. (And, had he chosen to forgive Billy, the unrealized value of administering justice would have remained.) Decisions not to realize certain values taint us.

We could now turn to the third characteristic of moral taints that I wish to highlight, which brings us back to the discussion of moral emotions. Moral taints are *distressing*. Moral taints cause us to experience certain moral emotions, which often constitute, at least experientially, evidence of the taints. Compare Vere as Melville portrayed him against a modified Vere who behaves just as Melville's except that he is not in the least distressed by what he did – a Vere, that is, utterly impervious and utterly unaffected by having executed the Angel of God. I think it is obvious which of these two Veres commands more moral respect. The sight of the modified Vere walking away after executing Billy whistling a happy tune, to put the point in Derek Parfit's felicitous terms (which I discuss in the appendix), would be chilling – *morally* chilling.

Despite the obvious difference between Agamemnon's killing of Iphigenia and the lorry driver's killing of the child – only the latter is completely faultless, not the result of the agent's conscious decision – the two cases are similar in at least one

[74] George Eliot, *Daniel Deronda*, New York, NY: Harper (1876), 15 (Book I, Chapter IV).

important respect. Both cases involve agents who are in the end not punishable: one because the agent was (*ex hypothesi*) justified and the other because it was completely faultless, only causally connected to the result. However, both types of action – the justified (or fully excused, etc.) and the utterly faultless – can generate taints. Yet the contemplation of the driver walking away whistling a happy tune (upon learning he was faultless) is as chilling as the contemplation of a relaxed and unaffected Agamemnon (say, upon realizing that he was justified in killing Iphigenia). Contemplating Vere unperturbed walking away whistling a happy tune would be not one bit less chilling.

There is room here to admit a distinction as to what exactly is fitting for Melville's Vere to feel and what is fitting for Williams's lorry driver to feel. After all, only one of these characters has *chosen* to do wrong (albeit in the context of facing an inescapable moral dilemma). The lorry driver was in a sense *passive*, a true victim of circumstances; he did not know he was killing a child and could not have expected to know it. Vere, in contrast, was much more morally active: he *chose* to hang the Angel of God. In this connection, Stephen de Wijze has insightfully suggested that in addition to Williams's "agent regret" (which, as we saw in Chapter 4, would attach to agents such as the lorry driver), we should recognize a different moral emotion called "tragic remorse" (which would attach to *choosing* agents such as Agamemnon or Vere).[75] I am sympathetic to de Wijze's suggestion. Insofar as the punisher has chosen to punish, I believe that the emotion that is fitting for a punisher to feel is more akin to tragic remorse than to agent regret. Vere's *innocence* has been blemished more, and at any rate differently, than that of the lorry driver – if for no other reason because Vere got his hands dirty in a way that the lorry driver did not. As de Wijze has put it, tragic remorse involves the realization "that our moral innocence can be destroyed despite our strenuous efforts to prevent this."[76] Vere, but not the lorry driver, strenuously tried to protect his moral innocence.

Other authors have forcefully suggested other important distinctions between different types of moral emotions.[77] I hope it is clear, however, why I do not need to adjudicate this issue. While I think that the case of punishment indeed calls for de Wijze's "tragic remorse" rather than for Williams's "agent regret," my main point would have been made either way. For despite the differences between agent regret and tragic remorse, they are both *moral* emotions, whose absence when they are fitting is, for my purposes here, sufficiently chilling. As P. S. Greenspan has put it: "[T]he hypothetical rehabilitated mass murderer who goes on to lead an exemplary

75  Stephen de Wijze, "Tragic Remorse – The Anguish of Dirty Hands," *Ethical Theory and Moral Practice* 7 (2004): 453–471.

76  *Ibid.*, 465.

77  See above all P. S. Greenspan, *Practical Guilt: Moral Dilemmas, Emotions, and Social Norms*, Oxford: Oxford University Press (2005). I do not need, either, to engage here with the distinction between (narrowly) moral emotions and (more general) piacular emotions: for this later distinction, see Roger Crisp, "Moral Luck and Equality of Moral Opportunity," *Proceeding of the Aristotelian Society* 91.1 (2017): 1–20.

life but never feels remorse gives pause, quite apart from deterrence considerations, even to those of us who would like to do without revenge."[78]

I think that it would be salutary if punishment theorists recognized that when we punish – even if we are justified in punishing – we are losing part of our innocence, in a way structurally similar to Vere's (again, even if not quite so dramatic). But if punishment theorists were to recognize that the innocence would be lost merely in the sense that the lorry driver loses it, that would do as well. No punisher, no matter how just, is ever fully morally innocent. A punisher is in the business of making people suffer, and this business, even when the suffering is deserved (or medicinally useful), simply cannot be done without – in admittedly different degrees – dirtying one's hands.

I wish to end this section by turning our attention to a real-life case that brings out the formidable moral horror generated by an impervious response to the moral dilemmas we have been considering. This is the case of Benjamin Murmelstein, the Viennese rabbi whom the Nazis appointed chairman of the *Judenrat* at the Theresienstadt concentration camp. Like other Jews appointed by the Nazis to internally manage the ghettos, Murmelstein is a very complicated figure.[79] Some see these men as heroes; others see them as collaborators. Murmelstein, the only one of these Nazi-appointed leaders to survive the war (the others either committed suicide or were killed by the Nazis), knowingly helped the Nazis murder thousands upon thousands of innocents. One of Murmelstein's specific contributions in Theresienstadt was to help the Nazis dishonestly prop up Theresienstadt in order to give the impression that Nazi concentration camps were humane. But he had to do much more too, including setting up stern policies and punishments and indeed preparing transports to gas chambers. As if to justify his actions, Murmelstein claimed that this was the *only* way to *save* thousands upon thousands of other innocents (a defense often invoked by other Jewish ghetto leaders as well).

There is no denying that Murmelstein faced unimaginably tragic choices. And I am not here interested in adjudicating Murmelstein's actions. What I wish to do is to consider Murmelstein's emotional engagement with his own behavior. Claude Lanzmann's *The Last of the Unjust* is built around an interview of Murmelstein.[80]

---

[78]  Greenspan, *Practical Guilt*, 113 ff. Interestingly, Greenspan sees some moral emotions as functioning as rewards and punishment: "[P]ride is self-administered reward" (125), whereas "guilt and blame come out as 'punishing'" (125), as "self-attributed responsibility for a wrong" (131), as "mental self-punishment" (147), and so on. This may help explain the role that some have attached to repentance, as we saw in Chapter 7 (although, as noted, if by repenting the repentant person is thereby punishing herself, then the decision not to punish her seems not to be forgiveness or merciful). This highlights, too, the inadequacy of the moral psychology of consequentialism, discussed in Chapter 3.

[79]  Similar cases involve, for example, Chaim Rumkowski and Adam Czerniakow, the Jewish leaders of the Lodz and Warsaw ghettos, respectively. On Rumkowski, see Steve Sam-Sandberg, *The Emperor of Lies*, London: Farrar and Farrar (2011); on Czerniakow, see Raul Hilberg, Stanislaw Staron, and Josef Kermisz (eds.), *The Warsaw Diary of Adam Czerniakow: Prelude to Doom*, New York, NY: Stein and Day (1979).

[80]  Claude Lanzmann, *Le Dernier des Injustes*, Paris: Synecdoche (2013).

Lanzmann's film opens with Murmelstein claiming that the literary figure with whom he most identifies is Sancho Panza because Sancho is "pragmatic and calculating while others are tilting at windmills," because "he's a calculating realist with both feet on the ground."[81] But Murmelstein's "pragmatism" – very much reminiscent of the sort of reasoning typical of the morality system – is more than chilling: it is downright terrifying. While Lanzmann shows considerable understanding and good will toward Murmelstein (and while he seems deeply aware of the complexities of Murmelstein's predicament), at some point in the interview, as if unable to hold his tongue any longer, he interrupts Murmelstein's ruminations on the topic. Lanzmann confronts Murmelstein on this overly "pragmatic" – but also rather disengaged and indolent – way in which Murmelstein relates the harrowing events and things he had to do in Theresienstadt:

> On listening to you talk about Theresienstadt, one doesn't have the impression that it was a place where misfortune reigned, a place of suffering where thousands of people died, and a stop on the way to Auschwitz for thousands more. Anyone would think you feel nothing as you talk about Theresienstadt.

Without the slightest sign of hesitation, Murmelstein responds:

> If, during an operation, a surgeon starts crying over his patient, he kills him. You don't get very far by weeping or wavering.[82]

Even after bracketing out the overall assessment of the behavior of those Jewish victims who, like Murmelstein, chose to obey murderous Nazi orders during the Holocaust, this exchange is morally disturbing. With ease, Murmelstein appears to stave off precisely the sorts of emotional conflicts that one would expect to find in any decent human being who may have done what he did (even if under duress). Even if Murmelstein *was* justified – though, again, I am not adjudicating that question here – one would have expected a person who did what Murmelstein did to be emotionally devastated and not to find such remarkable comfort in these purely pragmatic and medicinal considerations (again, even assuming them to be true and accurate). Furthermore, even if one could possibly imagine someone – a very committed "pragmatist" indeed – somehow succeeding in *suppressing* these emotional conflicts *at the time* of acting, one would at least expect that later, years after

---

[81]   *Ibid.*, 106.

[82]   These words are taken from the English subtitles of the film. Although the interview was conducted in German, the transcript of Lanzmann's movie appeared originally in French, and this passage is rendered as follows: "*Le chirurgien qui, durant une operation, se met a pleurer sur son patient le tue. En pleurant et en tergiversant, on ne va pas bien loin.*" See Claude Lanzmann, *Le Dernier des Injustes*, Paris: Gallimard (2013), 112. Medicinal considerations were common. Trying to convince parents to give up their children for deportation, in an infamous speech Chaim Rumkowski implored "I have to perform this bloody operation myself; I have to cut off limbs to save the body!," as reported in Leonard Tushnet, *The Pavement of Hell*, New York, NY: St. Martin's Press (1972), 73.

the fact, a decent person would be deeply emotionally distressed by having had to make these decisions – say, as Vere was.

Needless to say, just as Vere's predicament is not meant to be a model for the predicament each and every punisher must face, the discussion of Murmelstein is not meant to be a *model* for the discussion of punishment in general: punishers rarely face the sort of harrowing choices Murmelstein faced (even if some of Murmelstein's acts were punitive). Just as Vere's case underscores the potentially existentially devastating moral dilemmas punishers face, Murmelstein's case – harrowing as it is – underscores the peculiar horror of someone who, having faced such a dilemma, remains impervious to moral taints. While the taints of typical punishers are often admittedly much less significant than Murmelstein's, they are sometimes real. And punishment theory can hardly progress without recognizing the existence of these taints.

### 8.3 MORAL BRILLIANCE AND MORAL IMAGINATION

Gowans suggests that the moral distress caused by taints can come about in two ways.

> On the one hand, a person might be morally pained by the fact that there is a moral deficiency *in the world*, as when one reads in the newspaper about a morally admirable person who has fallen victim to disease or some senseless criminal act. Here the object of the feeling has no connection with anything the person having the feeling has *done*. One is simply morally pained to hear that this virtuous person has suffered at the hands of indifferent natural forces or vicious actions. It is clear that this is not the sort of feeling that is pertinent to the phenomenological argument. The argument requires that the focus of the moral distress be on something the person experiencing the feeling has *done*.[83]

There are at least three reasons to oppose Gowans's efforts to distance himself from the axiological turn.

First, the phenomenological argument simply does not require the focus of which Gowans speaks. Surely part of *Billy Budd*'s success, for example, is that we are moved by Vere's predicament without ourselves being *in* a dilemma as to what to do. Just as the phenomenological argument speaks to the tension between keeping to our diet and eating a cake, it speaks, too, to the distress we may feel when we witness, even from a distance, the undeserving getting what they do not deserve (or the deserving not getting what they do deserve) – even if we are not deontically involved in such situations. We do not need to undergo, say, Job's ordeal in order to feel the pull of his predicament.

In a famous response to Williams's seminal views on moral dilemmas, Philippa Foot stressed that the moral dilemmas of which Williams (and others) speak "are not necessarily ones in which anyone is *in* a dilemma about what to do." Rather, they are

---

[83] Gowans, *Innocence Lost*, 96. Emphases added.

dilemmas "between principles such as *keep promises* and *save lives*."[84] Furthermore, Foot concluded that, in the final – and most interesting – analysis, the conflict worth our attention is among "values." Echoing Isaiah Berlin's axiological pluralism (discussed in Chapter 3), Foot tells us that these conflicts obtain "when one really good thing which the man of virtue must cherish has to be sacrificed for another, a loss that is often reflected in a conflict of *oughts* or *obligations* but is not described [in full] simply by talking about such conflicts."[85] And I just cannot see why the loss of which Foot speaks could only be appreciated if we are ourselves deontically involved in the sacrifice.

Second, while some cases of punishment – say, Billy's – give rise to remarkable emotional upheavals, there surely are other cases in which punishment does not give rise to very serious emotional reactions at all. Imagine, for example, that Billy had not killed Claggart and that instead Claggart's perjury had been proven. I do not think Vere – or us – would have been as emotionally affected by seeing Claggart receive the suffering that he deserved as we are when we witness Billy's punishment. Or imagine seeing Ohlendorf or Hitler, etc., getting the punishment they deserve. Again, neither the punishers nor unrelated third parties in these cases are likely to be too emotionally affected by the fact that punishment was inflicted.

This variability may make it look as if the conflict that I claim punishment *necessarily* generates is somehow too contingent: sometimes it obtains, sometimes it does not. But this is to put the cart before the horse: emotional distress supervenes on underlying axiological conflicts. At the axiological level, punishment does necessarily generate the conflict I have been describing (between the value of justice and the value of empathy). Of course, it is possible that sometimes one of these two values is *much* greater than the other: say, the realized value of punishing Ohlendorf is much greater than the value of forgiving him. In these types of cases, the resultant *intensity* of the axiological conflict is extremely low, to the point of being negligible – and this negligibility then manifests itself at the emotional level as well. Sometimes the wrong being punished is so extraordinarily horrific – so "word-and-thought-defying," to again echo Arendt's words – that the importance of the unrealized value of forgiving it pales in comparison.[86] In other words, not every occasion in which we justifiably inflict punishment taints us in the same way or to the same degree. The suggestion that those who punished, say, Ohlendorf, should be as emotionally devastated as Vere was for punishing Billy is rather implausible, if not perverse. Still, in varying intensity, structurally the axiological conflict is there in both cases.

In cases in which the value that punishment realizes is not vastly greater than the value that forgiveness would have realized, even if punishment is justified, we are

---

[84] Philippa Foot, "Moral Realism and Moral Dilemma," in her *Moral Dilemmas and Other Topics in Moral Philosophy*, Oxford: Clarendon Press (2002), 37.

[85] *Ibid.*, 57.

[86] Hannah Arendt, *Eichmann in Jerusalem: A Study in the Banality of Evil*, New York, NY: Penguin (1994), 252.

more seriously tainted, and this taint, as we have seen, has emotional implications. Contemporary punishment theorists tend to operate as if all cases, or at least the paradigmatic cases, of punishment were such that the difference between the value of inflicting punishment is much greater than the value of its merciful remission. In light of its dysfunctionality, the contemporary criminal justice system in the United States offers many counterexamples and depressingly many occasions for serious taint. This is not to deny that even within the context of a dysfunctional system there may be clear-cut cases in which the contrast between the specific wrong being punished and its merciful remission is so extreme that the unsavory emotional consequences of the taint may be negligible. And it is not to deny, either, that state punishers in the United States can get dirty, to an extent that, say, those in Nazi Germany cannot: just as Hitler could not get dirty since he was dirty all over already, neither could his criminal justice system. As explained previously, this is not a point in favor of Hitler or his criminal justice system.

Third, failing to pay attention to the fundamentally axiological reality of the conflict may cause us to lose sight of its exact nature. For example, Gowans (like many others) takes Billy to be "innocent"[87] and "undeserving."[88] For the reasons I presented earlier, I believe that Billy is neither "morally" nor "legally" innocent but rather "angelically" innocent. If Billy were really morally or legally innocent, Vere's conflict would not be quite what Melville makes it out to be (and it would be hard not to see his killing of Billy as an unjustified, even malevolent act).[89] Given that he sees Billy as somehow morally innocent, Gowans further believes that Vere "ought to [have] show[n] Billy leniency."[90] Gowans believes that whatever other obligations he may have had, Vere had "a moral responsibility to Billy to be just and compassionate."[91]

As discussed already (above all in Chapter 5), the talk of *obligations* (duties, etc.) of forgiveness (mercy, compassion, etc.) is unhelpful. If Billy really is innocent tout court, then why refer to his non-punishment as *compassionate* – or as an act of leniency – at all? Where exactly is the leniency or compassion in not punishing someone who *is* innocent? Positing an alleged obligation to be lenient or compassionate resembles the counterintuitive and problematic notion of mercy that Tasioulas embraced and that it risks transforming the showing of leniency or compassion into yet another mechanism of the morality system.

Dismissing the fundamentally axiological basis of Vere's predicament creates another problem. By lumping together "justice and compassion," Gowans manages to then oppose this amalgam to Vere's "moral obligation to the king (and his country)."[92] Insofar as Gowans admits that Vere's obligations to king and country are

---

[87] Gowans, *Innocence Lost*, 12.    [88] *Ibid.*, 111.
[89] Perhaps a confusion between these different senses of "innocence" may explain Weisberg's odd reading of *Billy Budd* – aspects of which Posner finds downright "absurd" (in Posner, *Law and Literature*, 167).
[90] Gowans, *Innocence Lost*, 17.    [91] *Ibid.*, 18.    [92] *Ibid.*

moral,[93] his position is in fact an improvement upon the popular position whereby Vere's predicament involves a conflict between morality and something external to morality (typically: social or military expediency). Nonetheless, he still assumes that the central conflict is between the moral duties of justice and compassion, on the one hand, and the moral duties to king and country, on the other. Thus, Gowans in the end misses the central dilemma Vere faces: Vere cannot justly punish (and in his mind Billy's punishment *is* just) without creating an extraordinary amount of disvalue (by not forgiving him). And he cannot avoid creating such disvalue (were he to forgive Billy) without thereby creating the disvalue involved in failing to impart justice.[94] Vere's central dilemma is an instantiation of the same axiological conflict we have been discussing since Chapter 1: the "incongruity between destiny and merit," as Max Weber aptly called it.[95] Vere knew that he faced a situation in which no matter what he did he would contribute to make, from God's eye view as it were, destiny and merit more incongruous, not less so. And the resulting taint explains his deep existential anguish.

In order to further highlight how Vere's conflict is indeed about the incongruity between destiny and merit and how it bears on punishment theory, compare Vere's predicament to that of another famous literary character. Alexander Pushkin's *Mozart and Salieri* opens with Salieri's famous somber resignation: "They say there's no justice here on earth, But there's no justice higher up, either."[96] Salieri sees no justice because he sees so much talent in Mozart – a talent that he finds essentially undeserved. He, on the other hand, is not as talented as Mozart, even though he deserved – at least given his devotion and diligence – to have been rewarded with successes at least similar to Mozart's.

Admittedly, Pushkin's play is not about punishment. But it is not merely about envy or about envy *simpliciter*, either.[97] It is also, albeit indirectly, about axiology and about justice and about their contribution to a meaningful world. Salieri and Vere have something important in common. It is hard not to see Melville's piercing description of Vere as a man of "sterling qualities" but "without any brilliant ones" as also an extraordinarily fitting description of

---

[93] There is some ambiguity in Gowans's position. While his predominant position seems to be that Vere's dilemma involves two moral obligations (justice and compassion on the one hand against duty to king and country on the other), at times he seems to succumb to the temptation of seeing Vere's conflict as one between justice and compassion on the one hand and mutiny avoidance on the other. See, e.g., "Vere's argument ... made Billy's execution depend on grounds quite extraneous to the moral quality of his act" (Gowans, *Innocence Lost*, 62).

[94] This is reminiscent of Nussbaum's and Halbertal's dismissal of axiology as they react to the Talmudic stories discussed in the previous chapter.

[95] H. H. Gerth and C. Wright Mills, *From Max Weber: Essays in Sociology*, New York, NY: Oxford University Press (1946), 275.

[96] Alexander Pushkin, "Mozart and Salieri," in *The Little Tragedies* (Nancy K. Anderson, ed.), New Haven, CT: Yale University Press (2000): 55–65, at 55.

[97] Incidentally, I do not believe that Vere was envious of Billy (as Salieri was of Mozart). For a defense of that view, see Richard Weisberg, *The Failure ...*, *passim*.

Pushkin's Salieri.[98] Pushkin's Salieri was by no means a mediocre musician: Pushkin indeed portrayed him as a *sterling* musician, only not a brilliant one – just like Melville portrayed Vere. Granted, Vere did face a moral dilemma that condemned him to do wrong no matter what he chose, and nothing of the sort applies to Salieri. Yet, independently of what each of these two characters *did*, they were both morally distressed by the axiological disarray they *saw* in the world, by the mere *contemplation* of states of affairs conspicuously exhibiting the incongruity between destiny and merit. From Salieri's perspective, the organic whole in which the more devoted and diligent (and in his mind therefore more deserving) musician would be also the one rewarded with the most brilliant talents was more valuable than the other way around. From Vere's perspective, the state of affairs in which the bad person – Claggart – would have had to be justly punished was more valuable than that in which the Angel of God had to be justly punished.

The comparison between Vere and Salieri allows us to approach the limitations of the morality system from a different perspective. No matter how well thought out, sensible, intuitively appealing, or indeed "sterling" a morality system may be, it will never be "brilliant." Brilliance requires *transcending* the system. This is not to say that every instance in which someone transcends the morality system is brilliant – since one could, of course, go beyond the call of duty stupidly, rashly, or otherwise injudiciously. Worse yet: one could transcend it because one is a very bad person indeed. But it is to say that there is a sense in which any moral or legal system must have difficulty accounting for truly brilliant action. Brilliant action requires acting outside the system, and the admirability of brilliant action cannot stem from the rules of the system.

Evidently, trolley problems and other fashionable reductive schemas are utterly unenlightening regarding the rich texture of human life that this gap between the sterling and the brilliant presupposes. Just try imagining a trolley diagram capturing Vere's or Salieri's or Job's or indeed Murmelstein's predicaments. Moral brilliance cannot be plotted or charted in these reductive schemas. Even when they do not expressly rely on these sorts of schemas, contemporary punishment theories do not seem to have any room left for thinking about moral brilliance or about how the consideration of moral brilliance could perhaps temper our punishment practices and institutions.

This reflection on moral brilliance is not meant to be a thoroughgoing rejection of system, or even of a general systematizing ethos. A system that indicates – however generally – when punishment is justified is evidently not a bad thing at all. In general, there is nothing particularly awful (or even particularly bad) in doing what we are justified in doing. But the fact that we are justified in doing something is not to render such action particularly brilliant or particularly admirable, either.

---

[98]   Melville, *Billy Budd*, 310.

When what we are justified in doing is to make others suffer (however deservedly), reflecting on the nature of the gap separating the justified from the brilliant can only be salutary. Such a gap should remind us of the danger of following the system too mechanically or too unimaginatively.

*Billy Budd* ends with a news report, published in an imaginary weekly naval chronicle titled "News from the Mediterranean."

> On the tenth of the last month a deplorable occurrence took place on board H.M.S. *Bellipotent*. John Claggart, the ship's master-at-arms, discovering that some sort of plot was incipient among an inferior section of the ship's company, and that the ringleader was one William Budd; he, Claggart, in the act of arraigning the man before the captain, was vindictively stabbed to the heart by the suddenly drawn sheath knife of Budd ...
>
> The enormity of the crime and the extreme depravity of the criminal appear the greater in view of the character of the victim, a middle-aged man respectable and discreet, belonging to that minor official grade, the petty officers upon whom, as none know better than the commissioned gentlemen, the efficiency of His Majesty's navy so largely depends ...
>
> The criminal paid the penalty of his crime. The promptitude of the punishment has proved salutary. Nothing amiss is now apprehended aboard H.M.S. *Bellipotent*.[99]

To which Melville adds:

> The above, appearing in a publication now long ago superannuated and forgotten, is all that hitherto has stood in human record to attest what manner of men respectively were John Claggart and Billy Budd.[100]

Unquestionably, this is a very moving end for *Billy Budd*. For my purposes, however, it would have been even more useful had the report not been marred by obvious factual errors. That is, had the report not inaccurately asserted that Billy was the depraved ringleader of a mutinous crew or that he stabbed Claggart, it would have *still* grossly under-described what transpired on board the *Bellipotent*. *Billy Budd* painfully reveals what a report like this *necessarily* obscures – and this revelation would not have been entirely diminished had the report been perfectly accurate. What transpired on board the *Bellipotent* cannot be captured in a news report; to suppose that it could is to fail to appreciate both the complexity of the situation and the inherent limitations of *chronicles*. To the extent that a news report may succeed in capturing these events, to that extent it ceases to be a mere news report.

And it is in this context that we can make better sense of Nussbaum's view that we need a "legal, and especially judicial [and moral]" reasoning that is modeled after "the concerned reader of a novel."[101] Freed from the implausible (and unnecessary) supposition that literary and narrative imaginations invariably recommend

---

[99] *Ibid.*, 382–383.    [100] *Ibid.*, 383.    [101] Nussbaum, "Equity and Mercy," 110.

forgiveness (or mercy) rather than punishment – Nussbaum's point is importantly right. This narrative or literary form of thinking can capture much more of reality, and of reality's complexity, than other forms of thinking; and it can, too, help us avoid a mechanical bureaucratization of the distribution of suffering. This is not because concerned readers of novels are *necessarily* very deep and nuanced people but because novels tend to represent life with great complexity. Reading novels is, then, *likely* to nurture a certain engagement with this complex reality. Virtually any novel would do this better than trolley problems, since these are after all constructed with the specific aim of invisibilizing (even if only transitorily) the complexity of real human lives and real human choices. We need this type of thinking in moral philosophy generally but particularly acutely in punishment theory.

I do not wish to combat one caricature with another caricature. It is not that punishment theorists do not care about the emotional insides of wrongdoers at all. For example, the very point of the discussion of culpability (or *mens rea*) – a rightly prominent area of investigation among punishment theorists – is to examine the mental states (surely among the "insides") of wrongdoers in order to determine their degree of blameworthiness. Still, the mental states relevant to a theory of culpability are quite limited – mostly in relation to what wrongdoers *knew* and *intended* around the time·they acted wrongly. This explains, for example, Victoria Nourse's assessment: "[T]he individual implied by the modern law of *mens rea* is bare and alone, the subject of observation but bereft of emotions and motives and relationships to others." The point of view of culpability tends to be "rather empty, mechanistic," and it tends to reductively see the wrongdoer as a "rational calculator, [a] foreseer of risk, and [a] harborer of statistical probabilities."[102]

The solution to the problems Nourse diagnoses is not, however, limited to a revamping of culpability as such. (In fact, I have elsewhere argued in favor of the intimate connection between intentions and blameworthiness and thus in favor of traditional theories of culpability and against "new culpability" and "virtue jurisprudence" approaches others have recently proposed.)[103] After all, the problems upon which I have focused in this book are not always (or even often) matters of culpability. General matters of moral luck, of differentiated accounts of wrongdoing, of the distinction between punishment and revenge, of the foibles of micromanaging life, to mention just a few, can hardly be accommodated within the confines of a theory of culpability – even if this theory were to include motives and emotions. Moreover, specific historical considerations – say, the fact that in the United States slavery is a permissible punishment and what this says about its government's *standing* to punish anyone – are not matters of culpability either. As I have argued in this book, what is

---

[102]  See V. F. Nourse, "Understanding the New Culpability," *Buffalo Criminal Law Review* 6.1 (2002): 361–388, at 362.

[103]  Leo Zaibert, "A Non-Aretaic Return to Aristotle," *Archiv für Rechts- und Sozialphilosophie*, 97.2 (2011): 235–250; Leo Zaibert, *Five Ways Patricia Can Kill Her Husband: A Theory of Intentionality and Blame*, Chicago, IL: Open Court (2005).

needed is not merely a rethinking of culpability but a rethinking of punishment theory in general. A rethinking of culpability absent a rethinking of punishment theory more broadly is not likely to yield much fruit.

Independently of the existence of culpability, punishment theorists engage with the sorts of considerations I have discussed in this book (when they engage at all) with a remarkable lack of nuance. What is most appealing about Nussbaum's plea for novelistic reading has, for my purposes, less to do with novels as such and much more to do with the underlying complexity and nuance that such a reading often manifests. In my sense, Nussbaum's plea is similar to other pleas in which the role of novels as such is much less prominent. One such plea is Peter Goldie's criticism of mere chronicles, containing a "bare description of events"[104] and listing "one damn thing after another,"[105] we encountered in Chapter 2. Another plea relates to the value of *telling stories* – stories that, even if not novels, go beyond mere chronicles – which is central to Cheshire Calhoun's effort to explain how (aspirational) forgiveness can be justified.

Calhoun's (Strawsonian) effort takes place in the last two sections of her article, appropriately titled "Telling Stories" and "Telling the Aspirational Stories." At the beginning of the first of these sections, Calhoun tells us that "an aspirational story would begin by connecting misdeeds to the agent's true self. The protagonists of aspirational stories are thus always unclean, unworthy,"[106] and she adds: "[A]spirational stories appear impossible ones to tell successfully."[107] The uncleanliness and the impossibility of which Calhoun speaks, of course, evoke the axiological conflict between the value of punishment and of its merciful remission. When she explains what it is to treat someone as a *person* (and not as a mere caricature or placeholder), Calhoun does not mention novels at all:

> To treat someone as a person is, in part, to see her as continuously subject to moral requirements. It simply is not all that is involved in treating someone as a person. (In addition, to treat someone as a person is to treat her as someone for whom sustaining an integrated biography matters.)[108]

Another such plea can be found in a famous article by Gary Watson, in which he reflects on the (also Strawsonian) motif whereby we are not to see ourselves as "moral clerks, recording moral faults," as if from "a detached and austerely objective standpoint."[109] Watson's article revolves around the life of Robert Alton Harris, a ruthless criminal despised (and feared) even by his hard-boiled companions on

---

[104]   Peter Goldie, *The Mess Inside*, Oxford: Oxford University Press (2012), 9.      [105]   *Ibid.*, 13.

[106]   Cheshire Calhoun, "Changing One's Heart," *Ethics* 103.1 (1992): 76–96, at 86. I think that this is compatible with my suggestion that dirty hands dilemmas presuppose a certain amount of cleanliness, even if complete cleanliness is impossible. It is, in any event, hard to imagine constructing a plausibly aspirational story for someone as dirty as Hitler or Ohlendorf.

[107]   Calhoun, "Changing One's Heart," 87.      [108]   *Ibid.*, 96.

[109]   Gary Watson, "Responsibility and the Limits of Evil: Variations of a Strawsonian Theme," in his *Agency and Answerability*, Oxford: Clarendon Press (2004), 226, 227. I discussed these Strawsonian themes in Chapter 3.

death row. Although Watson describes the horror of Harris's crimes in full detail, he also describes the remarkably miserable and brutal life Harris had had ever since the moment he was born. Watson's point is not to exculpate (or excuse or justify, etc.) Harris but to compel us to see the "'whole' story" of his life, a story that is not a mere chronicle and that "forces us to see him as a *victim*."[110] The sense in which Harris was a victim bears resemblances to the sense in which Billy was a victim: while they were both, technically speaking, wrongdoers, they were also, in a different sense, victims – if only victims of the "jugglery of circumstances."

The imaginary author of the report in "News from the Mediterranean" displays exactly the "objective attitude" that Strawson (among others) so insightfully criticized. Melville too can be seen as criticizing it or at least as lamenting it. The "William Budd" depicted therein is but a sad caricature of Billy, the "Handsome Sailor," the "Angel of God"; and the reported "deplorable" events on board the *Bellipotent* are robbed of their complexity and of their tragic dimension. Reports and chronicles are unable to engage with the axiological complexity of maelstroms such as the ones on board the *Bellipotent*. Even had it been accurate, the story in "News from the Mediterranean" would have remained woefully simpleminded. In a sense, the *genre* itself is doomed to caricaturize (those it presents as) wrongdoers and (those it presents as) victims, even if no factual errors are committed. Unfortunately, contemporary punishment theorists, trapped inside the morality system, have uncritically relied on precisely these sorts of simpleminded caricatures.

Nussbaum, Calhoun, and Watson seem interested in avoiding these caricatures. And I agree with this interest. But I think that even they run the risk advancing caricatures of their own. These authors happen to be skeptical of "stories of desert" and of "retributive sentiments" more generally. As should by now be abundantly clear, I think that this skepticism is unwarranted. It is the result of the combination of two factors. First, these authors (like many others) exhibit a certain "panic" (in the sense discussed in Chapter 3) about the truly scandalous excesses of modern criminal justice systems, such as that of the United States. Second, by flatly rejecting the non-medicinal value of deserved punishment, they are (unwittingly) overly simplifying the axiological complexity of the problem of punishment.

## 8.4 CONCLUSION

In light of last section's reflection on the complicated narratives that are necessary in order to do justice in a complex moral world, I find the way in which Judith Shklar concluded one of her articles particularly pertinent here.

---

[110]  Watson, "Responsibility and . . .," 244. Part of Watson's strategy results from a mobilization of the notion of (moral) luck that, though not quite the same as my own in Chapter 6, is consistent with its spirit. Watson points out how it was a matter of (moral) luck that it was not us who had Harris's horrible life.

I am not good at conclusions. The desire to arrive at them strikes me, frankly, as slightly childish. A need for an "and they lived happily ever after" ending does not seem to me to fit a type of discourse that is unending.[111]

This book does not have that type of fairy tale ending either.

The substance of this book is unabashedly philosophical. I have argued that, independently of any consideration of policy or strategy, there is a purely theoretical problem relating to the axiological complexity of punishment. In suggesting ways of thinking about this problem, I have, moreover, systematically argued against extant justifications of punishment insofar as they presuppose (sometimes unwittingly) problematically monistic axiologies. I have suggested that punishment theorists have missed the central importance of the tension between the value of punishment and the value of forgiveness. And I have suggested that punishment theorists have misunderstood the *nature* of the very process of justifying punishment.

I would be satisfied if I have succeeded in making any of these theoretical points compellingly. But I claimed at the outset that I am optimistic regarding the ways in which my recommended reorientation in our thinking about the problem of punishment and its justification may perhaps affect some practical problems as well. The reasons for my optimism should by now be apparent.

There exists a very small number of cases in which the difference between the value of punishment and the value of forgiveness is truly enormous – say, cases involving inveterate wrongdoers such as Ohlendorf or Hitler. Most cases, particularly those occurring within the context of modern criminal justice systems, are not like this at all. In most cases, we simply cannot punish with clean hands. Underwritten by a neat formulaic story, simpleminded approaches to the justification of punishment – such as those I have criticized here – are incapable of even seeing the dirt that punishment almost invariably generates. The standard assumption has been that if so-and-so obtains, then so-and-so ought to be done; that if a given course of action is justified, then it ought to be done – and then all is good: end of story – "and they lived happily ever after." Typically, punishment theorists have no space for remainders, for conflict, or for dirt. But if I have been even partially successful in these theoretical aims, we should then approach the prospect of punishing wrongdoers (or of setting up punitive institutions) with more sober circumspection than we have tended to do.

---

[111]  Judith Shklar, "Obligation, Loyalty, Exile," *Political Theory* 21.2 (1993): 181–197, at 196–197.

# Can We Deserve to Suffer?

When published in 2011, Derek Parfit's *On What Matters* was one of the most highly anticipated and then one of the most enthusiastically celebrated philosophy books in decades.[1] Perhaps the central aim of the book is to argue for an unexpected "convergence" between Kantianism and utilitarianism – views that have traditionally been seen as if not downright irreconcilable at least very difficult to reconcile. Parfit was motivated by his beliefs that "Kant is the greatest moral philosopher since the ancient Greeks" and that "Sidgwick's *Methods* [*of Ethics*] is ... the best book on ethics ever written."[2] Parfit evocatively saw these authors (and their followers) "climbing the same mountain on different sides."[3]

Whether or not Parfit succeeded, it is beyond dispute that he did *try* – in earnest and in at least enlightening ways – to argue for this convergence. And this is enough to establish a remarkable contrast between Parfit's ecumenical efforts at the level of comprehensive moral doctrines and the insularity with which he treated punishment. Regarding this particular phenomenon Parfit sought no convergence whatsoever.

The last chapter of part two of *On What Matters* is explicitly titled "Why We Cannot Deserve to Suffer." Parfit thinks that the fact that a certain wrongdoer may deserve to suffer *cannot* play any role whatsoever in the justification of punishment. For, in his view, there simply is no such fact: there is no such thing as deserved suffering. If the possibility of deserving to suffer is rejected, then all we have is suffering *simpliciter*. And since suffering *simpliciter* is admittedly a bad thing, we should just try to reduce it. Punishment, for Parfit, could only be justified if it can be expected to reduce further suffering (or to lead toward greater pleasure). This is as good as a restatement of Bentham's simpleminded utilitarianism I have discussed in this book – and it inherits all problems attendant to it. Independently of these general problems, Parfit's arguments are intrinsically unconvincing.

---

[1] Derek Parfit, *On What Matters*, Oxford: Oxford University Press (2011). The enthusiasm transcended the confines of academia: see Larissa MacFarquhar, "How to Be Good," *The New Yorker* (September 5, 2011): 42–53.

[2] Parfit, *On What Matters*, Vol. I, xxxiii.    [3] *Ibid.*, 419.

## A.1 COMPATIBILISM À LA CARTE

The basic structure of desert claims is straightforward: "'S deserves X in virtue of F', where S is a person, X is a mode of treatment, and F some fact about S."[4] Thus, for example, Susan deserves a good (or bad) mark in virtue of her good (or bad) performance in the exam. Parfit believes that X can never be substituted with suffering, no matter what may substitute F.

It is crucial to underscore at the outset that Parfit explicitly claims not to disagree with this structure. Parfit is not a skeptic about desert in general: "[W]e can deserve many things, such as gratitude, praise, and the kind of blame that is merely moral dispraise."[5] It is only "suffering" (or being "less happy") that he thinks no one, no matter what she does, could ever deserve.[6] Unfortunately, however, Parfit nowhere tells us what it is about suffering – other than that suffering is bad – that leads him to conceptually isolate it so that it alone cannot be deserved. Parfit's route is rather circuitous.

Parfit's skepticism regarding deserved suffering is related to the general debate between free will and determinism. Shelly Kagan has neatly captured the widespread view that seems to animate Parfit: namely, that "there is an intimate correlation between desert and free will, so that no one could be correctly said to deserve anything at all, unless people have free will in some metaphysically robust sense of the term."[7] If all events in the world, including our actions and our thoughts, are determined, it is hard to see how we could be meaningfully praised or blamed: no one blames or praises water for boiling.

Famously, however, many different versions of *compatibilism* have been put forth, and some are evidently valuable in our efforts to preserve cherished moral practices, even if determinism were assumed to be true. Very roughly, the compatibilist suggests that even if in a metaphysically robust sense determinism turned out to be true, this would not affect the way life presents itself to us. Phenomenologically, we experience life as if we are, often, unproblematically free, in the sense of subjecting ourselves and each other to praise or blame or to reward and punishment.

Parfit's engagement with the general debate between free will and determinism is framed in Kantian terms.

> Suppose that, while I am standing in some field during a thunderstorm, a bolt of lightning narrowly misses me. If I say that I could have been killed, I might be using 'could' in a *categorical* sense. I might mean that, even with conditions just as they actually were, it would have been causally possible for this bolt of lightning to have hit me. If we assume determinism, that is not true, since it was causally inevitable that this lightning struck the ground just where it did. I may instead be using 'could' in a different, *hypothetical* or *iffy* sense. When I say that I could have been killed,

---

[4] Joel Feinberg, *Doing and Deserving*, Princeton, NJ: Princeton University Press (1970), 61.
[5] Parfit, *On What Matters*, Vol. I, 272.   [6] *Ibid.*
[7] Shelly Kagan, *The Geometry of Desert*, Oxford: Oxford University Press (2012), 12.

I may mean only that, *if* conditions had been in some way slightly different – if, for example, I had been standing a few yards to the West – I would have been killed. Even if we assume determinism, that claim could be true.[8]

Armed with these two senses of "could," Parfit then suggests that Kant misunderstood them. Kant believed that only the categorical sense of "could" could save morality. In fact, Kant refers to the compatibilist sense of "could" as "a wretched subterfuge."[9] Kant was, in short, an anti-compatibilist. But Parfit argues that Kant's anti-compatibilism rests on the mistake of confusing determinism with "a quite different view":[10] fatalism, which Parfit characterizes as the view that "it is inevitable that we shall later act in certain ways, *whatever* we decide to do."[11] The crucial difference between determinism and fatalism, for Parfit, is that determinism is consistent with recognizing that our presently potential actions could affect our future choices. Only fatalism denies this. Insofar as it allows for our decisions to meaningfully affect our future choices, Parfit concludes that "[f]or practical purposes, this compatibilist kind of freedom is all we need," that this is "the kind of freedom that morality requires."[12] So, Kant rejects compatibilism, and Parfit rejects Kant's anti-compatibilism.

But if Kant believed that determinism precludes moral responsibility (and, a fortiori, the notion of moral desert altogether) and if Kant was a determinist (who rejected compatibilism), then at least the uninitiated may have difficulty understanding how Kant could countenance moral desert at all. The explanation is Kant's (in)famous division of the world into a phenomenal and a noumenal realm. In the phenomenal realm, that is, in the realm of events that happen in time, determinism is true; but in the noumenal realm, where "events" do not happen in time, determinism is false. Given Kant's metaphysical commitments, morality can only be salvaged by positing the existence of the non-deterministic realm of the noumenal.

Unlike Parfit, however, Kant never denied that people could deserve to suffer. By salvaging morality via the positing of the noumenal realm, Kant, *eo ipso*, salvaged desert in general, *including deserved suffering*. Only Parfit singles out suffering as undeservable. And this reveals a certain instability in Parfit's view which is not found in Kant's. Independently of whether or not postulating the existence of a noumenal realm is intelligible or useful, Kant is perfectly straightforward about the fact that determinism is true in the phenomenal realm and false in the noumenal realm. Similarly, Kant straightforwardly claims that compatibilism is unacceptable in the phenomenal realm and that it simply has no place in the noumenal realm. If it turns out that the noumenal realm does not really exist, then so much the worse for Kant's overall philosophical project. But, structurally, there is nothing odd in the way that determinism operates within the Kantian philosophical system: the phenomenal

---

[8] Parfit, *On What Matters*, Vol. I, 260.    [9]  *Ibid.*, 261.    [10]  *Ibid.*, 262.    [11]  *Ibid.*, 261.
[12]  *Ibid.*, 263.

realm is irremediably deterministic; if there is no noumenal realm, there is no morality, and that is that.

To be clear, I am not here endorsing Kant's distinction between the phenomenal and the noumenal. In fact, about this, I would agree with Parfit (and many others) in believing that all events take place in time and that Kant's noumenal realm may, problematically, be one in which we enjoy "some kind of incomprehensible freedom."[13] The distinction, however, does allow Kant to offer a cogent explanation as to when determinism operates and when it does not.

Parfit, in contrast, does not have access to any explanation as to why, even though there is only one world (akin to Kant's phenomenal realm), compatibilism is enough for moral responsibility in some cases (say, in cases of deserving anything except suffering) and not in others (in cases of deserving suffering). Parfit cherry-picks when compatibilism operates and when it does not. Interestingly, then, Parfit actually *agrees* with Kant's anti-compatibilism, albeit in one case only: the case of deserved suffering. And Parfit never explains this idiosyncratically selective deployment of compatibilism, even though it creates problems for his views.

For example, Parfit's thinks that discussing children and the insane can help his case against deserved suffering. In Parfit's view, children and the insane are not "responsible for their acts in some way that could make them deserve to suffer."[14] Unfortunately for Parfit, the facts that explain why children and (some of) the insane may indeed be incapable of deserving to suffer also explain why they are incapable of deserving anything else. As it turns out, Parfit joins Kant in rejecting "what we can call the *compatibilism about desert*."[15] But notice that what Kant rejected (again, in the phenomenal realm, which is the only realm Parfit countenances) was *compatibilism about global desert*, not only about deserved suffering. When he claims that Kant believed that "if our acts were merely events in time, we could not be responsible for our acts in this suffering-deserving way" (a view which Parfit considers a "profound truth"),[16] Parfit is being understated to a fault. Kant's view is that *if our acts were merely events in time, we could not be responsible for our acts in any deserving way*.

It is hard to understand Parfit's turn to Kant in the context of deserved suffering. Parfit needed something special – something that would show suffering (and suffering alone) to be undeservable. But Kant offers Parfit no help on this point. In Kant's view, if the noumenal realm does not exist, then desert does not exist *at all* either; and if the noumenal realm exists, then desert – including deserved suffering – exists. There simply is nothing special about suffering in Kant's views about responsibility and desert.

Parfit's discussion of children and the insane suggests that what Parfit really rejects is desert across the board – even though his main line is that he only rejects deserved suffering. So, for example, when Parfit claims that Nietzsche is right "to deny that we

[13] *Ibid.*, Vol. II, 583.   [14] *Ibid.*, Vol. I, 264.   [15] *Ibid.*, 265.   [16] *Ibid.*, 264.

can deserve to suffer," he does so as a commentary on Nietzsche's *general* view that "the history of moral sensations is the history of an error, the error of responsibility, which rests on the error of free will."[17] In this passage, Nietzsche is expressly denying free will and moral responsibility *tout court*: we cannot deserve anything. As in Kant's case, there is nothing special about suffering at play in Nietzsche's.

So, Parfit's views are not merely unstable as a result of his capricious deployment of compatibilism, they appear invalidated by a full-blown contradiction. For Parfit claims that he only wishes to cast doubt over desert in the case of suffering, and yet he casts doubt over desert in general. While I believe that this contradiction is a veritable leitmotif in Parfit's book, I shall henceforth (try to) assume that the contradiction could somehow be explained away. Even with this charitable assumption in place, Parfit's case against deserved suffering remains unpersuasive.

### A.2 TO HELL AND BACK

According to Parfit, then, Kant subscribed to the following "profound truth":

(J) If our acts are merely events in time, we cannot have chosen our own character, or be responsible for our acts in any way that could make us deserve to suffer.[18]

Since it is clear that Kant also believed that

(R) We *are* responsible for our acts in a way that can make us deserve to suffer,[19]

Kant had to conclude that

(S) Our acts are not merely events in time. We are responsible for our acts because, in the timeless noumenal world, we freely choose to give ourselves our character, and to act as we do.[20]

Insofar as this argument is valid (provided we ignore the second proposition in the conclusion) and insofar as Parfit rejects its conclusion S, he needs to reject either premise J or premise R. Of course, as we by now know, Parfit rejects R. But it is, I think, instructive to take a look at what Parfit has to say about those who, rather than rejecting R, would reject J.

There are, obviously, many reasons why someone may decide to reject J rather than R. One may fear that jettisoning R may force an across-the-board rejection of moral responsibility, as Parfit himself, contradictorily, appears to have done. Or one may find that R coheres with folk psychology, with considered moral intuitions, or with our efforts at inferring to the best explanation.[21] Moreover, some of us might be inclined to believe that the type of compatibilism that Parfit sometimes claims to

---

[17] *Ibid.*, Vol. II, 583.  [18] *Ibid.*, Vol. I, 268.  [19] *Ibid.*  [20] *Ibid.*, 269.

[21] See, for example, the famous results of the Yale University's Infant Cognition Center (https://campus press.yale.edu/infantlab/our-studies/), which suggest that even preverbal infants seem to acquiesce with the deserved suffering of perceived wrongdoers.

endorse – namely: compatibilism about everything under the sun, except suffering – actually applies to everything under the sun, including suffering. But Parfit does not discuss any of these possible reasons for rejecting J. Instead, he focuses on one idiosyncratic reason.

Among the people who might reject J (let us call them *the people who believe that we can deserve to suffer*), Parfit focuses on a subset of them who believe that even if all events take place in time, "we could deserve to be sent by God to suffer in Hell."[22] Let us call this group *the people who, on theistic grounds, believe that we can deserve to suffer (in Hell)*. Parfit further zeroes in on yet another, even smaller subset of people who believe that we can deserve to suffer: this last group is as theistically oriented as the previous one, except that its members also believe that God's justice is "incomprehensible."[23] Let us call this last subset *the people who believe, on theistic and dogmatic grounds, that we can deserve to suffer (in Hell)*. So, in the end, Parfit only discusses dogmatic and obscurantist people who would reject J because they believe that there is a God making sure that deserving people suffer in Hell. (Dogmatic and obscurantist since incomprehensibility prevents rational discussion of their view.)

Not surprisingly, then, Parfit concludes that compared against these positions, even Kant's noumenal realm appears plausible: after all, "[w]e have no reason to expect such moral truths to be incomprehensible."[24] I share Parfit's rejection of dogmatic obscurantism.[25] But Parfit does not realize that this obscurantism is his own creation. Surely there are people who are dogmatic obscurantists – Parfit has not invented *them*. But it is nonetheless Parfit's decision to focus on them and to pay no attention to people who may have tractable (and plausible) reasons for believing that we can deserve to suffer.

Parfit, however, claims that he does engage with the *people who, on theistic grounds, believe that we can deserve to suffer (in Hell)*, that is, people who, although believing that God makes wrongdoers suffer, are not dogmatically committed to the view that this aspect of God's wisdom is beyond our capacity to comprehend. I shall immediately suggest that Parfit does not really discuss this other, larger group. But I would like to underscore, once again, that this group of non-dogmatic theists, while surely more interesting than the group of dogmatic theists, is still a subset of the *much more* interesting group of people that Parfit does not discuss at all: those who believe that we can deserve to suffer and who are neither theists nor dogmatists.

According to Parfit, the (allegedly non-dogmatic) theists endorse the following argument:

(W) God makes some people suffer in Hell.
(X) God is just.

[22] Parfit, *On What Matters*, Vol. I, 270.   [23] *Ibid.*   [24] *Ibid.*
[25] I distanced myself from this type of position when I discussed theodicies in Chapter 1.

Therefore

(R) We can deserve to suffer.[26]

This argument is not valid. And it is not the argument Parfit needed to attribute to the theists anyway. From (W) and (X), what we can validly conclude is something like:

(B) God acts justly when he makes wrongdoers suffer in Hell.

This conclusion would then appear as a premise of another argument, which is the one Parfit needed:

(A) If God acts justly when he makes wrongdoers suffer in Hell, then wrongdoers can deserve to suffer.[27]
(B) God acts justly when he makes wrongdoers suffer in Hell.

And from *these* premises we can indeed validly conclude:

(R) Wrongdoers can deserve to suffer.

Still, this "deserving to suffer" needs further refinement, in the sense that Parfit's argument is only about what God does to wrongdoers in Hell. More accurately, the conclusion that follows from (A) and (B) is something along the lines of

(R') Wrongdoers can deserve to suffer, at least in those cases when God punishes them in Hell.

But let us continue, assuming that some tinkering with Parfit's argument, along the lines of (R'), does salvage the essential bits of his endeavor.

Of the very premise that fuels his own argument, however, Parfit says: "But we don't, I believe, know that (W) is true." This should have given Parfit even more reason to cease discussing God and Hell. But he perseveres and claims that "if we believe in a just God, we must accept either

(Y) God acts justly in making wrongdoers suffer in Hell, though it is unintelligible how such acts can be just,

or

(Z) God does not make anyone suffer in Hell."[28]

Parfit believes that we have more reason to accept (Z) than to accept (Y). Even if he is right, however, this, again, is insufficiently related to what was supposed to be

---

[26] Parfit, *On What Matters*, Vol. I, 271.
[27] Do notice, however, that Parfit recognizes that punishment *can* be justified by attending to values other than desert – say, by its fairness (Vol. II, 649–651); but he apparently thinks that matters are different in Hell.
[28] Parfit, *On What Matters*, Vol. I, 271.

the issue at hand: whether we could ever deserve to suffer and not whether we could suffer *in Hell*. Perhaps there is no God. Perhaps there is a God but no Hell. Perhaps God in fact does not make anyone suffer in Hell; perhaps God does not do this in spite of the fact that some people do deserve to suffer in Hell, perhaps no one can deserve to suffer *in perpetuity*, as the idea of punishment in Hell traditionally presupposes, and so on.[29] None of this resolves the question as to whether we can – in this world – deserve to suffer. This question can, and should, be asked independently of the discussion of Hell.

Moreover, it would be a mistake to think that with this last argument Parfit is somehow discussing the views of a group of people different from the dogmatic obscurantists who endorse the idea that God's justice is "incomprehensible." For Parfit's talk of "unintelligibility" in (Y) suggests that those wishing to accept (Y) rather than (Z) are just the same dogmatic obscurantists we encountered earlier.[30] In the end, Parfit engages only with a position held by a smallish and uninteresting subset of a subset of people, chosen in such a carefully self-serving way so as to slyly suggest that the idea that we can deserve to suffer is somehow irrational.

## A.3 SUFFERING, ITS BADNESS, AND ITS CONTEXT

Toward the end of Parfit's book, there is a section titled "The Double Badness of Suffering." Parfit begins the section by offering these two claims:

(A) It is in itself bad to suffer
(B) It is bad when people suffer in ways that they do not deserve

Immediately Parfit adds: "[T]hese claims describe what we may call the *double badness* of suffering."[31] The first claim is supposed to capture the sense in which suffering is "bad *for the sufferer*," or, in other words, *personally* bad. The second claim is more complicated. Since, as we have seen, Parfit believes that no one can deserve to suffer, (B) does not really add much to (A): (B) can, within the Parfitian context, in fact, be reformulated this baldly: *it is bad when people suffer*. Be that as it may, Parfit wants the second claim to capture a sense in which suffering is also "*impersonally* bad, or bad, *period*."[32] So, for Parfit, the double badness of suffering has to do with its being both personally and impersonally bad. Above all, Parfit seems intent on emphasizing how bad suffering is – a point that need not be denied in order to insist that we can deserve to suffer.

Parfit then turns to discuss those people who deny the impersonal badness of suffering, those who, in his words, believe that

---

[29]  Recall our discussion of Bennett's famous criticism of Jonathan Edwards's theology in Chapter 4.
[30]  It takes effort to see how someone who *ex hypothesi* believes (X) (or indeed the first part of (Y)) can also believe (Y) without *thereby* already being a dogmatic obscurantist – for it would be very hard to understand what (given her endorsement of (Y)) she could possibly mean by "just" in (X).
[31]  Parfit, *On What Matters*, Vol. II, 565.      [32]  *Ibid.*

(C) Suffering is in itself impersonally good, or is at least not in itself [impersonally] bad, when and because this suffering is deserved.[33]

Parfit's engagement with this position strikes me as tendentious. Again, he chooses to focus on a smallish and peculiar subset of people who may believe (something along the lines of) (C). For example, he tells us that "though some people have seemed to deny the double badness of suffering, these people were either not really denying (A) or (B), or they were under the influence of some distorting factor, or both."[34] As examples, Parfit briefly discusses the Stoics, Albertus Magnus (particularly in connection to his views regarding the medieval doctrine of the transcendentals), and Kant when he was most prone to (obscurantist) theodicy and to the defense of Stoicism. (To be sure, Parfit also devotes a whole chapter to Nietzsche and to the Nietzschean view that "pain and suffering are good."[35] In part because some of these claims by Nietzsche are in fact claims about the *instrumental* goodness of suffering, thus not really contradicting the claim that suffering is intrinsically bad, and in part because Parfit focuses on what he thinks was Nietzsche's waning mental competence, Parfit concludes that Nietzsche is not to be counted among those who "deny that suffering is bad" after all.)[36]

Once again, Parfit manages to discuss only a certain group of arguments that link this specific issue to theological considerations having to do with grandiose, metaphysically rich discussions of the Problem of Evil or to other rather large-scale investigations. Given his plain claim that suffering cannot be deserved, Parfit should have engaged with negations of this claim that do not involve "distorting influences." Moreover, Parfit also recognizes that not all of those who deny the claim that "no one could ever deserve to suffer" have been "obviously affected by some distorting influence."[37] So, why not engage with *their* arguments? (As I have suggested – above all in Chapter 2 – the view that the suffering of the deserving is intrinsically good has been defended in non-obscurantist ways by many thinkers.)

Parfit concludes his section on the double badness of suffering in stunning fashion. First, he appears to admit that he has not really presented any argument for his belief that no one can deserve to suffer:

Though I have claimed only that

(B) undeserved suffering is in itself impersonally bad,

I [happen to] believe that

(H) no one could deserve to suffer.[38]

Second, Parfit merely *hopes* that "in ideal conditions," "some undiscovered argument" may convince people ("not affected by some distorting influence") to accept the claim that no one could deserve to suffer.[39] Again, had Parfit actually presented

---

[33] *Ibid.*   [34] *Ibid.*, 555–556.   [35] *Ibid.*, 571.   [36] *Ibid.*, 568.   [37] *Ibid.*, 569.   [38] *Ibid.*
[39] *Ibid.*

arguments why he thinks that we cannot deserve to suffer (in this world), perhaps the people he had in mind would have been convinced.

Those who believe that we can indeed deserve to suffer can agree with the claim that *undeserved* suffering is both very bad and that it is even doubly bad in Parfit's sense. Granted, a particularly unimaginative reader may ask: *How can anyone ever deserve something that is so bad, and bad in all these ways?* But why worry about the particularly unimaginative reader? The obvious answer should suggest itself: *someone could deserve something as bad as suffering by doing something that is itself very bad.* And how this is so was illustrated by the discussion of organic wholes in Chapter 2.

Parfit pays no attention to the fact that suffering, bad as it undoubtedly is, can occur in contexts – as part of *organic wholes* – in a way that these wholes are made better by its presence. Or, in other words, that although suffering's *default* value is bad, this is not *invariantly* so. Parfit' silence regarding organic wholes is as odd as it is significant. Perhaps one could speculate that Parfit's seeing Sidgwick's *The Methods of Ethics* as "the best book on ethics ever written"[40] sometimes comes at the expense of due attention to other important books on ethics, such as G. E. Moore's *Principia Ethica*, where organic wholes figure prominently. Parfit believes that "Moore's clouds, for many decades, hid the light from Sidgwick's sun."[41] While Parfit evidently does not like Moore's *Principia*, he still declares that "with the exception of the 'doctrine of organic unities' [organic wholes], every interesting claim in Moore's *Principia* is either taken from Sidgwick or . . . obviously false."[42] Notwithstanding Parfit's (indirect) recognition that Moore's discussion of organic wholes is worth our attention and notwithstanding the fact that this doctrine supports essential aspects of Parfit's own general views, concerning e.g., non-naturalism and intrinsic value, organic wholes are conspicuously absent from *On What Matters*.

Parfit's neglect is also striking in that he seems to come very close to admitting that there are wholes in which there is more value when they contain some suffering than when they do not. For example, consider a case he presents (precisely in the course of asserting his view that no one can deserve to suffer):

> When people treat us or others wrongly, we can justifiably be indignant. And we can have reasons to want these people to understand the wrongness of their acts, even though that would make them feel very badly about what they have done. But these reasons are like our reasons to want people to grieve when those whom they love have died.[43]

While Parfit says nothing about *why* we may want people to grieve (i.e., to suffer), he seems to admit that we have reasons to prefer a state of affairs in which people mourn their loved ones when they die over one in which they

---

[40] *Ibid.*, Vol. I, xxxiii.   [41] *Ibid.*, 464–465.   [42] *Ibid.*, 465.   [43] *Ibid.*, 272.

did not mourn them.[44] Given many of his other views, Parfit seems to be, moreover, committed to the view that, quite independently of the instrumental goodness of living in a society in which people mourn their loved ones when they die, there is intrinsic value in the mourning itself. But it is *axiomatic* that if you compare two groups of people who are *ex hypothesi* identical in every respect except that one of them is mourning and the other one is not, there is more suffering where there is mourning.

Correctly, in my estimation, Parfit admits that the state of affairs in which there is mourning is better than the one in which there is no mourning. It is better because there is more intrinsic value.[45] And admitting that this is better need not conflict with the view that suffering is both personally and impersonally bad. This example highlights the complexity and the depth of both our moral and our emotional lives. The mere sight of someone who is perfectly happy after her loved ones die is repulsive.[46]

Recall the thought experiment we discussed in Chapter 4 regarding the lorry driver, to which Parfit insightfully reacts admitting that we would find it "chilling" if a man who just *blamelessly* killed a child "drove away, whistling a happy tune."[47] The chill need not have anything to do with the consequences of the whistling – it is the very whistling the happy tune after having killed a child, *itself*, that fittingly repulses us.[48] To be sure, it is not that mourners deserve to suffer or that the deceased deserve to be mourned or that the child (or her parents) deserve that the blameless driver suffer or that the driver deserves to suffer: desert itself is not crucial (at least not directly) in these examples.[49] But the examples effectively highlight how some organic wholes can be better than others even though they contain more suffering. And we are thus back to theodicy. We do prefer a world in which people suffer when their loved ones die over one in which they do not and a world in which even blameless drivers are agent-regretfully – or tragically remorseful – over one in which people simply whistle happy tunes, whatever the occasion. Arguably, Parfit shares these preferences.

---

[44] As we have seen, there are differences between the suffering involved in mourning and the suffering involved in regretting and between the suffering involved in agent regret or in tragic remorse and the suffering involved in being punished (by someone else). But for current purposes, it is enough to underscore that these are all cases of suffering.

[45] Not all skeptics about desert agree: recall Tadros's position, discussed in Chapter 3.

[46] Of course, the assumption here – shared by Parfit and by me – is that those who do not mourn their loved ones exhibit callous indifference. Perhaps an enlightened Buddhist, for example, can come to see that mourning loved ones is clingy and egotistical. But, like everyone else, Buddhists must nonetheless recognize a difference between callous indifference and enlightenment.

[47] Parfit, *On What Matters*, Vol. I, 461.

[48] Again, what repulses us is that the driver is callously indifferent, not that he is somehow extraordinarily enlightened.

[49] Williams's view was precisely that there is something beyond the "morality system," something not fully captured by what he thought were the overly "narrow" categories of praise and blame, and desert, which explains the appropriateness of the suffering, via agent regret, of the blameless driver.

But if Parfit admits that it is good that the *blameless* driver should suffer, why should he not also admit that it is good that a *blameworthy* driver should suffer? Granted, as we discussed earlier, there are important differences between the suffering involved in moral distress (produced by agent regret, by tragic remorse, or in self-punishment) and the suffering caused by being punished by someone else. But these differences do not support the view that it is good that the blameless driver should experience the suffering associated with these forms of moral distress but that it is not good that the blameworthy driver should experience the suffering associated with punishment. Yet even if this (extraordinarily implausible) supposition were assumed to be true, it would not help Parfit much. First, this would beg the question as to why it could be good for the blameless driver to suffer but not good for the blameworthy driver to suffer. Second, it will not refute that the state of affairs in which the blameless driver suffers (albeit via agent regret) is preferable to one in which he does not – and this undermines Parfit's view that, since suffering cannot be deserved, it ought to be eliminated at all costs.

## A.4 SUFFERING AND ITS DISTRIBUTION

By way of conclusion to the long second part of the first volume of his book, Parfit offers the following thought:

> If Kant had seen that no one could deserve to suffer, or to be less happy, his ideal world would still have been a world in which we were all virtuous and happy. But he would have changed his view about less than ideal worlds, since he would have ceased to believe that it would be bad if some people suffered less, or where happier, than they deserved.[50]

It is not entirely clear whether when Parfit says that "it is bad if some people suffer less than they deserve" he is presenting one of his own views or one of Kant's. If it is one of his own, he would thus appear to be recognizing that people could after all deserve to suffer. And this would be yet another contradiction in *On What Matters*: while Parfit repeatedly states that "no one could deserve to suffer," he would also be stating that "it is not bad when people suffer less than they deserve" – thus recognizing that people can after all deserve to suffer.

If we instead assumed that the view that "it is bad if some people suffer less than they deserve" is Kant's, this would reveal that Parfit cavalierly attributed a contradiction to Kant. If Kant truly believed that no one could deserve to suffer (as Parfit's hypothetical has it), then he would not replace his belief that "it is bad that people suffer less than they deserve" with (Parfit's) "it is not bad

[50] Parfit, *On What Matters*, Vol. I, 272. Kant's understanding of happiness was not hedonistic. But, following Parfit, I will here ignore this point.

when people suffer less than they deserve." Whether it is bad for people to suffer less than they deserve is a question that is only *intelligible* if it is granted that people can indeed deserve to suffer. So this passage is problematic either because Parfit contradicts himself or because he proposes a tendentious hypothetical that involves Kant contradicting himself. In other words, Parfit's hypothetical is problematic independently of which of these two possible interpretations we favor. No one, on pains of self-contradiction, can simultaneously hold that (a) we could not deserve to suffer and that (b) it is bad/good/not bad/not good for people to suffer less/more than they deserve.

But, as we did in the case of another contradiction in Parfit's position, let us proceed as if this contradiction could also be somehow explained away. Let us instead focus on the fact that Parfit lumps together cases of people being happier than they deserve and cases of people suffering less than they deserve. Parfit's view seems to be that whether there is a match between people's lot and the lot that they deserve does not matter; what really matters is for people to be as happy as possible.

Parfit believes, again with Kant, that a world in which we are all supremely virtuous and supremely happy would be ideal. (In this context, "the virtuous" can be equated to "the deserving of happiness.") It is hard to imagine who would disagree with the desirability of such a lovely world. As Parfit realizes, however, the philosophically interesting question concerns non-ideal worlds – that is, worlds like ours, in which we are neither supremely virtuous nor supremely happy. And this is what Parfit thinks:

> In considering worlds that are not ideal, we would again have to decide which worlds would come closer to the ideal. It would always be better, I believe, not only if there was less suffering and more happiness, but also if more of this happiness came to people who were less happy, or who suffered more.[51]

The way in which Parfit considers less-than-ideal worlds is tendentious yet again. For while he recognizes that it is important to discuss "how we could get closest to Kant's ideal," Parfit suggests that, as we "compare the goodness of virtue and happiness,"[52] there are only two views worth our attention:

> On one view, the goodness of virtue is infinitely greater, so that if anyone became slightly more virtuous, or slightly less vicious, this change would be better than the achievement of any amount of happiness, however great, or the prevention of any amount of suffering.[53]

A series of interrelated questions immediately suggest themselves. Why be so extreme? Why should a view that considers *either* virtue *or* happiness as "infinitely greater" than the other one be attractive at all? Why not consider more nuanced views that may hold that the goodness of either virtue or

[51] Parfit, *On What Matters*, Vol. I, 409.    [52] *Ibid.*    [53] *Ibid.*

happiness is (at times or even always) *somewhat* greater than the goodness of the other? As presented, Parfit's view is implausible. Oddly, however, Parfit appears to believe that the view could be made plausible relatively easily: by assuming "that we have some kind of freedom that could make us responsible for our acts in a desert-implying way."[54]

Since Parfit believes too that "there could be no such freedom,"[55] he does not find the view plausible. But even someone who, unlike Parfit, believed that we can deserve to suffer and that, moreover, people should in principle get the suffering that they deserve, could, and probably *should*, find this view implausible (or even abhorrent) as well. The implausibility of the view is not related to the question of whether people can deserve to suffer. Rather, its implausibility rests on the exaggerated difference between the goodness of either virtue or happiness – and on the way in which it invisibilizes the complexity of moral life. This is wholly Parfit's contribution.

The other view, which, according to Parfit, "we ought to accept," is "very different."[56]

> If someone is morally bad, by being a cruel murderer for example, this would be bad for the murderer, his victim, and others, and this would also be a bad state of affairs, which we would all have reasons to regret and to try to prevent. But the badness of someone's being a cruel murderer is, I believe, relevantly similar to the badness of someone's being insane. Such badness can be easily outweighed by the badness of great suffering.[57]

I will sidestep here Parfit's apparent endorsement of the much discredited "humanitarian justification of punishment."[58] I will focus instead on Parfit's suggestion that great suffering (such as the one some would inflict on a cruel murderer) is worse (more weighty) than the actions of the cruel murderer and that, since "no one could deserve to suffer," adding any suffering simply augments, pointlessly, the amount of suffering in the world. Paraphrasing Parfit's formulation of the view he rejects, the view he endorses is that *the goodness of happiness is "infinitely greater," so that if anyone became slightly happier, or slightly less unhappy, this change would be better than the achievement of any amount of virtue, however great, or the prevention of any amount of vice.* This extreme view is, I believe, not one bit less implausible than the extreme view that Parfit first put forth only to then (rightly) reject.

By claiming that people could never deserve to suffer, Parfit is in effect eliminating the most important way in which suffering may enter into organic wholes and increase their value. As we have seen, many authors recognize that

---

54    *Ibid.*, 409–410.
55    *Ibid.*, 410. Notice how the specter of the earlier contradiction reappears: Parfit here sounds like a skeptic about desert *in general*.
56    *Ibid.*      57    *Ibid.*
58    For problems with humanitarian justifications of punishment, see Michael Moore, *Placing Blame*, Oxford: Oxford University Press (1997): 85–87.

the intrinsic value of an organic whole that includes a cruel murderer may in fact be increased if we add the suffering involved in punishing this cruel murderer. But, given his extreme and implausible sublimation of happiness at the expense of virtue, Parfit cannot accept this.

It is possible, then, to agree with Parfit that a world in which there is great happiness despite there being some less-than-perfect correlation between this happiness and what people deserve is better than a world in which there is great misery but a perfect correlation between this misery and what people deserve. Much more fruitful, however, is to consider the nuanced ways in which happiness and virtue may be interrelated with each other and may, on this or that occasion, "defeat" each other – and the remainders that these defeats generate. Parfit wants us to compare a world with maximal happiness albeit with not a very sensible distribution of said happiness against a world of maximal misery very sensibly distributed. It does not take great doses of hedonism to agree that the first world is clearly preferable. But it does not take great perspicuity either to see that Parfit's is a tendentious, unhelpful contrast.

As he reflects on his own discussion, Parfit says "this rejection of desert may seem to take us far from Kant's view." Parfit does not wish, however, to be too far from Kant's view, and so, on the strength of two brief remarks by Kant, he suggests that Kant (in those two passages at least) can be seen as asserting "a hedonistic version of Rule Consequentialism."[59] Whether or not Parfit is right about Kant, something is clear: when it comes to punishment, Parfit is – like the consequentialist punishment theorists we have discussed in this book – indeed a classical utilitarian. For Parfit sees the suffering constitutive of deserved punishment as invariably bad. And this classical utilitarianism leads Parfit to the uninspiring positions we have discussed already. To repeat a passage in part cited at the end of Chapter 3:

> If we are not Retributivists, we do not believe it to be in itself bad when murderers are not punished. Though we believe that innocent people do not deserve to be punished, we also believe that *guilty* people do not deserve to be punished. On our view, all punishment is in itself bad.[60]

So, when it comes to punishment, Parfit sees vanishingly little difference between guilt and innocence. The difference is so little and so elusive that it is indeed hard to see what "desert" could possibly mean for Parfit. The suffering of a saint and the suffering of a villain are, for him, equally undifferentiated: equally undeservable and equally and invariably bad.

---

[59] *Ibid.* The early contradiction (Parfit allegedly being a skeptic only about deserved suffering but actually being a skeptic about desert in general as well) reappears yet again.

[60] Parfit, *On What Matters*, Vol. II, 651.

## A.5 CONCLUSION

If I am right in the preceding arguments, Parfit's views on suffering and punishment are remarkably weak. As in other cases I have discussed in this book, this weakness can be explained by the exaggerated "panic" caused by all the misery that dysfunctional contemporary criminal justice systems regrettably generate. Consider Parfit's assertion in Appendix E, toward the end of the second volume of *On What Matters*:

> We often have more reason to be sorry, not for the victim of some crime, but for the criminal. Compared with their victims, criminals have often lived more deprived and wretched lives. When we imprison such people, in order to deter future crimes, we should greatly regret what we are doing. We should regard these criminals as like people who are quarantined, because they have some dangerous and infectious disease. Any criminal's well-being matters just as much as ours.[61]

Given the distortions in contemporary criminal justice systems, it is sadly true that sometimes we should feel sorrier for the "criminal" than for her "victim." In fact, given the proliferation of victimless, nonviolent crimes, it is often hard to know who exactly the victim is or why the behavior in question is considered a crime in the first place. But there are cases and there are cases. Imagine a real wrongdoer – say, Ohlendorf, from Chapter 2: it is scandalously implausible to say that when he gets punished, we are sorrier for him than for his victims. Those problems with criminal justice systems that understandably saddened Parfit are not caused by the recognition that the value of suffering can vary from context to context.

Since Parfit begins this paragraph cautiously, by saying that it is only "often" that we have more reason to feel sorrier for the criminal than for his victim, it could be argued that the cases such as Ohlendorf's are not among those he has in mind. But he ends the paragraph by explicitly reminding us of his overall view: "[A]ny criminal's well-being [including, evidently, the well-being of Ohlendorf] matters just as much as ours" – and this is just another way of saying, as we saw in the last section, that neither the guilty nor the innocent deserve to be punished and that their suffering is equally bad. And it is to refuse to engage with the complexity of moral life – a complexity that generates deep axiological conflicts and remainders but that (when it comes to thinking about punishment) seems, as in the case of so many other authors we have discussed, to have escaped Parfit's purview.

---

[61] *Ibid.*

# Index

justification of punishment (cont.)
  endorsement of, 79–80
  forgiveness and, 147–148
  future crimes and, 93
  introduction to, 3, 25, 210–211
  moral emotions and, 222, 223, 224
  moral philosophy of, 155
  retributivism and, 115–117
  retributivism *vs.* consequentialism, 4, 12–20
  Tasioulas *vs.* Duff, 144, 145
  unitary theory of punishment, 124, 125–126
  utilitarianism and, 218

Kagan, Shelly, 62, 244
Kant, Immanuel
  deserved suffering and, 244–246, 254, 257
  Moore and, 114
  retributivism and, 28, 32, 88, 89–92, 98, 105–106
  suffering in Hell, 247–250
Kantian ethics, 77
Kolnai, Aurel, 203

Lanzmann, Claude, 231–232
Last Judgment example, 43
*The Last of the Unjust* (Lanzmann), 231–232
legal moralism, 91
Leibniz, Gottfried Wilhelm von, 5, 8
leniency, 3, 137–138, 220, 235
*lex talionis*, 91, 179, 186–187, 188
liberalism, 129–130, 174–175
logic of mercy, 132
logic of punishment, 132, 142, 143, 144, 149
lorry driver thought experiment, 96–98,
    229–230, 253

magical thinking, 61–62, 179–188, 208, 209
malevolence, 110, 213, 215, 235
martial utilitarians, 217
meaning in punishment, 9, 10–11
meaning in suffering, 77
Melville, Herman. *see Billy Budd, Sailor*
mercy
  communicative approach to punishment,
    126–133, 137
  counterintuitive idea of, 142
  duty of, 141, 162
  forgiveness and, 4, 119–120
  introduction to, 3
  logic of, 132
  pluralism and, 132
  retributivism and, 180–182
  Tasioulas *vs.* Duff, 143–144
*Mercy* (Dworkin), 180, 185
mercy killing, 4

merit
  desert and, 59, 62, 64
  destiny and, 236, 237
  fate and, 150
  meaning and, 10–11
  organic wholes and, 50
  utilitarianism and, 61
messiness in pluralistic axiology, 173–174
metaphysical naturalism, 50
metaphysical organic wholes, 49
*The Methods of Ethics* (Sidgwick), 252
micro-management of life, 195–201
Mill, John Stuart, 79–80, 92, 184–185
minimalist forgiveness, 203, 204
misery, 5, 84, 257, 258
mixed justifications of punishment, 4, 12–15
moderate holism, 54, 57–58
monism *vs.* pluralism
  axiology of punishment, 26, 27, 71
  communicative approach to punishment, 134
  overview of, 15–20, 22–23, 26
  reductionism and, 133
  retributivism and, 17, 19, 21
  retributivism *vs.* consequentialism, 17–18, 19
  simplemindedness, 69
  welfare and, 84
monistic axiology
  of classical utilitarianism, 80, 194
  of deontic retributivism, 223
  justifications of, 19, 172, 209
  messiness in, 173–174
  problems with, 78
  punishment theorists and, 177
  suffering and, 56
Moore, G.E.
  axiological views of, 32, 49–51
  classical utilitarianism and, 38–39
  Dancy and, 53
  "Heap of Filth" thought experiment, 37
  organic wholes and, 49–51, 252
  principles of ethics, 33
  problem of beauty, 45
  wickedness and pain, 42
Moore, Michael S.
  emotional engagement and, 93–94
  external justification and, 116
  internal justification and, 116
  justification of punishment, 28, 115–117
  Kant and, 114
  retributivism and, 18, 88, 92–93, 95, 98,
    105–106, 187
moral brilliance, 237–238
moral costs, 227–228
moral dilemma